THE MYSTIC EXPERIENCE

The Mystic Experience

Bhagwan Shree Rajneesh

Translated by:
DOLLY DIDDEE

Edited by:
MA ANANDA PREM

**MOTILAL BANARSIDASS PUBLISHERS
PRIVATE LIMITED • DELHI**

First Edition: Delhi, 1977
Reprint: Delhi, 1997

ISBN: 81-208-1377-4 (Cloth)
ISBN: 81-208-1378-2 (Paper)

Also available at:

MOTILAL BANARSIDASS
41 U.A. Bungalow Road, Jawahar Nagar, Delhi 110 007
8 Mahalaxmi Chamber, Warden Road, Mumbai 400 026
120 Royapettah High Road, Mylapore, Chennai 600 004
Sanas Plaza, Subhash Nagar, Pune 411 002
16 St. Mark's Road, Bangalore 560 001
8 Camac Street, Calcutta 700 017
Ashok Rajpath, Patna 800 004
Chowk, Varanasi 221 001

PRINTED IN INDIA

BY JAINENDRA PRAKASH JAIN AT SHRI JAINENDRA PRESS,
A-45 NARAINA INDUSTRIAL AREA, PHASE I, NEW DELHI 110 028
AND PUBLISHED BY NARENDRA PRAKASH JAIN FOR
MOTILAL BANARSIDASS PUBLISHERS PRIVATE LIMITED,
BUNGALOW ROAD, DELHI 110 007

FOREWORD

(Translated from the original Hindi edition)

The quest for Truth is a quest for life and the mysteries of Existence.

There is this life, there is the Existence, there is sensitivity and the senses, as well as the intellect.

In spite of all these, the reality of life remains unknown and unfamiliar.

This ignorance of life, this unfamiliarity with life, is very painful.

The stage of growth that man has reached in the passage of time is inadequate and incomplete.

In comparison to his enormous potential, man is but a seed.

A great deal of potential lies dormant and hidden within him; a long chain of possibilities awaits awakening within him. Man's consciousness has to pass through many stages and dimensions in the course of its growth.

There are many layers and obstructions which man's consciousness has to pierce before it reaches its ultimate peak.

Then alone is Truth attained and suffering transcended.

In the long history of man's culture, very few have reached the ultimate stage of the inner growth.

We can count them on our fingers—Krishna, Mahavir, Buddha, Lao Tse, Christ, Mohammed and others.

There have been still other sons of the earth who have attained the peaks of knowledge and immortality.

But history has not kept their memory alive.

Since thousands of years, men of courage and daring have toiled in search of the secrets of life and existence and have made extensive journeys into the bottomless depths of their inner being in order to experience and know them.

There is a long chain of tradition of such men.

From the modes and methods discovered and recognized in the course of man's journey into the mysteries of Existence and inward growth, religion was evolved.

Just as science has unfolded the mysteries of matter and the physical world, so has religion evolved the occult science of the inner world and uncovered the inner consciousness and secrets of Existence.

Religion calls this quest "sadhana" and its various methods by the name of yoga.

Yoga has been developed in many dimensions. There is hatha yoga, Raja yoga, Taoist sadhana (spiritual practice), Christian sadhana, kundalini yoga, etc.

It is the science of yoga that has travelled to far-off lands in these various forms of spiritual practices.

Among all the various methods of yoga, kundalini sadhana has proved to be the most practical and significant.

For kundalini yoga contains the means for the growth of almost all types of individuals.

The kundalini's journey starts on the physical gross plane and journeys upwards toward more and more subtle planes, finally transcending the most subtle of the subtles, to reach the Utimate Truth.

Through kundalini sadhana the human personality can be developed in its entirety.

Kundalini sadhana, in the heights of its development, envelops within itself the various methods and dimensions of yoga. Therefore this sadhana is known as "siddha yoga" or "maha yoga".

Kundalini yoga is a scientific method for inner awakening and transformation.

Existential transformation takes place within a person in the course of kundalini sadhana, and the dormant seed of the spirit breaks and sprouts within him.

And then the sapling grows and develops into the gigantic tree of Divine life.

And then flowers appear on this full grown tree of man —flowers of meditation, of Samadhi—and then the fruits of bliss, serenity and love.

And then there spreads a fragrance and splendour from within—of liberation, of grace.

And then the individual is lost—in the infinite mysterious Existence !

He becomes One—with the very source of life.

Then all the limitations of life—its contradictions, conflicts and agonies—are dissolved when the Ultimate Truth is attained.

But the seeker has to set out in search of this attainment.

He will have to travel within.

He will have to labour with the existence of his own being. He will have to work with his inner psyche.

He will have to awaken the dormant energies, the psychic centers within himself.

It is a long journey.

But for the steady, earnest and the courageous seeker, the distance proves no distance at all.

With an inner jump into meditation time ceases to be.

Then God's grace takes over the task of complete transformation.

Then one day we find that without any effort or struggle from the ego, without the "doer" attitude, the Ultimate Truth has manifested itself.

Then each atom of one's being—nay, the whole of Existence—is filled with gratitude and prayer, and it dances with ecstasy and sings "Thy grace Infinite !"

Some wonderful, unique and unparalleled discourses on kundalini yoga by Bhagwan Shree Rajneesh are compiled in this book. They are an invitation as well as a challenge for all to take this inner journey.

Seekers of the Ultimate Reality will find these discourses not mere intellectual information, but the manifestation of real, living experiences as well as a firsthand encounter with the Divine.

These discourses are pure and unadulterated and they have been tested thousands of times on the touchstone of experience. They represent an immediate encounter with the Truth.

In comparison to the literature available to date on kundalini yoga, this book is a unique offering.

It is devoid of the burden of scriptures and doctrines.

All the discourses are a living flow.

Each word comes from the very life and depth of the Being of Bhagwan Shree Rajneesh.

You will find yourself deeply touched and shaken out of your spiritual sleep by his words. You will be inspired to begin your own journey.

The first five discourses are from a meditation camp held at Nargol (Bulsar, Gujarat, India). The remaining thirteen are question and answer sessions with special seekers in Bhagwan's Bombay residence.

The discourses in this collection contain many hints and suggestions for experimentation which will inspire the seeker to dive deeper into the depths of Existence.

There are hints and suggestions about the esoteric dimensions of kundalini yoga and the tantra, but further details of these are only for the initiates.

These lectures throw a light not only on kundalini yoga, but also on the ways to transcend kundalini through the kundalini itself.

Shaktipat, grace, and the planes of the seven bodies have never before been explained in this clear and scientific manner.

Behind these discourses lies the personal knowledge and experience of countless experiments in meditation gained in previous lives by Bhagwan Shree Rajneesh.

Whatever has been said regarding the awakening of the spiritual body, the Cosmic body and the Nirvanic body will prove to be an unparalleled and unique offering—not only to Hindu literature, but to world literature as well.

Generally, kundalini yoga has been practised by a few chosen seekers within the precincts of an ashram or a monastery. The general masses have been entirely unfamiliar with it and untouched by it. The reason behind this was that the known kundalini methods had their own dangers, and, therefore, they had to be limited to a chosen few.

But in the words of Bhagwan Shree Rajneesh : "The coming years in the history of mankind will prove highly significant. The presence of just a few men of spiritual wisdom will not do. If a worldwide spiritual movement is not born in which millions of people are influenced, it will be impossible to save the world from the chasm of materialism. In the coming fifty years the fate of human culture will be decided. Either religion will be saved or dead materialism will triumph."

Says Bhagwan, "The struggle that has been going on for centuries has now come to a decisive point. As things are today, there seems to be no hope for anything better. But I have not given up hope, for I feel soon a way will be evolved—a simple, natural method—that will become a source of spiritual mutation for millions of people . . ."

"The Mystic Experience" contains the answer to this compassionate goal.

The method of meditation used is a unique attempt of its own kind. This method can be practised alone by a person or even amidst thousands. Thousands of people have practised this meditation technique in the course of many meditation camps held under Bhagwan's guidance.

Thousands of people are getting the advantage of practising this method in India, and now its message has started to reach various countries abroad as well. In the near future, this method will greatly benefit thousands and thousands of seekers from abroad.

In this method the possible dangers of kundalini yoga are removed. Reactions take place according to the worthiness and capacity of the sadhak (seeker). At the same time this system makes him strong and competent for more intense inner transformations.

In this meditation technique lies the scientific alchemy for the total transformation and spiritual awakening of the individual.

This method can be practised with complete self-reliance and freedom. As the sadhak progresses the path ahead opens of itself, and the necessity for direction or guidance is minimal.

This technique of meditation is so simple that any person of any age can learn it within three days and practise at home. It can be learned even from a tape recorder or from the radio.

This method has much to offer toward the physical, emotional, intellectual and spiritual growth of the student. The new generation can obtain a tremendous direction from this method.

This method of sadhana has a great therapeutic value also.

Before the seeker enters into higher stages of intensity in this meditation, this method initially has the effect of healing any physical ailments and emotional disorders that would otherwise interfere.

The spiritual forces released by this meditation technique are very useful for mass healing. If the afflicted are made to sit in silence among hundreds of meditating persons, freedom from illness can be attained to a large degree.

This book, "The Mystic Experience," unfolds a new occult and esoteric dimension of Bhagwan's personality, and together with it the world of his profound experience and attainments come to light.

A Final word :

In the absence of a living worldwide spirituality, all of mankind stands precariously on the brink of insanity and destruction. The higher truths of religion and spirituality and the words of Godmen are today nothing more than mythology.

The claims of spiritual attainment are becoming illusory and merely verbal. The long absence of persons like Krishna, Mahavir, Buddha and Christ makes it difficult even to believe that they ever existed. Also, science and so-called communism are working hand in hand to destroy mankind completely. The distance between spirituality and present-day civilization seems to be getting wider and wider. Distressed by this chaotic and militant state of the world, Bhagwan in His utter compassion, warns the world, calls out to its people, solicits them :

"We need people like Krishna and Christ, Buddha and Mahavir. If we fail to produce men of this calibre in the next fifty years, mankind will enter into an age of total darkness in which there will be no hope in the future . . .

"Therefore, there is a great challenge ahead for those of you who think you can do something for mankind. I will go from place to place challenging all people, and wherever I find an eye in which I feel that the Divine flame can be lit, I shall do my very best. I am ready—on my part. Let it not be that at time of death I too will have to say that I looked for a hundred men but never found them."

Hearing his call, many seekers from far and wide have begun to arrive. That many more will come is the silent, prayerful awaiting.

Finally, seekers should remember that spiritual quest is not a subject for mental reflection or for intellectual analysis. These are but ways of escaping sadhana.

Sadhana is the courage to jump into the unknown depths of one's own self. It is the determination to effect a radical transformation of one's self. It is a preparation to pass through the pangs of a new birth.

Thousands of seekers will find a deep inspiration to enter the world of spiritual quest through this book. With this feeling and hope, and also with an invitation as well as a challenge, we present you "The Mystic Experience".

Swami Yoga Chinmaya
Bombay, India
26.1. 1971

PREFACE

Kundalini is the greatest mystery ever revealed to man. Through its awakening man has an opportunity to totally transform his personality into that which he really is : into his Divine essence. And this experience of kundalini is such a total metamorphosis from how man currently experiences himself, that unless one has known it, it cannot be communicated. It is a metamorphosis of his total being—an alchemy from rusty old iron into pure gold.

Until one has had the experience of kundalini one cannot imagine what a great potentiality lies hidden within. It is an experience so overwhelming that the one who discovers it feels that it is worth anything at all. That is why seekers have often renounced everything of this world in order to sit at the feet of a spiritual Master. Once they have tasted its nectar, they want to plunge into it as totally as possible. Thus, seekers go on searching for the right Master—a Master who can help them to awaken their own dormant Divine energy—through techniques of meditation, through their own surrender, devotion and receptivity, and through Shaktipat (the transmission of this energy through the medium of the Master himself). The entire tradition of Master-discipleship in the East is, in fact, based on these very three things.

The kundalini can be awakened in a variety of ways if the disciple is ready. "Love" in itself is a path that helps to awaken it. If one can love deeply and intensely, to the point where 'the other" is seen as God by the disciple, he can awaken his kundalini just by the purity of his surrender and devotion, Bhagwan tells us in "The Mystic Experience". Then love alone is enough and no other method is needed. And generally, he tells us, this path is best suited for females and for passive and receptive personalities. But it is not so easy as it seems as today man has lost this purity of heart. To regain it seems like a very difficult task for most. Rare is the one who can love with a pure, total heart.

Love can be focused on any object appealing to the seeker. If one is capable of loving anyone or anything, this opportunity can be utilized to take one into the experience of the Divine. Many seekers focus their devotion on the Master himself, as it is easy with a living Master. And by attuning oneself to the Master in this way, they are able to receive intense transmissions of energy through him—a mystical technique known as "Shaktipat". Still others can focus their love and devotion on a form of God on the subtle planes (Christ, Buddha, Ganesh, Divine Mother etc.) The lost science of "idol worship" was really a path of this type. In "The Mystic Experience" Bhagwan reveals the lost secrets behind the science of idol worship. He tells how certain idols can be used as a medium for transmission of energy—what kind can be utilized and what kind cannot.

Another method based on the heart is tantra—another secret science of the East. In tantric methods, the seeker sees his or her beloved as the Divine and unites with the inner Self through love for the beloved. Through this love and through the utilization of certain tantric practices, the kundalini is awakened and the seeker discovers a wonderful hitherto unknown bliss.

So those capable of "heart" methods find it easier to awaken the sleeping energy. The pure heart is the easiest door, says Bhagwan. Surrender, devotion, worship, love, are all doors to the Divine—easy entries into meditation.

There are also many methods of yoga and meditation which can be utilized. If practised intensely and with totality, these also awaken the force of kundalini and bring the seeker into a deep blissfulness—an experience far beyond anything he has ever known. As far as methods of meditation go, Bhagwan not only has seekers experimenting with ancient known methods, but he has also devised a series of methods of his own for awakening the energy. Bhagwan's basic methods, which are explained in this book, have been found more effective in the modern age than many ancient practices.

It is difficult to describe the experience of kundalini in a way that the uninitiated can understand. It can be understood intellectually, but the feeling of it can only be known after one has had his own kundalini awakened to same degree. Once it is awakened, meditation becomes possible. Meditation is a moving inward into the depths of one's soul, purifying all layers of the being until one arrives at infinite bliss. It is with the energy of kundalini that this moving inward takes place. First it must be awakened in a seeker, and then the inner journey begins.

The awakening happens when one is ready. But it is made easier by the presence of a living Enlightened One like Bhagwan. For instance, just by sitting at his feet during his inspiring lectures, a seeker begins to feel something totally mysterious taking place beyond the words. A subtle energy begins to flow throughout the seeker, and before he knows it he has entered the state of bliss.

As an Enlightened One, Bhagwan is the purest of mediums. His own consciousness is totally Void, totally empty, totally non-attached. He warns us against persons who exploit these esoteric secrets. "Shaktipat" (transmission of Divine energy) just happens, he tells us. No one is a doer. Thus, there is no guru—only disciples. The Master is empty and the happening just happens through him. He is not "doing". Often, false gurus have claimed that THEY are doing and have used this to exploit and bind the disciple.

When the experience of Shaktipat happens, says Bhagwan, be in a deep gratitude. But do not seek it, and never let it bind you to anyone or anything. To bind a disciple is a great wrong, he says. This book reveals many things about the science of kundalini that have until now remained secret. It is a clearcut explanation of many of its aspects from Bhagwan's own experiences and infinite wisdom. Most books on kundalini represent explanations drawn from ancient scriptures. Thus, they tend to be vague, ritualistic and irrelevant to modern man's needs.

"The Mystic Experience" is a very rare book for spiritual literature. Never before has a book on this important subject appeared based on the experiential wisdom of an Enlightened One. It is revolutionary, disarming, revealing, and practical as well. As far as Bhagwan's own literature goes, it is one of his best books thus far.

Ma Ananda Prem
Editor

CONTENTS

THE MYSTIC EXPERIENCE

Eighteen discourses by Bhagwan Shree Rajneesh on the deeply esoteric subject of kundalini. Given May to June 1970. Lectures 1 to 5 were delivered at a meditation camp held in Nargol, Gujarat (India) under Bhagwan's guidance, and lectures 6 to 18 were given in Bombay (India).

1

THE ASCENT OF KUNDALINI

Blessed Souls:

I do not know why you have come here. Perhaps you also do not know, as most of us live in a manner that makes it impossible to know why we are living, where we are going and why we are going.

The whole of life is spent without our asking these questions, so it would not surprise me if most of you have come without knowing why. Maybe some of you have come knowingly, although there is little possibility of it. We all move about, hear and see in such a state of hypnotic sleep that we do not see what is, do not hear what is spoken and cannot touch an experience which surrounds us everywhere—within and without.

So most likely, you all have come unconsciously. We do not know why we are living, we are not aware of our karmas, nor are we mindful of our breath. But I very well know why I have come, and that is what I would like to talk about this evening.

Man's quest (for truth) continues through many lives. Then after countless births, he has a glimpse of that which we may call bliss or *shanti* (peace) or Truth or God or *moksha* (liberation) or nirvana, or call it whatever you like, though there is no word that is able to convey this experience. One achieves it after so many births, and those who search for it think that they will experience relief after achieving it. But those who succeed in finding it, however, discover that their success is only the beginning of a new travail, without any relief whatsoever.

What was a race for achieving until yesterday now becomes a race for distributing that which is achieved. That is why Buddha appears right at our door, and Mahavir and Jesus are found very anxious to convey their message to us. Truth, once found, gives birth to a fresh labour. As a matter of fact, whatever is worthwhile in life gives as much pleasure in achievement as it gives in its distribution. The bliss of distribution is many levels deeper than the bliss experienced in achievement. One who experiences it becomes anxious like a flower which must distribute its fragrance, like the cloud which must rain or like the breakers of the sea which must strike against the shore. Likewise, what is achieved is meant to be distributed and scattered. The very *prana* (of the liberated soul) becomes anxious to expand itself.

I know what has brought me here—and if you and I can meet somewhere, if your purpose in coming here and mine could be identical, then our presence here can be meaningful. Often, however, it is found that we cross paths but do not meet. So if you nave not come for the same reason as I, then we will be in close physical proximity without meeting.

I would like you to see what I am seeing at this moment. It surprises me indeed that you are unable to observe that which is so near. Many times I have had doubts that you have closed your eyes deliberately. You do not want to see—for how else could that which is so near escape your notice? Jesus had said so many times that people have eyes but see not, have ears but hear not. It is not only the deaf that are deaf and the blind that are blind: those who have eyes and ears are also blind and deaf.

The Divine is so near and cannot be seen! So near and cannot be heard! It surrounds us from all sides and cannot be touched! What is the matter? Perhaps there is some impediment somewhere, but not a big hurdle. There is so much of talk going on in this world about God, so great a bliss which, it is said, is experienced by the successful seeker. There are so many *shastras* (doctrines); there are so many people praying and singing *bhajans* (spiritual songs) in the temples. Still, they do not appear able to experience the Divine. It does not appear that He can be visible to us; it does not appear that He can be heard; it does not appear that His heartbeats are audible to us near our vital breath. It seems as if all this is just talk—only talk and talk and nothing but talk.

We continue to talk about God, perhaps, because we think we can belie the experience of God. We think that we can find Him just by mere talking. Now if the deaf talk about musical notes and tunes and if the blind talk about light for so many lives together, they will not gain anything. The talk can only lead to the illusion that they are not deaf or blind, and the blind may only come to think that they know what light is.

The temples and mosques, consecrated to the Supreme Being, have succeeded in creating a similar illusion. Those who surround them, or are seated inside them, are subject to nothing but illusion. At the most, we only acknowledge the existence of the Divine, but we do not know Him. And acceptance is not more than mere talk. If the talk is convincing, we just accept it. When someone argues vociferously and "proves" the existence of God, then we accept it and yield. If one "proves" that God does not exist, then again we accept it. But mere acceptance is not knowledge. Even if a blind man were made to accept the reality of light, this acceptance will not be equivalent to knowing.

I have come here fully aware that knowing is possible. There are certain psychic centers within us which are lying dormant—centers which a Krishna comes to know, and he begins to dance in ecstasy; centers which a Jesus comes to know, and he cries out from the crucifix, "Father forgive them, for they know not what they do". A Mahavir comes to know them and also a Buddha. There is certainly a center, and an eye or an ear which is lying unawakened. I have come here to see to it that the centers which are lying unawakened may be activated.

The electric bulb which hangs also radiates light. If you snap the wire in two, the bulb is not touched, and it stops radiating. The bulb that does not receive the electric current becomes dark, and where at one time there was light only darkness will gather. The bulb is the same, but it has become inactive. The current of energy flowing to the bulb has ceased to flow to it. When the flow of energy has stopped, what can the bulb do?

There is a center inside us through which we know that which is called the *Paramatman* (Supreme Self). But our vital energies never reach that center, so the center lies inactive. If the vision is intact, but the eyes do not receive the vital energies, then the eyes become useless.

Some of my friends brought a young girl to me. She was in love with someone, but members of her family, having come to know about it, erected a wall between the girl and her lover. We have not been able to fashion a world up until now in which we do not have to erect walls between two lovers. They erected the wall and prevented the girl and the boy from meeting each other. As the girl came from a rich family, a wall was erected on the roof so that the lovers could not see each other. The day the wall was erected, the girl all of a sudden became blind.

In the beginning, the parents were suspicious. They chastised the girl and threatened to beat her. But threats, however, do not cure blindness. Opticians were consulted. They said the eyes were all right, but also that the girl was not lying. The girl was unable to see. The doctors further said that she was suffering from psychological blindness and that they were quite helpless. The vital energies in the girl's body had indeed ceased to reach her eyes. The energy that reaches the eyes had stopped. Though the eyes were intact, it was the vital energies that did not reach them.

The girl was then brought to me. I knew at once what was wrong with the girl. I asked her what was the matter. She said, "If my eyes cannot see the one for whom I have these eyes, then they are useless. It is better for me to be blind. My mind was occupied with only one thought the whole night last night. I dreamt that I had gone blind, and I was delighted to know that I was blind. For if my eyes have been denied the privilege of seeing the person who brings them delight, he for whom they are meant, they must perish." She had willed herself to be blind. The energies which would have enabled her to see stopped reaching the eyes.

There is a center hidden within each of us from where the Divine is recognized and known, from where we get a glimpse of truth, from where we become related to the primordial energies of life and from where music bursts forth which no normal instrument can ordinarily produce. It is from here that one comes to feel a fragrance which is ineffable that one finds the door to that which is called *mukti* (liberation), where there is no bondage, where there is supreme freedom, where there is no boundary, but where there is the expanse of the infinite; where there is no *dukkha* (suffering) and where there is bliss and bliss and bliss and nothing but bliss. But, unfortunately, our vital energies do not reach that center. Something obstructs their flow.

It is necessary to understand this rather clearly because what I would call *dhyana* (meditation) for these three days is but an attempt to direct the energy (kundalini) to the above-mentioned center from where the flower can bloom, the lamp can be lighted, the inner eye can be opened and from where all men should be able to see. But it is not necessary for the seed to grow into a tree. Every seed has a potential to grow into a tree, but all seeds do not become trees. They have the potentiality, but the soil has to be manured and the seed has to be sown : it has to die, to break, to scatter. The seed that is willing to break and to scatter and obliterate itself grows into a tree.

If we examine the seed by placing it near the tree, it will be difficult to discern how a tiny seed could grow into such a big tree. It would appear impossible. How can such a small seed grow into such a big tree ? This is how we have felt from time immemorial. When we stand near Krishna, we have the same feeling—that we can never be like him ! So we say, "Whereas you are Bhagwan (Divine), we are ordinary beings, so how can we fashion ourselves after you ? Whereas you are an avatar, we are ordinary men creeping on this earth. It is beyond our capacity to be like you." When a Buddha or a Mahavir has passed by, we have touched their feet and said, "You are a *teerthanker* (one who helps others cross from this world into the next), an avatar, a son of God. We are just ordinary folk."

Had the seed spoken to the tree, it also would have said,

"You are my Lord, my *teerthanker*, my avatar, whereas I am an ordinary seedling and cannot, therefore, be like you." How can the seed imagine that such a big tree lies hidden in it ? This big tree, however, was once a seed, and that which is a seed today may one day become a big tree.

Infinite possibilities lie hidden in us all. But so long as there is no awareness within us of these infinite possibilities, no doctrine can prove them. For we can never trust that which is to be expected, for to put our faith in that which is unknown to us is sheer deception. It will be better for us to say that we know not whether there is a God. But some have known Him. And some have not only known Him, but have also transformed their lives through knowing Him. They have observed all around them celestial flowers blooming.

All religions have stopped with *poojas* (worship rituals). How can new seeds bloom into flowers by only worshipping them ? And however much the river worships the ocean, it can never expand itself into that ocean. And however much the egg worships the bird, it can never flap its wings in the expanse of the sky. The egg must crack. And when the bird forces itself out from the shell, it does so without self-confidence. When it finds birds winging in the sky, it does not believe that it can also do the same. Sitting on the fringe of the branches, it musters courage. Its parents fly and push the nestling up into the air, but its feathers and feet tremble. How can he who never flew believe that his wings will flap in the heavens and that he too will be able to begin the journey to the infinite and the unknown ! But I know that you too will sit on the fringe of these trees all of these three days, and however loudly I may shout and invite you to take a leap, to jump, to fly, as you sit on the fringe of the tree, you too will not trust yourself—you will not have self-confidence. How can the wings that have not flown believe that they are capable of it ? But since there is no other way, one has to take a leap in the dark.

If one who wants to learn swimming wonders "How can I get into the river without knowing swimming ?," he is not wrong. For how can he step into the river without a knowledge of swimming ? But his teacher would say, "How can you master the art of swimming unless you step into the river ?"

And the debate may go on endlessly while the two stand on the river bank. What then is the solution? The teacher would say, "Jump!" For how can he learn without stepping into the water? In fact, learning begins with the pupil's descent into the river. Everyone knows swimming. They do not have to learn it. If they have learned it, they will also be aware that swimming is not learned: they already know it. But they do not know it properly. When they stumble into the water they learn the technique. At the outset, they toss their hands and feet about haphazardly, then more skilfully. We all know how to toss about our hands and feet. But we learn to move them about skilfully only after we step into the river. Those who know, therefore, say that swimming is not learned but it is memory and a recollection.

That is why those who know say that the experience of the Supreme Self is a memory, not an experience which we will "learn". The day we come to know we will exclaim, "So this is swimming! We were already able to toss about our hands and feet, even before. This tossing about of hands and feet had nothing to do with learning the skill in the river. We never gathered courage, but we remained standing on the shore. We must jump into the river. The work begins as soon as we jump in.

The center I am talking about is hidden in the mind. If you ask the psychologist, he will tell you that only a small segment of the mind is active, a large part inactive. It is difficult to ascertain what lies hidden in the larger segment. In fact, even in the great geniuses of the world, only a very tiny part of the mind functions. The center described as the inner eye is located in the mind. The center is hidden, but the moment it is revealed we begin to see life in different facets. Matter will disappear and the Divine will reveal Himself. With the disappearance of form, the Formless will make its appearance. Death will be reduced to nothingness, and the door to the elixir of life will open. But the center which would have enabled us to see is lying inactive. How shall we activate it?

I have said that if the electric current does not reach the bulb, the latter does not radiate light. If it manages to connect with the current, the bulb awakens. It has been waiting for the current to reach it. Even if the current continues to flow, light will not appear. It needs a bulb through which the current can manifest. We all have the vital current within us, but it is not manifesting. So long as it does not reach the center where the possibility of its manifestation is great, it remains hidden.

We are only nominally alive. Would you call mere breathing living? Is digesting food the same as living? Are sleeping at night and waking up in the morning the same as living? Are growing into youth and then into old age living? Are being born and dying the same as living and leaving behind sons and daughters the same as living? No, this could just as well be done by machines : if not today, then tomorrow, and children will be born in test tubes. Childhood, youth and age are extremely mechanical processes. When a machine is made, it also passes through youth and age. When we buy a watch, we are guaranteed that it would work for ten years at a stretch. It grows young and old and then finally dies. In fact, all machines are so born, then they grow and they die. What you call living is nothing more than such a mechanical process.

If the bulb remains unaware of the existence of the electric current, it would regard its present condition as living. A gust of wind would come and push it about, and the bulb would exclaim, "I am vibrantly alive bacause I am experiencing being blown about". The bulb would take death for life. But what would it say if, were it gifted with speech, the day came when it received the electric current for the first time. The bulb would exclaim, "It is indescribable ! I don't know what it is. I was filled with impenetrable darkness, but now everything is so radiant and light rays are flowing from me and spreading all over". How would the seed react the day it grows into a tree? It would say, "I do not know what has transpired. I cannot describe it. I was a mere seedling, but now I do not know what has happened to me. And it is equally difficult to say that I have been instrumental in bringing about this change"

Thus, those who Realize the Divine do not say that they have Realized. All they say is that "there is no palpable relation between what we were before and what we have realized. Where we were surrounded by darkness, we are now in light. Where we were thorns, we have now become flowers. Where we were frozen in death, we are now flowing in life. No, we have not

Realized anything whatever". Those who Realize will say, "It is all His grace. What we have attained is through His grace, not through our own effort". This does not, however, mean that there has been no effort.

When one Realizes one's Self, one feels that it was all due to His grace. But to be able to reach the point where grace is received one has to go on a journey involving a great effort. And what is that effort ? It is a small effort in a particular sense, but a great one in another sense. The effort is small because the inner center is not very far, because the spot where the energy is gathered and the spot from where the eyes, which would enable us to see life in its proper perspective, are located are not far apart. At the most, the distance between them is a matter of two or three feet, not more than that. Because we are five to six feet tall, the whole life pattern is confined to an area of five to six feet.

The spot where life's energies are gathered is close to the sex center and lies like a *kunda* (reservoir of water). That is why this energy is called "kundalini", as if it is just a small pool of water. And it is so called also because it is like a coiled, serpent, asleep. If you have observed a sleeping serpent, you must have found it lying in coils with its hood on top. If, however, you disturb the sleeping serpent, the hood will be raised up and the coils opened, and the serpent will uncoil and raise up his hood. This energy is also called kundalini because it lies precisely near the sex center where the *kunda* of energy is stored as a seed.

One should bear in mind that the little pleasure we derive from the sex act is in reality a pleasure born not of sex, but of the vibration in the *kunda* of vital energies. The sleeping serpent is slightly disturbed, and one begins to look upon sexual pleasure as the real pleasure of life. We are not in the least aware of what we can possibly Realize when the whole serpent is awakened, and its hood reaches the psychic center in the brain after having transcended all the layers of the psyche.

We all live on the first step of life. There are other steps too which lead to the Supreme Self. The distance of two-three feet lying within us is in a sense a very great distance: it is the distance between nature and God, matter and the spirit, wakefulness and sleep, death and the elixir of life. The distance is, therefore, both great and small, but we CAN travel inwardly.

To awaken the energies lying dormant within us is not less dangerous than disturbing a snake. As a matter of fact, disturbing a snake may not be very dangerous, especially because 97% of the snakes are non-poisonous, and you can, therefore, easily disturb them. And if anyone dies from the bite of a non-poisonous snake, he dies not from the bite but from his assumption that he has been poisoned. Ninety-seven per cent of the snakes do not kill anybody, although many people die of their bite. Moreover, disturbing the poisonous snakes may also not be dangerous, because all they can do is deprive you of the body. But the kundalini *shakti* (force) I am talking about is "dangerous" if it is disturbed. There could be nothing more dangerous. What is the danger? It is a kind of death. When the energy inside you awakens, that which you were before its awakening will die, and a totally new person will be born inside you—a person you never were before.

It is this danger that prevents people from becoming spiritual. This fear (of death) is the same fear which keeps a seed a seed. The greatest danger for the seed is to fall to the ground, to be manured and irrigated, to die. Similarly, the greatest danger for the egg is to break the shell and let the bird escape into the freedom of the skies. As the egg has to die, we too are in the early stages of something yet to hatch. But we look upon the egg as the whole. We nestle to it.

When this *shakti* begins to rise you will disappear. Nothing can save you. If you are frightened, something will happen which Kabir speaks about in a beautiful couplet. He says:

"He who dives deep succeeds in finding. But I the madcap went out seeking and on the bank remained sitting."

Someone asked him why he remained sitting. Then, said Kabir,—

"Those who went out seeking dived deep into the water and found, so I sat on the bank, as I the madcap was afraid of getting drowned."

Those who have sought have done so in deep waters. What is necessary is the preparation to be drowned, to be obliterated. In short, we must be ready to die. He who is afraid of drowning will, of course, be saved, but will be just like an egg, not like the bird that roams the firmament. He who is afraid of drowning will, of course, be saved, but he will be like a seed, not like a tree, under the shade of which multitudes may relax.

Is living like a seed worthwhile ? No death would be worse than living like a seed. So I say there is great danger. It lies in the fact that what we were yesterday would not be today. When the energy will be roused, it will completely transform us. New centers will be awakened, a new person will come into being, a new experience will be undergone—everything will be new. If you are ready to welcome the new, you must have courage enough to abandon the old. But the old has so tenaciously bound and fettered us that the energy is not roused. The journey to the Divine is actually a journey into insecurity. The flowers of life and of beauty bloom in insecurity. Let me, therefore, tell you a few special and a few non-special things about this journey.

First of all, when we meet here tomorrow and proceed to awaken this energy, I hope that you will throw everything you can into the process. This is not going to be a minor gamble. He who risks the most gets the most. Even an iota of energy withheld will cause you to miss the target—for no seed which withholds a part of its being from flowering can ever hope to grow into a tree. If the seed dies, it dies totally. And if it remains, it is alive in its totality. There is no such thing as partial death. If, therefore, you fail to stake everything you have, your labour will be wasted. Very often a little saving is responsible for the loss of everything.

I am told that when gold mines were discovered for the first time in Colorado the whole of America rushed there. News was received by people that they would find gold wherever they bought a plot of land. People did so. A multi-millionaire staked all his assets and bought an entire hill. Huge machines were installed to dig out gold. The smaller people who had bought small plots were likewise busy in mining this precious metal, but the millionaire brought huge machines for the purpose.

The actual work of mining began, but no gold was found anywhere. The news spread like a wildfire, and the millionaire became nervous because he had staked everything. He told his family members that they had gone completely broke. He had staked all his assets and yet there was no news of gold. Then, he advertised that he would sell the hill along with all the mining machines and instruments. The family members said, "Who is going to buy them? Everyone knows that the hill is empty and that you have squandered away your millions. Only a madman will agree to buy the hill". The multi-millionaire said that there must be a madman somewhere who would offer himself for the purpose.

At last a customer was found. It struck the seller that he must warn his customer and tell him that he should not be so mad as to buy the hill. But he could not muster enough courage to give him this warning—for what would happen, he thought, if the hill was not sold. So the hill was disposed of. After the process was completed, the seller said to his customer, "You seem to be a curious madman. Do you not realize I am disposing of the hill because it has ruined me?" Back came the customer's reply that life itself was uncertain and that he may find gold where the millionaire had failed. How could the millionaire say that there would be no gold where he had not applied his instruments? The millionaire had to acquiesce to what his customer had said.

The unexpected happened. Mining was begun one foot deep. The multi-millionaire, who had reason to weep when he discovered there was no gold, now had double reason to weep out his heart. They were all stunned to find that the whole hill was one solid mass of gold. The multi-millionaire went to see his erstwhile customer and said, "Look at your good luck". The man replied, "It is not a question of good luck. It is that you did not stake everything you had. You turned your back on the hill before you had done enough digging. You should have dug a little deeper".

Events similar to this happen almost every day of our lives. I know of countless men and women who try to dig to the Divine. Since they do not dig with their whole might they have to return disappointed. It is their superficial digging that causes the disappointment. Sometimes they miss by just an inch. Before they cover the distance of an inch, they return.

Many a time have I observed some aspirants returning just when they were on the brink of success.

One must, therefore, be reminded that one must not hold anything back. What is there to be bought that is more precious than the Divine? But most of us are miserly even with matters of Divinity, where miserliness will not do. There is no place for close-fisted men at the door of the Divine. There one has to stake one's all. No, it is not that we have much to stake. The question of what one posesses does not, in fact, arise. The question is whether one has or has not given all, because as soon as all is given one reaches the point where the energy dwells and from where it begins to ascend. Why indeed are we stressing this point of staking everything? When we apply ourselves with all our might, then and then alone does that energy, collected in its reservoir, feel the necessity of rising up —and not before that. So long as there is some energy left in us, we go on exploiting it. The reserve energies are used only when there is no other energy left. That center is activated only when we apply all our might. We feel the necessity of tapping that source when we find all other energies thoroughly exhausted; otherwise, we do not use it.

Suppose I ask you to run and you begin to run. Then I ask you to run with all your might, and you begin to run with all the strength you have at your command. But while you think that you have applied all your might, it seems to me that you have not done so. Tomorrow when you have to take part in a racing contest, you will find that your speed has increased. Why? Where has this extra energy come from? Yesterday you said that you were running with your entire might. Today the competition has added to your speed. Today, your speed has increased because of the competition.

But even this is not the application of your entire strength. Tomorrow, when someone with a gun in his hand will pursue you, you will find your speed better than ever. You never knew that you could run so fast. From where has this strength come? This strength too was lying dormant inside you. But even this, however, is not enough. Your speed, even when you were being pursued by the man with a gun in his hand, was inadequate. You shall have to stake more than that in the act of meditation. You shall have to stake your utmost! And the moment you reach that point where your entire energy is employed, you will find that you have become related to some other force, and that some energy inside you has begun to rise upward.

Suddenly, you will experience its awakening. It is like experiencing an electric shock: some energy within begins to rise up from below, from the sex center. It is like a flaming fire, and it is at the same time extremely cold. It is like the prick of thorns on all sides, but also as delicate as flowers. And you feel as if something is rising upward. And when that something rises upward, so very much can happen. Then, at that moment, you do not have to withhold yourself at any point. Let yourself go, no matter what may happen, like a man flowing along the current of river.

Another point: you must first stake everything, and then when that something within you begins to occur, you must let yourself go and float as if you are floating on the surface of a river. You must be willing to be led to whatever place the current takes you. We have to evoke our energies only up to a particular point, and when they are aroused we have to relax ourselves. For then, since we are in greater hands, we should not worry about anything. We must float along.

And now the third point: when the energy begins to ascend from within, and many things begin to happen at once, do not lose your head. The new experience will certainly unnerve you. When a child is born from the womb of its mother, it is extremely anxious. The psychologists say its experiences are traumatic—unforgettable, something from which he will never be free. Anxiety in the child begins with the birth from its mother's womb, because for nine months it was in a world which was completely secure. It had no worries: it didn't have to breathe, to eat, to cry, to sing. It had to do nothing whatsoever; it was at complete rest.

As it emerges from the mother's womb, it enters into a new world. From that time onwards, the child is gripped by the first trauma of life and anxiety. That is why people are afraid of new things and feel like clinging to the old. It is our childhood experience that the new lands us in difficulty and that the mother's womb was a better place. Most of our modern contrivances are modelled after the mother's womb: our cushions our sofas, our cars, our rooms, have been fashioned after the womb. We try to make them as cozy as possible, but we do not succeed. So the first experience, that which begins from our emergence into the world, is an experience of anxiety—anxiety due to the new.

This awakening of *shakti* (kundalini energy) is a still newer experience, because the experience of the new that one has on one's birth is purely physical. But this one is on the plane of the Atman (Self). Therefore, it is a totally new birth. We call people so reborn Brahmins. A Brahmin—one who has been reborn—is a *dwija* (one who is twice-born).

So when that *shakti* awakens in full force, the man in whom she so does is reborn. In this kind of rebirth, you are both the mother and the child in one. You feel, therefore, the pangs of childbirth and those of insecurity as well. You may be anxious and frightened. You will experience the same labor pains as the mother, because here you are both the mother and the child rolled into one. Here there is neither a separate mother, nor a separate child. You are being reborn, and that is happening from yourself. The pains may be very acute.

Many cases have been reported of persons who cry aloud, as if in excruciating pain, and who groan. I have been advised to stop them from doing so. But they must cry and groan. Let them do so. They alone know what is happening within them. How can a woman who never experienced the pangs of childbirth advise a woman who is crying in pain to stop doing so? How can such a woman stop crying and groaning? How can she be told that crying is futile? However, a woman who never had the experience of childbirth may mouth such trifles. Men will never know the pangs which women have to experience in childbirth. They can never even imagine them, for they are beyond their imagination. Nor is there any way for them to know what it is to give birth to a child.

Both men and women are alike in meditation, however, and in a certain sense become mothers—because the new will be born within them. It is not necessary, therefore, to stop their anguish, their wailing. It is not necessary to stop those who fall down, who roll on the ground and scream. Let that happen which is happening. It is not necessary to stop, but rather everyone must be allowed to flow along. And many types of diverse inner experiences can be had. Some may feel that they have levitated, others that they have become expanded, and yet others that they have become contracted. Thus, diverse new experiences can be undergone, experiences which I will not enumerate.

Many things can happen. Each one of us can have our distinct experiences, and these should not cause any anxiety or fear. And if any have to report to me, they should do so at noon. These experiences should not be talked about with others. There is a reason for my asking you to do this. The reason is that what is being experienced by one may not be the same as that which is experienced by another. And since the other is not experiencing it, he will simply laugh and say, "This is sheer madness. I am not experiencing anything of the sort". For every man, the man himself is the measure. If correct, it is none but he, if wrong, it is none but the other. He will, therefore, either laugh at you or else he will skeptically remark that he is not experiencing anything, like it.

This type of experience is so personal and subjective that it need not be talked about with others. Let not the husband divulge it to his wife, for in this regard no two persons are close to each other. Nor can any two persons understand easily each other in the matter of meditation. Understanding is so difficult in this case. Anyone can, therefore, declare another mad. People will call Jesus mad and will not exclude Mahavir either. The day Mahavir had stood naked on the paths, people must have declared him mad. Mahavir himself could know what it meant to be naked: he would be mad.

You should not, therefore, talk about your experiences to others. Moreover, as soon as you speak to others, they will not be wise enough to keep quiet. They would babble things out, and whatever they will say will be an obstacle to you. And you might also be affected by their suggestions.

The fourth point which I would like to stress is that you should not talk with one another. If one wishes to report one's experiences, one should come straight to me.

Before we assemble here for meditation tomorrow morning, no solid food should be taken—only liquids like tea and milk. And those who can forgo even these should do so. The effect of meditation will then be easier and quicker. Talk should be reduced to the minimum. Aspirants are required to avoid all unnecessary talk. Preferably, they should go to the meditation place with an empty stomach and in garments which are loose. Nothing should be tied to the body. No one should go without having taken his or her bath. Especially, nothing should be tied to the waist. When sitting, garments should be loosened around the body. Our dress has caused so much trouble to the body: it presents an obstacle. When some energy begins to ascend, the clothes impede its flow on various planes.

Another point to be borne in mind is that the aspirant should not speak for at least half an hour before coming to the meditation place. Those who can maintain *mouna* (silence) for three days should do so. And if anyone else is *mouna* (silent), others should not present any hindrance. The greater the number of silent *sadhakas* (aspirants), the better. If complete silence is impossible, there should be only minimum talking in telegraphic language. When we go to the telegraph office to despatch a telegram, we see to it that it does not exceed more than eight words. We keep on curtailing the words in the telegram, until only the most important ones remain—for every word in a telegram costs money. So use only those words which are indispensable.

Similarly, the use of the five physical senses should also be reduced to a minimum. When using the eyes, for example, try to direct them downward or toward the sea or even toward the sky, but not toward the people—because most of the associations in our minds are related to human faces rather than to the trees, the clouds and the sea. Direct your gaze to these, and you will find that they do not stir any thought in you. Human faces, on the other hand, immediately arouse all kinds of thoughts. Your vision should encompass only four feet, while your eyes are only half open. The tip of your nose should be visible, and cooperate with others so that they too may see and hear as little as possible.

Switch off your radios and transistors and do not look at

newspapers. Let your senses have as much relaxation as possible. This is desirable because it will enable you to conserve energy which can be used for meditation. Otherwise, you will be completely exhausted. Most of us are almost depleted in our energy—like used cartridges. We spend everything we have in twentyfour hours so that nothing is left over. Whatever little is left in the morning after a good night's sleep is wasted on newspapers and radios. We have no idea of what conservation of energy means, of how much energy can be conserved and used for meditation. Remember that one has to apply all one's might when meditating. If one does not conserve one's energy, one is easily tired out.

Some people report that they get exhausted after an hour's meditation. Their exhaustion is not due to meditation, but due to the fact that they live constantly on the point of exhaustion and continue to keep on expending energy indiscriminately. When one raises one's eyes then also energy is spent—as it is spent when one raises one's ears to hear. Even when one thinks or speaks or does anything, one expends one's energy. A little energy is conserved at night because one has stopped working, but some of that is even spent in dreaming. In the morning, a little of one's energy is left over, causing one to feel fresh. Conserve your energy for three days so that you may apply the whole of it. I am giving you this information so that I do not have to give you any other information for the next three days.

When sitting, you must sit quietly. I have been communicating through words, but at this sitting I will communicate with you through silence. So please assemble here at three o'clock. No one should come after three o'clock, because his late arrival will be harmful. I will be sitting before you. What will all of you do between three and four ? There are two things which should be borne in mind. First, you must sit at a place from where I can be seen, though you do not have to see me. Then you should close your eyes. If you want to keep them open you can do so, but closed are preferable.

We have to wait for an hour for the unknown in silence. You do not know who it is who would come, but someone is expected. You do not know what you will hear, but you will certainly hear something. You do not know what you will see, but you will see something. You should sit quietly, just awaiting the unknown, unfamiliar guest whom you never met, never saw, never heard. If you feel like lying down, lie down; if you want to sit, then sit. Be in total receptivity during the hour. Be passive, but alert and anticipating. I would communicate to you in that hour of silence what I want to communicate. Perhaps speechlessness might be able to communicate what wordscannot.

Again at night I will answer your queries for an hour. We will have nine sittings during these three days. You shall have to apply your entire strength right from tomorrow morning so that your entire strength is actually applied to the ninth sitting. What will you do in your spare time ?

Go and lie down on the beach and hear the waves. It would be better if those who want to sleep go to the beach quietly with their bedding and sleep on the sand beneath the trees in solitude, away from one's circle of friends. In fact, one should not try to form such circles of friends. Be alone for three days, because if you want to meet the Divine, no one can keep you company. You are lonely and you have to travel alone. Be alone as much as possible, and remember—these are my last instructions.

Do not do any grumbling. Eschew all grumbling for three days. Let the food be unsatisfactory; let the mosquito bite. But do not grumble. There should be total acceptance of all that is happening. The gain you accrue will be more than that of the mosquitoes. If you grumble against the food, the harm caused to you will be more than to your physical body. There are reasons for this : a grumbling mind is never at ease. Our complaints are minor, but our loss is major. So do not grumble. Keep your mind free from all grudges. That which is, is. Accept it in its totality.

These three will be wonderful days. If you go beyond griping for three days, if you become filled with delight and accept that which is, you will cease to harbor any complaints after these three days, for you will realize how delightful and peaceful it is to be without any grudge.

Abandon everything for three days, and if you feel like asking anything do so tomorrow morning. And remember when asking that it should be a question for the common good. Ask that which is essential, that which is in your heart and mind.

I told you why I have come and that I do not know why you have come. From tomorrow, however, I shall be meeting you with the hope that you too have come with a similar purpose. Our habits, in fact, have been spoiled. Even if Buddha were to stand at our door, we would feel like sending him away. (*Wailing is heard*). We believe that all who come, come with some request. We ignore those who come to give and ask them to leave. Thus, we commit a grave error. I hope you will not henceforth be repeating this mistake.

Do something to the atmosphere here for these three days so that a transformation may take place. This transformation is possible, and upon every individual depends the creation of a charged atmosphere. Let the whole forest of pine trees be charged with unknown forces, with unknown energies. All these trees, all these grains of sand, these winds and the sea, can be filled with a new *prana*. We can cooperate in producing it. Remember not to be an obstruction, nor to be a mere spectator. Let no one sit like a spectator; abandon all inhibition, fear and concern with what others say or feel. Then alone can you reach Him.

I wish you did not have to say what Kabir said. You could proclaim, "No, I am not afraid," and so saying could take a plunge. I am grateful to you for having heard me in silence and in so much love. I bow to the Divine seated within you all. Please accept my obeisance.

[The inaugural discourse, given on May 2, 1970 at a meditation camp held in Nargol, Gujarat, India.]

2

THE SLIPPING OF THE DROP INTO THE OCEAN

Blessed Souls:

The cosmos is an expansion of energy, and life is the crystallization of it. That which is seen as matter is also energy. That which is seen as life, that which is experienced as thought and that which seems to be like consciousness is also a transformation of that energy. The whole cosmos—be it the waves of the sea or the pine trees of the forest or the grains of sand or the stars of the sky or that which is in us—is the infinite manifestation of the same energy. It is difficult to say precisely where we begin and where we end. It is also difficult to say where the body ends. The body, which seems to be a boundary, is not the real boundary for the body. If the sun, which is a hundred million miles away, cools down, we will also cool down with it. That is, the sun is ever-present in our beings; it is a part of our bodies. With the cooling of the sun, we also cool down. And the heat of our sun is the heat of the body.

We receive our *prana* (vital energy) from the ocean of currents all about us. If it were not available, we will immediately die. The breath we are inhaling relates us, therefore, not only to ourselves inwardly, but also to the world without.

Where does the body end? If a thorough investigation is undertaken, the whole cosmos is shown to be the body. The body is infinite and endless, and if we made a thorough search we would find that the center of life is everywhere; it is ubiquitous. To experience this, however, it is extremely necessary for us to be alive with energy.

What I call *dhyana*, or meditation, is another name for liberating in all possible ways the streams which have stopped moving or which have stagnated. Therefore, if you enter into meditation, the energy lying hidden within you may be roused with such a force that it may be connected to the cosmic energy outside. And as soon as it is connected to the outside force, we become like leaves trembling in an infinite wind. Our own obliteration is effected; we become one with the cosmos.

What does one experience when one is completely immersed into the cosmos ? Man has tried his best to describe this experience, but he has found it incommunicable. Kabir says, "I have gone out in quest of Him; I searched for Him. But while engaged in the quest, I found myself lost. I did certainly find Him, but then I was completely obliterated." Who could, therefore, say what is achieved? How can one verbalize it?

What Kabir had experienced for the first time and what he had said to describe it was later changed by him. What he had initially felt was as if the drop had slipped into the ocean. His own words are, "When seeking and seeking, oh friend dear, Kabir lost himself. The drop slipped into the ocean, so how can it be regained ?"

Kabir lost himself in the search, and the drop slipped into the ocean. How can that be regained? Kabir, however, changed the couplet later and the change is quite valuable. He later said, "No, no, it is not the drop that slipped into the ocean, but the ocean that fell into the drop".

If the drop fell into the ocean, someone might regain it. But if the ocean slips into the drop, then recovery becomes impossible. And if the drop slips into the ocean, it might somehow say something. But if the ocean itself slips into the drop, it would find itself speechless. So, modifying the couplet, Kabir says, "Seeking and seeking, oh friend dear, Kabir lost himself. The ocean slipped into the drop, so how can it be regained ?"

When we remain a pure vibration of energy, it seldom happens that we fall into the ocean, when we become living vibrations, the infinite ocean of energy slips into us. Indeed, it is difficult then to say what actually transpires. This does not, however, mean that we are not aware of what actually takes place. And, remember, that there is not necessarily a connection between speech and experience. Our capacity to experience is infinite, but that of communication is limited.

Even small experiences are incommunicable, not to speak of great ones. If I have hated, I would not be able to describe exactly how I feel. And if there is in my heart the ache born of love, I would still be unable to describe the feeling. These, however, are minor experiences. But when the Supreme Self descends upon us, something utterly indescribable happens —something that we know, but cannot explain.

It is necessary, by all means, to remain a pure vibration of energy, as if one is an overflowing fountain. Let us vibrate with so great an intensity, and let every fiber of our beings, every beat of our hearts and every breath be filled with so insatiable a thirst, prayer and anticipation that we become nothing but thirst and anticipation. Let our very beings be completely obliterated. It is in such a moment that a union will be effected, a union that is brought about within ourselves. The sleeping centers are within ourselves. It is from these sleeping centers that *shakti* (the life force) will rise upward and spread throughout the upper regions of the body.

The seed is lying, then a flower will bloom. The tree has to spread out branches and make twigs in order to connect the flower and the seed. The flower, which was hidden in the seed itself, does not spring from without. But in order to make it manifest, there must be a connecting branch between the seed and the flower. The branch itself will stem from the seed—as does the flower. In us too lies energy in seed form. It will rise up. It needs branches which are also available within us.

At the base of what we outwardly know as the spine is the root from where the energy will rise and reach the flower—the flower which has diverse names. Those who have experienced it describe it as a thousand-petal lotus. Something inside our psyches blossoms forth like a lotus of a thousand petals. Something flowers within us, but it is necessary for the *shakti* to rise up before this blossoming.

When this *shakti* begins to ascend, the whole personality of the *sadhak* (seeker) experiences an earthquake, so to speak. He must not stop that quaking, but should rather cooperate with it, though ordinarily one would feel tempted to restrain it. Many people report to me that they are afraid and do not know what will happen to them. One cannot make any progress if one gives way to such fears. There is nothing more outrageous than a sense of fear, nor is there anything more sinful.

Fear is perhaps the greatest obstacle in the way of the *sadhak* and it is most responsible for keeping him at the bottom. And fears are very curious and negligible. People come to me and say that they are afraid of the opinion of their neighbours. Fear of public opinion can alienate us from the Divine. The polite and civilized man has stopped laughing and crying wholeheartedly. There is no emotion or feeling in which he can drown himself heart and soul. He always stands outside of every situation, and he is like a pendulum. When he laughs or cries, he does so in fear.

As it is, males have stopped weeping. They do not realize that weeping is also an important dimension of life. They do not realize that he who cannot weep will find something fundamentally lacking in his personality. He will find a part of his being crippled forever, and that part will always be lying heavy upon him like a stone. Those who want to get into the world of energy, to travel to the supreme energy, must give up all fear and allow their bodies to tremble, vibrate or dance with total simplicity.

It is necessary to know, though it might surprise you, that all the *yogasanas* (postures) have been derived accidentally from positions in meditation. They have not been deliberately invented by any person. When the body adopts those postures during meditation, people come to know about them. And gradually it was revealed that the position of the body automatically follows that of the mind. Then it was concluded that if the body is driven to a particular position, the mind will follow.

We know, for example, that if we cry inwardly the eyes are filled with tears, and if the eyes are filled with tears one is crying inwardly. These are two aspects of the same phenomenon. When we are filled with anger, the fist is closed, the teeth gnash, the eyes redden, and the hand lifts itself to strike. When, on the other hand, one is filled with love, the fist does not close, the teeth do not gnash, and the eyes do not redden. In fact, some other signs are observed then : Even if the fists had been closed, they open. Gnashing teeth relax, and burning eyes become serene.

Love has its own ways. Similarly, the body has its own ways in every position of meditation. Try to understand it in this way, that if you hinder the body in its assumption of natural positions, there will be a hindrance in the position your mind would like to assume. For example, if someone provokes you into losing your temper, and your eyes do not redden and your teeth do not gnash, you will not be able to express your anger.

How can one lose one's temper without the cooperation of these physical parts? If someone provokes you to be angry and you do not let your body react, you will not be able to be angry. If someone asks you to love without letting your eyes shower ambrosia, without your hands feeling the currents of love, without your heart responding with the beats of love and without your breath changing, you will not be able to love.

Therefore, when your body begins to twist and turn in some specific manner during meditation, let it do so—for if you hinder it in any way, you will cripple what is taking place inside. That expression will not make any progress.

All the *yogasanas* are derived from positions in meditation. There have been a large number of *mudras* (gestures). You must have seen the statues of Buddha in different yogic *mudras* which originate from distinct conditions of the mind. Eventually, a special *shastra* (scripture) dealing with these *mudras* came into being, and it became easier to prognosticate what was going on within the *sadhak* after looking at his external *mudras*. If one is not faking, but actually flowing in meditation, then the position one will assume will eloquently express what is transpiring within.

It seems to me that dancing also originated from meditation, and I feel that whatever is valuable in life has had its original source in meditation. Meera did not go anywhere to learn dancing. People mistakenly assume that Meera Realized the Divine just by dancing. But the fact is that her feet began to dance because she Realized. No one can Realize God just by dancing, but one can certainly dance when one Realizes God. And when the ocean slips into the drop, what else can the drop do but dance? And when countless treasures rain upon the door of a beggar, what else can a beggar do than dance?

But civilization has so much fettered and cribbed man, that he cannot dance. It seems to me that if that world has once again to be made religious, its spontaneity will have to be regained. So it is just possible that when the energy of meditation awakens, you may begin to dance with your whole being. You should not in that moment restrain your body. Otherwise everything will cease, and that which is imminent will not happen. But most of us are very frightened people. Some worry about what their wives or sons will think if they dance. Similarly, if a woman dances, she worries about the reactions of her husband whom she feels might take her to be mad. If there is fear, no progress in the journey within can be expected. And remember that many other things reveal themselves side by side with the physical *mudras* and *asanas*.

There is a thinker who went to, I know not how many, sannyasins and sadhus and ashrams. He came to me about six months ago. He said that though he understood everything, nothing experiential happened to him. So I said, "You might not have allowed it to happen". This caused him to think, and he said, "That had not occurred to me. Maybe you are right. Once though I heard someone crying, I sat upright and took pains to control my own feelings, for I was worried about what would people say if I did likewise !"

What have you to do with others ? Who are these people who are pursuing us all? And, remember, when you die they will not come to save you. When you are in sorrow they will not come to share it, when you lose your way in the dark, they will not light the lamp for you. But when your lamp is on the verge of becoming lit, suddenly they will halt you. Who are these people ? Who is there to stop you? You yourself turn your fear into these anonymous people. You yourself scatter your fear all about.

So the gentleman in question began to say, "Maybe I was frightened when I heard someone crying, and warily I sat to prevent all such reactions from expressing themselves". I advised him to go into solitude for a month and to cooperate with whatever happens to him. Chagrined and surprised, he said, "What do you mean?" I answered, "If you feel like yelling or abusing or like roaring, or crying or dancing or running, do any of these. He said, "I am sorry, I cannot." "Why?" I asked. His answer was that he was frightened, and that if he let himself go, madness would result. Then I said that this would be just as bad as if he just repressed his madness. If it expresses itself, it will be out. If it is repressed, it will continue to live. If it is repressed, it would remain forever with him.

Most of us have suppressed ourselves. We have neither wept, nor laughed, nor danced, nor played, nor run. We have closed all the doors inside and we have become watchmen sitting at the doors. If we have to go out to meet the Divine, we must open the doors. There may be a fear lurking that what had been repressed will be revealed. If you have repressed weeping, then tears will flow out. If you have repressed laughter, then you shall have to laugh. Let all these be washed away.

Let yourself go completely, and allow that which is happening inside to happen. If you feel like dancing, dance. If you feel like running, run. If you want to fall, then fall. You must give complete freedom to yourself. When you let yourself go in this way, you will suddenly experience a new energy moving within that is ascending upward. Some new force will be rising within you and the doors will have begun to give way. Do not harbor any fear at that moment. Become one with it, and let yourself go into the movement which is born inside you—into the energy that begins to gyrate within you. Then alone can the happening be expected to happen.

It is very easy for it to happen, but we are not prepared to surrender ourselves. If by chance you succeed in your quest, you will laugh at all those petty things which once hindered you. Were these things significant, there would be some meaning in being hindered. But the things that hinder us are much too small and insignificant. If you have to ask anything or if you want to talk to me you may come and do so for a while. We will then sit for meditation. Ask me whatever you have to ask.

Questioner : *Is nature purposeless ?*

Bhagwan : Why should we be led by any purpose ? If you can give up all purposes, nothing would be more purposeful. If you can be like nature, then you will have achieved all there is to achieve. Man, however, has become unnatural, for which reason he has to make a purpose of returning to nature. This is a great misfortune, and what I have been telling you is that you must abandon everything. But our hold over everything is so tenacious that even loosening the grip has come to be a purpose. Even this has to be given up. We have gripped so tightly that loosening the grip will involve labor, though it should not require any effort. What labor is needed in giving up a thing ?

It is true that there is no purpose anywhere. But why is there no purpose ? That there is none is not due to nature being purposeless, but because there is no purpose beyond what is.

Suppose a flower has bloomed. It has not bloomed for anyone. Neither has it bloomed because it wants to sell its beauty in the market, nor because it wants the passersby to stop and inhale its fragrance. It blooms not for any gold medal, nor for any state honor. It blooms because blooming is a source of bliss; it blooms for the sake of blooming. We can, therefore, also say that the flower has bloomed without any purpose whatsoever. When it blooms without any purpose, it blooms fully, because where there is a purpose there is some impediment.

If the flower blooms with the motive of exhibiting its beauty, it will not bloom when someone does not appear to appreciate it. But the flower which keeps its petals shut may not be able to bloom forth even when an admirer comes, because the habit of remaining closed will be too strong. No, the flower blooms fully because it does not have any purpose whatsoever.

Man too should be like the flower. But the difficulty with him is that he has ceased to be natural and spontaneous. He has to be brought back to his natural spontaneity, and this bringing back is also a kind of purpose. When I speak about purpose, I speak of it as if it were a thorn in your leg, and the thorn has to be taken out with the help of another thorn. Now if someone comes to me and says, "There is no thorn in my leg, so why should I take it out ?" I would tell him, "Since the question of taking out the thorn does not arise, why should you consult me ?" If there is no thorn in the leg, then there is nothing to discuss. But if there is a thorn one must use another thorn to take it out.

My friends might tell me that it is not proper to advise the use of a thorn when one has already been pricked. The first thorn was causing trouble, but it has to be taken out with the help of another. It is necessary to bear in mind that the second thorn does not have to be lodged in the wound caused by the first thorn, and one does not have to be grateful to the second because it has taken out the first one. Once the first thorn is out, both the thorns should be thrown away.

When, however, unnatural lives become natural, we must throw away the concepts of both unnatural and natural so that the sense of naturalness can be complete. The very thought of being natural will make you unnatural. No, I do not say that a purpose is necessary. But I speak about purpose because we have been clinging to purpose and have sown thorns. It is, therefore, necessary to take out these thorns with the help of other thorns.

Another friend asks whether mind, intellect, ego and psyche are separate entities or just one. He wants to know whether these are separate from the *Atman* (Self) or one with it. And he wants to know whether these are unconscious or conscious, what is the difference between the conscious and unconscious, and where they are distinctly located !

The first thing is that there are no two separate entities like unconscious and conscious in this universe. What we regard as unconscious is sleeping consciousness, and that which seems to be conscious is but waking unconsciousness. Only one exists, and that one is called the Divine, the Brahman or whatever name you may give it. When asleep the same one seems to be unconscious, and when awake it seems to be conscious. I would, therefore, advise you not to dichotomize existence into conscious and unconscious, as these are merely convenient terms; there are no such separate entities. And science too has reached the conclusion that there is no matter which is unconscious.

It is interesting to note that about fifty to sixty years ago Nietzsche declared that God was dead. And fifty years hence science shall have you declare that God may or may not be dead, but matter has certainly died and is not. As science began to probe into matter and went deeper and deeper until it reached bottom, it found that there was nothing but pure energy. What remains behind after the explosion of the atom are merely particles of energy. What we know as electrons, protons and neutrons are mere particles of electricity. In fact, even the word particle is not appropriate because it connotes matter. The scientists had to, therefore, coin a new word, "quanta," which has altogether a different meaning: it signifies both a particle and a wave simultaneously. It is difficult to comprehend how a thing can both be a particle and a wave simultaneously, but "quanta" is that which behaves as both. Sometimes it appears to be a particle and sometimes a wave—a wave which is energy and a particle which is matter.

When science went deeper, it found that there is only energy; and when spirituality went deeper, it found that there is only the *Atman*, and the *Atman* is energy. Very soon, therefore, that synthesis will be effected in which there will be no gap between science and religion.

When the gap between matter and God has been proved illusory, it will not take long to bridge the distance between science and religion. If the unconscious and conscious are not separate entities, then religion and science cannot remain separated either. They were two because God and matter were considered to be two. But there is no such duality. To me, there is only one; therefore, the question of conscious and unconscious does not arise. If you favor the language of unconsciousness, you might say that everything is unconscious. If, on the other hand, you favor the language of the conscious, you might as well say that everything is conscious. I prefer the language of consciousness because one should always prefer a language which emphasizes the higher possibilities.

We may for instance say that only seeds exist and not trees. It would not be wrong because trees are only seeds transformed. But this involves a danger—especially when some seeds may say, "If we are seeds, then let us remain seeds. Why should we grow into trees?" No, it would be better for us to say that only trees are and not seeds. Then the possibility of the seed growing into a tree is revealed.

I like the language of consciousness, as what is sleeping may be awakened and the door to possibilities may be opened. There is a kinship between the materialist and the spiritualist in that they acknowledge the existence of oneness. The difference is that the materialist acknowledges a primary substance and thus remains deprived of the Ultimate, while the spiritualist accepts the Ultimate. However, this also includes primary substance. The spiritualist accepts the last which includes the first. I prefer the language of spirituality, and therefore, I say that everything, all Existence, is consciousness.

Questioner : *Are the mind, intellect, psyche and ego separate* ?

Bhagwan : No, they are not. They are the different facets of the same mind. It is like asking whether the father, the son and the husband are separate individuals. We know that the same individual is a father in relation to his son, a son in relation to his father and a husband in relation to his wife. The same individual is a friend in relation to his friend and an enemy in relation to his enemy. He is beautiful to some and ugly to others, a master to his servant, a servant to his master. Those unacquainted with his family would be surprised and confused if they are told that there was a master, a servant, a father and a husband all sitting in the house. In fact, the same man is all these rolled into one.

The mind acts in various ways. When it becomes obstinate and regards itself as superior to everything, it appears as ego, which is only one of its manifestations. When the mind cognizes and thinks it is the intellect, and when it just flows along undirected it is the psyche. Direct thinking is the function of the intellect. And when the thinker dreams of riches or of becoming the President of the country, and when his thinking is purposeless and useless, the psyche—which is but a discordant and uncoordinated jumble of currents or waves—is functioning. When the mind moves along a definite course, it is certainly intellect. These are the different ways in which the mind acts, but they are mind all the same.

And I have been asked whether mind, intellect, ego, psyche and *Atman* are separate or only one. When there is a storm in the ocean, would you consider this storm to be separate from the ocean ? When the ocean is disturbed we call it stormy.

When the *Atman* is strirred it is mind, and when the mind is quietened it is *Atman*. Mind is thus the disturbed state of the *Atman*, and the *Atman* is the tranquil state of the mind. In other words, when the consciousness within us is disturbed and tempestuous, it is mind. That is why so long as there is awareness of the mind, there is no awareness of the *Atman*, and that is why the mind is lost in meditation. What does losing the mind mean ? All it means is that the waves arising on the surface of the *Atman* are stilled, and after falling down they are at rest. Then one Realizes that one is the *Atman*.

So long as one is disturbed, one finds oneself to be nothing but mind. The disturbed mind manifests itself in different forms—sometimes as ego, then as intellect and still again as psyche. These are the many facets of the disturbed mind. The *Atman* and the mind are not separate, nor are the *Atman* and the body—for the substance is only one, and all these are the transformations of the same substance.

If we know the One, all disputes and conflicts disappear. It is known neither with the body nor with the mind. Once you recognize it, then it alone will remain. It is as much in Ravan as in Ram. It would, therefore, be wrong to bow to Ram in obeisance and to burn Ravan to ashes, wrong not to bow to both in obeisance or to burn both, because the same substance is immanent in both. There is only one substance, but its manifestations are infinite. There is only one Truth, but many forms; only one Existence, but it has many aspects and many *Mudras*.

If, however, we try to understand it philosophically, we will find it beyond comprehension. We should understand it experientially. I am talking to you with a view toward making you understand—but when you plunge into Truth, only then will you Realize that what is known as the body was also He, and what was known as the mind or was also He, as well as the *Atman*. When we come to know, only one remains for us. Only one remains and so much so that the gap between the knower and the known also disappears. The knower and the known are reduced to one.

One of the *rishis* (sages) of the Upanishads asked, "Who knows ? Who is He who is known ? Who saw Him there ?

Who is He who was seen there ? Who was he who experienced ? Who is He who was experienced ?" No, there is no duality there. Even the experiencer ceases to exist, and all gaps are closed.

But thought must create gaps and must say, "This is my body, this is my mind, this is *Atman*, and this is the Divine." Why does thought create gaps ? It creates gaps because it cannot embrace the total Existence in its entirety all at once. Thought is a very small window through which things can only be observed piecemeal. Suppose there is a palatial building with a small opening through which I try to see what is inside. I would thus be able to see chairs, tables, then the master of the house himself, or his photograph, and then the clock on the wall. All these will be observed separately in a fragmented way through the small opening. The whole chamber will not be seen at once for the simple reason that the opening is very small. If I demolish the wall and get into the house, I will be able to see the whole chamber in one sweeping vision.

Thought is a very small opening through which we try to search for Truth. When seen in this manner, everything appears fragmented. When we plunge into emptiness, however, into meditation, when the mind is free from all thought, the total is observed. And the moment it is observed fully, the *sadhak* is struck with wonder that what was only one had manifested itself in its infinite variety. But this is possible only through experience.

My friends ask me how many years I took to find an easy entrance into meditation. The entrance into meditation is a matter of the moment, though one may have to take innumerable births outside the door. But entry through the door does not take more than a fragment of a second. In fact, a second too is not an appropriate word. Even a second is too long. We should say, rather, one thousandth part of a second. But even this is not a correct calculation. In fact, it is in timelessness that one enters into meditation. Then there is no sense of time, but a complete transcendence of it.

If someone says, therefore, that it took an hour or a year to get into meditation, he is wrong, because when one enters into meditation he transcends time. Truly you may spend numerous lives outside the temple of meditation, but that is not an entrance into its inner sanctuary. I too have spent lives thus, but that was not an entry. But when I entered, I entered outside time.

The question is, therefore, very difficult to answer. If we try to calculate the time spent outside the temple, we will find it incalculable. Then we will have to calculate countless lives. And if we take just the phenomenon of entrance into account, it cannot be expressed in the terminology of time, because it is an event occurring between two moments. It happens when a moment has passed but before the next second has arrived. It takes place, we may say, when your watch has struck a second past one: the gap between one and a second past one is the interval for this occurrence.

It invariably happens in gaps or intervals between two moments, and, therefore, one cannot say how much time it took to get into meditation. It does not take much time. It cannot, because one cannot enter into the eternal through the temporal, through time. That which is beyond time cannot be known through time.

I understand what you say. You can loiter about outside the temple as much as you like. One has to do so because one is always moving on the periphery. We have drawn a circle as it were—a circle with a center, and are trying to reach the center by moving on the periphery. We may spend countless lives in this manner, but will never reach the center. No amount of fast running will do; even an aeroplane will not be helpful. If one continues to run around in a circle, the center will remain remote and equidistant from the periphery. The amount of running done is, therefore, meaningless. Wherever one would stand, he will be as far from the center as he ever was. If he wants to reach the center, he must stop running on the circle. He shall have to leave the circle behind and take a leap to the center.

One may ask him on his reaching the center, "How many days of journeying on the circle did it take to bring you to the center?" What would he say? How would he answer? If he says that he travelled on the circle as much as he could without reaching anywhere, he will again be asked, "How many miles did you cover before you reached the center ?" His answer would be that he covered as many miles as he could without any effect. If at all he reached the center, it was by taking a leap from the circle. The question of miles does not arise.

This is true also of meditation. It does not take place in the dimension of time. We have all lost so many opportunities and so much time. The day it happens to you too, you will not be able to say how much time it has taken. No, the question of time does not arise.

Someone asked Jesus, "How long can one stay in your Heaven ?" Jesus said that the question was difficult because "There shall be time no longer. You ask me how long one can stay in Heaven. It is a difficult question because there is no time there—so how can time be calculated ?"

It should be clearly understood that time is inextricably connected with our sufferings. In the state of bliss, time ceases to be. The sense of time is proportionate to the intensity of sufferings. When at night someone is on the point of death, he will find the night lengthened in duration, though on the calendar, on the clock, it will remain unchanged. But he who is sitting near the bed of the dying kinsmen will find the night endlessly long. He will wonder whether the sun will ever rise. Though the night is long, the watch points to the same hour. The one looking at the watch will wonder if the hands are moving or not. The leaves of the calendar are just on the brink of falling and the day is breaking, but it appears as if the night is long.

Bertrand Russell has said, "Whatever sins I have committed, and whatever sins I have wanted to commit but have failed to commit, do not deserve to be punished with more than four or five years of imprisonment. But Jesus said that one has to have eternal punishment in hell. This is not right. Let even those sins which I have not committed be added to those which I have committed". "Even then," says Russell, "the strictest court of law will not inflict a punishment of more than four to five years of imprisonment. The court that Jesus talks about will make a sinner suffer until eternity. This kind of punishment seems to be excessive."

But Russell died. If he had not, I would have told him that he did not understand Jesus. He did not understand Jesus's meaning. What Jesus is saying is that if one has to stay even for a moment in hell, the moment seems to be eternity. There is so much of suffering that it seems endless. It appears as if it will not come to an end.

Dukkha (suffering) prolongs time, while *Sukha* (happiness) shortens it. That is why we say that pleasure is momentary. It is not necessary that pleasure is momentary. There is only a feeling that it is so. Pleasure has its own duration, but it seems momentary because time is shortened in the experience of pleasure. It seems as if the beloved has not even been met when suddenly the moment of separation comes. The flower did not even bloom when it withered. The sense of pleasure is thus momentary, because time is shortened in the experience of pleasure. The clock does not change andthe calendar remains unaffected. But it is our sense of *sukha* that makes time so brief.

In fact, time is completely obliterated in bliss. It is neither shortened nor lengthened. In bliss, it does not at all exist. When one is in bliss, one will not be in time. In fact, time and *dukkha* are two names for the same thing. Time is another name for *dukkha*. In the psychological sense, time is *dukkha*. That is why we say that bliss is beyond time, and that which is beyond time cannot be attained through time.

I too have made as many circles as you. But the most interesting thing is that this race has been long—that it does not matter who has run the most circles and who has run the least. Mahavir as well as Buddha realized 2,500 years ago, Jesus 2,000 years ago and Shankara 1,000 years ago. But if someone says that Shankara circled and circled 1,000 years less than I he is wrong, because there is no end to this circular movement. Here is an illustration:

When you went to Nargol from Bombay, you covered 100 miles, but you did not travel at all to the star that is infinitely far away from you. You are where you were for this star. It does not make much difference for the star that you have travelled 1,000 miles away from Bombay. If you look at yourself from the angle of the star, you have not travelled at all. At Nargol, your distance from the star is the same as what it was when you were in Bombay. Wheresoever you go on the earth, you will be equidistant from the star, because it is so remote that all these terrestrial distances do not make any difference.

The journey of our births and deaths is so long that it does not make much difference whether someone reaches after 2,500 years or 5,000 years or five days or even five hours. The day one reaches the center one exclaims, "Aha, here is Buddha coming and Mahavir and Christ are about to enter, and here we are !" But these are incomprehensible matters, because in the world in which we live time is very important.

Therefore, the question of how long it takes to get into meditation arises so naturally in the mind. Do not talk about being late: stop moving about in a circle which will cause you delay. Do not idle about outside the temple, but get into its innermost sanctuary. But most of us are afraid of doing so and do not know with what we will meet inside. We are all acquainted with what is outside the temple: with friends, with kinsmen, wives, sons, houses, doors, shops and the like. Everything outside the temple is our own. There is only one condition for our entry into the temple—namely, that one has to enter it alone. No two persons can in any way pass through its door together. One cannot, therefore, get into the temple with his wife, son, wealth and safe. Reputation and honour—these must be left behind. I, therefore say, make a few more revolutions outside the temple. We are waiting for that moment when the door will open a little more, enabling all of us to get inside.

But remember that the door does not open wide enough to enable more than one person to enter. Also you cannot enter it with a sense of rank in mind, because that would mean two trying to enter—you and your rank. You also cannot enter with your name because that too will mean two entering—you and your name. It is not possible to carry anything in there. You shall have to be totally naked and alone to find access to it.

So we keep on idling about and pitching our camps outside the temple. We say, "We are in close proximity to God" not very far from Him. But it does not make much difference whether you are a thousand yards away from Him or a thousand miles, or if you are a yard away from the temple. If you are outside the temple, you are outside it. If you want to get in, you may, even in the 1,000th part of a moment.

Look upon this as a last question, and if any other question is left unasked, ask in the evening : It has been asked whether knowledge is obtained in a state of no-thought whether it disappears in thought and whether it appears in a state where the mind is free from thought.

Higher knowledge is Realized when the mind is free from thought, and once it is Realized it remains through all states of mind. It remains even when the mind is full of thought. The question of using it thereafter does not arise, but remember that this knowledge is obtained only in a state of no-thought. Its expression is possible through thought, but its Realization through no-thought. If you want to Realize it, you shall have to go into no-thought. Why is this necessary ? Because the waves of thought will not allow the mind to be a mirror.

Suppose you have to take a photograph with a camera: you shall have to be careful that no light gets into the camera and that the instrument does not shake. Once the photograph has been taken, you can shake the camera as much as you like and can allow it to be exposed to light. This does not make any difference to it. But if the camera is unsteady in the moment when the photograph has been taken, it is spoiled. Once the picture is taken, however, the matter ends. You can do whatever you like with the camera; it will not affect the photograph.

Higher knowledge is obtained in a state of the psyche where everything is tranquil and silent. Then alone is the picture of knowledge imprinted. Once it is imprinted you can dance, you can tremble, you can do whatever you like without it making any difference. Higher knowledge is attained in the state of no-thought, and once it is attained your thoughts cease to be an obstacle. But if you are under the impression that you can Realize it through thought, you are mistaken, thought is a great obstacle in its Realization. Thought becomes thoroughly impotent after the Realization of higher knowledge; it becomes absolutely powerless and ineffective. It is interesting to note that in the Realization of higher knowledge, the most essential thing to begin with is quietude. After it is Realized, nothing remains important. But these are things which we should discuss later. The first thing must be taken up first. Great harm is done by discussing initially what should be discussed later. The harm lies in our thinking that if a thing can be discussed later, we can just as well discuss it now. This attitude will be harmful. Then the camera will shake. It will take the picture, but the picture will not be authentic. Unsteady cameras can also take snaps, but the picture thus taken is not authentic. One comes to possess knowledge even in a state of thought, but that is not authentic because it is produced in a mind which is unsteady. Thus, it distorts everything.

Imagine that the moon has come out and the sea is turbulent. The reflection of the moon will, of course, be there, but a thousand fragments of it will be scattered about on the surface of the sea, and he who has not seen the real moon in the sky will not be able to form any idea of it by looking at her multitudinous fragments. The moon will break into a 1,000 pieces and will lie pell-mell on the waves. Her silver will suffuse the sea, but her image will not be formed. Once this image is formed, we can easily recognize her among the waves of the turbulent sea. We should at least observe it once. Once its physiognomy occurs to our mind, it can easily be recognized in all other physiognomies. But it can never be recognized if it is not known to us even once. You may come across her every day, but you will not recognize her.

Let me narrate an incident before we sit for meditation. A Hindu sannyasin had spent many days in the company of Sai Baba, who lived in a mosque. No one knew whether Sai Baba was a Hindu or a Mohammedan. Nothing is certain about such men. When people wanted to know, he would just laugh away the question, and his laugh would not reveal anything except that the questioner was stupid. As the monk was Hindu, he did not live in the mosque, but had chosen a temple outside the village as his abode. Since he adored Sai Baba, he used to bring his food every day, cooked by himself. Having brought him food, the monk would return to his temple and feed himself.

Sai Baba once told him, therefore, that since he himself passed in the direction of the temple every day, it would be better for the monk to feed him in the temple itself. The monk replied, "Is that so ?" I never saw you pass by ! Thereupon, Sai Baba said, "You should be on the look out. I will pass through your temple and you will feed me there. I will present myself tomorrow."

The next day, the Hindu monk prepared the food and waited for Sai Baba to appear. He did not come, did not come, did not come. The monk was worried. When it was two o'clock, he could not restrain himself. Thinking that Sai baba must be very hungry like himself, he ran with the dishes in his hands. When he reached Sai Baba, he told him that though he had been waiting for him, he (Sai Baba) had refused to oblige him. But Sai Baba said, "I had gone to you as usual, but you refused me." Said the monk, "Refused you !" "Only a dog had appeared." Then said Sai Baba "The dog was me." The Hindu monk began to wail and cry and said, "How stupid of me not to have recognized you. I will certainly do so tomorrow."

But the monk again did not recognize him. Had he appeared as a dog, this recognition would have been easier. But finding a leper in the way, the monk said, "Get away from here. I have prepared food for Sai Baba, so do not come here." The leper gave a smile and went away. At two o'clock the monk again came to the mosque and told Sai Baba, that he had again waited for him. He said, "I had again gone to you, but your mind is so restless that you cannot recognize me. You are so unsteady ! A leper had gone to your house, but you had driven him out. What could be stranger than this ? When I go to you, you send me away, and then you come here grieving that I did not go".

The monk began to cry. He said, "I am sorry I did not recognize you". Sai Baba said, "Since you could not recognize me up until now, how can you recognize me with other faces ?"

Once we get a glimpse of Truth, falsity disappears forever. Then nothing remains but Truth. Once we Realize the Supreme Self, nothing other than He remains. But such a glimpse of the

Supreme Self is possible only when we are quiet within. Then all questions will die. All thoughts, passions and tendencies disappear in Him and they rise in Him, but initially all these have to come to a dead end in order to know and recognize Him.

[Text of a question and answer session held on May 3, 1970, at a meditation camp in Nargol, Gujarat, India.]

3

DEATH : THE DOORWAY TO THE DEATHLESS

Questioner :

If the awakening of Kundalini involves danger, what is the nature of the danger ? And if there is danger, why should one awaken it ?

Bhagwan Shree Rajneesh :

There is certainly great danger. In fact, the danger may involve the loss of everything we consider to be life. We will not remain as we are after the Kundalini is awakened. Everything will be transformed—everything. Our relationships, our emotions, our world and all that we knew until yesterday will change, and the danger lies in this transformation. But if the coal has to change into a diamond, it must annihilate itself as coal. There is great danger : there is danger for the coal. If it changes into diamond, the coal will die. Then the diamond can be born.

Perhaps you may not be aware that there is no generic difference between diamond and coal. They are the same substance in two different forms. After a long, long time coal is transformed into diamond. In fact, there is no basic chemical difference between diamond and coal. But if the coal desires to be a diamond it must cease to be coal. Thus, the coal shall have to face the danger of annihilation.

Man too has a similar danger. One who moves on the path toward Existence must die as man. The river runs toward the ocean, but its meeting the latter is dangerous, as it involves its total extinction. What does danger mean ? It is nothing but total extinction. Only he who is prepared to die and become extinct can travel toward the Supreme Self—the Existence.

Death does not obliterate one as completely as does meditation, for death only severs us from one body and connects us with another. One does not change in death. In fact, only the raiments are changed, but the man remains the same as before. Therefore, physical death is not so dangerous. Most of us, however, look upon death as being extremely dangerous. But I say that meditation is more dangerous, for while death deprives you of your clothing, meditation snatches away your very self. Meditation is total death.

In past ages those who knew used to say that meditation is total death, and that it brings about a complete change—not just a change of clothing. If the river has to merge into the ocean and become one with it, it has to risk its life. But it does not lose anything when it falls into the ocean. It just becomes the ocean without losing anything whatsoever. When the coal becomes a diamond, it just becomes a diamond without losing anything. However, so long as it is a piece of coal it is filled with fear of complete annihilation. And so long as a river is a river, it is frightened of losing itself. It does not realize that by merging with the ocean it will just be the ocean.

Man has to face the same danger. And the same friend asks me further, if there is danger why should one deliberately involve oneself in it ? Here it is necessary to understand my meaning. We are alive in proportion to the amount of danger we have to face, and we are dead precisely in proportion to the fear that dangers invoke in us. In fact, the dead do not have to face any danger. One great danger which they do not have to face is that the dead cannot die again; only the living can die. The more alive a person is, the greater is the intensity with which he can die.

Suppose there is a stone and a flower blooming beside it. The stone may say to the flower, "How stupid you are ? Why do you risk your life to be a flower ? Do you not realize that you will wither away before sunset ?" There is indeed great danger in being a flower, while it involves no risk to be a stone. The stone will go on lying exactly where it lay in the morning, but the flower will have withered away by the evening. The stone does not have to face much danger because it does not have much life.

The more a person is alive, the greater the danger. The more a person is pulsating with life, the greater the danger he will face. Meditation is the greatest danger because it is the doorway to the most profound achievement of life.

My friend asks me, "If there is danger why should one go there ?" My answer is one should go there because there is a danger. It would not have been necessary had there been no danger. Never go to a place where there is no danger, for you will find nothing but death there. Always go to a place where there is danger because then there is also a possibility of life. However, we all love security. If there is insecurity, we become frightened, we run away from it, we hide ourselves. This is how we find life's labour lost.

Many a man loses his life in his attempt to save it. He alone really lives his life who does not try to save it, but who goes on sporting with it. There is danger indeed, and you must go there only because there is a danger. And the danger is very great. In fact, climbing the Mt. Everest or going to the moon is not as dangerous as is entering into meditation. Only recently the moon travellers have lost their way. The danger is great, but it pertains only to garments. It is only that the body may be changed. The danger in meditation is great, very much greater than what it is to go to the moon.

Why do we fear danger ? Have you ever thought why you fear danger ? There is ignorance behind every such fear. We fear because we think we might be reduced to nothing or we might be lost completely. We fear because we may have to cease. That is why we try to save ourselves, to secure ourselves, to erect walls and fortify ourselves against all dangers.

I have heard the story of a certain Emperor who had a remarkable palace built—remarkable because it had only one door. It was so securely built that no enemy could enter it through any window or any door. All the entrances except one were closed, so that the palace had become a veritable tomb. The only difference was that it had at least one door, and that one could go in and come out through it. But no less than a thousand soldiers were stationed to guard the single door. A neighbouring monarch, having heard of this unique palace which was secure against all dangers, came to have a look at it. He was glad that the palace was secure against all adversaries and dangers. He said that he too would have a similar palace built.

The Emperor and his friend went out. The master of the palace bid a hearty farewell to his friend. When the friendly monarch got into the chariot, he reiterated that the palace was beautiful and secure and that he too would have a similar palace erected. He gave his friend thanks and bid the charioteer to drive on. A fakir sitting on the roadside gave out a ringing laugh which made the Emperor ask the fakir, "Why are you laughing, you madcap?" The fakir said, "I am aware of an omission in this palace, your Majesty. I have been sitting here from the day the palace was being built and have had the feeling that if I were to get a chance, I must apprise you of this omission."

The Emperor said, "Tell me all about it". Back came the fakir's reply that the only door the Emperor had built for the palace was a dangerous spot. "No one," he said further, "could get into the palace," but there was one exception to the rule. Death could easily get in. Therefore, the fakir advised the Emperor to keep this door closed with bricks so that he may be perfectly safe and keep death away.

The Emperor said, "Death will not in that case need to enter my palace, because as soon as this door is closed, I will die and the palace will become my sepulchre". Thereupon, the fakir said, "The palace is already a tomb, except for that door. You also admit, your Majesty, that as soon as the door is closed the palace will become a tomb". Said the Emperor, "I admit it". The fakir then pointed out that the palace was a tomb because the more doors one closes the more of a tomb it becomes. He said, "There was a time when I too had tried to hide myself in my own dwelling, but then I found that living in a hide-out was tantamount to dying. As you say, when the last door is closed the house becomes a tomb, so I had all the walls demolished and began to live under the open sky." Remember, therefore, that where all is closed, there is death. By the same token, where all is open, there is life. Therefore, I say living means living in the open, living in the midst of danger, but living fully and completely.

There is danger, but it invites. Danger is always in inviting. It is a challenge and you must respond to it. And know that the danger involves the life of the coal and not that of the diamond; it involves the river and not the ocean; it involves you and not the Supreme Self within you. Now think, if you must save yourself you will lose yourself in the Divine, and if you want to Realize the Divine you must be prepared to lose yourself.

One night someone asked Jesus, "What should I do to Realize the God about whom you have been talking?" Jesus said, "You do not have to do anything. You just lose yourself." He said, "What are you talking about. What will I gain by losing myself?" Then said Jesus, "He who loses finds and he who saves is lost".

If you have any other question, you may ask me.

Questioner : *When the Kundalini is rising upward, and when there are certain impediments in its way at some of the centers that block the Kundalini from rising, what may be the reasons for it and how can we give it an impetus?*

Bhagwan : There is only one reason: namely, we do not invoke Kundalini with all our might; we do not awaken it with full force. We are always incomplete and fragmentary, and when we do anything we do it half-heartedly. Nothing is done wholly and with a totality of one's being. There is no other obstruction than this. If we could do it wholeheartedly there would be no obstruction. But throughout our lives we do everything half-heartedly. Even when we love, we love partially and allow hate to mingle with our love. It sounds rather strange that we should hate the person we love, and wish to kill the person we love and live for. It is difficult to find a single lover who has not desired or wished for the death of his beloved.

This is how the mind is split in half. It works in fragments. Although our left and right feet move in the same direction at one time, the feet of our mind move in different directions each, causing great tension. The great disquiet of our lives is that we are everywhere partial and fragmented.

A certain youth came to me and said that he had been contemplating suicide for about twenty years. I said, 'Why did not you do it, you mad fellow. Twenty years is certainly a long period. As you have been contemplating suicide for twenty years, when will you do it ? Will you do it after you are dead ?" He was taken aback. He said, "What are you saying ? I came to you with the hope that you would counsel me not to commit suicide." I said, "Why should I have told you not to do so when you have not been doing so for the last twenty years ?" Thereupon the young man said, "Whomsoever I met advised me not to commit suicide." My final answer was, "It is due to these counsellors that you are neither able to live nor able to die. You are not doing either. You should either live or die. If you want to live, you must live and you must give up the idea of committing suicide. If you want to die, you must die and give up the idea of living."

He stayed with me for two or three days. I told him everyday that he should give up the idea of living, and that if he had been thinking for twenty long years to commit suicide, it was better for him to do so. But on the third day he said, "What a strange thing you have been suggesting. I want to live." So I said, "When did I ask you to die ? You have been telling me that you had contemplated suicide for no less than twenty years."

It is worthwhile considering that someone who has thought of committing suicide for twenty years and has not done so, has not been able to live either, because how can he who is thinking of death live ? We live divided in halves and this becomes the habitual pattern of our lives. We ourselves make neither friends nor foes; we are nothing wholly and completely. But the wonder is that if one is able to be a foe fully it is more blissful than being a friend halfway.

In fact, everything done completely brings joy, because whenever the whole of man is involved all the energies latent in him cooperate with him. However, when the personality is split, we are at war with ourselves. Therefore, when the kundalini does not rise upward, but is obstructed halfway, all it means is that one is both desirous of awakening it and frightened lest it should begin to rise.

You are proceeding toward the temple but do not have courage enough to go in. You are doing two things simultaneously—proceeding and resisting. You are preparing to enter into meditation, but you cannot gather adequate courage to take a leap into it. You want to swim, you have reached the riverbank, but you are in a fix while you are standing there. You want to swim without getting into the river. It is like wishing to swim in the room itself, to enjoy the delights of swimming just by tossing about your hands and feet on the cushioned bed. No, you cannot get any pleasure by swimming in the bed. The real joy of swimming is inseparable from danger.

Half-heartedness is a great impediment in the upward rise of the Kundalini. That is why many must have felt that it has stopped somewhere in the middle. If it stops, there is only one thing to be borne in mind and that is that you are not whole-heartedly engaged in awakening it. Do not try to find other pretexts. We are experts in finding one pretext or another and in believing that the obstructions are due to the karmas of a past life or due to bad luck or the untimeliness of the endeavour. None of these pretexts are valid. The fact of the matter is that your endeavour is not total. If there is an obstruction from any quarter, know that your leap is half-hearted, that you are not jumping with the totality of your being.

Apply yourself heart and soul. Stake all that you are and all that you have. Then the Kundalini will not stop at any of the chakras (centers). She can complete her journey in a moment. And if we are half-hearted, it may take years. If we are whole-hearted, a second is enough. If she is blocked anywhere, it only means that we are not total. You must, therefore, cooperate with her fully and totally and apply your entire strength.

Know that we possess within ourselves an infinite source of energy, an infinite potentiality, and that we have never exerted ourselves to the maximum. Rather, we live superficially, we have never invited our very roots to join us in the endeavour. The blockage is due to this and not to any other reason.

Questioner : *We feel hunger, sleepiness and thirst right from the day of our birth, but why do we not feel the same insatiable thirst for God from birth?*

Bhagwan : It is useful to understand what I am going to say on this point. The thirst for God is there right from the day of our birth, though it takes such a long time to recognize it. Children, for example, are born with the sex instinct, but it takes fourteen years to recognize it. The sexual hunger is concomitant with birth, but this recognition comes after fourteen to fifteen years. Why is such a long period needed ? The thirst is within, but the body is not ready. It takes fourteen years for the body to get ready and for the sexual thirst to be felt; otherwise it lies dormant. The thirst for God is also present in us at birth, but the body is callow. When it becomes ready, the thirst at once comes up.

Kundalini is the preparation of the body. But you might as well say, "Why doesn't it happen by itself?" Sometimes it does happen spontaneously. But try to understand it this way : certain things in man's development happen first to individuals and then to the group. For instance, go through the Vedas, read the whole of the Rig Veda, and it will appear, as if the *rishis* (sages) did not have any sense of smell. All of the *shastras* (scriptures) throughout the world, written during the Rig Veda period, do not contain any reference to the sense of smell. There are, no doubt, references to flowers, but not to their fragrance. Those who know say that until the time of the Rig Veda man's thirst for fragrance lay dormant. Then it was roused in a few persons.

Even today fragrance does not seem to have much meaning for many people. Even today, the sense of smell in all of us is not fully awakened. It is not awakened in undeveloped communities. There are a few tribes in the world even today who do not have any word for fragrance. At first the sense of smell was roused in a few individuals, and then very gradually and steadily it became the possession of the collective mind.

There are many other things which did not exist in the past, but which have come into being today. The sense of colour is also quite amazing. Aristotle in his books has alluded to only three colours. The Greeks in his day were aware of only these three colours. They did not know of any other. Gradually, other colours too appeared. And remember that the colours which we observe today are not the only colours. There are many others besides these, but we are not alive to them. That is why one who is under the influence of LSD or mescaline or hashish or ganja begins to see many colours unknown to others. And the number of colours are a very large number. Awareness of color has grown very slowly.

And there are still quite a few people who are totally colour-blind. If there are about a thousand listeners here, at least fifty out of them will be blind to one colour or another. They themselves will not be aware of their colour-blindness. There are some people who cannot distinguish between green and yellow colours. This is true not only of ordinary men, but very often of extraordinary men too.

A man like George Bernard Shaw could not distinguish between green and yellow, and until he reached his sixtieth year he did not know that he could not make this distinction. On his sixtieth birthday he came to realize he had this colour-blindness. Someone presented him with a green suit. The man who had brought him the gift had forgotten to give him a tie. Bernard Shaw, therefore, went to the market to get a matching tie and asked for a yellow one. The shopkeeper pointed out that the yellow tie would not match his green suit. The amazed Shaw said that the tie and the suit were quite matching.

The shopkeeper took it for a joke, for he knew that Shaw was an excellent jester. He said, "Are you joking? Do you think that the tie and the suit are of the same colour, whereas the tie is yellow and the suit green"? Shaw insisted that both were the same. He had to get his eyes examined, after which it was disclosed that he was blind to yellow.

There was a time when no one could see yellow. This colour is new to man's consciousness. Many new colours have appeared to him. Music is not meaningful to everyone. Some people find its nuances very rich in depth, while to others it is just a a jolting of one's head. These latter do not have a deep sense of musical rhythm. In fact, music has not yet become a collective experience for mankind.

God is a very remote and ultimate transcendental experience. That is why very few people become awakened, though the ability to awaken is present in all of us. Whenever someone in our midst is awakened, many of us find our latent thirst stirring because of his awakening. Whenever a Krishna appears in our midst, his very presence begins to awaken that in us which is sleeping.

Though the thirst and the hunger (for God) is inborn in us, they are seldom allowed to be roused. There are many reasons, the most important of them being that the huge crowd all around is completely destitute of that thirst. Even if it is felt by an individual, he suppresses it because he considers it to be madness. When people around us are filled with the thirst for wealth and fame, that for religion will certainly look like madness and make people suspicious that a man thirsting for God is slightly deranged. Man, therefore, suppresses himself. The feeling is nipped in the bud. And the world we have built is devoid of a place for God because, as I said, it is dangerous to leave a place for God in this world. We have not, therefore, given him any place here.

The wife is frightened lest her husband should become God's vehicle, because as soon as God enters into his life the wife disappears. Similarly, the husband does not want his wife to be wholeheartedly attached to God, because if God enters into his wife's life what will happen to him who had made himself a veritable God for her ? What will happen to the substitute God, the husband ? What will be his place in his wife's life ?

So there is no place for God in the world that we have created, maybe because God will prove Himself to be a disturbing element here. His presence in our midst is bound to be disturbing. It would upset the status quo; it would disturb our long sleep. A world with God in it will have to change many things, and we will cease to be what we are. That is why God has been kept out of our homes. But just in case a thirst for Him should be aroused in us, we have created false gods and kept them in our homes. Then, even if this thirst is aroused, it will be a thirst for these false gods. We keep stone idols and exhort people to worship them because we do not want people to direct their thirst toward the authentic God. Man has thus created substitute gods who only testify to his exemplary cunningness and conspiracy against God.

The most cruel conspiracy against God is these man-made Gods. It is on account of this that the thirst which might have been directed to the quest for God becomes wasted around temples and mosques which contain nothing in them. And when we do not get anything in these so-called places of worship, we not only feel disappointed, but we realize for once that our homes are much better than the temples and mosques. What is there in a mosque and temple ? Things that disappoint. The one who goes there returns empty-handed. He should have realized that these temples and mosques are the most extremely deceptive inventions ever made by man.

I am told that Satan returned home one day and said to his wife, "Since there is no work left for me, I am thoroughly jobless". The wife was taken aback, as all wives are when the husbands lose their jobs. So the wife said, "You are unemployed ? How did that happen ? Is not your work eternal ? Weaning people away from God and corrupting them—a work of this routine does not ever cease. How did you lose your job ? How is it you are unemployed" ? Then said Satan to his still wondering wife, "It is in a very difficult and strange manner that they have rendered me unemployed. My work has now been taken over by the temples and mosques, by the Mullas (Mohammedan priests) and Pundits. Now I have ceased to be useful. It was my duty to waylay people from the Divine path. Now no one directs his steps toward God. They all are waylaid by the temples and mosques. So I do not have the opportunity to lead them astray from God."

There is in all of us a thirst for God. But the way in which people begin to condition our minds from early childhood and teach us about the Supreme, causes great harm. Before we know God we slip into the illusion that we know Him, that every man knows Him. We are thus made to drink before the thirst is awakened. This leads to boredom and bewilderment, and makes God distasteful. Mainly it is our education that is responsible for this loss of interest. Instead of fostering an interest in God, it stuffs our minds with the Gita, the Koran and the Bible. Our heads are so crammed with the names and sayings of mahatmas (so-called great souls), sadhus and saints that we long to get rid of them all. In these circumstances, therefore, the question of journeying to God does not arise at all.

Our systems and organizations are antagonistic to God. That is why the thirst for the Divine is so rare—so difficult. And even if it arises in someone, he appears to be mentally deranged. At once such a one is declared a lunatic, because he becomes so different from us and lives so differently. His mode of breathing, his demeanour, his dealings, all change and he ceases to be a man who is earthy in our midst. He becomes a total stranger.

The world we have created is anti-God. There is a deep conspiracy going on, a conspiracy in which we have until now been successful. We are still continuing to be successful and have absolutely ousted God from His own world. The trap we have made does not have any opening through which He can enter, so how can our thirst be awakened? Though the thirst is not awakened and felt, yet throughout one's life one's restlessness is eddying within. One may become widely known, but there is still something within which remains unfulfilled. One may become very rich, but he feels that something still remains unattained. One may win love, but he feels that something has eluded his grasp, something has remained unrealized—something that he will never perhaps attain.

What is that something which always remains so elusive? That something is a thirst within us which we have suppressed, which we have not permitted to be quenched or to grow and rise. That is why it raises its head and looms so significantly from place to place, becoming a question mark in whatever path we tread. It is all on account of this thirst that we say to ourselves, "You acquired so much wealth and yet have acquired nothing. You have acquired so much fame, yet you have acquired nothing. You have acquired all the treasures of the world, yet you find yourself absolutely empty". The thirst pinches us, digs into us and pierces us from moment to moment and from different vantage points, but we belie it and we busy ourselves in our work with a greater intensity so that we may not be aware of it.

That is why one who is engaged in earning money goes on accumulating wealth, and he who is engaged in widening his sphere of reputation speeds up his endeavour to win more and more fame. He plugs up his ears so that he may not hear his own disappointments murmur that all was vanity. All our systems and our doings prevent the thirst from being aroused; otherwise the day would come when the children of the earth will be born with a thirst for the Divine, as they are born with natural urges such as hunger, thirst and sex. Such a world is not a very remote possibility. It is worth creating, but who will do so ? Many thirsty seekers engaged in a quest for the Divine may create this world. This could be possible, however, only if all this conspiracy against God is exposed and defeated. There is, therefore, an acute natural thirst. But man has been devising artificial means to slake it.

For thousands of years in China women had to wear iron shoes in order to keep their feet small. Small feet were a symbol of beauty and respectability. The smaller the feet, the more respectable the girl's family. Sometimes the feet remained so small that it was difficult for the women to walk. While their bodies would grow in size, the feet remained proportionately tiny, making it impossible for women to move. Such a one who found it difficult to move was looked upon as belonging to a royal family. A poor woman could not afford to have her feet so small. Since she had to use her feet for longer hours and work, she had to have longer feet. Only the regal women could do without their feet, and instead moved with the support of others. Though crippled, they were considered to be beautiful. No Chinese girl, however, would do the same today. A modern Chinese girl would summarily dismiss her ancestors as being mad. But the vogue of small feet lived for thousands of years.

When a thing is in vogue, it is difficult to see and evaluate it in a proper perspective. When thousands of people adopt it, when the crowds endorse it, then one cannot judge it as good or bad. When the entire populace wore iron shoes, the girls had to follow suit. Those among them who could not wear them were dubbed mad and were unable to get handsome husbands from good families. They were looked upon as helpless paupers. Whenever such a girl's feet were seen, people at once took her for an illiterate and uncivilized creature, only because her feet were large. Large feet in China were thus associated only with illiterate folk. The cultured women had small feet. This conception of culture kept women in China lame for thousands of years. Nor had they any idea what all that madness was about, but the madness continued. With the abolition of the practice, they did not take long to realize that it was all madness.

The entire mind of humanity from the point of view of Divinity has thus been crippled. That thirst which should have taken us to God was suppressed from all sides and has not been allowed to grow. Even when it begins to arise from time to time, false substitutes are shown. If you want the Supreme, get into the temple; if you want God, read the Gita, the Koran and the Vedas. But the seeker does not find anything there except words. He does not find anything in the temples except rocks and stones. This compels one to think that the thirst itself was perhaps unreal. And, remember, that thirst is one of those feelings that come and go. As soon as you enter the temple, your thirst disappears. As soon as you have read the Gita, your thirst for the Divine melts away. Gradually, the thirst is suppressed and frustrated. And when a thirst does not have a chance to be satisfied, it dies out very slowly.

If you decide to fast for three days, you will experience acute hunger on the first day. It will be still more acute on the second day and the most acute on the third. It will be less acute, however, on the fourth day and still less on the fifth. And on the sixth, it will not be acute at all. By the fifteenth, it will stop being felt altogether. If you fast for a month, you will hardly know that you are hungry. During this period you will continue to grow weak and thin. You will lose weight and you will digest your own flesh, but you will stop feeling hungry. If the hunger is not allowed to be satisfied for a month, it dies out.

I am told that Kafka wrote a small story about a big circus. There are many types of people in it, as there are many types of sports and entertainments. The ringmaster features a man who is fasting. The man exhibits his fasting to the spectators. He has a small hut. People who go to witness the performance see wild and strange animals and also this strange man who survives fasting even for months. He has presented himself as one who could live without food for no less than three months at a time. Naturally, people came to see him as well. But how many times can they stand it? In a certain village, the circus stayed for six to seven months at a stretch. Inquisitive people came to watch the performance for fifteen to thirty days, but after that, they said, "All right, if he fasts let him fast. Why should people be interested in him, and how long will they go on seeing him?"

There are circuses and sadhus and sannyasins, and they must keep on changing villages. If they stay in the same village for long, they have to face difficulties. How long can people afford to watch their antics? That is why it is fit that they change the site of their performance after two or three days. As soon as they go to another village, people again flock around them.

The circus (in Kafka's story) came to stay in that village for quite a long time. People stopped coming to see the fasting man. They forgot all about his hut, and he himself was so weak he could not inform the manager. He would hardly get up. He lay and lay, and since the circus was huge, people forgot him altogether. After about four to five months they suddenly remembered him and wanted to know what happened to the man who used to fast. The manager rushed toward him, already in fear that he might be dead. He too had forgotten him. When he went there, he found that the bundle of grass on which he lay was all that remained there. There was no trace of the man. He called out though his nervousness had almost rendered him speechless. When the grass was removed, the man was found reduced to a bare skeleton with his eyes bulging out.

The manager said, "Dear friend, pardon me. We had all forgotten that you were here. But was it not mad of you to keep lying here ? You should have begun to eat—and more so when people had stopped coming to you." The man who was fasting replied, "But I no longer have the habit of eating, nor am I driven to hunger. I am no longer playing a part in the circus, and in fact I am now a prisoner of the game I played for others. I am not jesting. I am really no longer hungry. Now I do not know what hunger is or what people call hunger. I do not sense it within."

What has happened to this man? If you resort to fasting systematically for a long time, hunger dies out. We do not allow hunger for God to be roused because there is nothing in the world more disturbing to us than God. We have, therefore, made all possible arrangements to block His way, lest He enter into us. We carefully keep Him out of our lives. Nonetheless, every man is born with an innate thirst for God. And if facilities were provided for the thirst to awaken, all other thirsts, such as those for riches and fame, would automatically disappear. The only thirst that would remain is the thirst for God.

There is another reason : you can either thirst for God or thirst for worldly things. These thirsts—the spiritual and the material—cannot live together. So one has to inhibit his thirst for God in order that one can encourage his thirsts for wealth, fame and sex. The moment this spiritual thirst awakens, all other thirsts either disappear or are assimilated into it. It alone remains. The Supreme is very jealous. When He comes, He allows no others to stay. When He makes you His temple, minor deities cannot linger there. There are so many of these deities in you. The monkey God Hanuman is there along with other gods and goddesses who will not be allowed to stay there. When He appears, all these deities are expelled; He alone remains. He is very jealous.

Questioner: *Is not what the individual does actually done by the Supreme* ?

Bhagwan : The point made in the question just asked is quite correct. So long as man is the doer, his acts are not done by God. So long as man feels that he has been doing, he is not aware that the Supreme is the doer. But the moment the individual feels that he is not, that things are just happening, that his work is consecrated to God, it becomes Divine.

As long as the notion of doing, of being a doer, remains, the work is not Divine. When doing becomes a spontaneous happening, as if it is not being done, the momentous event occurs. Ask the wind, "Are you blowing ?" The wind will say,

"No ! I am being blown." Ask the trees, "Are you growing ?" The trees would say, "No ! We are being grown." Ask the waves of the sea, "Are you breaking against the shore ?" They will say, "No ! Breaking just happens." This is what is called consecrating one's actions to God. But when man says, "I am doing," then and there comes a dividing door, and he is sorrounded by his ego, his "I"-process. It is there that man pits himself as a separate entity against everything else.

Just as the winds blow, as the waves of the sea break, as trees grow, as the flowers bloom and as the stars in the firmament twinkle, so is man driven, so does someone within him move and speak, so is he not a separate entity. And the moment someone realizes this, the Divine enters. The illusion of being a doer is the cause of our suffering. It acts like a dividing wall. The moment we cease to be doers, the veil is lifted and He alone remains. Even now only He is. You are not the doer only because you believe you are. If you think that you are the real doer, you are just under some illusion. Only He is, but you are not aware of Him.

It is like this : You go to sleep, say here at Nargol, and you dream that you have reached Calcutta. But however much you may dream you would not actually reach Calcutta. However, the dream has taken you to Calcutta, and you are asking, "Which train shall I catch to go back to Nargol ? Shall I travel by train or by plane or on foot ? How can I reach there ? Where is the way ? Who will take me there and act as my guide ?" But when you wake up from slumber you find that you are in Nargol, and then you do not consult a map. Then you realize that you had not gone anywhere. Now you do not need a guide. Were someone to ask you then whether you would return to Calcutta, you just smile and say, "I never went to Calcutta, but had just been in a dream".

Even when man looks upon himself as the real doer, he is not the doer. He is still dreaming that he is doing. In fact, things are just happening. When this dream is broken, that which is called Knowledge or Awakening dawns. And when we say that we are made to act, the illusion persists because, the statement implies an acknowledgment of being separate. I am acknowledging that I am and He is. While He makes me to act,

I am the actor. No, when you really wake up, you will not say that you have just returned from Calcutta. Rather, you will say, "I have never been there."

The moment you wake up from the sleep of thinking you are a doer, the sleep of your ego, you will not say that He is impelling you to do and that you are the doer. That moment you will admit, "He alone is and I am not; I never existed. The dream has vanished". But one can dream for countless lives. There is no end to dreaming, and the most wonderful thing about dreams is that when you dream them they seem to be absolutely real. You must have dreamt so many times. You dream every night, and you know every morning that it was a dream and that it was false. You will dream again tonight, and it will not occur to you again that all this is a dream and, therefore, unreal. You will again find your dream absolutely true and will again find it unreal in the morning.

How weak is the human memory. We wake up in the morning and dismiss all dreams as false. Then we dream again and find reality in the dreams. The morning realization of the unreality of dreams is again lost. Obviously, the realization had nothing very profound about it. It was all very superficial, and deep within the same illusion remained.

Our understanding of things is certainly very superficial. For instance, we read in books that God is doing everything. For a moment, we have the superficial realization that we are not the actual doers—that God is doing everything. But even now we say, "I am not the doer. It is God who is making me act." The "I-process" is still alive and strong. In a moment, this statement that "I am not the doer" will be completely lost. Give a person a blow, and he will be filled with anger and will blurt out, "Do you not know who I am ?" He will forget that he had just been saying that he is not a doer, that he does not exist, that he is no one, and only God is. Give Him a blow, and he will forget everything. In a moment, his humility will disappear and his God will likewise bid him goodbye. His "I-sense" will return.

I am told that a certain sannyasin spent thirty years in the quietude of the Himalayas. He spent his days in peace and solitude and he became egoless. The other is necessary for the ego to be. When the other is not there, how can we make our age felt ? So the other is imperative. The age is able to exist only when you peep into the eye of the other with pride and haughtiness. If the other is not there, into whose eyes will you peep and be haughty ? To whom will you say "I am" ? The "you", therefore, is needed to strengthen the "I". Another false entity is needed for my false "I". The other false entity is "you", without which, my "I" cannot stand.

A net system of many falsehoods is needed for the survival of one falsehood, Truth, on the other hand, stands alone. False-hood always needs other falsehoods as props. If you want to establish the falsehood of "I", you must also establish the falsehood of "you", "he" and "they", amidst which your "I" will stand conspicuously.

So the sannyasin was alone in the mountainous forest, and there was no other person—no "he" or "they" or "we"—so he forgot his "I-sense". During the period of thirty long years he became still. People from the valley now began to flock around him. They made a request to him : "Since a fair is being held in the village, please come down and give us *darshan* (a spiritual encounter). The mountain is high and people may not be able to reach you." The sannyasin thought that since his "I-sense" was dead, there was no harm in meeting people.

We are often prone to such delusions. The sannyasin climbed down where a great crowd had collected and had formed a fair-like gathering of hundreds of thousands of people. They were all strangers, none of whom knew him. He had retired to the Himalayas thirty years before, and so people had forgotten him. When he moved in the crowd, someone trampled upon his feet with his shoes. Though the shoes had touched only his feet, he grabbed the trampler's neck and said, "Do you not know who I am ?" The thirty years he had spent in the Himalayas were wiped away with the twinkling of an eye, as if they were a dream. Those thirty years and that mountain, that solitude, that emptiness, that egolessness, that constant commu-nion with the Divine, all disappeared in a second. He gripped the man's neck and repeated, "You should have known who I am."

Then suddenly it occurred to him that he had blundered. Now he recollected that while in the mountains he had forgotten his ego, and he wondered how his "I-sense" had come back. Then he begged those people's forgiveness and sought their permission to go away. They said, "Whither ?" Said the sannyasin, "Not to my mountain retreat, but toward the plains." The eager masses wanted to know why ? He said, "That which I did not realize during the last thirty years of my sojourn in the solitude of the mountains was realized in contact with man. Now I am going toward the plains. I will spend my days there and will try to understand whether I exist or not." The thirty years the sannyasin had spent in the solitude of the Himalayas were but a dream. He thought he had become egoless. But everything was in its place; nothing had been lost.

Thus are illusions born, but illusions will not do.

Let us now prepare for meditation.

[Text of a discourse given on May 3, 1970, at a Meditation camp held in Nargol, Gujarat, India]

EXPERIMENT IN DYNAMIC MEDITATION

Meditation Camp at Nargol, Gujarat, India
Evening, May 3, 1970.

Now let us sit for meditation, for there will be a change from tomorrow. From tomorrow, we will meditate in the mornings and spend the evening listening to discourses. But today, we will follow the scheduled program. Now, stand apart and add some distance from one another—not a great distance, because as I saw this morning those who had gone far away had deprived themselves of the charged atmosphere created here. You are, therefore, advised to keep apart from one another, but not at a great distance. Let there be no spacious gap between one aspirant and another. Those who want to lie down should make enough room for themselves and lie down. Those who want to sit down should sit, but not at a great distance. Let there be no talking at all. Let our work be carried out without conversation; there is no need to converse.

(. . . *A few stones from an unknown direction fall on the meeting grounds, but Bhagwan continues to speak in a serene voice*) : What is the matter ? Stones are being pelted ? Nothing is the matter; just welcome them. Someone has thrown them out of love. Those who are talking in the rear should at once stop. If they want to sit let them do so quietly, or else they should quit. No one should sit here in the capacity of a spectator, and even if he does sit as a spectator he should at least sit silently. Remember that one should not cause any obstruction to another. It appears as if some unknown friend has been throwing stones. He has already thrown a couple of these. If the stones need to be thrown, they should be directed at me, not at any one else.

The First Stage :

Remain sitting where you are. Close your eyes. You have to give your entire strength for an hour. Close your eyes and begin to breathe deeply. Look how the sea is intensely breathing, and so are the pine trees ! Breathe like them. Let the whole breath be drawn inside and forced out. There should be only one occupation for ten minutes—breathing in and breathing out. Breathe in and breathe out, and be a witness within. Just watch inside. The breath has gone in and gone out. Descend as deeply as possible into the process of breathing for ten minutes. Now begin.

Take in a deep breath, and exhale a deep breath, take in a deep breath, and exhale a deep breath, take in a deep breath and exhale a deep breath, take in a deep breath and exhale a deep breath. Do it with your entire might. We have this evening and this opportunity. We may or may not have them again. Apply your entire strength. If anything can be achieved, it can be achieved only if the entire energy is applied. If you withhold yourself even by an inch, it will not be achieved. Take a full deep breath and be like a machine. Let the body breathe as if it were a breathing machine, let the body breathe as if it were a breathing machine. You are now only a breathing machine. And watch ! Do not hesitate or care for others, but only for yourself. Draw in your breath as deeply as possible for ten minutes, and exhale deep breaths. Be as if you are only a breathing machine—a breathing entity. Draw in a deep breath, draw out a deep breath, and continue to watch within like a witness. Watch within. The breath has gone in and out, in and out, the breath has gone in and out. Apply . . . apply your entire energy.

Apply your entire energy. Do not draw in a few deep breaths when told to do so and then slacken your breathing afterwards. Do it with your utmost energy for ten minutes and concentrate on breathing. Draw in a deep breath and exhale a deep breath. Let the whole body and every fiber of it tremble. The whole body will be charged with electricity; some energy within you will begin to rise and diffuse and spread through every part of your body. Apply your entire might. Take in a deep breath, exhale a deep breath. Take in a deep breath, exhale a deep breath. Take in a deep breath, exhale a deep breath. Take in a deep breath, exhale a deep breath. Take in a deep breath, exhale a deep breath. Take in a deep breath, exhale a deep breath. Take in a deep breath, exhale a deep breath.

Let the body be a mere breathing machine. Be one with the roar of the ocean and with the gusts of the mind. They are all breathing; you do not have to do anything else : just breathe in deeply and breathe out deeply. Breathe in and breathe out, breathe in and breathe out, and be a witness within. Apply your entire might. Breathe in and breathe out mindfully, and keep on watching inwardly in full awareness. The breath has gone in and out, the breath has gone in and out. Do not withhold any part of yourself; do not withhold yourself. Instead, apply yourself with the totality of your being. Deep breaths and deeper and still deeper. Let nothing remain other than breathing in and breathing out. Deep breathing, deeper breathing and deeper, deeper breathing. Deep breathing, deep breathing, deep breathing, deep breathing, deep breathing.

See that you will not have to repent later that you did not do your utmost, that you withheld yourself. Let there be no stopping. Apply your entire might. Tire yourself out before we switch to the second stage. Apply your entire might. Deep breathing, deep breathing, deep breathing, deep breathing, deep breathing. You are just your breath. Deep breathing, deep breathing, deep breathing, deep breathing, deep breathing, deep breathing, deep breathing. And continue to observe within. The breath has come and gone, and we are just witnesses. The breath can be seen coming in and going out. Keep on watching within. Faster and still faster and still faster (*people dance, shake and scream*). Do it more vigorously before entering into the second phase. When you are most intense, I will let you enter into the second phase. Apply your entire strength, apply your entire strength. Apply your entire energy in every possible way. Deep breathing, deep breathing, within, deep breathing, deep breathing. Only breathing remains and nothing else. Do it with your utmost energy, and go deeper and deeper, deeper and deeper, deeper and deeper, deeper and deeper, deeper and deeper. (*The sound of crying and wailing is heard*). You can go still deeper. Do not restrain yourself, but make breathing deeper, and still deeper.

Let the body vibrate. If it sways, let it do so. If it gyrates, let it gyrate. Draw in a deep breath. Let it be as deep as possible (*sounds of mmmmmmmmm are heard*). Deep breathing, deeper breathing (*wailing and crying*). Deep breathing, deeper breathing. Before entering the second phase draw in a deep breath for the last one minute (*different sounds are heard*). Draw in a deep breath. The last minute is left, so apply your entire being. Deep breathing, deep breathing. Change at the climactic point is welcome. Deep breathing, deep breathing, deep breathing, deep breathing, deep breathing, deep breathing, deep breathing, deep breathing, deep breathing. Let breathing consume your entire energy. Only breathing is left, only breathing is left, and nothing else.

The Second Stage :

Now we have to enter into the second phase. Continue to breathe deeply, and let the body do whatever it wants to do. Let it assume whatever postures it wants to assume; let it do whatever *mudras* it wants to do. Let it vibrate, gyrate, cry; let it go. Let the body completely go. The breathing will be deep, and the body relaxed. If it falls down, let it fall. If it rises up, let it rise. Do not worry if it begins to dance. Let the body go completely, and let it do whatever it wants to do. Do not restrain it. Instead of restraining it, cooperate with it. If it gyrates, you must also gyrate. If it sways or falls, or cries or laughs, you must also sway and fall and cry and laugh. Let it go, whatever happens to the body must be allowed to happen. Breathing must be deep and the body relaxed.

(*Hundreds of people are heard crying, wailing and shrieking; some of them are seen dancing and reacting intensely, while Bhagwan continues to guide them*). Let the body go completely for ten minutes. Deep breathing, deep breathing and a relaxed body. If it weeps, let it weep. If it screams, let it scream. You should not impose any restrictions on it, but should, rather, cooperate with its reactions. Let the body do whatever it wants to do, and allow that to happen which is happening. The body will assume *mudras* and will gyrate. When the *shakti* will wake up, many things will happen in the body. Different sounds may be produced, and the body may weep. Do not worry. Let it go—let the body go. Now you have to tire out the body. You have to exert it to the utmost before going to bed. Let the body go; cooperate with it. Deep breathing, deep breathing, deep breathing, deep breathing, deep breathing deep breathing, deep breathing, deep breathing, deep breathing, deep breathing, deep breathing, deep breathing.

(*The tape recorder receives a blow and goes out of order, but Bhagwan continues to direct the experiment. The aspirants continue to breathe fast for another ten minutes and to intensify their physical reactions by cooperating with them.*)

The Third Stage :

Fast breathing, and with it yelling and dancing and singing continue for ten minutes. The aspirants were directed to ask within, "Who am I? Who am I? Who am I?" The yogic reactions, spontaneously being performed by the sadhakas, went on unabated and soon reached the climax.

The Fourth Stage :

The aspirants were asked to abandon doing everything and to rest. Neither deep breathing nor inner inquiring of "Who am I?" Only a relaxed, quiet and mute emptiness, as if they are all dead—as if they are not. Hundreds of these *sadhaks* had an easy entry into deep meditation. The whole pine forest was filled with the waves of meditation, and it appeared as if *the sadhaks* had merged with Cosmic Consciousness.

As soon as the fortieth minute was over, the meeting of the meditators was dismissed. Many *sadhaks*, however, still continued to be absorbed within themselves. They continued to dwell in the same unknown inner world. Slowly, people went back to their abodes, but several of the seekers remained absorbed in meditation—some for half an hour; others for an hour or two. Afterwards they also left the scene of meditation.

****

4

SPIRITUALITY : A PATH OF COURAGE AND DETERMINATION

Questioner :

Can meditation be attained through the grace of God?

Bhagwan Shree Rajneesh :

It would be useful to understand this point which has caused so much understanding. I do not know how many men are under the impression that if it can be attained through the grace of God, they do not have to do anything. If this is what they take God's grace to mean, they are certainly deluded. Another delusion to which they are prone is the belief that God's grace is not equally available to all. That belief is wrong. Grace showers upon all equally. There are no chosen ones. If God had favourites, there would be no justice in this world.

By "God's grace" it is understood that God is kind to some and unkind to others. If this is how it is interpreted, the interpretation is absurd. It has another meaning which is its true meaning. That it (meditation) is achieved through the grace of God is not the statement of those who have failed to achieve it. It is the statement of those who have already achieved meditation. They make such a statement, because when meditation is achieved, the *sadhak's* (seeker's) own efforts seem to be absolutely irrelevant. When it is achieved, the efforts appear so negligible and the achievement so huge that the *sadhak* hesitates to take credit for his actions.

When it is achieved, the humble *sadhak* feels, "How did I achieve it? What did I do for it? What did I give? What did I sacrifice? What did I do? What did I have to offer? What action was there which I was capable of performing?" When He showers infinite, infinite bliss, at that moment when bliss rains down, the aspirant feels, "It is thy compassion, Lord. It is thy grace alone that has rained upon me. I myself am helpless, hopeless, before your might."

This then is the experience of the one who has attained it. Those who merely cling to words go astray. They have to make efforts. What happens after one succeeds in one's efforts is like opening the door of a dark room to let in the sunshine. When the door was closed and the sun had risen, the room remained dark and effort was needed to open it. One cannot tie sunlight into a bundle and carry it in. It enters by its own grace. It is interesting to note that while our efforts cannot bring the sun in, we can certainly make efforts to prevent it from coming in. We can shut the door and close our eyes so that the glory of the sun cannot penetrate our closed eyes.

We can stop the sun's rays outside the door. We are able enough to stop them, but not to bring them in. But let the door be opened, and the room is at once flooded with sunlight. When sunlight floods the interior we cannot claim that WE have brought it in. All we can say is that we opened the door and it entered. All we can say is that it was by our own grace that we did not keep the door shut.

Man can be an open channel for His descent. Our efforts merely open the door. His advent is a matter of His own grace, but His grace is forever waiting at every door. But if some of these doors are kept closed, what can He do? He knocks at many doors, and when they do not open he withdraws. Those doors are closed. We have kept them so. When he comes and knocks, we content ourselves with numerous explanations just to deceive ourselves.

Let me tell you a story which is dear to me. There was a temple with a hundred priests in it. The head priest dreamt one night that God told him He would be coming to visit the temple on the following day. The priest, of course, could not believe that He would come, for it is difficult to find a greater non-believer than a priest. Besides, those who run temples as a business can have no faith in religion. There is no one more faithless than the one who uses faith as a means of livelihood. The priest had no faith in the dream. For years he had been in the temple, and God never came. Whatever offering was made to the Divine by way of food or clothing had always been passed on to him. He knew that all the praises he sang to the Divine were addressed to the winds and nothing else, for he was certain no one heard his prayers. So the priest comforted himself that after all, it was only a dream. But he could not rest. He feared that if the dream were true, then what ? For sometimes dreams do come true, and sometimes what we know as reality becomes a dream.

So he thought it better to tell his associates. He called the other priests and said, "Although it seems funny to me, let me tell it to you. Last night, I dreamt that God spoke to me and said that He will visit our temple tomorrow." They laughed and advised him not to tell it to anyone else, for he would be taken as mad. But he said, "Let us at least make all preparations in case He does come. If He does not come, it does not matter. But if He does, He should not catch us unprepared." So the temple was washed and cleaned. Fresh flowers were arranged and all the lamps were lighted. They sprinkled all kinds of fragrances and burned incense. All types of *prasad* (food offerings) were prepared. The priests were thoroughly exhausted by the end of the day. Many times they looked out at the street and saw no one. They were disappointed and said, "A dream is a dream after all. We are really mad to do all this. It is good we did not tell this to anyone in the village. We would have made a laughing-stock of ourselves."

By evening they gave up all hope. They decided, 'We will have to eat the offerings made for God, as usual. No one is going to come. It was mad of us to believe a dream." They wondered how they were so easily led astray by such madness, for they knew very well that God never comes. It is for the foolish devotees to believe in such things. After all, where is God ? This idol in the temple is all that is left of Him. "There is this temple, this idol and our prayers, and that is our vocation," they felt. "What made them give in to this mad idea ? They were filled with shame at their foolishness. The priests ate the food offerings, and since they were tired they went to bed early.

In the middle of the night, a chariot drew up at the temple door. The head priest heard the wheels stop at the door, but he was not sure, for he was half asleep. He quickly called out to the others, "Get up, get up ! He has come. I heard His chariot at the door." "Go back to sleep," the others said. "Have you not made us look foolish enough during the day ? Do you now want to spoil our night also ? It is not the sound of any chariot wheels. It is the rumble of thunder that you hear." So they went to sleep again.

Then they heard the chariot stopping at the temple and the sound of feet climbing the temple steps. Then someone knocked and another priest woke up. He shook his neighbour shouting, "Get up, get up. Someone is knocking at the door. It must be Him." Again the others rebuked him. "What is this ? Won't you let us sleep in peace ? No one is knocking. It is only the wind making sounds against the door. Go to sleep." Again they reassured themselves and snuggled back into their beds. They got up in the morning and went to the door. There they found strange footprints on the steps, and sure enough there were the wheelmarks of a chariot on the road.

Now they were filled with remorse. They began to beat their breasts and wail. They would fall to the floor, get up, then fall again. A crowd from the village gathered and began to ask, "What is the matter ?" "Do not ask what has happened," said the head priest, "We are damned. He came, and we did not open the door. He knocked and we said to ourselves, it was the wind. We heard his chariot and passed it off as the rumbling of the clouds. The fact was we did not want to disturb our sleep, so we invented explanations for everything in order to explain it away."

Thus He knocks at the door of each and everyone. His Grace is always waiting at our doors, but our doors are closed. And even if sometimes we hear a knock, we explain it away.

In India, in the olden days, people used to say that, "Guests are Gods". It is slightly wrong. It should be, "God is the guest," for He comes as a guest to our door every day. His grace forever awaits us. But the door must at least be open. Therefore, do not ask whether we attain by His grace. We attain through HIS GRACE ALONE. Our effort only helps to open the door—to remove the obstructions that are in the way. When He comes, he comes of His own.

Questioner : *You have talked about the four stages of meditation. Can you explain the meaning of these four stages in detail ?*

Bhagwan : Please understand first of all that the first three steps are merely steps to meditation and not meditation. The fourth step is meditation. The first three are not the openings. They lead to the opening. The fourth step—that of total relaxatoin, tranquillity, emptiness, surrender, death, extinction—is the door. The basic use of the first three steps is to bring the body to such a peak of tension that it easily slips into relaxation.

When a man toils the whole day long, he sleeps well in the night. The greater the toil, the deeper the sleep. Now if we argue that sleep and work are two opposite things and, therefore, one cannot lead to the other, we are wrong. The rule is that the opposites follow each other. Therefore, the one who remains in bed the whole day long finds it difficult to sleep at night. This is why the more comforts increase in the world, the more difficult it becomes for people to relax. And the irony of it is that we increase our comforts so that we may sleep comfortably. But what do we find ? Comforts are increasing, but sleep is decreasing. Sleep requires labour. The greater the labour, the deeper the sleep.

Similarly, as soon as tension reaches its climax, it leads into deep relaxation. The first three steps are completely opposite to the fourth. It appears that we are using all our strength, all our power to create the maximum possible tension. We are working ourselves to a pitch of madness and creating a storm within, spending our energy completely. Now how can we hope to silence this storm and relax ? But it is THROUGH this that you will slip into relaxation. The higher the mountain, the deeper is the canyon below.

Remember, where there is a mountain there is bound to be a canyon. In fact, a mountain cannot be without a canyon, for as it rises upwards it creates a canyon below. As you create the tension within you, you are also gathering energy for relaxation. That is why I ask you to apply all your strength so that you can reach the climax of tension. In this way, when you fall from that height of tension you will lose yourself in the bottomless chasm below. There you will find repose and relaxation. And in this moment of relaxation, meditation is attained.

The basic thing is that I want your tension to reach its maximum so that you can then let it all go. Many people come and ask whether relaxation is not directly possible, without all this tension. No, even if it were possible, the experience would be very shallow. The deeper you want to dive, the higher you will have to go.

Look at these pine trees. They are about forty feet above the ground and their roots reach a similar depth below. The higher the tree rises, the deeper the roots will go. Now these pine trees can ask, "What is the harm if I let my roots grow only six feet?" Indeed, there is no harm. However, the tree would only rise to six inches.

Nietzsche has somewhere made an observation which shows great insight. He has said, "Those who wish to reach the peaks of heaven must touch the depths of hell." It is a very deep observation. An ordinary man is never able to touch the heights of religion, but a sinner often manages to do so. The deeper he falls into the abyss of sin, the greater becomes the possibility of his touching the heights of virtue.

This technique involves change through extremes. All transformations take place at the climax point. You have seen the pendulum of a clock going to the left and to the right. As it moves to left, it is gathering momentum to go to the right. It will go as far out to the right as it goes to the left. The pendulum of your psyche must be drawn to the maximum tension so that in the moment of relaxation the release will be complete. If you do not go into tension, you will not be able to relax.

And people have been asking me strange questions. It seems as if they want to gather flowers without taking the trouble of planting seeds. They do not want to sow the fields, but are eager to reap the harvest. One friend came to inquire whether there was any harm if he did not move his body or allow it to tremble. There is no "harm". If you do not do anything at all, there is no harm whatsoever. If you are so afraid of the body trembling, what will happen when the trembling energy begins from within ? What will you do then ? No, you would like that something inner should happen to you, but at the same time you want to maintain a refined, cultured appearance outwardly. You would like to keep your wax outer image while something else happens within. This is absurd. When the energy arises within, this image of wax will melt away. It must melt away and make place for something else.

Try to bring your tension to the maximum so that your relaxation also may be maximum. Tranquillity will follow by itself. You concentrate on the tension and God's grace will bring about relaxation. Let the wave of tension go high. When it falls, you will become peaceful. There is no peace like the peace that comes after a storm. The peace that is born out of a storm is a living tranquillity. For this living tranquillity, I insist on a complete state of tension. No part of this technique can be dropped. Therefore, henceforth, please do not come and ask me whether you can do it without moving the body or without deep breathing—whether you can merely ask, "Who am I ?" These three steps have been developed in a regular, scientific manner to take you from one extreme of tension to the other.

And only when each step reaches its climax can it be carried into the next step. It is just like driving a car. Each gear has to be raised sufficiently to put the car in the next gear. And if the speed in the second gear is slow, you cannot put the car into the third gear. All changes are made at maximum speed. The transformation of the psyche also takes place at maximum intensity.

You should understand fully the meaning of these three steps. The first step is to breathe deep and also fast. You have to breathe as deep as you can and as fast as you can. What will happen with this ? Breathing is the most mysterious factor in man's existence. It is the connecting bridge between the soul and the body. Therefore, man is alive as long as he breathes. The moment the breath stops, man ceases to live.

Recently, I visited a house where a woman was lying in a coma for the last nine months. The doctors said she will never gain consciousness again, but that she could still live for at least three years. She was kept alive with glucose and all sorts of drugs. I told her mother, "She is now as good as dead." She replied, "Not yet. As long as she breathes, there is always hope." The doctors are certain the case is hopeless, but who knows? Many a time a person has recovered when the doctors gave up hope. The breathing is intact, the bridge has not fallen. She can yet return.

Breathing is the bridge that connects the body to the soul. Deep and intense breathing not only causes the body to tremble, but also the very threads of the soul. If some liquid is kept in a bottle for a long time in one place, the contents of the bottle and the bottle itself will not appear as two different things. Their separate identities become clear only when the bottle is shaken. Similarly when you breathe with as much vigour as possible, you create a storm within yourself—a storm which causes not only the body to shake and tremble, but also the soul. It is in this moment that we feel the body to be something apart from ourselves.

Then you come and ask me, "What if we do not breathe hard?" If you do not, you will never know yourself apart from the body; that will be your only loss. And that is precisely why you are asked to look within. When you begin to see the breath coming in and going out, not only will you experience your body to be apart from you but you will also feel that the breath is apart from you. You will then know yourself as the witness—as something completely apart from the body and the breathing.

Deep breathing will make you aware that you are separate from the body, but that you are also not the breath becomes clear when you watch the movement of the breath as a witness. Therefore, the first two stages involve these two things, and these two continue until the third step.

In the second step I ask you to continue deep breathing and to let the body go. There are a lot of implications involved in this, and I shall talk of two or three of these. First and foremost, you have collected thousands of tensions within yourselves of which you are completely unaware. Our way of living has made us so unnatural that we smile even when we are seething with anger within. The body does not understand what is going on. The body wants to clench its fists and break the head of the other person, but you go on smiling. So you do not clench your fists, and the nerves that had been geared up for them to clench become confused. They do not know what has happened. A curious situation has thus been created in the body, as the fists are preventing from being closed.

Those who have studied anger in detail and understand it advise us, as I also do, not to suppress. When you are angry, instead of putting on a false smile you should clench your fists a number of times, with all your strength, under the table. This will relieve your tension, and your smile will be of a totally different quality.

The body does not know that man has become civilized. The body works mechanically, but man has put many restrictions on its working. Because of these restrictions, innumerable tensions are accumulated within, and too many tensions cause complexes. So when I ask you to let go, if you do so all these complexes which you have gathered from childhood will begin to scatter and melt away. It is essential that these melt away; otherwise you will never be able to transcend the body so that you can become as light and as weightless as a flower and free from all complexes.

Perhaps you have heard of a wonderful name attributed to Mahavir. The name is "Nirgranth" and it means "without complexes or tensions". It means one who is free from all inner knots and whose complexes have disappeared, one who has become absolutely simple and innocent.

When the body wants to be freed from these complexes, you hold it back. Your culture, your education, your habits, your inhibitions, your being somebody's wife, your being in a high position, your being this and that: all these have such a strong hold on you that you do not let you go. It was this morning that a lady came to me and said that she is afraid somebody's hand might touch her (during the meditation experiments). Today, she must be sitting far away. But how far can she go ? Suppose someone happens to roll up near her and bump against her : she will again be disturbed in her meditation. She came to ask me whether she could sit far away from everyone. "There too someone might come near you," I said. "And it is good if someone comes. You sit where you were sitting. Do not worry even if someone touches you," I told her.

Our women are such that even if by chance they met God, they will wrap their sarees closer lest He might touch them. The whole female body is full of complexes. From childhood they are taught to look upon the body as a disease that they must bear. They do not live in their bodies. The body is a shell that a woman is busy protecting all the time, although there is nothing about it which is worth saving. Such minor preoccupations do not allow the happening to take place.

A certain highly educated gentleman has asked me, "All this can happen to an emotional person, but how can it happen to an intellectual person ?"

If someone has learned to read and write a little, he considers himself to be an intellectual. If his mother dies, will he not cry ? Will he never fall in love now that he has become an intellectual ? Just because he has obtained a certificate from a university, when he makes love he will think twice whether or not he should indulge in kissing because some germs may become transferred. He will begin to calculate and he will refer to books before he decides whether to be or not be emotional. Intellectuality has become a sort of disease. The intellect does not have a fragrance, lightness. It has become not an asset, but a disease.

Some think that because they are intellectuals the happening cannot happen to them and that it can only happen to those who are emotional. Why ? Is it undesirable to be emotional ? Whatsoever is meaningful and significant in life comes through emotion. The intellect has never given birth to anything of value, nor will it ever do so. For mathematics and for keeping account books intellect is all right, but whatever is significant in life comes through emotion. It is amazing that the most significant discoveries in science, which are said to result from a highly intellectual process, actually spring from emotion rather than from intellect.

If Einstein was asked how he came upon the theory of Relativity, he would say, "I do not know. It just came, it just happened." This is a very religious statement : "It happened." If someone should ask Madam Curie how she discovered radium, she too would say, "I do not know. It just happened. To describe it is beyond my capacity." Whenever a great scientist has been questioned on how he came upon his discovery, the answer is always this : "What has happened is not through my search. It just happened. I cannot explain. It is the work of something beyond me. I was only a medium—an instrument—in its manifestation." This is a very religious language.

Emotion reaches profound depths; intellect is merely on the surface. It is only a utilitarian arrangement. The intellect is like the motorcycle officer who heads the procession of the Governor merely to clear the way for him. Do not mistake the motorcycle officer for the Governor. The intellect is nothing more than a policeman. The policeman clears the street from pedestrians and other motorcars so that nothing should disturb the Governor. The Governor is way behind—and that is emotion. All that is beautiful and noble in life springs through emotion. But there are many persons who are bowing to the policeman and who insist that he must be the Governor. They are the persons who insist that they are intellectuals. They consider the policeman to be the Governor. Let them. Even the policeman is laughing at their foolishness.

Some think that all this (meditation) happens only to weak-minded people and that for people with strong minds it is not possible. "How can it happen to us ?" they ask. They do not know anything. Meditation happens to the strong, and the weak ones are left behind. To persist with determination for half an hour requires strong will-power. The weak ones breathe hard for two minutes and then they give up. And these poor intellectuals insist it is happening to the weaker minds and it does not happen to them because they are strong. They cannot even breathe fast for half an hour. They cannot even ask "Who am I?" for ten minutes. They do not even have the courage to drop their false faces.

These rationalizations are nothing but excuses to escape. These are mental tricks by which we try to save ourselves. We say, "These things can happen only to weak-willed people. We are strong-willed, so how can this happen to us?" This is a very surprising statement. Anything which is of any importance is brought about by strong people. And meditation ? Meditation demands your ultimate strength. They will say that it happens to weaker minds and it does not happen to them because someone standing beside them is crying loudly. But the man to whom this is happening is utterly indifferent to whosoever is looking at him or to what anyone thinks of him. He is lost fully in that happening. Such a strong determination needs great strength. It is definitely not for the weak-willed.

Therefore, do not engage in the futile effort of safeguarding your ego by thinking that you are strong-willed, that you are an intellectual, and that, therefore, these things cannot happen to you. Simply know that it is not happening to you. There is no need to glorify the fact. You might begin to enjoy these arguments, and then the happening will never be possible. Just know that "It is not happening to me". And if it is not happening to you, there is some weakness on your part somewhere. Know this weakness, recognize it, and try to overcome it. Do not glorify the fact by thinking that your "strong intellectual mind" does not allow it.

Now one person has come and asked, "This is mass hysteria. Why are all these people becoming hysterical?" He does not know what is hidden in us. By looking upon this as hysterical, he detaches himself. He considers all of them as insane and weak-minded. If this is so, then Buddha, Mahavir, Jesus, Socrates, Rumi and Mansoor were all insane. But it is much better to join the tribe of these maniacs than to be one of "strong-willed" intellectuals, for what these "mad people" have attained the latter can never have.

When the energy rises in full force, it creates a terrible storm within the person. This is not madness, for if it were it would be impossible to become quiet afterwards. If we are capable of becoming tranquil soon after the first three steps, it cannot be hysteria. If a hysterical person is told to be quiet, to relax, he cannot, for he is not in control of his senses. Whatever happens in this experiment is well within your control. Whatever is happening takes place with our full cooperation. This is why the experience leaves you as soon as you stop cooperating.

There is only one way to distinguish a healthy person from a mad one. He who is the master of himself is healthy; he who is not is mad. Now this is an interesting situation. When I tell those who participate in the experiment to be quiet and to relax they immediately do so, whereas the so-called strong-willed intellectuals find it impossible to still their thoughts when they are asked to. They say, "We simply cannot. Howsoever hard we try, we cannot do it." This is proof of madness. It is they who are mad and weak. One who has no control over his thoughts is no better off than a mad person, but one who is his own master is truly a healthy person.

When the moment comes when you will be able to switch your thoughts on and off at will, you will be a healthy person. The moment you order your mind to stop, it must obey immediately. That is the sign of a healthy personality. But the fact is that you order the mind to stop, and it goes on and on doing just what it wants to. You are moving heaven and earth, but the mind is doing just as it wishes. You go to the temple and sing praises to the Divine, but the mind is sitting in the cinema rebelliously saying, "You go on singing as much as you like. I will sit here, as I like it here."

But man is very cunning. He hides his shortcomings with highsounding phrases and belittles the abilities of others with derogatory remarks to ease his conscience. Beware of this. My advice to you is do not think of others. It is difficult to tell what is happening to the other. Life is so mysterious that it is very difficult to judge others. Think only about yourself; it is enough. Think about yourself; "Am I mad? Am I weak or strong?" But we are so habituated that we are always curious about others. This is wrong.

As I told you, by letting the body go there is a catharsis of the complexes, and the blocks which are obstructing melt away. Another thing: when the body moves with its own momentum, without interference from you, the fact that it is separate from you becomes apparent. You are witnessing and the body will be moving. You are witnessing and the body will be swaying. The body will be trembling and you will know that it is the body trembling and not you. Then, for the first time, you come to realize that your being and the body are two different things. Then you will also come to know that it is the body which becomes young and not you, that it is the body which becomes old and not you. And when the experience becomes more and more profound, you will know that it will be the body that dies and not you. When the body begins to gyrate mechanically, you will come to realize its separateness from the Self. Allow the body complete freedom, and you will know it.

In the third step we ask, "Who am I ?" Even when one knows that "I am not the body, I am not the breath", one still does not know, "Who am I ?" This is a negative approach: "I am not the body, I am not the breath." But what about the positive aspect of "Who am I ?" Thus, the third step in which we ask "Who am I ?" is necessary. We flood ourselves completely with this question. The day this question fills you totally, the answer will come from within your own self. It is not possible that in your innermost depth you do no know who you are. If you are, you must also have a knowledge of who you are. But the question has to be carried to the innermost depth.

Deep within the earth there is water, but we are standing above on the ground and are thirsty. It is necessary, therefore, to dig down at least thirty feet in order to reach this water. If you are inquisitvie to know, "Who am I ?" you should know that the answer is lying thirty feet under somewhere within you. But there are many layers, and the answer will be obtained only if these are removed. So this "Who am I ?" acts like a spade. The greater the speed and force of the question, the deeper you dig within yourself. One has only to ask with a powerful force.

Many a time strange things happen. One friend has been undergoing a strange experience for the last two days and it is worth noting. He asks with all his might. There is nothing lacking in his effort and nothing wanting in his determination, but there are so many layers to the mind. He goes on asking the upper layers, "Who am I ?." He asks with a very great force, but while the upper layers are repeating "Who am I ?" something else within him is also asking simultaneously, "What will you get out of this ?"

One layer of the mind is asking, "Who am I ?" and another questions, "Of what use is all this ?" Who is asking, this second question ? You are asking, "Who am I ?" but who is asking, "What will you get out of this ?" This is the second layer of the mind speaking.

If the mind is split into two, one part taking part in the experiment and another opposing it, you will not be able to go very deep. Therefore, I say put all your strength into the asking so that the whole mind becomes involved and engrossed in the question. When only the question remains, piercing through you like an arrow, the answer will immediately come. The answer will come ; it is within you.

Knowledge is within, but we have never asked, we have never awakened it. It is ready to be awakened; thus, we need these three steps. But these three steps lead only up to the door. They take you up to the gate and leave you there. You enter within in the fourth step. But he who has not crossed the first three steps cannot possibly enter this door. Therefore, be very careful. Tomorrow is our last day. You have to put all your strength and energy into these three steps. Then the fourth will happen of its own. This fourth step will not be your doing. It will happen on its own. Three you will do, the fourth will happen.

Questioner: *Will the first three steps definitely drop away upon the attainment of the fourth* ?

Bhagwan: When the fourth step happens, this question does not arise. Then how one reacts will depend on the individual. If one will feel like continuing the efforts, he will do so; otherwise not. Nothing can be said beforehand about when the first three stages will drop. If we raise the question of whether to drop the first three stages before the fourth is attained, it shows that we want to escape from them. That is why we are unable to do the technique properly.

We are very eager and anxious to get rid of the first three steps. I will not promise that they will drop or become unnecessary, for if I do you will not go into them wholeheartedly. You will be finished with them, but only when you step into the fourth stage. We should not even talk about this in the beginning.

The mind deceives us in a thousand ways. When you ask, you do not know why you ask. You are asking only to know when you can get rid of the first three stages. But the fourth step cannot be reached merely by going through the first three with the idea of being rid of them as soon as possible. If that is the attitude, the fourth will not happen. But why this fear of the first three steps ? There is a fear, and it is to expel this very fear that these three steps must be gone through.

There is a fear that the body might do something irrational and reprehensible. But what can it do ? At the most, it will dance, cry or shriek, and after all what is the difficulty about that ? Continue that intense breathing in the first stage; in the second, together with deep and fast breathing, allow the body to let go. There is absolutely nothing to hinder you in this. In the third stage breathing will continue, the body will remain in a let-go and you will question within you with all your might, "Who am I ?"

You do not have to do anything to dance. Any action on your own will create a hindrance. For instance, if you dance, the breath will be obstructed. But if the body begins to dance on its own, that is a different matter altogther. You are not to dance, but if the body feels like dancing let it. Our trouble is that we either prevent the action or do the action. We never allow anything to happen on its own.

Man's entire culture is suppressive. We have suppressed a lot within ourselves and we are afraid this will all bubble up to the surface. This is the fear that holds us back from expressing ourselves totally without reserve. Thus, the question of dancing does not arise. Our fears are very deep-rooted. We have suppressed a lot within ourselves, and we are quite aware of all that we hold within. The son has wanted to kill the father. Now he is afraid that this thought might come out in the experiment. The husband has longed to strangle his wife, though at that very moment he might be expressing his faithfulness to her. Now he is afraid. If this comes out, others will know of it.

Gurdjieff was one of the most peerless men of our age. When anyone went to him for guidance, the first thing he did was to make him drunk every day for fifteen days. In that period he studied the man by making him bring out all his suppressed feelings. Then he knew what sort of a person he was and directed him into meditation accordingly. If anyone refused to undergo this treatment, he would show him the door. Rarely has a Master tried such a unique method. He was a very wise man and his understanding was invaluable. He knew well how much we keep suppressed within us. Our suppressions are unlimited.

Because of our suppressions we are afraid that something might come out—something we do not want others to know about. If someone has committed theft, it is possible that when he asks the question "Who am I ?" his mind may reply, "You are a thief." It can erupt loudly : "You are a thief, you are dishonest—a black marketeer." So this person will come and ask me whether he can drop this step. He will feel that he should ask this question in a low voice, for he already knows who he is : He is a thief and someone may hear it. He is afraid that this might break loose from his mouth loudly. And, really it is possible. So he is afraid to ask. And this is exactly the reason why he asks me when one can stop drop this questioning. But he will have to go through this. Let whatever comes from within come out. A lot of filth lies hidden within : let it all come out. The masks that we are wearing are not our real faces; that is why we are frightened.

Now a man who has a totally false face will naturally be afraid to drop it, for if he does so his real face begin to show itself. He is afraid that someone will discover its ugliness. He has taken great pains to make up this false face, and if he drops it the result will be chaotic. So he continues to be afraid. He will want to save it at any cost. All our faces are false, masked, made-up. Do not think that those who do not use make up have real faces. The make-up is very deep, and there is no need of any beauty aids. So you are afraid that if you let go completely, your real face may come out. You are afraid that someone might see it. But these fears are dangerous and they will not allow you to go deep. These fears have to be dropped.

Questioner : *What is meant by energy transmission* (*Shaktipat*) ? *Can anyone do it* ?"

Bhagwan : No one can transmit energy, but energy can be transmitted through someone. Anyone who says that he can transmit energy is uttering a falsehood. No one can do it, but it can happen through someone at some moment. If there is a person who is totally void, totally surrendered to the Divine will, then in his presence a transmission of Divine energy can take place. He becomes the medium, the conductor of energy, but he does not do this knowingly. However, the Divine energy can enter through him into others.

No one can knowingly become a medium, for the first condition to be a transmitter of energy is to be unaware of the fact that you are transmitting. There should be no sign of ego present. Ego disqualifies a person for this. So when there is a person who is in all respects completely void within, who is not doing anything himself, then through the emptiness in him (which acts as a passage) the Divine energy rushes forth and reaches you, and your progress will be intensified by this process. Remember this when you come tomorrow for the afternoon meditation session.

Transmission of *Shaktipat*, Divine energy, denotes the descent of the Divine force. The explosion of energy can become possible in two ways : Either it arises from within you and reaches up to the Divine or else the Divine force descends and flows into you. The result is the same; it is only viewing it from two directions. It is just as if there is a glass half filled with water, and some say the glass is half full while others say it is half empty. The issue cannot be decided because both views are correct. But philosophers can go on arguing without ever reaching a conclusion. Energy can descend from above and it can also rise from within you. When the dormant energy within you meets with the Divine energy, the explosion takes place.

Nothing can be predicted about this explosion. The outcome of it cannot be foretold. Those who have experienced this explosion have been crying for ages, "Come ! Pass through this explosion and see for yourself what happens, for it is inexpressible."

Shaktipat transmission of energy, is the descent of energy from above. It can descend. In fact, it descends daily. And when it comes across an individual who is completely empty within, it uses him to transmit it further. The happening is as simple as that. But if the slightest trace of ego remains in a person, if he thinks he is bringing down the power, then he cannot be a conductor and the energy will not flow from him.

There are two instructions for tomorrow morning and evening. Tomorrow is the final day and a lot is possible. We shall begin our experiment tomorrow assured of new possibilities. Firstly, those who begin to feel a new sensation anywhere in the body should stand up during the experiment, for the process is accelerated while standing.

Mahavir used to meditate entirely in a standing posture. The flow of the energy is faster when you are standing. So far I have not asked you to stand. Because you were hesitant even to sit, how could I have asked you to stand ? The impact of the energy while standing is tremendous. You may go entirely mad and break into a mad dance. This is possible only when standing. Tomorrow is the last day, and some ten to twenty-five friends have passed through a deep experience. Thus, they should stand up. I need not name them; they should stand up from the beginning of their own accord. If others feel like standing up during the experiment, they can do so. Then allow whatever happens to happen.

Secondly, in the session of silent meditation to be held in the afternoon, leave more space in front of me. Then I will place my hand upon the head of whosoever comes up to me, and they should allow any happening to take place. Perhaps they may scream or their hands and feet may tremble. Or, they may fall or they may stand up. Whatever happens, allow it. So leave some space in front of me, and those who have courage enough will stand from the very beginning. Before I come, stand silently. Do not take support from any tree or railing. Stand on your own without any support.

Shaktipat, the transmission of energy, can take place, and the energy can descend into many in the standing posture. The atmosphere is very charged and could be put to a very great use. Tomorrow, since it is the last day, you have to make your best effort. Now, let us deal with some more questions.

Questioner: *Do the first three stages have any effect upon the states of mind and the physical condition of the body* ?

Bhagwan: Yes, many changes take place. (*Someone says in between* : "*The heart may fail.*" *There is laughter all around*).

If that were the case, it would be the best thing that could happen. That is the only thing that does not happen, but if it should happen, let it happen. Do not try to save your heart, for one day it is going to fail. The bliss of experiencing that it failed on your path to the Divine is enough—more than enough.

This friend inquires about what effect the experiment will have. This meditation experiment will bring about many physiological changes. Many illnesses of the body will vanish and the life span can also increase. There will be many chemical changes within the body. Many centers that lie dormant within the body will spring into life.

Physiologists and psychologists say that in anger the body secretes particular poisons, but up until now they have not been able to discover any chemical reaction for love within the body. In love the body secretes nectar—but as it is rare that anyone is truly in a state of love, love has not been detected in scientists' laboratories.

When meditation is complete, the nectar of love begins to flow like a spring within the body. There are many other reactions. Those who go a little deep within themselves begin to see wonderful colours, smell wonderful fragrances and hear enchanting music. Sometimes they see streams of light flowing or they hear Divine music. These are all chemical reactions. The whole chemistry of the body changes. The body begins to see, think and discern things in an altogether different way. All the electrical circuits within the body undergo a change.

Just as a great deal happens within the body, so also does much happen to the mind. This needs elaboration, and the friend who has asked may meet me later on for further discussion. There are very many possibilities.

Questioner : *What is the effect of deep breathing on the heart, or on the brain, etc.* ?

Bhagwan : As soon as you begin to breathe deeply, the ratio of oxygen and carbon dioxide in the body changes. No sooner does this ratio change when consequent changes take place in the brain, the blood and in all parts of the body. The entire personality depends upon the ratio of oxygen and carbon-dioxide, and any change in this ratio will bring about a change within the body. That is why I say we may discuss it separately later, for this is a technical matter and is not likely to interest everyone.

Questioner: *Is this meditation experiment like the auto-hypnosis?*

Bhagwan : It resembles hypnosis to a great degree, but their paths change at the last point. The first three stages are the stages of hypnosis. The witnessing state alone is non-hypnotic. Throughout this experiment, the witnessing has to be kept up, and one should be fully aware of all that is taking place within. You should be fully aware—that the breath has come, that the breath has gone, that the body is trembling. There should be an awareness that "I know, I see it". This feeling, this state, is not of hypnosis. This is the difference, the only difference, and it is a very fundamental difference. All the rest is a process of hypnosis.

But the process of hypnosis is very valuable. Together with awareness, it becomes meditation, but without awareness it is a state of unconsciousness. If you make use of hypnosis alone, you will fall unconscious. But if you practise awareness along with it, you will be awakened. There is a great deal of difference between the two. Though the path is the same for a long way, they part at the last stage.

Some questions remain. We shall deal with them tomorrow night.

[Text of a discourse given May 4, 1970, at a meditation camp held in Nargol, Gujarat, India]

EXPERIMENT IN DYNAMIC MEDITATION

Meditation Camp at Nargol, Gujarat, India
Morning, May 5, 1970

In today's experiment, put in all your effort and determination, and have faith that you will succeed. Know that the happening will take place. Just as the sun has risen, so will the inner light flood you. As the flowers have opened in the early morn, so will the flowers of bliss bloom inwardly. He who sets out with full hope reaches, and he who calls out with total longing attains.

Those who can go through the experiment standing will remain standing throughout. And those who are sitting near them should leave a little space so that if someone falls it will not be on them. The momentum of the process will be very great and the whole body will dance in ecstasy. Therefore, those who are sitting too close should quickly move a little bit away. Gather all your courage. You are not to hold back even the slightest part of yourself.

The First Stage :

Close your eyes and begin deep breathing. Take a deep breath in and exhale out deeply. Look within : the breath comes, the breath goes. Inhale a deep breath and exhale a deep breath. (*The sadhakas, both men and women, begin to shriek and cry. Many begin to tremble and reactions begin to happen involuntarily*). Deep breathing, deep breathing, deep breathing. Put in all your effort. Breathe hard—in and out—for ten minutes. (*Many of the seekers begin to dance, jump, scream, cry and shriek loudly . . .*)

(*Bhagwan's directions continue*) : Deep breathing, deep breathing. Breathe in deeply and breathe out deeply, and keep looking within. Put in all your effort. (*There are shrieks and shouts, etc.*) Breathe in deeply, breathe out deeply. Keep looking within. See the breath coming, see the breath going. Apply your utmost effort. Breathe deeper, still deeper, yet more deep. Put all your strength, in your breathing for the next ten minutes. Deep breathing, deep breathing, deep breathing. (*There is some loud and hysterical laughter among the seekers*).

Deep breathing, deep breathing, deep breathing. Keep on looking within. The breath comes, the breath goes. Apply all your strength; hold back nothing. Deep breathing, deep breathing, deep breathing, deep breathing. The body will become a reservoir of energy. Breathing and only breathing will remain. The body will become a current of electricity. Deep breathing, deep breathing. (*More cries and shrieks are heard. One person shouts, "Rajneesh"*).

(*Bhagwan continues his directions*) : Deep breathing, deep breathing. No one should be left behind. Devote your entire energy. Deep, deep, deep breathing. (*The seekers laugh, scream, dance and jump*). There are only five minutes more, so do your utmost. Then we shall enter into the second stage. Deep breathing, deep breathing, deep breathing, deep breathing, deep breathing, deep breathing. Let the body become a mere breathing machine. Let there be breath and breath alone. Deep breathing, deep breathing, deep breathing, deep breathing. (*A meditator lets out a piercing shriek*). Apply all your strength. Deep breathing, deep breathing . . . deeper . . .deeper. Only the breath remains, only the breath remains. Do not give in to fatigue. Do not stop; apply all your effort. Save nothing; give your all. (*All kinds of sounds are heard from the meditators*). Apply all your strength. . .all. . .all. . .all. . .all. (*The seekers let out all kinds of sounds. They pant and shriek, jump and skip*).

(*Bhagwan goes on guiding*) : Apply your all. Do not be left behind; do not go back. The surroundings are becoming charged. Apply every bit of your strength and the happening will take place. Put all your effort into deep breathing. Deep breathing, deep breathing. Still deeper . . . deeper . . . deeper, deeper . . . deeper. (*Some cry and shriek. Many kinds of movements of the body take place.*) Apply all your energy; see that you do not stop. I am with each one of you. Give your all. There should be no regret later on that you could have done better. Apply all your effort . . . all your effort. Deep breathing . . . deep breathing. . .deep breathing. . .deep breething. . . deeper, yet deeper. The deeper the breathing, the easier it will be for the energy to awaken. The kundalini will begin to rise upwards with every stroke of the breath. Breathe deeply, breathe deeply, breathe deeply, breathe deeply. (*Some cry out aloud, some shriek*).

The kundalini will rise up . . . up. Take deep breaths. *A meditator cries out aloud* : "*Ahahahahahahaha.*" All around the seekers are going through all kinds of movements. Some do postures, others go through pranayams (breathing exercises). Some cry, others laugh. It is a strange scene. Bhagwan remains silent for some time, then again starts his encouraging directions.

Now two minutes are left. Apply in all your effort. Deep breathing . . . deep breathing . . . deep breathing. The kundalini will rise upwards. Breathe hard . . . breathe deep . . . breathe as deeply as you can. Apply all your effort for these two minutes. Then we shall enter the second stage. Deep breathing, deep breathing, deep breathing. Something is rising within. Let it rise, let it rise. (*Some seekers shriek, some utter a variety of sounds, some dance*). One minute more. Apply your all. We are now ready to step into the second stage. Deep breathing. Double your effort . . . double your effort . . . double your effort. The energy is rising within. Do not let yourself stop. Apply all your effort, all your strength. Deep . . . deep . . . deeper . . . yet deeper . . . JUMP. Put in all, put in all, apply all your strength . . . deep . . . deep . . . deep . . . deep breathing. Let the breath strike deep within and the energy will awaken. Deep breathing, deep breathing, deep breathing, deep breathing, deep breathing. Now we are about to go into the second stage. Deep breathing. . .deep breathing. . .deeper. I am telling each one of you alone to apply all your strength. Deep breathing, deep breathing, deep breathing, deep breathing, deep breathing. Now enter the second stage.

The Second Stage :

Deep breathing will continue. Now let go of the body. Whatever happens to the body, let it happen. If the body wants to cry, let it cry. If it wants to laugh, let it laugh. If it feels to shout and shriek or jump and dance. let it do what it pleases. Leave the body alone . . . Leave the body alone. (*All kinds of noises and movements take place with great intensity.*) Leave the body completely. Let it do what it pleases. For the next ten minutes, do not interfere with its movements. (*The speed of all body movements increases with renewed vigour as Bhagwan continues his encouragement*). Let go of the body—totally, completely. It will dance, it will jump; leave it, let it go. (*Some laugh aloud, others beat their own bodies, some cry, some dance. One woman lets out a loud shriek and begins to cry. All kinds of sounds and calls emerge from the meditators*).

(*Suggestions continue*): Let the body relax; continue to breathe deep and hard. The energy will rise within. The body will remble, dance, jump. Leave it free to do as it pleases. Let it roll on the ground or dance or shout. Let it go, let it go. Leave the body completely to itself so that you may see that it is apart from you—that you and the body are not one. Let the body go, let the body go, let the body go, leave it alone. The body has become a mere electrical tool. The body dances, it jumps, it shouts, it trembles; let it go, let it go. Leave it alone. The body laughs, the body cries; leave the body alone. You are not the body; it is apart from you. Leave it to itself; let it do what it pleases.

(*Cries, shouts, sobs, strange noises, come from the meditators*). Let go, let go, let go of the body completely. Do not stop it. Some friends are holding back. Do not, do not. Do not interfere with the body at all no matter what may happen. (*Someone lets out a piercing cry*). Tire out the body completely. Cooperate with it and reach the point of total exhaustion. Leave the body, cooperate with it and help it to reach the breaking point. The body has to become exhausted. Let it go. Whatever happens, let it happen. (All kinds of sounds, shrieks, shouts, loud cries and sobs are heard). Let go. Do not hold back; see that you do not hold back. Let go, let go. (*A wailing shriek*). Let it happen, let it happen. (*All around the soft and loud noises from the meditators create a strange and uncanny tumult. Bhagwan's directions continue*).

Only five minutes more. Cooperate fully with whatever is happening to the body. Let the body do as it pleases. Let it cry if it likes, let it laugh if it likes. Do not come in its way. Let it dance and jump or do whatever it wants. (*Some meditators are jumping and running about*). Let go, let go completely. Help the body all you can. The energy is rising within. Let go of the body. Leave it; leave it alone. Five minutes more. Let go of your hold on the body completely. (*A great deal of shrieks and sounds and all types of movements take place. The microphone goes out of order. All those in charge of the arrangements are lost in meditation. The loudspeaker operator had to be shaken back into consciousness to set the microphone right. Bhagwan continues his directions all the same*).

Let go completely. Allow the body complete freedom to go through the reactions. (*All sorts of sounds from the seekers arise—cries, guffaws, shrieks, wails*). Leave the body completely. You are different from the body. For two minutes, let go completely. You are not the body, you are not the body. Let the body do whatsoever it pleases. Two minutes and we shall enter into the third stage. Let go, let go, let go completely. Exhaust the body completely. Let go, let go, let go of the body. Make one final Herculean effort before we step into the third stage. Let the body go, let go. One more minute to go. Let go, let go. (*Long sounds of braying, crying, laughing and guffaws.*). Let go, let go completely. Let the body do what it wishes. Let it shout or cry or laugh; leave it alone to do as it pleases. You will see clearly your separate identity from the body. Let go entirely, completely. Cooperate with all reactions. Now leave the body completely aside and enter the third stage.

The Third stage :

Ask within, "Who am I ? Who am I ? Who am I ? Who am I ? Who am I ? Who am I ? " For ten minutes let the body be free to do what it pleases. Keep up the pace and the intensity of breathing and ask within, "Who am I ? Who am I ? Who am I ?" (*Seekers pass through various reactions, crying, shrieking, groaning, sobbing. One seeker calls out continuously, "Who am I? Who am I?" Bhagwan goes on repeating, "Who am I? Who am I?" All kinds of sounds come out of the seekers. There is crying and sobbing, shouting, shrieking and dancing. One person lets out a blood curdling cry : "Ahahahahahahahaha".*) Go on repeating, "Who am I ? Who am I ? Who am I ? Who am I ?" (*There are sounds of roaring, bellowing and shrieks that rent the skies : "Who am I? Who am I? Who am I? Who am I? Who am I?" One seeker groans in agony, "Ahahahahahah.")*

(*Bhagwan goes on repeating, "Who am I? Who am I? Who am I? Who am I? Who am I?" One seeker calls out, "Who am I? Who am I? Who am I?"*). Ask with all your might, "Who am I? Who am I? Who am I?" (*Cries, and shouts are heard, there is rolling and wriggling, dancing and jumping, and asking, "Who am I? Who am I? Who am I?" From various directions as Bhagwan continues his directions*). Apply all your strength, give your all and ask, "Who am I? Who am I? Who am I? Strive hard, strive relentlessly, Who am I? Who am I? Who am I?" Ask, Ask relentlessly. Do not stop. (*Many cry out and fall to the ground, many roll on the sands, yet others jump and dance in a frenzy*). "Who am I? Who am I? Who am I?"

Only five minutes more. Do your best; then we shall relax. Let the body go completely and ask within, "Who am I? Who am I? Who am I?" Try your best, put your all into the question. (*A long loud wail. . . cries from many and shrieks and shouts*). "Who am I? Who am I? Who am I?" Ask with all the strength at your command. Ask, ask, "Who am I? Who am I?" Apply all your strength and energy into that one question, Who am I?" All your strength and all your energy into that one question, "Who am I? Who am I?" Three minutes more to go; then we shall relax. Tire yourselves out completely. The energy is awakening within. (*Cries and shrieks, jumping and running among the meditators*).

(*Bhagwan continues*): "Who am I? Who am I? Who am I?" Apply all your energy; do not spare yourself. Two minutes more: "Who am I? Who am I? Who am I?" (*All kinds of body movements. There is a lot of noise and all kinds of sounds from the meditators. A long shriek is heard*). "Who am I? Who am I? Who am I? Who am I?" Last two minutes: Make a last strong bid, "Who am I? Who am I?" Then we shall rest. The energy is awakening within; let the body free to do as it likes. "Who am I? Who am I? Who am I?" (*There are cries of A-a-a-ah*). Let the energy awaken completely: "Who am I? Who am I? Who am I?" Go absolutely mad and ask, "Who am I? Who am I? Who am I?"(*One person calls out Ba-a-a-aha*). "Who am I? Who am I?

Who am I ?" Reach the point of complete exhaustion; then we shall rest. "Who am I ? Who am I ? Who am I ?" One minute more : "Who am I ? Let the body dance. (*A loud shriek. . . cries*). "Who am I ? Who am I ? Who am I ?" (*Intense activity among the meditators*). "Who am I ? Who am I ? Who am I ?" We have to pass into total relaxation, so put all your energy in this last moment. "Who am I ? Who am I ? Who am I ?"

The Fourth Stage :

Enough ! Enough ! Now leave everything. Stop asking, stop the deep breathing. Lie where you are; stand where you are. If you feel like falling down, fall down; if you feel like lying down, lie down; if you feel like sitting, keep sitting. Let everything be quiet and empty. Do not ask, do not do anything. Lie as if you are dead, as if you are not. The storm has passed and peace prevails within. All is erased, all is quiet. The storm has passed. Now relax. Lie quietly for the next ten minutes. It is in this tranquillity that the coming of He whom we are seeking takes place. Lie in complete peace. There is nothing to be asked, nothing to be done. Leave everything. If you are standing, keep standing, if you have fallen, remain so. Be absolutely dead for the next ten minutes, as if you do not exist. The storm has passed. (*All around the meditators are quiet and still. Sometimes someone lets out a cry, another sobs, then there is peace again*).

(*Bhagwan goes on talking*): It is in this void that the happening takes place, that some flower will bloom, that some light will spread. A stream of peace may spurt forth; some strains of bliss may be heard. The Divine comes in this Void. Await HIM, await HIM. Keep lying; lie still, lie still, and wait—await His coming. There should be only a silent awaiting. Everything is exhausted, everything is empty. (*Sounds of groaning are heard*). Await, await. Now I shall be quiet for the next ten minutes. Lie absolutely still. (*The birds sing in the trees. Someone moves, someone sobs, someone breathes heavily. One meditator cries out loud, "Oh Lord ! Oh Lord !" Some cry out, "Hoo, Hoo," while others groan. One person shouts, "Sinner, sinner." After some time, another voice calls out, "Who says I am a sinner ?" Again someone groans, "Ooh. . .Ooh. . .Ooh." The crows caw, the wind rustles in the pine trees and the ocean roars. Then for a while, there is complete silence all around, as if the pine forest was absolutely deserted. Then a woman cries and sobs*).

(*Bhagwan*) : Do not make any more sounds. No more expressions now. Be as if you are no more, as if you are dead and there is nothing but emptiness. Everything is extinct, destroyed; everything is quiet, everything is peaceful. In this silence is HIS coming. (*A woman cries out*). This Void is His entrance. Expect HIM, await HIM. (*A woman sobs bitterly. A man cries, "Hoo. . . Hoo. . .Hooo !" Another seeker who is sitting at a distance undergoes processes of pranayam. Someone shrieks, someone groans. Another calls out, "Sinner." Some mumble, some moan. The microphone is put in order once again and Bhagwan's voice comes clearly*). Be as if you are dead, as if you are no more. The storm has passed and now silence prevails. Expect HIM now.

It is in this moment that the happening takes place. Await in silence, await in silence, await in silence. Await, await, await; be as if you are no more. But within SOMEONE is awake. Everything is not, but within a flame is lit that sees, knows, recognizes. You are no more, but there is an ANOTHER who is fully awake. There is only light within. Streams of bliss flow within. The Divine is very near. Await HIM, await HIM. (*One person begins mumbling, "sinner, sinner, sinner." One seeker calls out, "Keep the sadhana going, keep the sadhana going. Someone claps, another calls out, "HELP."*) You are dead; you are no more. You are dead; you are no more. As the drop falls into the ocean and loses itself, lose yourself. Await, await. In this losing of yourself, you shall attain HIM.

A tranquil, silent light prevails within. A profound bliss has begun to sparkle within. A deep bliss will start within and flow all over. Wait for it—await. (*"Lord, Oh Lord, Oh Lord," someone calls*). Bliss will flow within, light will penetrate within. Await, await, await, as if you are dead; as if you are finished, as if you are no more.

It is in this Void that He appears, it is in this Void we get a glimpse of HIM, it is in this Void that He is attained. Await silently—await, await. See within : someone is entering. See within: someone is awake. See within : some joy has manifested itself—a joy that was never known before, that is wholly unknown and unfamiliar. Every pore of the being is filled with something

Divine. Await. . .await. . .await. (*The sound of the birds, the rustling of the leaves, everything, has stopped. All is quiet; everything is peaceful*). There is bliss and bliss. . .and bliss alone. There is light. . .there is nothing but light. Nothing but peace prevails. Await. . .await. It is in these moments of peace that He comes. It is in these quiet moments that meeting with Him is possible. Await. . . await. . . await. (*One seeker begins breathing heavily; another groans*). He whom you seek is near at hand. He for whom you search is close by. Await . . . await. (*Bhagwan becomes silent for a while*).

(*Bhagwan*) : Now return back to this world from the world of bliss—very slowly. Retrace your steps very, very gently from the world of light. Open your eyes gradually. If they do not open, put your hands on them first and then open them. Do not be in a hurry. Those who have fallen down and find it difficult to get up should take a few deep breaths and then get up slowly. Get up silently, without a word. Those who are standing may sit down silently and then open their eyes. Come back—gently. . . very gently. (*One woman sobs loudly*). Our morning session is now over.

5

THE SPIRITUAL SEARCH

My Beloved Souls :

Many questions have been received during these three days. I shall try to answer as many as I can by dwelling upon them briefly.

Questioner :

Vivekananda had asked Ramakrishna, 'Have you seen God ?' And he had replied, 'Yes. As I see you, so have I seen God.' Can we put the same question to you ?

Bhagwan Shree Rajneesh:

First and foremost, Vivekananda did not ask Ramakrishna's permission if he could ask the question. (*Laughter*..) Vivekananda ASKED; you are not asking. You are merely inquiring if you may or may not ask that question. In order to ask that question, a Vivekananda is required. And such an answer Ramakrishna would not have given to another. Remember that the answer given by Ramakrishna was given for Vivekananda alone. It could not be given to another.

In the realm of the spirit, all answers are entirely personal. The one who answers is, of course, important, but the one to whom the answer is given is not less important. The questioner is equally important. So many come and tell me, "Vivekananda experienced Divine knowledge at a mere touch from Ramakrishna. Will you touch us so that we too may have the experience ?" They do not realize that there were thousands of others whom Ramakrishna touched, and they did not have any experience. In the experience of Vivekananda, Ramakrishna is 50% responsible and Vivekananda for the other 50%. They are both equally responsible. Also, if Ramakrishna had touched him at some other moment he would not have necessarily had the experience. The happening took place at a particular moment.

You are not the same person throughout the entire 24 hours of the day. Within those 24 hours, your personality changes a countless number of times. The happening is the outcome of a particular moment. Vivekananda asked, "Have you seen God?" It seems to be a very simple question. We think we understand what Vivekananda had asked, but we do not understand. "Have you seen God?" These words are not so simple; otherwise even a child in the first standard at school would understand. These are very difficult words, and the answer is not to Vivekananda's question but to his thirst—to his longing. Answers are always given to the thirst of the seeker and never to his question. The quality of the questioner behind the question decides the answer.

Buddha was passing through a village. Someone asked, "Does God exist?" Buddha replied, "No." By midday, another man approached him and said, "I think that God does not exist. What do you say?" Buddha replied, "God is." By evening a third confronted him and said, "I do not know whether God is or is not." Buddha replied, "Then be silent." To this one he said neither yes nor no. The *bhikkhu* (monk) accompanying him was terrified. He had heard all the three answers. Before going to bed, he told Buddha, "I am utterly confounded with your answers. In the morning you said 'God is not', by midday you said 'God is,' and by evening you refuted both the answers. What am I to understand?"

Buddha replied, "None of the answers were given to you. They were each given to the person concerned. You had nothing to do with them. Why did you hear them? When you did not ask, why should you get the answer? You will get the answer when YOU ask." However, the *bhikkhu* insisted, "But I heard all the answers."

Buddha replied, "Those answers were for others, and they were given according to their need. The one who asked in the morning was a theist and he wished that I would confirm his view. He had no idea whether God existed or not. He only wanted to satisfy his ego by being able to feel that 'even Buddha believes in what I believe'. He only came to me for confirmation. Therefore, to him I said, 'No! God is not. I shook him by his very roots. He had no idea about the existence of God, or else why should he ask ? He who has realized God needs no confirmation. Even if the whole world denies God, he will stand by his belief and never give in. Now this person is still searching; he does not know. He asks, 'Does God exist?' So I have to say 'no'. His search had stopped and I had to start it again for him.

"The man who came in the afternoon was an atheist. He believed that God is not. I had to say to him that God is. His search was also at a standstill. He too had come to confirm his atheism. The man who came in the evening was neither a theist nor an atheist, and I did not wish to bind him with either—for 'yes' binds as much as 'no'. Therefore, I told him neither yes nor no, but to be silent; then he will reach. And there is no need to answer you, for, as yet, it is not your question."

Religion is a very personal matter—like love. When a lover says something to his beloved, he does not shout it in the market place. It is entirely personal, and when declared in public it loses its value. Truths that have been spoken about religion are just as personal. They have been spoken by a specific person to a specific person, and never in general. Therefore, the day you become a Vivekananda, you are welcome to ask. But Vivekananda did not first ask for permission to ask.

I was in a village sometime back, and a youth came and asked, "Shall I take Sannyas?" I told him, "As long as you feel that you should ask this question, do not take it, for then you will repent. Besides, why do you want to bother me about it? If you want to take it, then take it; if you do not want to take it, then do not take it. (*Laughter*...) The day you feel that you must take Sannyas, even if the whole world stops you, take it—for then only can Sannyas be joyful, not before this. "What about you?" he said. I said, "I never asked anyone—at least not in this life."

If one has to ask, one should ask one's own self. Why should we go and ask others? And how can we trust what others say?

It is impossible to put our trust in others, no matter how trustworthy they may be.

If I say to you that "God is", what difference will it make? Now you read in the book that Ramakrishna answered: "Yes. God is, and I can see him more clearly than I see you." But what difference has it made to you? You may write a book—or a thousand books—based on your asking the question and my giving the answer, but what difference will it make? All assertions from books that "God is" are useless. They are useless unless they come from within you. The answers of others do not help. The system of credit and debit works in all other transactions, but not in our transaction with God.

So why do you ask? And what is the value of my answer whether it is yes or no? Ask within your own self, and if no answer comes then know that fate ordains it to be so. Then await silently. Live with this awaiting; live without the answer. Someday it will come. Besides, if we know the art of right questioning, all answers are within us. If we do not know the art of right questioning, no amount of questioning will bring the right answer.

When a man like Vivekananda questions Ramakrishna, it is not the latter's answer that works on Vivekananda. Vivekananda is so filled with the thirst of knowing that when the answer comes from Ramakrishna it seems as if it has come from deep within his own self. Hence, the answer works, but not otherwise. When we ask from the very depths of our entire being, the answer that comes is our very own. It cannot be another's. The one who answers then becomes a mirror to prove the authenticity of the answer that came from within. If Vivekananda found Ramakrishna's answer authentic, it was because Ramakrishna acted as a mirror. He heard the echo of the sound of his own intrinsic being in the answer of Ramakrishna.

Vivekananda had asked another person before he asked Ramakrishna. That person was Ravindranath's grandfather—Devendranath. He was called Maharshi Devendranath. He used to stay in a boat on the river and used to practice meditation in his secluded surroundings. Once, in the middle of a night of the dark moon, Vivekananda swam across the river and climbed into his barge. The barge shook, and Vivekananda pushed open the unfastened door. It was dark. Within, Devendranath was sitting with his eyes closed in meditation. Vivekananda caught him by the collar and shook him. The Maharshi was shocked by the sudden violence of this youth, who, soaking wet, intruded on his privacy in the middle of the night.

No sooner had he opened his eyes when Vivekananda asked, "I have come to ask you, 'Does God exist?' " The Maharshi hesitated. You can imagine the plight of a person thus accosted in the middle of the night in a lonely place. He said, "Please wait a minute. Who are you? From where do you come and what is the matter?" Vivekananda let go of his collar and jumped back into the river. The Maharshi called out to him to come back, but he did not come. "Your hesitation gave me the answer," he shouted back from across the shore.

The Maharshi's hesitation was enough for Vivekananda. He was so taken aback that he forgot the question. Devendranath said later on, "I was truly frightened, for never before had I been approached in such an outlandish manner." When people asked him in meetings and in temples and mosques, he explained to them with the aid of the Gita and the Upanishads. But he had never been treated in this way before. "I was really shocked by the youth's behaviour. I was so startled I couldn't think anything, and before I could pull myself together the youth was gone. My hesitation made me aware of the fact that I do not know. This episode to me was an eye-opener."

Ask—certainly ask. But ask the day you are prepared for the question. Be fully prepared, for the matter does not end by getting the answer. Ramakrishna answered, and then the one who listened was not the same person who asked. The one who asked was Narendranath; the one who heard and went back was no longer Narendranath. When Ramakrishna said, "Yes, and I can see Him more clearly than you; I can even claim that you are false, but HIS existence is very much true," Vivekananda did not say, "Yes Sir. Your answer pleases me and I shall quote you in my examination." Then Vivekananda was drowned in the answer. The same boy did not go back home. He was a different person now.

The answer can be had; there is no difficulty in answering. But you will find YOURSELF in difficulty. The day you feel like asking, come. And it would be better if you too ask in an outlandish manner. On some dark night, come and catch me by the neck and ask me. But remember, although you will be catching hold of my neck, it will be yours that will be in the noose. (*Laughter*...) Then you cannot run away. This is not an intellectual matter that you may ask and go your way. That would be nothing. You have to put your whole life at stake.

Questioner: *When we sow a seed, it takes time before it sprouts. You say that man is God in seed form, but how is it that at the same time you say that he can sprout into Divinity this very moment?*

Bhagwan : This is exactly what I say. We sow a seed and it takes time to sprout, but time is required only for the seed to break. Then no time is needed for the shoot to sprout forth, for that is an explosion. It certainly takes time for the seed to break; you may take time to break from your shell. But it never takes time for God to appear. It is just like water which takes a long time to be heated. But once it reaches the boiling point, it takes no time to turn into vapour. That is a jump. At 100 degrees centigrade water jumps and turns into vapour; it loses itself. It is not that a part of the molecule of water turns into vapour and the other part remains water. The whole turns into vapour at once. It takes time, but the change is immediate. Also, until it completes the 100th degree it still remains water.

God is an explosion—a jump. Before that, you are man whether you are at the 98th degree or the 99th. When you reach the 100th degree point, God begins and you are no more.

Therefore, I say it can happen this very moment. Where is there a question if we are ready to reach the 100th degree? And is it not a long time since we are in the cauldron? For numerous lives we are trying to reach the Divine. We have placed ourselves on the fire since many a birth, and we have not yet reached the 100th degree. How much more time do you want? Enough time has been spent, and still we have not known how to reach the 100th degree. Even when the 99th degree is reached in some cases, the person quickly turns back and cools down. We are very much afraid of the 100th degree. I noticed this during meditation : many of you turned back from the 100th degree.

What useless things cause you to turn back. I am shocked at this. It must be your own urge to turn back, for the excuse is worth nothing in itself. It is just as if a man boards a train to go to Bombay but comes back saying that there were two people talking so loudly in the train that he could not bear the disturbance. To such a man we would naturally say, "You did not wish to go to Bombay, for there were bound to be disturbances and discomforts on the way." He who wants to go goes. And if he finds the disturbances overbearing, he increases his pace so that he may not have to go through the ordeal too much longer.

"Someone pushed me" or "someone fell down" or "someone cried aloud" are the reasons one gives for slackening his pace in meditation. They wait for any excuse in order to cool down, even the least excuse—that "So and so shouted and my meditation was disturbed". What has another person's shouting got to do with you ? And have you ever thought of what you lose by these excuses ? You do not know what you are saying.

One person met me on the way today. He said, "Please cool down these people, for a very explosive situation is being created. Two people even became naked." He told me very kindly that some people were upset on account of this.

Everybody is naked under his clothes and nobody is upset about it. Two people shed clothes and everyone is disturbed. This is a great irony. It would be understandable if someone had stripped you. But someone removed his own clothes and you are upset. If someone snatches your clothes, then too you should. not complain. Jesus has said, "If someone snatches your coat, give him your shirt as well." Perhaps in his inhibition he snatches less. It looks as if you were waiting for someone to do something so that you could slacken your tempo in meditation, and then you put the blame on the other.

Now this is strange, that someone becomes naked and your own meditation is spoiled. Were you watching someone becoming naked ? Were you meditating or what ? You should have not known at all what is happening around you. You should have been within your own self. Are you a laundry man or a tailor that you are worried about other people's clothes ? Your distress is senseless.

Now the one who sheds clothes does not stop to think. If someone tells you, forces you to shed your clothes, we can understand. But because of some unique happening within, a person sheds his clothes of his own accord. If someone offers you a 1,00,000 rupees, you will not remove your clothes. But some person discards his clothes without any such bribe, and you are upset. There must be a reason for his action, but it is not in us to understand life with mutual understanding for one another and sympathy.

When Mahavir shed his clothes for the first time, he was stoned; now he is worshipped. And all those who worship him now are cloth merchants. (*Laughter on all sides.*) The followers of Mahavir are all cloth merchants. This is strange, and it must have been these very people who stoned him. That is why perhaps they sell cloth—so that no one should go nacked. Mahavir was driven away from place to place because he was naked. He was not allowed to remain in one place. Wherever he went, people drove him far away from their village because of his nakedness. Now the same person who was denied a place in the village *dharmashala* (a place of free lodging provided by a religious group in India), or even the village burning ghats, is worshipped. They let loose wild dogs on him so that he would not stay in their village. What was troubling these people? Mahavir's nakedness.

What is the fear behind someone discarding his clothes? The fear is terrible. We are so perverted within ourselves that another man's nakedness reminds us of our own pervertedness and fills us with distress. There is no other reason. To be innocently devoid of clothing is one thing and to be pervertedly naked is quite another. Looking at Mahavir! No one could say that he was pervertedly naked, whereas we, in spite of all our clothing, cannot hide our pervertedness.

Have you observed closely those who discarded their clothes? You may have snatched a glimpse or two, but you could not dare to look at them longer, and it is because you only dared to snatch a glance that you are upset. Now this friend who met me has said that ladies were distressed. What does that mean? Did the ladies come with the purpose of seeing others remove their clothes? They should have engaged themselves in their own meditation. Instead of looking within themselves, instead of meditating, they were looking at others. Then the situation is bound to be explosive. Who asked you to keep an eye on others? If someone stands naked, let him stand. He is not looking at you and you were supposed to shut your eyes. If the naked man had complained that because of the ladies he could not carry out his sadhana (spiritual practice) fully that could be understood, but here the ladies are in an explosive state because of this man.

If you had to see him you should have observed him closely, and then your mind too would have been filled with the peaceful joy, the simple, guileless innocence, of the state he was in. There was much to gain; your mind would have been light and unburdened. But we forever resist all that is worth gaining. We always tend to embrace all that is harmful, and to that end we have developed countless insane theories.

A stage comes in meditation, and it comes unavoidably to some, when they must shed their clothes. They have taken my permission, so if you must you can hold me responsible. These people came and told me that during the course of meditation they have felt that if they do not shed their clothes something within will be blocked. I told them to go ahead and discard their clothes when this happened.

This is pertinent only to these persons. Why are you worried? If anyone has reproved them for this, he has done wrong. You have no right to say anything to anybody. You should understand that a time comes when many things become a hindrance to an innocent mind. Clothes are the most apparent indication of man's inhibition. They are a sign of his greatest taboo. They represent a very deep-rooted blind tradition, and they have a very powerful hold on man—so much so that clothes even become the symbol of one's culture. But a moment comes when the mind feels clothes to be an unnecessary burden. This happens to few, however, and not to everybody.

Buddha wore clothes and so did Jesus, but Mahavir discarded them. In the time of Mahavir, no woman dared to discard clothes in spite of the fact that his women disciples were more than the male ones. Ten thousand men and forty thousand women followed Mahavir during his lifetime. Yet, not a single woman dared to discard her clothing. Therefore, Mahavir had to say that these women will have to be reborn again as men or else there is no hope for their liberation. How can one who is afraid of shedding his clothes not be afraid of leaving the body? Therefore, Mahavir had declared a principle that a woman could not reach Divine bliss. She has to take birth as a man first.

But there have been brave women. One such was born in Kashmir. Her name was Lalla. If you ask a Kashmiri, he will say, "We know only two words: Allah and Lalla." This woman, like Mahavir, had discarded her clothes. All of Kashmir revered her. In her nudity, there was seen for the first time a wonderful beauty, a wonderful innocence, a wonderful joy—that of a child. If Lalla had met Mahavir, this blemish against women would not have been on Mahavir, for then he would not have said that it is imperative for a woman to be born as a man before she attains Realization.

Actually, the source of the accusation against Mahavir are the women around him and not he himself. He felt that since none of the women dared to discard clothes, it was impossible to expect them to let go of the body. If the outer attachment is so great, inner renunciation is impossible.

I do not exhort you to shed your clothes, but if someone else sheds them do not stop him. If in a meditation camp we do not allow a person complete freedom, where else can we hope to attain freedom? Meditation camps are for sadhaks and not for spectators. As long as no one comes in the way of another, he is free to do what he pleases. If someone trespasses on another, then alone is there cause for complaint. If a man becomes naked and begins to push you or harm you, then he should be stopped. But as long as a man is lost in his own self, you have no reason to complain; you are no one to do so.

We create strange hurdles. Someone becomes naked and the meditation of others goes to the wind. Of what worth is such cheap meditation? You feel that if there were no outer disturbance (like someone becoming naked), then only would you be able to go into meditation. How? No, these paltry excuses will have to be denounced. Sadhana is a matter of great courage, for in it we have to peel off each layer one by one.

In its deepest meaning, sadhana is to lay bare your innermost self. It is a nakedness of your inner being. An outward discarding is not absolutely necessary, but at some moment someone might reach a stage of shedding clothes.

Remember also that when this happens to someone, you can never know, nor have you any right to decide, whether it is right or wrong or the why and wherefore of the happening. Who are you ? And how will you know the implications of this situation ? It was people like you who pelted Mahavir with stones—clever, well-mannered moralists who decided that such a man should not be allowed within the precincts of their society. Time and again we repeat the same mistakes.

My friend who met me on the way explained very lovingly and earnestly to me that I should make things more clear or else not very many people will come for meditation in Bombay. Let the attendance fall; let not a single person come. There is no need at all for wrong type of people. Let only one come : What is the difference ? My friend has said, "Ladies will not come at all." Let them not come. Who asked them to come ? They may come if they want to, but only on my conditions. The meditation camp cannot be directed by their rules. The day I hold a camp on your terms do not come at all, for then I shall not be worth a cent. Then you should have nothing to do with me.

The meditation camp will be conducted on my terms. I do not come for you and according to your wishes. Therefore, I shall not work according to your directions. This is why dead gurus are so much in demand. You can direct them as you like. If a guru is alive, there is trouble. That is why only a dead Mahavir is worthy of worship. If he is alive, he is stoned. This is very natural. Therefore, the dead are worshipped all the world over. A living guru is very troublesome : you cannot bind him. No motive is of any worth to me. Who comes, who does not, is of no consequence to me. Whoever comes, let him come with full knowledge and understanding as to why and for what he has come.

Questioner : *Bhagwan, can you elaborate on what is "sahaj" (spontaneous, effortless and easy) yoga ?*

Bhagwan : This is the most difficult of yogas, for there is nothing more difficult than to be "sahaj". What is the meaning of "sahaj"? It means let whatever happens happen. You should offer no resistance. Now one man has become naked (in the meditation camp). This may be a spontaneous happening for him, but to us it is very difficult. To be "sahaj" means to be as natural as water and air. Do not allow the intellect to interfere in whatsoever is taking place.

The mind interferes and we begin to be unspontaneous. As soon as we start debating what should be and what should not, we become unspontaneous. When we are ready to accept whatsoever comes, we become spontaneous. Therefore, first and feremost, understand that sahaj yoga (easy yoga) is the most difficult yoga. There is a misconception about this yoga. People repeat Kabir's words. : "Sahaj Samadhi is best." It is best, but very difficult, for nothing is more difficult for man than to be natural and spontaneous. Man has become so unspontaneous, has gone such a long way from being natural, that it is easy for him to be unspontaneous and most difficult to be spontaneous.

Some facts have to be understood. Whatsoever I am saying pertains to sahaj yoga only. To heap doctrine and dogmas on life is to deform it, but that is what we do. One who is violent by nature tries to be non-violent; one who is of a violent temper strives to be tranquil; some thief tries to be a generous person : such are the rules and principles that we have made in life. We are forever striving to add on to our personalities something that we are not. If one succeeds in this one is just as great a failure as when he does not succeed. A thief cannot be generous no matter how hard he tries. He may give to charity, but that will only serve to create an illusion of generosity in him. A thief's mind finds means and ways of stealing even as he donates in charity.

Ekanath once set out on a pilgrimage. A thief in the village begged him to take him along with him. He wished to bathe in the Ganges to be absolved of his burden of sins. Ekanath said, "I do not mind in the least since there are others with me who are also thieves, though of different sorts. But there is one hitch. These other thieves have requested me not to take you along as they are afraid you will steal their belongings on the way. If you sincerely promise not to indulge in stealing, you may come along." He swore he would not rob the others, either while coming or while going. The journey started, and the thief joined the party which consisted of thieves of various kinds. Is there one type of a thief? There are thousands : someone is a magistrate, someone an advocate, someone something else.

Now the poor thief soon began to feel uncomfortable. The day passed somehow, but the night became more and more impossible to go through. One night, two nights passed. When the night came, everyone would go to sleep, but he became very tense, for it was his time for business. After two days he could hold out no longer. He said to himself, "I will die this way. How will I manage to get through the three to four months of this journey ? If things continue this way, I might even forget the art of stealing. Then what shall I do on return ? After all, a pilgrimage is not a lifelong affair." (*Laughter* . . .)

The third night, trouble started—trouble that was orderly and religious. He committed theft, but with great ingenuity. He removed one person's things and put it in another person's bag; he did not take anything for himself. (*Loud laughter*. . .) Everyone was upset the next morning, for each found his things in the other's bed or baggage. There were fifty to a hundred people, and it was difficult to locate things. Everyone was surprised. It was a strange situation. Nothing was lost, but everything was interchanged. (*Laughter*. . .)

Then it occurred to Ekanath that it must be the doing of the thief. He kept awake that night. At about two a.m. the thief got up and began mixing up the belongings of the others. Ekanath caught him and questioned him : "What is this you are doing ?" He said, "I had promised that I wouldn't steal and I am not stealing. But at least I must keep up the habit of removing things. (*Laughter*. . .) I do not keep things with me; I merely displace them. Besides, I did not make a vow to you that I would not do this." Ekanath used to say later on that a thief can never improve, no matter how hard he tries.

All the unnaturalness in our lives is due to the fact that we are always attempting to be different from what we are. No, sahaj yoga says—do not try to be other than what you are. Be what you are, know what you are, and live accordingly. If you are a thief, then know yourself to be a thief. Then live wholly and entirely as a thief. This is a most difficult task, for a thief also gains satisfaction and consolation from the fact that he is trying to overcome his tendency to steal. This tendency does not leave him, but he lives in the hope that if not today then tomorrow he will be an honourable man. His ego consoles him that though today he is driven to steal, a time will soon come when he shall no longer feel compelled to stoop to such an act. Thus, in the hope of tomorrow, he indulges in stealing today without any qualms. Sahaj yoga says, "If you are a thief, then steal with the full understanding that you are a thief and not with the hope that tomorrow you will not be thief."

If we understand what we are and accept ourselves as such, a revolution takes place instantly. If a thief fully understands the fact that he is a thief, he cannot remain a thief for long. By considering himself to be a good man driven to thieving, he is simply devising a method for remaining a thief. He deludes himself with the thought that his conditions have made a thief out of him, and as soon as he can he will get out of them. Thus, while trying to clear his image in his own conscience, he goes about his task of stealing without the slightest hesitation. So also does a man commit violence while vowing to be non-violent. Another swears that he is serene of nature and that it was the other person's abuses that incited him to anger. Then, when his anger abates, he even goes to beg the forgiveness of the person concerned. He is amazed how those words ever crossed his lips, for he is "a peaceful man". Thus, the ego is safely maintained. Remorse is a remedy to reinstate the ego : Ask forgiveness for the excess committed and save the ego.

No, sahaj yoga says, "Know yourself exactly for what you are and not just in part; do not try to escape from the knowledge of what you are." And the moment you are aware of the pain, the agony, the sinfulness, the hellfire that you are, you will immediately transcend it; you will have to jump out of it. If a thief knows himself fully to be a thief and does not delude himself with the thought of not being a thief; if he realizes within himself that "I am a thief and will always remain a thief"—that "if I am a thief today I shall be a bigger thief tomorrow, for my practice will have increased by 24 hours";

if a person becomes fully aware of his inner tendency to be a thief; then do you think such a person can remain a thief for long ? It will be difficult for him even to breathe, for the awareness of his being a thief will pierce him like a sword, and he will lose no time to get out of it all. Thus, a revolution will take place within him—that very moment !

We are clever, and we have evolved clever methods : We are thieves who are always dreaming of not being thieves. These dreams help us to remain thieves forever. They are like the buffers between train bogies that absorb the shocks of movement. Thus, travellers do not even know of them. Or, they are like the shock absorbers of a car which absorb the jolts along a bumpy road. We have made buffers and shock absorbers out of doctrines and dogmas in the same way as we do for train bogies and cars. I may be a thief, but I follow the doctrine of non-stealing. I may be violent, but I wear an emblem reading "non-violence is the ultimate religion" around my neck. This helps me to remain violent. Whenever the awareness comes about my violence, I can say, "What ! I violent ? But I believe in non-violence ! If I have not attained it today because of my weakness, I shall attain it tomorrow; if not tomorrow, then in next life. But my doctrine is *ahimsa* (non-violence). I will carry the flag of non-violence all over the world."

But within I remain violent, and the emblem of non-violence becomes my support. Wherever you see a sign that reads "*Ahimsa* is the Ultimate religion", be sure that there are violent people around it. That is the only reason for the signboard to be there. It is a trick of violent people. Man has evolved so many tricks and methods that these alone remain and man himself is lost.

The meaning of being "*sahaj*" is to be in a condition where that which is, is with no escapes from it—simply to remain in it. But this is so painful that we cannot live in such a way. If we were thrown into hell, our dreams would help us to pass our time there. If we fast for one day, we have to shut our eyes and dream of all kinds of delicious foods. On fasting days, it is these dreams that help us to pass through the torturous period. If these dreams are broken, the fast too will break.

There was a professor who was with me in the university. We were together for a long time. Sometimes, in the course of our talks, he would suddenly begin talking about various delicacies. At first I did not notice it, but as this began to happen many times at regular intervals I was curious to find out the reason behind it. Then I began to note the intervals, and I found that on every Saturday he would talk about sweets and other things to eat. (*Laughter. . .*) One Saturday, as soon as he came, I told him, "Today you will definitely talk about sweets." He was takena back with surprise. "Why do you say that ?" he asked. (*Laughter. . .*) I said, "I have been observing you these last two months. Every Saturday you talk of sweets. Do you fast on Saturdays ?"

"Who told you ?" he asked. "There is no need for anyone to tell me," I replied. "I have made my own calculations." (*Laughter. . .*) He said, "I do, but how did you find out ?" "Why else should a healthy man, who always eats well, suddenly begin to talk of sweets ?" I asked. You are a normal, healthy person, but on Saturdays you never fail to talk about sweets under one pretext or another." "You are right," he admitted. "On Saturdays my mind always plans what it is going to eat the next day, and that is how I can manage to pass the day. On Saturdays I fast." (*Laughter. . .*) I advised him to fast without thinking of food, but he said that it was impossible. It was absolutely necessary to keep the mind occupied in this manner, and then only did he manage to drag through the day. (*Laughter. . .*) The hope of tomorrow helps us to go through the agony of today.

A murderer passes life in violence hoping to be non-violent. A vindictive person passes his life with the hope of developing patience and kindness. A thief passes through life with the hope of doing charity. A sinner, likewise, goes through life with the hope of becoming virtuous someday. These hopes are very irreligious. Break them ! That which is, IS. Know this and live with it. Live with the facts. They are hard; they are harsh and very agonizing. It gives the mind a great deal of pain to realize that "I am this or that sort of a person". Now a man who is filled with thoughts about sex passes his days reading about celibacy. He is filled with thoughts of sex, but he reads books on "brahmacharya" (celibacy) and believes that he is practising it. The book is a great help and support toward keeping him sexual. Every day he consoles himself by thinking, "Just this day I shall indulge in sex; from tomorrow I shall be firm in my vows of celibacy."

Once I was a guest in a family. The old man of the house told me that he was initiated three times into brahmacharya by a sannyasin. "Thrice?" I questioned. "The vow of brahmacharya is only taken once. Now did you take it again?" (*Laughter. . .*) How can the vow of brahmacharya be taken thrice?" I asked again. "I have told this to many people." The old man replied, "But no one else has caught me like this. No one has asked me why I took it thrice except you." I persisted in my questioning : "What happened that you had to take it a second time?" He said, "My vow broke, so I took it again. Again it broke, so I took it for a third time." "Then what about a fourth time?" I asked, "I lost confidence in myself," he replied. (*Laughter. . .*) But by the time he was through with taking vows, he had reached the age of sixty, and so he had passed his span of sexual life. He passed through his period of sexuality vowing celibacy all the time.

We are very strange people, and what is actually happening is "a-sahaj (unnatural) yoga." We remain sexual, but we study brahmacharya. Books on brahmacharya serve as buffers for our sexuality. You console yourself by thinking, "Do I not read books on brahmacharya? Who says I am sexual? Right now I am weak; the actions of my past birth are coming in my way. Perhaps the time is not ripe for me yet; hence, the indulgence. Otherwise I am a "brahmachari" (a celibate); I believe in brahmacharya." We train our minds into thinking and believing in this way. On the one hand there is a hankering for sex, and on the other there is a claim of brahmacharya. Both go side by side. The belief in brahmacharya becomes a buffer, a shock absorber, while the seat of sex within continues on without any bumps and jolts. In this way the journey of sex continues comfortably.

This is an unnatural state. The natural state would be to remove all buffers. If there are potholes on the road, we should be aware of them. The inner car should be without any shock absorbers. Then, at the very first jolt, we would jump out of the car and bid it goodbye. We will never sit in it again. (*Laughter*. . .)

"Sahaj Yoga" means that which is, IS. Do not make any effort to be unnatural. Accept and know things as they are, recognize them, and be prepared to live with them. Then the revolution is a certainty. He who lives with that which is, is bound to change. Then there shall be no need to contrive ways to spend sixty years in sexuality. If you take a vow, you shall find ways and means of evading it.

Suppose that you have lashed out at someone in anger. However, you do not ask pardon. On the contrary, you say, "I am a wrong type of person, and if you want to remain friends with me keep in mind that I may lash out at you again." Then all friends will fall away, all your relationships will break. You will then have to live alone with your anger. Anger alone will be your friend. There will be no one to vent your anger upon, no one to hear it and no one to give you an opportunity to be angry. Then you will have to live with this anger. Will you be able to live with anger ? You will jump out of it. You will then see the madness of anger. But we have found ways and means of avoiding this realization and nurturing our weaknesses.

The husband is angry with the wife in the morning. After an hour, he makes up with her and goes and buys a saree for her. The poor woman thinks he is very loving, but this fellow is repenting for his anger and making arrangements to reinstate it back into its old place again. (*Laughter*. . .) He goes back to the starting point. The saree returns the wife to her old place again, his remorse takes him back to his previous line of attack, and so the old conditions are kept alive for the future. Then the same thing will be repeated in the evening, and then again they will make up at night, and then day after day the same cycle will go on repeating. Thus the whole life passes, and neither of the two realize what is the truth of the matter. What is happening ? What is this maze of improbity ? Each continues deceiving the other. We pass through life not only deceiving each other, but also deceiving ourselves.

"Sahaj yoga" means not to deceive yourself. Know yourself for what you are and accept it to be so. The moment you look upon yourself in this way there will be an instant change. It will be simultaneous; you will not have to wait for it. If someone's house is on fire and he knows it, will he stay there ? He will jump out immediately. The moment we understand life as it is, the turning point comes and the situation is created for the jump. But our house is on fire and we decorate it with flowers. We do not look at the flames at all; we only look at the flowers. Our hands are fettered and we have polished them with gold. We do not see the chains; we only see the ornaments. We are ill and wounded, but we cover our wounds with colourful bandages. Then we look at the colours and not at the wound which they hide.

The deception has been going on since long. The whole life passes and the moment of change does not come. We keep on postponing it. Death comes, but this moment never arrives. Ultimately we die, but we are unable to change. The change can take place anytime. Sahaj yoga is a wonderful process to bring about this change. Sahaj yoga means, "Live with that which is and you will change ; there is no need to make any effort to change." Jesus says, "Truth liberates." But we do not know truth at all. We colour everything with falsehoods instead. Falsehoods bind, truth liberates. The most painful truth is better than the most pleasant falsehood, for a pleasant falsehood is very dangerous : it binds.

Truth liberates, howsoever painful. Even the pain of truth liberates. Therefore, live with an agonizing truth, but do not nurture falsehoods, howsoever pleasant. This is all of sahaj yoga, and this will lead to Samadhi. You will not have to go looking for Samadhi : it will come on its own.

When you feel to cry, cry. Do not stop your tears. When you feel to laugh, laugh : do not hold back your laughter. Let whatsoever happens, happen, and know that it is happening.

It is said that in Japan there was a very well-known saint. He died, and thousands of persons flocked to pay homage to him. He had a disciple who was even better known than he. In fact, the Master was known because of this disciple. Now the disciple sat outside the door crying and beating his breast. People asked him, "You are crying? We thought you have attained Knowledge." He said, "You fools, I shall not stop my tears because of any Knowledge. Crying is a different matter altogether. Keep your Knowledge to yourself. I have no need for it."

But they tried to make him understand : "What will people say ? Go inside or else there will be a scandal. We were under the impression that you are the wisest man—one who has reached a state of balance within. We thought nothing can ever affect you." He said, "You have not understood me. At first my feelings were less sensitive ; I was impervious to feeling. Now every thing affects me and passes through me. Thus, I will cry to my heart's content. Take your wisdom ! Throw it out of the window !"

Still, the well-wishers tried to stop him. They formed a circle around him, for they thought that his reputation would suffer if people saw a man known far and wide for his knowledge crying bitterly in such a manner. "You used to say that the soul is eternal," they tried to explain. "Then why do you cry ? Who is it that is crying for the Atman (Soul) ?" The disciple wailed, "The soul shall always be, but I cry for the body. The body that was so dear to me has fallen away. It will never again come on this earth. The temple in which the Atman resided was very, very lovable, and now it will be no more. I cry for the body of my beloved Master."

"You cry for the body ?" People rebuked him. "Will you make conditions for crying ? Will you not let me even cry in peace ?" said the disciple. (*Laughter*..).

A liberated mind is a mind that has become truthful. A truthful mind is a mind that is authentic under all conditions. Its tears are bona fide, its laughter is genuine, and so also is its anger. If an authentic mind is angry, the anger should be so complete that the person and all who are around him come to realize what anger actually is. Such an anger will be liberating. Instead of being angry in small quantities throughout life, it is better to be completely angry once and to know it. Then the fires of anger will burn you, and you, together with those around you, will know once and for all what anger really is.

All our emotions and actions are such that we are hardly aware of them. One minute we are in anger, the next minute we are not. It is as if we take one step forward and another backward. We go nowhere, we return nowhere. We stand and dance in one place ; there is no going anywhere. Sahaj yoga means to accept life as such, to live it and know it as such. This knowing, living and accepting of life as it is, brings about a mutation, and through this mutation you reach to the Divine.

What I call meditation is the very method of this Sahaj yoga. In it you fully accept whatsoever is happening and let yourself go, allowing all reactions. Otherwise, it would be difficult to imagine educated, well-to-do, sophisticated people standing here shrieking, clapping their hands, stamping their feet, and dancing madly. This is not an ordinary happening. This is priceless—extraordinary. This is why the mere spectator cannot understand what is happening. He laughs at what he sees. He does not know that if he too were to take part in it sincerely the same thing would happen to him. It is also possible that his ridicule is simply a defense measure. He laughs it off by saying, "I will not be able to do all this." But his laughter betrays him. It shows that he too is concerned with what is happening, but he has held himself back ; he has repressed himself. He has not cried, he has not laughed, he has not danced.

Bertrand Russell once said, "Man's civilization has snatched some priceless things from him, one of which is the ability to dance." Russell said, "Today, I cannot stand in the middle of Trafalgar Square and dance—and we say we have attained independence. They say independence has come to the world, but I am not free to dance where I please. The traffic police will put me behind bars right away, and I would be accused of causing an obstruction on the road. He will even say, "You seem to be mad. A crossing is no place to dance."

When I see the backward tribals dancing under the stars with gay abandon, I wonder if we have gained something or lost something by civilization. We have gained something from civilization, but lost much. We have lost our simplicity ; we have lost our naturalness. We have become immune to nature and have acquired a lot of complexes. Meditation is a method of taking you back to a natural state of existence.

Before we end, I would like to tell you that whatever has happened here in these three days is very significant. Some people have gained wonderful experiences ; some have had glimpses of the beyond ; others made the effort though it was not complete. They were very close to the experience, and entrance was possible. Everyone has made an effort except for a few who are under the illusion of being wise and intelligent. Everyone participated except these few who are filled with book knowledge. A special kind of an energy has been created in these surroundings in spite of many obstructions. A lot has taken place, but this is just the beginning.

If you devote one hour out of every 24 hours to meditation a door will open in your lives. Shut yourself in a room and warn the members of your family not to worry about whatever may happen within that room during that hour. Strip yourself of clothes within the room. Throw all clothes away and meditate standing. Put a mattress down so that you won't get hurt if you fall. You must warn people in the house not to be worried if they hear cries or shrieks. A lot can happen, and they should be forewarned to prevent anxiety and worry. Practise meditation for one hour every day before we meet again in the next meditation camp. If all those who have taken part keep up the practice daily, I shall be able to hold a separate camp for them.

The possibilities are great. They are infinite, but you will have to put in the effort. You take one step forward and the Divine is always ready to come a hundred steps toward you. But if you are not ready to take a single step, then there is no remedy. Many inhibitions will try to obstruct you. Small children will laugh and say, "What has happened to father that he shouts and dances ? When we make a racket he scolds us. Now what is he up to ? (*Laughter . . .*) They will certainly laugh. You must ask their forgiveness for ever having stopped them from these natural expressions. Tell them to keep alive their ability to laugh and sing, for it will be very useful later in life. We make our children old too soon.

Do not talk about what you are doing; do not discuss it with others. Only mention it to warn the family members—and then no more. After a day or two, they will get used to it. Then, not only will the result begin to show in you, but also in the members of your family.

If it is possible, have a separate room for your meditation. No matter how small. Do not use that room for any other purpose. Look it from within and use it just for meditation. If other members of the family also want to meditate, they may join—not otherwise. If it is not possible for you to have a separate room it is all right, but there are many advantages to having a special room. If it is used for meditation only, the room will become charged with Divine energy. Then you will feel this energy daily, for you will be radiating Divine energy all around you.

Rays are constantly being emitted from the mental plane on all sides. The room or the place where you are, absorbs these rays. That is why, for thousands of years, a place can remain holy. If Mahavir or Buddha or Krishna have sat in a particular place, that place has been exposed to a different sort of vibration which it holds for thousands of years. By standing in such a place, it becomes easier for you to enter into an altogether different world.

Those who are well-to-do—and by that I mean those who can and would have a temple within their homes (all others are paupers) —should keep a room aside which can be used as a temple and which can become a door to a different world. Do not use that room for anything else. Enter the room in silence and use it only for meditation. The other members of the family will also be gradually affected, for the mutation that will take place within you will begin to show.

Now, even in this very camp people have begun to inquire about those in whom this change has taken place. They come and ask me what they should say when people ask them what has happened to them. So at home, your children, your wife or husband, your friends, will begin to be curious about the changes in your disposition. They too will be eager to find out the cause of this. And if you continue your sadhana, that day will not be far when the happening will take place within you —the happening for which we have to pass through infinite lives and for which we lose infinite lives.

The coming years in man's history are very significant. Now, nothing can be accomplished with only a few spiritual people. If an enormous spirituality is not born, if a massive spiritual movement does not take place upon the earth in which millions of persons are affected, it will be impossible to save the world from the doom of materialism. There will be momentous moments during the coming fifty years that will decide the fate of mankind. Either religion will be victorious or materialism. These fifty years will be years that will properly evaluate Buddha, Mahavir, Krishna, Mohammed, Ram, Jesus and others of their kind. All these luminaries will be on our side of the scales, while the other side of the scale will contain all the neurotic politicians, various sorts of worldly people, and the deluded, ignorant masses as well.

The struggle that has been going on since long will soon reach a climax. On our side of the scale, there are very few people, as you can see. And there is little to hope from things as they are now. But I am yet not disheartened, because I feel that very soon a way that is simple and natural will be found which will act as a revolutionary ray of transcendence in the lives of millions of people.

In olden times, it was enough for mankind if only one man attained Godhood. Now this will not do. Such a terrible explosion of population has taken place that a single individual is but a helpless non-entity. Now only a massive wave of spirituality involving millions of people can be effective. If a few people form a nucleus and begin the work, then India can play a decisive part in this momentous fight. No matter how poor, how miserable, how enslaved or how strayed from the path this country may be, it still has within its bosom some well-guarded treasures. Such great persons have trodden on this land and consecrated it ! The very air carries the vibrations and flames of their being, and their cherished wishes have blossomed forth on every leaf.

Man has gone astray, but the grains of dust on this earth yet have the memory of Buddha's footfalls. Man has erred, but the trees still remember the sacred moment when Mahavir sat beneath them. Man has forgotten, but the oceans have heard voices of a different kind. Man has fallen, but the skies have still not given up hope. If man alone can retrace his steps, everything else is ready.

I pray ceaselessly with the hope that I may be instrumental

in bringing about a spiritual explosion in the lives of millions of people. You can be of help in this. The explosion within you will not be valuable only for you, but for all of mankind. With the hope and prayer in mind that you will kindle the flame within yourselves and also be instrumental in lighting it within others, I bid you farewell.

May I thank you for having heard me with such love and serenity for these three days? And now I bow to the Divinity that resides within all of you. Accept my obeisance.

[Text of a discourse given on May 5, 1970, evening, at a meditation camp held in Nargol, Gujarat, India]

6

SHAKTIPAT, GRACE, AND THE AWAKENING OF KUNDALINI

Questioner :

Bhagwan, please explain the relationship between deep breathing and the asking of "Who am I?" on one hand, and the process of the awakening of the kundalini and its piercing of the various "chakras" (centers) on the other.

Bhagwan Shri Rajneesh :

There is a relationship—a very deep-rooted relationship. In fact, it is the breath that joins the body to the soul. Breath is the bridge, therefore : As soon as breath is gone, life is gone. If the eyes or the limbs go life still remains, but if the breath is cut off we are no more. Breath is the link between the body and the soul. The place where the body and soul meet is the place where this energy which we call "kundalini" lies. But whatever name we call it by, it is the same energy.

This energy has two forms. If the kundalini energy flows toward the body it becomes sex energy. If it flows toward the soul it becomes the kundalini. While flowing toward the body it descends, and when flowing toward the soul it ascends. But the place where it is can only be stimulated by breath. You will be surprised to know that that is why the breath cannot remain tranquil in the sex act. There is an immediate change in the pace of breathing. As soon as a person becomes sexual, the rate of breathing is accelerated, for sex energy will rise and flow only when the breath strikes the sex center. Without the pounding of the breath the sex act is impossible. Samadhi is the ascending point and the sex act is the descending point. The breath strikes equally in both directions.

When the mind is filled with sex, slacken the pace of breathing; allow it to relax. When the mind is filled with anger or some other passion, breathe slowly, reduce the pace of breathing, and the passion will leave you immediately. Passions cannot be sustained without energy, and this energy can only be there if there is the strike of the breath. Therefore, no one can breathe slowly and be angry. If he can, it is a miracle, not an ordinary happening. This is not possible though, anger leaves as soon as pace of breath slackens, and so does the sex urge. So when the mind is filled with anger or sex reduce the pace of breathing, and when the mind is filled with the desire for meditation increase the pace and the intensity of the breath. When the mind is filled with a desire for meditation, if the breath is deep and intense the energy begins to flow along the channels of meditation.

Deep breathing has a profound effect on the kundalini. "*Pranayam*" (the science of Yogic breathing) was not evolved without a reason. After numerous experiments and experiences, it was discovered that a great deal could be accomplished due to the hammerstrokes of the breath. The harder the blows, the swifter the flow of energy. In ordinary people like us in whom the kundalini is in deep slumber since many births, very hard blows are required for it to be awakened. One's total force must be applied to the breath in order to make the impact as strong and hard as possible.

The basic center of the kundalini is hit by deep and intense breathing. As your experience deepens, you will be able to see clearly, with your eyes closed, where the breath is striking. Therefore, it happens many a time that with the hammerstrokes of breathing the sex center is stimulated. Because your body knows only this one experience, when the breathing pace accelerates and strikes at the "*kunda*" (the reservoir of dormant energy), the experience of sex is felt. Thus, the body begins to work in the groove of the experience already known. This is why many seekers feel the effect on the sex center.

Many people used to feel this in the presence of Gurdjieff. Many women felt that their sex centers were stimulated when they went near him. This is very natural, but Gurdjieff was badly criticized for this though it was not his fault at all. The fact is that the vibrations around a person whose kundalini is awakened begin to work on the kundalini of those who approach him. But the kundalini in you lies asleep near the sex center, therefore, that center is affected first.

Deep breathing has a tremendous effect on the kundalini, and that which you refer to as "*chakras*" (centers) are "stations" on the path of the kundalini. The kundalini will pass through them on its journey upward. There are many such points which you can count, but broadly speaking there are seven main centers where the kundalini pauses awhile to rest. So at each center there will be some happening. The first effect will be on the center which is most active within the person. For instance, if a man has made maximum use of his brain, his head will become heavy after deep breathing—for his brain center is the most active one in his body. The breath will attack the most active center first. If a man is sexual, his sexuality will become increasingly active. If a person is very loving, his love will increase. If a person is emotional, he will become more emotional.

So the most active center within a person will be the first target of the kundalini. But the other centers are also affected simultaneously. Therefore, the individual begins to feel a transformation in his personality almost immediately. He will begin to feel that he is not the same man that he was before. We do not know how many persons reside within us. We only know the one that lives in the center that is inwardly active. Therefore, when a second center becomes activated, one feels as if one's basic personality has gone and as if it has been replaced by another. One does not feel to be the same person that one was previously. It is just as if you know only of this one room in this house. Then your mind will have an image of this room only. Then suddenly a door opens and you find another room. Then your whole image of the house will change, for the old concept has to give a place to the new arrangement.

So, as the various centers are stimulated, new dimensions of your personality will begin to manifest. When all the centers are activated, that is, when the energy flows steadily through all the centers, then for the first time one begins to live in one's total personality. No one lives in his total personality, and the upper centers in all persons are normally left untouched. But the breath will hammer at these centers.

The asking of "Who am I?"* also does the work of helping us to know our total personalities, but this is an attack from a different direction. This needs to be understood. We can understand the effect of breathing, but how does the asking of "Who am I?" work on the kundalini ?

You may not have observed that when you close your eyes and visualize the picture of a naked woman in your imagination, the sex center immediately becomes activated. Why ? You are just imagining, and yet your sex center is affected. In fact, every center has its own point of imagination—and if you touch the point of imagination of any of these centers, that particular center immediately becomes activated. Therefore, no sooner do you think of sex when the sex center becomes active.

You will be surprised that the thought of a naked woman has a greater effect than an actual naked woman. The reason is that the thought of a naked woman will take you into your imagination, and then the sex center will be hammered. A naked woman standing before you does not take you into flights of imagination, for she is there before you in substance. Her persence will only be able to influence you outwardly, and this will not be as deep as the effect of imagination which works on the inner center.

The push from within has a stronger effect than the push from without. Therefore, there are many men who, though very virile in imagination, are impotent before women. In thoughts, their potency is boundless, because the force of imagination works directly on the center within. An external impact does not touch the center directly, and hence it is not as effective. As man lives in his mind, he can therefore work more effectively on these centers through the mind.

---

* (In the dynamic meditation method taught by Bhagwan, the third stage of repeating "Who am I?" can be replaced by shouts of the Sufi mantra "Hoo-Hoo-Hoo". The fast breathing can then be dropped after the first stage of ten minutes, upon entering the second stage of cooperating with one's bodily, psychic and emotional reactions).

So when you ask "Who am I?" you are making an inquiry. You are asking something to your imagination; you are raising a question. Which center will this question touch? It is bound to touch some center. When you ask the question, when you are filled with inquiry, filled with the desire to know, when every hair on your body is filled with this question "Who am I ?" then you are going within, and some center within will begin to be affected. "Who am I?" is a question you have never asked, and, therefore, it will not affect any of the known or already active centers. You have never asked, you have never inquired. You have always inquired, "Who is this? Who is that ?"

"Who am I ?" has remained an unasked question, and hence it will work on an entirely unknown center. This unknown center is the basic center, for this question is a very basic question. It is a very existential question. "Who am I ?" is a question that arises out of the entire depth of your existence. It will take you where you were before you ever took any births—beyond the infinite births you have thus far taken to the beginning of your Being. The profoundness of this question is unfathomable. Its journey is into the very depths of the Being. Therefore, this question strikes at the most deep-seated center—that of the kundalini.

Breath has a physiological impact whereas "Who am I?" has a mental impact. One strikes with your physical energy and the other strikes with your mental energy. So generally you have only two ways of attacking the centers. There are other ways also, but they are complicated. Another person can be helpful to you also. Therefore, when you practice before me, the impact will be greater, for then there is an impact from a third direction of which you are not aware. This is the impact from the astral world. When you breathe hard, that is the impact of the physical world; when you ask "Who am I ?" it is the impact of the mental world.

If you are near a person through whom your astral body can be influenced, then a third journey begins. That is why, if fifty people meditate together, it will be more effective than one person meditating. The vibrations created by the earnest longing of fifty people, together their intense breathing, will fill a place with an "astral" atmosphere. Then a new type of electrical vibration will begin to operate. This will begin to throw its impact onto the various centers.

Normally, there are these two clear ways for you—that of the body and that of the mind. The impact of "Who am I ?" will be more forceful than the impact of deep breathing. We start with the breath because it pertains to the body and is not difficult. "Who am I ?" is a little difficult, for it pertains to the mind. When the body becomes completely vibrant and charged, the mind becomes ready to ask. A very special situation is required for this asking. It will not do to ask just any old way. All questions, in fact, must be well timed and well placed. Now when your whole body trembles and shakes, you automatically begin to wonder within, "What is all this ? What am I doing ? It is not I that am doing all this. I am not turning my face, I am not lifting my legs, I am not dancing, and yet all this is happening."

Now if all this is happening without your will, your identity with the body will begin to loosen. Then a new question arises before you—"Who am I ?" If the body is doing all this and not "I", then who is doing this ? "Who am I" then ? So this is the correct opening from which the question of "Who am I?" can arise within. Therefore, it is very necessary to ask at the right moment. Every question has its proper timing, and to discover the correct moment is very important. If you ask at any time, it is of no consequence. If sitting here you begin to ask, it will be lost in the air; it will not penetrate anywhere. An opening is required from where the question can penetrate.

With the impact coming from these two planes (the physical and the mental) the kundalini will awaken. And with its awakening unique experiences will begin to happen, because your entire experiences of all your past lives are connected with your kundalini. Your experiences when you were a tree, your experiences when you were a fish, your experiences when you were a bird, all the myriads of experiences that you passed through in the course of your evolution lie on the path of this journey. Your kundalini has absorbed them all. Therefore, many happenings will take place, and you may identify your self with these experiences. Any kind of happening can take place.

Many subtle experiences of which you are not at all conscious are also connected with the kundalini. For instance, take a tree standing in the garden. There has been a strong wind followed by rain, but you will never know the wind and the rain as the tree has known it. You will know it only as you can know it. But at sometime, in the course of your evolution, you must have been a tree also. Now if the kundalini reaches the spot where your experiences as a tree are collected, you will suddenly come to feel what the tree feels when there is rain or when the wind blows. You might feel very frightened then at what is happening. Similarly, you might experience the feeling of the ocean or the air. In this way, your aesthetic sense and many other possibilities that you never suspected within yourself might unfold before you.

Van Gogh has painted a picture in which a tree is shown touching the skies. The stars are placed very low, and the sun and the moon lie on the ground depicted as small and insignificant. But the tree is up high—high into infinity. Someone asked him, "Are you out of your mind? Are trees ever so high that the stars and the moon lie way below?" Van Gogh replied "How would you know? You have never known a tree. I know the tree from within its depths. It may not be able to reach the skies; it may not be able to touch the stars and the moon. But it longs to all the same." The tree does not and cannot grow that high, but inwardly its being is forever soaring far above to the heavens.

Van Gogh used to say, "The trees are the longing of the earth to meet the skies." The earth tries to extend its hands to touch the skies. And so, we can have glimpses of our past experiences which were like that of a tree, though they may not be as clear now as the tree is experiencing. All these experiences are within us; therefore, anything can happen. Also, we will begin to experience our future possibilities. What we shall be in future, that too begins to come within our experience.

On entering the path of the kundalini's journey, man's story is no longer an individual episode but the story of the Universal Consciousness. Sri Aurobindo used to speak in this language, and therefore he was not clearly understood. Then the subject matter is not of one person alone, but of the whole Cosmic

Consciousness. You are no longer alone. Within you is that part of the Infinite that is of the past and also that part of the Infinite which is to follow. It is like a seed that is forever unfolding and manifesting itself. Then, when you see the endless expanse of yourself—that which is lost in the infinity behind you and that which is merged in infinity before you—your state will be something very different; everything will change. All this lies hidden in the kundalini.

Many colours will be seen that were never seen before. In fact, there are not nearly so many colours outside of you as you can experience within. And at sometime or other, you have known these inner colours—but that happened in altogether different kinds of situations and in an altogether different manner. When a kite hovers in the skies, it sees all the colours in a different manner. We see colours in one way, but an artist will see in an altogether different manner. He will see a thousand colours where we see only one. For instance green is not one single colour. There are a thousand shades of green and a thousand variations in each shade. So when you enter within, you will experience thousands of minute details.

Man is a very weak creature when it comes to his sensory perceptions. Animals and birds have a more powerful sensory system. The depth and distance of their experiences and perceptions are very great. Their only drawback is that they cannot grasp them together in their consciousness and think about them. But their experiences are very profound and their sensitivity is great. There is a very common bird in Japan. This bird leaves the town 24 hours before an impending earthquake. When that bird is not seen, the people of that place know that an earthquake is bound to occur within 24 hours. Even with modern scientific implements we are not able to forecast an earthquake more than six hours in advance, and that forecast too is not 100% correct. But these birds are never wrong. This shows that the subtle vibrations of a forthcoming earthquake are felt by these birds, and they leave the town. But you too can feel these vibrations in the journey of your kundalini, if you have been that particular bird.

You might see colours you have never seen before, hear music you have never heard—that Kabir refers to as "*nada*" (the inner sound). Kabir says, "Dance my friend, for nectar is pouring." And the friend asks, "Where is it pouring?" This nectar is not pouring from anywhere outside. Kabir says, "Friend, hear the enchanting strains of the *nada*". And the friend asks, "Where is the music?" Kabir says, "Can you not hear?" This very music that Kabir heard, you too can hear. You may also experience such tastes as you have never known before in your entire life.

The vast world of subtle experiences is joined to the kundalini. All this will become active; all this will awaken and confront you from all sides. This is why, in this particular state, a person appears to be mad. When we all sit quietly, he breaks into laughter—for he sees something that we cannot see. When we laugh, he might break into sobs : something happens to him that we cannot see.

So ordinarily, there are two ways of striking open this vault of energy. There is also a third, uncommon way—through the transmission of energy. This method requires a medium. When another person cooperates, the intensity of your effort increases. The other person has to do nothing: his presence is enough; he acts as a medium. Infinite energy exsists spread out all around us. Now we can fix a rod on our house so that when lightning strikes it can pass through the rod, and then the house will not be affected. Lightning has always been striking the earth, whereas the lightning rod is a recent innovation.

Infinite powers are present all around us, and these can all be used for man's spiritual progress. However, a medium is required. You yourself can be a medium, but initially this is dangerous. Your body must be able to withstand the high voltage of this energy. Some of the delicate sinews of your body may be damaged if the voltage is too high for you to bear. So through a medium the voltage can be controlled according to your capacity. Now such a person can only be one on whom the power has already descended. Then only can he direct the flow toward you according to your requirements. He does nothing, but his presence acts as a catalytic agent. This is why if anyone says that he transmits energy, he is wrong. No one can transmit energy, but the transmission of energy may take place through the presence of a person.

I think that this transmission can happen with full force if seekers go still a little deeper. There is no difficulty ; nothing is to be done. It will happen of its own accord. You will suddenly feel energy rushing into you from without. When you have the experience of kundalini you feel it rising from within you, and when you have the experience of "Shaktipat"—of transmitted energy—you feel it to be coming from the outside. It is as clear a feeling as when water falls on you from above. When the energy rises from within you, it is the same as if you are standing in a river where the waters begin to rise and you are being drowned.

So the experience of the kundalini rising is always like that of drowning—like something rising from below and drowning you, like something engulfing you. But whenever you experience Shaktipat—the transmission of energy—it will come like a rainfall. It is like "nectar raining" according to Kabir. This nectar rains down from above and makes you soaking wet. Now if both these happen together, the pace of your progress will be accelerated. Then the skies rain from above and the river rises from below. You are drowning from both sides and you are no more. So it can happen simultaneously from both sides ; there is no difficulty in that.

Questioner : *Is the effect of transmitted energy temporary or long lasting? Does it take us to the final stage of the journey or are many such transmissions required?*

Bhagwan : The fact is that only the effect of that which rises within you is long lasting; transmitted energy is only a help. What happens within you is the principal thing ; that is your personal property. Transmitted energy will not increase your overall energy, but it will raise your energy temporarily. This difference must be properly understood. Transmitted energy will only intensify the pace of your progress and help your energy to rise and spread over your being quickly. It cannot be your property.

It is somewhat like this : you are running and I am after you with a gun. Now the gun can in no way add to your power of running, but because of my gun you will run faster. In both the cases it will be you who runs. It is your energy that is being expanded, but because of the gun you will be bringing into use more energy than you normally would. No energy is provided by the gun. There will be no difference in the gun, for it loses nothing. But because of the gun your speed will be accelerated. Where you were walking leisurely, you will begin to run. So Shaktipat accelerates the speed of your progress, but it does not add to your overall energy.

Though a single experience, one flash of lightning, does not illuminate the way for all time, though it does not become a lamp to light the way, it gives a glimpse of the road ahead. It strengthens your feet, it strengthens your resolve and your desire, and you make a firm decision to reach. Then you are convinced that the path is there and you are not groping in the dark. One flash and you get a glimpse of the temple that is your goal : then the light is no more. But now you are a different person altogether, and though you still are where you are you will set out with renewed energy. The road is clear, the goal is near. So what if it can no longer be seen ! You are fully convinced, and this conviction will increase and fortify your resolve.

So the result of Shaktipat is indirect, and hence it is required time and again. Once is not enough. With a second flash of lightning the road will become more clear ; with a third still more clear. What you may have missed the first time you might see in the second flash, in the third flash. One thing is certain : your conviction will get stronger and stronger. So the goal cannot be attained by Shaktipat. That will be your own effort alone.

You can reach without Shaktipat, but it might take you a little longer. It will only mean that your confidence will be less because of the darkness all around. You will have to gather more courage, more strength. Fear will catch hold of you, doubts and uncertainties will engulf you, and you will hesitate. All the same, you will reach. Shaktipat is a definite help though.

With a group that has advanced in progress, this transmission of energy can be carried out simultaneously on many at a time, for the energy takes the same amount of time to descend on one person as on ten thousand persons.

Questioner : *If a link with the medium is not maintained, is there a possibility of the effect of Shaktipat wearing off?*

Bhagwan : The effect will definitely be reduced ; all influences wear off gradually. The very meaning of "influence" is the effect of an outside agent. So it will wear off, but your own experience, your inner happening, will remain the same—for it is your very own. And that which comes under the influence of this inner happening of Shaktipat will also remain the same. What you have basically acquired remains the same ; the influence wears off.

Questioner : *Is there a possibility of our losing this possession by keeping bad company? Do we then fall to a lower state?*

Bhagwan : There is no way of falling back. This too you must understand well. It is funny, but nonetheless a fact that you cannot fall lower. You can be raised upwards from the point you have reached ; you can be made to remain where you are. But there is no way of making you fall from your position. The reason is that when you proceed upwards YOU change completely. If you have risen even an inch beyond your initial personality, you cannot fall back ; it is impossible.

It is just like a child who gets promoted to the second standard from the first standard by being given added tutoring. You cannot find a teacher who can make the child forget what it has learned in the first standard. Also, if the child falls into the company of dull and foolish boys, at the most he will fail. He may keep failing again and again and fail to go to the third standard, but there is no way of putting him back to the first. He will stagnate; that is all.

In spirituality, there is either going ahead or stagnating, but no going back. And going back means, in spiritual language, stagnating. Thus your motivation can be broken, but you cannot be made to fall back.

Questioner : *Is Shaktipat—energy transmission—different from grace?*

Bhagwan : There is a great difference. Shaktipat is a technique ; it has to be planned. It cannot be brought about anytime and anywhere. The seeker must be in a state to receive and the medium should be in perfect condition to transmit. When these two conditions are in order, then at the right moment the happening will take place. Grace, on the other hand, is an unexpected descension. For it, there is no call, no preparation—and it happens sometimes. The former is as if we were to press a button and the bulb is lighted, and the latter is like a sporadic flash of lightning. The difference between Shaktipat and grace is the same. One is brought about by a technique : we press a button and the light comes ; we press it again and it is cut off. But the lightning in the skies cannot be ordered.

Grace is like liohtning. It flashes at some unexpected moment. And if you are in the required state, the happening can take place. But you cannot call this a transmission of energy, though the power is the same. In grace there is no medium. It is direct, sudden and accidental. One can make no preparations for grace, whereas for Shaktipat one can make the necessary preparations. I can tell you, "Come tomorrow at five p.m. duly prepared." But for grace, your coming at five p.m. will have no meaning. It may happen, it may not happen, but it is not in our hands : this is the difference.

Questioner : *If energy is transmitted in an egoless state, how can preparations be made for it?*

Bhagwan : Preparations can be made in an egoless state. The ego is not connected with the preparations at all. Ego is a different matter altogether. Now when we decide to sit prepared for Shaktipat, the seekers are not required to be egoless at all. The point is that the medium must be egoless. But for Shaktipat to happen, one cannot be egoless at one moment and not at other times. If you are egoless, you are egoless forever ; if you are not, you are not. If I am egoless, I am egoless forever; if I am not, I am not. It is not that tomorrow at five p.m. I shall become egoless. (*Laughter*...) How can I ? There is no way. If I am egoless now, I shall be egoless at five p.m. tomorrow—

whether any preparations are made or not, whether you come, or whether I am asleep or awake. If I am egoless, I am so for all time ; if I am not, I am not.

All our thinking, in fact, is in degrees. If a person's body temperature is 98 degrees Fahrenheit, we say he is absolutely all right. But if his temperature rises to 99 degrees, we say that he has fever. Actually, 98 degrees is also temperature, but it is normal temperature. At 99 degrees it becomes abnormal. When the temperature returns to 98, we say that the person's temperature has returned to normal and he is all right. Temperature is there, but what we mean is that it is as much as it normally is in everyone. A slight change here or there causes confusion. The same is the case with the ego. It is our fever. If it is of the same normal degree as that of others, we say the man is very humble and good. If the degree is a little higher than ours (99), we say the man is an egoist. If it goes down to 97 degrees, we call him a mahatma and feel that he has become "absolutely humble." (*Laughter...*)

The states of ego and no-ego are different things altogether. They have no connection with degrees. To have temperature or not to have temperature is not a matter of 98 and 99 degrees. Only a dead man can be said to have no temperature, for as long as there is warmth in the body there is bound to be temperature. It is only a difference of normal and abnormal temperature, and in the latter situation inconvenience is experienced. If someone else's ego hurts your ego then he is an egoist to you, and if it pleases your ego that man becomes egoless in your eyes.

How are we to measure? How shall we know? A man comes to me and talks in a haughty manner, and we say he is an egoist. Another comes and touches my feet, and we say he is humble. (*Laughter...*) What other measure do we have to judge by? We have only one method : if a man upsets your ego he is an egoist, and if he flatters your ego then he is humble : he has no ego. Whether the other person has an ego or not, the measure is your own ego.

Therefore, we cannot understand the state of no-ego ; we only understand in terms of degrees. But when there are no degrees, we find ourselves in difficulty. Shaktipat, however, requires a non-egotistical medium. It would be more correct to say a medium who is EGOLESS.

Remember, on such a person grace pours all the twenty-four hours. He will make arrangements for you to receive grace, but on him it pours constantly. That is why he can make preparations for you so that you may open your door and allow a drop or two to enter within yourselves.

Questioner : *Is the effect of direct grace permanent, and does it take us up to the attainment of Realization ?*

Bhagwan : Direct grace is only received on attainment and not before. When ego departs, grace descends. Ego is the obstruction. Attainment is the state in which where there is no longer anything left to be attained.

Questioner : *Is Kundalini sadhana (practice) psychic or spiritual ?*

Bhagwan : You know that eating is a physical act, but by your not eating the soul will soon take flight. So though eating is a physical act, the "Atman" (Soul) can only stay within the body under certain conditions. In the same way, if the kundalini is in a particular state, we can reach up to the Divine. If it is in the wrong state, this is not possible. So though kundalini is psychic, it acts as a step to the spiritual; it is not spiritual in itself. If someone calls it spiritual, it is wrong, just as calling food spiritual would be wrong. Yet both are supports for the spiritual.

Breath is physical and thoughts too are physical. All is physical. Their subtle forms are called psychic, but they are in the form of matter. All these are only supports though. They are the jumpboards from which you jump into the non-physical. Now when someone jumps into the water from a diving board, someone else might argue that since the board is not a part of the pool it is not correct to use it to jump into the water, that if you want to jump into water you should stand within the water. How can this ever be possible ? In order to jump into the pool, we have to use the diving board, and the diving board is a totally different thing from the water.

So the jump you have to take is from the body, from the mind, and you have to jump into the Atman which will only be attained after you jump. But first you will have to make arrangements from where you stand, so you will have to jump with the help of the body and the mind. Verily, when the jump is taken, you will reach that which is spiritual.

Questioner : *In the beginning when you taught meditation, you used to direct seekers to be tranquil, relaxed, silent and aware, in the witnessing state. Now you are using the method of fast breathing and exhorting the seekers to put all their energy into the effort. But the seeker who has practised the first type of "sadhana" (spiritual practice) finds himself unable to carry out the second type. So which method is good for him?*

Bhagwan : There is no question of good or bad here. Just observe in which method you are tranquil and have made progress, because methods will be different for different people. There are some people who can only relax if they run until they are exhausted ; there are some who can relax at a moment's notice. But such persons are very few. To go directly into silence is very difficult, and it is only possible for very few. For the majority of people, movement and tension is necessary first. The purpose is the same ; they lead to the same goal.

Questioner : *About intense breathing you have said that it is a method of mutation by extremes—that we have to reach the ultimate point in tension in order to attain the state of complete relaxation. Then should we take it that kundalini sadhana is a sadhana of tension?*

Bhagwan : It is absolutely a tension sadhana. Truly speaking, all "shakti sadhanas" — energy awakening sadhanas—are tension sadhanas. "Energy awakening" means tension; energy is born only where there is tension. We have created such a powerful energy by breaking the atom and causing a state of tension between its two parts. Likewise, all energy-awakening sadhanas are sadhanas of tension. And if we understand correctly, tension means energy.

Questioner : *You speak of two methods of sadhana—positive and negative. Is kundalini sadhana negative or positive?*

Bhagwan : Positive—absolutely positive.

Questioner : *Why has Buddha not talked about the chakras and kundalini sadhana ?*

Bhagwan : Actually, Buddha's statements and discourses have not been recorded; that is the biggest problem. Most of the things that Buddha has said have deliberately not been recorded. And whatsoever has been recorded was not until 500 years after Buddha. For 500 years the *bhikkhus* (monks) who were the guardians of Buddha's knowledge refused to record it. Then a time came slowly when one by one these *bhikkhus* also began to disappear. Then a big meeting was called and the matter was discussed. It was agreed that if they did not put the knowledge on record from the few *bhikkhus* that were remaining, Buddha's treasure of knowledge would be lost to the world for ever.

As long as they could memorize, they refused to record the knowledge. The same happened in the case of Mahavir and Jesus. This was very necessary though, and many reasons were behind this refusal. These people passed on the knowledge by word of mouth, and in so doing different things were spoken to seekers who were on different levels. For instance, all that was spoken was not necessary or useful for seekers of the first level; rather, many things would prove harmful. What happens is that knowledge about steps other than that upon which we are standing prevents us from standing firmly on the step upon we are. Such information diverts our attention to the steps ahead, with the result that we do not even stand on the first step properly.

There is another problem too: Many things that are essential for the first step become wrong and useless for the second. Now if you come to know what is wrong on the second step, it will appear wrong for the first step too. Then it will not be possible for you to cross the first step, as these things are absolutely essential for the first step. Only with them will you be able to go forward.

We teach little children that "g" is for "Ganesh" (a popular Hindu God). Now "g" could be for a gadha (donkey) also, and there is nothing common between a gadha and Ganesh. (*Laughter...*)

There is no fraternity between them. "G" has no connection with either of them, but it will not be advisable to tell a child of the first standard so. But if the father of this child tells him, "You useless fellow. "G" has nothing to do with Ganesh; "G" can be used for a thousand other names too. What has "g" got to do with Ganesh ?" then this child will never be able to learn the letter "g".

It is very necessary that he should first grasp that "g" is for "Ganesh"; he should not be burdened with more than this. At this stage, even if his concept of Ganesh is only "h", let it be so, for tomorrow a thousand other things will also come into "g", and then he will invariably know by himself that "g" is not necessarily only for "Ganesh". That was one relationship; there are others also. Then, later on when he comes across "g" in other words, the "Ganesh" will drop and only "g" will remain.

So there are thousands of things on thousands of levels. Besides, some matters are very personal and very serious. Now all that I am saying is such that it can be talked about openly, but there are many things that cannot be openly disclosed and I shall not talk about them in public. I will talk about these matters only to those alone whom I think to be qualified for it.

So Buddha has spoken a lot, but it is not recorded, and all that I say will be recorded. Thus, I too will say in the open only those things that can be said. (*Laughter. . .*) What cannot be said openly will have to be memorized.

Questioner : *Then do you mean to say that the matter of kundalini and chakras must remain secret and should not be recorded?*

Bhagwan : No, No ! There are other factors that must be taken into consideration. That which I have spoken already can safely be recorded, but there are many other things. Twenty-five hundred years have passed since Buddha, and man's consciousness has changed a lot during this period. That which Buddha felt should not be revealed openly, I believe can now be made known to all. Many fundamental changes have taken place in the course of 2,500 years. However, whatever Buddha said cannot be disclosed to all, but I feel that a great many of those secrets can be safely disclosed. Even now, everything that

I tell to persons cannot be disclosed publicly. Perhaps after another 2,500 years, it will be safe to tell certain things openly —that is, if man progresses in the area of spirituality.

If even Buddha were to come back today, he would safely prescribe many things for public consumption that he previously held back. He had singled out eleven questions which he had ordered that no one should ask him, for if these questions were asked he would have had to give an answer. If he gave a wrong answer that would not be correct, and the right answer was not to be given to the questioner. So he decided that he would not answer these eleven questions. Before Buddha entered a village, it was publicly announced that no one should ask any of these eleven questions, for he would not answer them. There was a reason : If he answered, it would prove harmful for the questioner; if he did not, the questioner would feel he had kept the truth hidden. Therefore, the best way out was to declare that no one should ask these questions.

So the *bhikkhus* proclaimed beforehand in each village that Buddha was coming and no one must ask these questions. People were distressed, but these questions were then accepted by all as unanswerable and were never asked. If someone opposed him and insisted on asking, Buddha would tell him, "Wait a few days and practice sadhana, and when you are qualified I will answer you." But it never happened that he answered these questions. So the Jains and the Hindus accuse Buddha of not knowing anything. They argue, "He could not answer these eleven questions, whereas our *shastras* (scriptures) answer all." It seems these poor people do not know that as much as was written in their *shastras* Buddha could reveal. In fact, the real answers are not given in *shastras* and they cannot be given.

Thus, the question of why Buddha did not talk about kundalini and the chakras does not arise.

[Text of a question and answer session held with Bhagwan on June 15, 1970, evening, in Bombay, India].

7

THE PATH OF KUNDALINI

Questioner :

You have said in the Nargol meditation camp that kundalini "sadhana" (practice) is a preparation of the body. Please explain this clearly.

Bhagwan Shree Rajneesh :

First and foremost, the body and the soul are not separate. Also, their difference is very superficial. When Truth is fully experienced, we no longer see the body and soul as two separate entities. Then we discover that the body is that part of the "Atman" (soul) which can be grasped by the senses and the Atman is that part of the body which is beyond the grasp of the senses. The invisible extension of the body is the Atman and the visible extension of the Atman is the body. This becomes known in the Ultimate Experience.

The ordinary person too goes about believing that the body and soul are one, but for him this is only an illusion, as he has no knowledge of the soul whatsoever. What he takes to be the soul is only the body. But there is some truth behind this illusion, and in some unknown corner of our being we have this feeling, this knowledge, of oneness.

This idea of oneness has created two kinds of errors, however. On one hand, there are the spiritualists who say that the body is not, and only the Atman is, and, on the other, there are the materialists like Charvak and Epicurus who say that only body is and the soul is not. These misconceptions are created by the same intrinsic feeling, and the ordinary person, the one whom we call ignorant, who is unenlightened, also feels that he is only the body. Once the inward journey begins, this will be the first illusion to break, and he will come to experience that the body is separate and the Atman is separate. As soon as an awareness of the Atman is established, the body and the Atman will be experienced as separate. But this is the middle stage. If you go deeper . and deeper and deeper, when you reach the Ultimate Experience you will find that there is no "other". Then the body and the soul are not two, but they are just two forms of the same entity.

It is just like I am one person with both a left and a right hand. If someone says that my right hand and the left hand are one and the same, that would be wrong. The left and the right re absolutely separate from each other. When the right is in pain, the left is not. If the right is cut off, the left remains. Thus, the two are obviously not one. But if someone goes inside of me, he will find that "I" am the one who has a right and a left hand. When the left is hurt, "I" feel the pain; when the right is hurt, "I" feel the pain. When the right is lifted up, it is "I" who am lifting it; when the left is lifted up, it is "I" who am lifting it.

So in the Ultimate Experience, the body and soul are not two. They are two sides, two hands, of the same Truth. I have given this example so that you may understand what I mean; then it will be easier to start the journey from anywhere. If we start with the body and go deeper and deeper, we will reach the soul. If someone catches hold of my right hand and proceeds further and further along, he is bound to reach my left hand. If someone wishes to start from the other direction, from the Atman to the body, he can do this also. However, it is very difficult, since we have no knowledge of the Atman.

We are standing on the physical plane, so we must start from the body. There are methods which start directly from the soul but normally, these methods are only for very few. One in a million can use these methods. The majority of us have to start from the body, for that is where we are standing. And for the journey of the body, the preparation is kundalini. Kundalini is the deepest experience of the body, and the basic centers of experiences are in the body. The body actually is not only as we know it or as the physiologists know it: it is much more.

If we take a fan and break it to pieces, we will not find electricity anywhere. Based on this information, it is possible that the most intelligent person may deduce that there is no such thing as electricity in the mechanism of a fan, for it is not present anywhere within it. Yet the fan works on electricity. The moment the current is cut off, the fan stops. In the same way, physiologists have studied the body by dissecting it, but they have been unable to locate the kundalini—and they never will. Yet the body works on the electrical current of the kundalini. It cannot be discovered by external analysis, for that causes it immediately to disintegrate. It can only be experienced within.

There are two ways of knowing the body. One is to know it from the outside as a physiologist knows it; the other is to know it from the inside. He who resides within the body knows it from within. Remember, we know our bodies from the outside only. If I know my left hand, I know it as my eyes see it. This is knowing as a physiologist would know. But if I close my eyes and feel the left hand from within, that inner experience is my own experience. So when a person sets out to know his own body from within, he will soon reach the source from where all the energies of the body arise. The power that lies dormant in the "kunda"—the reservoir of energy—is called the kundalini. The person going within will begin to experience that everything rises from this and spreads all over the body, just as a lamp burns and lights a whole room. And if we continue the search, we may come to the lamp itself and discover that all the rays of light are emanating from the flame alone. These light rays have spread far and wide, but they issue forth from this single point.

So when we talk of the kunda—the reservoir of life energy—we mean that place within the body from where the life energy spreads throughout the body. There must be a center for this energy. No energy can be without the source. If the sun is 90,000,000 miles away from us, then from the evidence of a single ray we can infer that there must be a center from where that ray began its journey. No energy can ever be without a source. If there is energy there is a center, just as if there is bound to be a center in a circle.

So the body is a collection of energy—and this needs no verification, for it (the body) walks, it sits, it talks, it sleeps. Also, this energy does not perform only one type of work: it is sometimes more and sometimes less. When you are angry, you might be able to pick up and throw a big stone that you would normally not be able to move. When fear grips you, you can run faster than you would if you were taking part in the Olympics. Energy flows in proportion to how it is required. This also proves that there is a reservoir within from which the energy is drawn or not drawn, as is required. When needed, it comes into action; otherwise it lies dormant at the source.

So you have a source from which you can draw energy for your ordinary day-to-day requirements as well as for extraordinary tasks; yet this reservoir is never spent, nor do you ever make full use of it. Those who have carried out research in this direction have discovered that the most extraordinary genius does not make use of more than 15% of this energy. The most ordinary man does not use more than 2-2½%, and the rest of this energy goes wasted. As far as capacity goes, there is no difference in the potential of an ordinary man and an extraordinary man. The seed force is the same; the difference is only in its use. The same force that the greatest of men employ is also present in the most ordinary of men. It is only lying in disuse. It has never been drawn upon; it has never been roused.

The ordinary man has never bothered to awaken it. He is content with whatever he has and takes it to be the maximum of his potential. But actually, it is the most minimal. And though we make do with this minimal force of energy, in times of stress and crisis we often exhibit extraordinary strength. It is then we know of our own capabilities.

THE KUNDA — THE SOURCE IN THE UNCONSCIOUS

There is a center where this energy lies hidden and asleep, like a seed in which everything that is dormant can become manifest. This is what is referred to as the "kunda" (reservoir).

The word "kunda" is very significant. The first meaning implied is "the place that is without a single ripple". If there is the slightest ripple the force becomes active. So "kunda" means the place where there is neither the slightest tremor, the slightest stir nor the slightest ruffling—where everything is in a deep slumber. The second meaning is "there where everything is asleep but can be awakened any moment". The kunda is not dead or empty or dry : it is full. But because it is sleeping it is quite possible that we may never be aware of what is asleep within us. We will only become aware of it up to the degree to which we awaken it.

This must be clearly understood. Until it is awakened we cannot be aware of it, and we shall only be aware of it to the extent that we have awakened it. Only as much energy as you awaken will come within the grasp of your consciousness. The non-activated part of it will remain asleep in your unconsciousness. This is why the greatest of men have no idea of their greatness before they become great. Neither Mahavir nor Buddha nor Jesus were aware of their potential until they reached the height of their knowledge.

Therefore, when the happening suddenly takes place within, it seems like the compassion of the Divine. Then we wonder from where this gift has come or who has given it to us. Then we feel it has come from whoever is nearest to us—whether it is the guru or the idol we have worshipped. The attainment is always from within, but we attribute it to a *Teerthankar* (world teacher of the Jains) or to some God up above or to something or someone who has preceded us.

I was reading a story the other day in which two farmers set out in a train journey for the first time. It was their birthday, so the people of their village thought, "What could be a more fitting present than a train trip ?" So they bought tickets for their journey. Now it was a very new experience for both these men, for trains were as yet a new invention. They were excited about everything that was happening around them. A vendor of soft drinks happened to pass by, so they bought one bottle and decided to share it. They agreed that if they liked the taste they would buy another one.

The first one began to drink, and as he finished his half-share the train entered a tunnel. The second one then tried to snatch the bottle from him, saying, "Do not finish all." The first one said, "Don't touch it ! It is poison. It has struck me blind." The one who drank first, warned the other not to touch the bottle or he would be struck blind. This is natural, for that which precedes an event always appears to be the cause. In the same way, we do not know where the energy comes from and we are not at all aware of it until it rises within us. Thus, we are not conscious of this source of energy or of its magnitude.

The energy that is awakened within this sleeping, unconscious "kunda" is called the kundalini. The kunda is unconscious; the kundalini is conscious. The sleeping energy comprises the kunda; the awakened energy is the kundalini. That which awakens and rises above the kunda is referred to as kundalini. Kundalini is not the entire kunda. It is merely a small wave that has risen out of it. Therefore, the search in this journey is twofold. The kundalini awakened within you only heralds the news of a source within you where a great deal more is asleep. One ray emanating from the kunda discloses a possibility of infinite rays. So one way is of awakening the kundalini to make you conscious of the energy of your body—and having awakened this energy, you will reach those centers, those openings in the body, from where you can easily enter the invisible form of the body, the Atman.

This too should be well comprehended, for whatever we do it is the energy within us that is doing it with the help of certain openings. If your ears have gone bad, the energy will come up to the ears and recede. Then you will not be able to hear. Then by and by, the energy will stop coming to the ears, for energy flows only where it has an opportunity to flow. The opposite can also happen. If a deaf person makes a keen resolve to hear through his fingers, he can hear. There are people even today in the world who have developed the power to hear through different parts of their body. There are also people who can see through different parts of the body.

Now what is that which we call the eye ? It is a part of the body. Since time immemorial, man has been looking out from this particular part of the body. When the first creature that was to become man began to look from the eyes for the first time, it must have been very coincidental. He might have also been able to see from some other part of his body. Other animals have seen from other parts of the body, and so their eyes are located in other parts of the body. There are birds and animals and insects that have false eyes and real eyes. They see with the real ones, and the false ones are to deceive the enemy so that the real eye is spared when they are attacked.

The ordinary fly has a thousand eyes. Its one eye is a group of a thousand eyes, and its capacity of looking is great. There are fish that have eyes in the tail, for they have to protect against the enemy from behind. If we study the eyes of all living creatures, we will find that it is not imperative that the eyes should be where we have them.

The same is the case with the ears. They too could be anywhere. They are now permanently situated on the head because for ages and ages man has repeatedly used that place for hearing. The accumulated memories about them have gone so deep within man's consciousness that the body has grown the organs of hearing in that particular place. Now if any one of the organs senses which we have is out of commission, that opening toward the world will be lost to us. If we lose the eyes, we cannot experience light. No matter how sharp our ears or how sensitive our hands may be, the world of light will be closed to us. Then, no matter how sharp the ears or how nimble the feet, they cannot help us to experience light.

So when the kundalini begins to rise, it also knocks at doors that are beyond the ordinary, from which you begin to experience things that you could not experience with the ordinary eyes and hands. Correctly speaking, it begins knocking at the doors of your extrasensory perception. The power that operates your eyes and ears is also the power of the kundalini. A very small amount of kundalini operates them. If the amount of kundalini is increased, you will have additional energy that can strike at new doors. A small stream of water flows in a single stream, but if the water suddenly increases new streams break out in all directions—for the single stream is unable to bear the load of the extra water.

So in the physical sense, awakening the kundalini means that you have so much energy that your normal openings will be unable to contain it. Then the energy, out of necessity, will have to knock at new doors, and new faculties of perception will begin to come into action. Many kinds of perceptions will open: you will experience telepathy, clairvoyance; you will begin to see and hear without your eyes and ears; you will begin to experience things without the help of any of your known sensory organs. New faculties will begin operating within. The most profound result of the activation of these faculties is that you will begin to experience the invisible world within—that which we call the Atman—which is the most subtle extension of the body. So with the awakening of the kundalini your potentialities grow, but the work will initially begin from the body.

There is another method of which I have not spoken. Ordinarily, we talk about ways of awakening the kundalini. But the kundalini is not the whole kunda. There is another method on which we shall talk separately sometime. Very few people have experimented with this method in which instead of awakening the kundalini we have to drown ourselves in the kunda. It is not to raise a wave or two of energy, but to plunge the whole consciousness into the kunda. Then no new doors will open, nor will there be any extrasensory experiences. And the consciousness of the Atman will also disappear. Then there will be a direct experience of the Divine.

When the kundalini is awakened, the first experience is that of the Atman, and with this will be the feeling that, "My Atman is distinct from the Atman of others." So those who have awakened the kundalini believe in the individuality of the soul. They will say that within each person, there is a soul, and hence there are as many souls as there are people. Those who have plunged straight into the kunda, however, say that there is no Atman—that there is only God : not many, but ONE. When you jump into the kunda, it is not your own kunda alone. It is the universal kunda that you plunge into—for the kunda of each person is not individual : the source is ONE. Therefore, the kunda is infinitely powerful. No matter how much energy you draw from it, it remains the same. Like the ocean, it is infinite. But when we fill our own vessel and bring it home, then I call the water in my vessel "mine" and you call the water in your vessel "yours", though the water is the same.

We have brought up something of the ocean by experimenting with the kundalini, but those who plunge in directly declare that there are no separate vessels and all the water is of the same ocean. You cannot keep it as your own for very long, for it will return to the source Soon the sun will shine, and the water will evaporate and become a cloud. Everything will go back to the ocean. Similarly, by experimenting with the kundalini you go through extrasensory experiences which are wonderful manifestations of the psychic, and the experience of the Atman from where you touch God is only a part.

It is just as if I touch the ocean from one end and you touch from the other—from millions of miles away. Then how am I to believe that you are touching the same ocean? You are touching from your shore and I from mine, so mine becomes the Indian ocean, yours the Atlantic and a third person's the Pacific. The ocean will be the same, only we draw our dividing lines where we touch it. Then we make our own oceans and our own shores.

So the experience of the Atman is to touch God from a corner, and this can come about by awakening a small wave of the kundalini. Thus, we are walking on this path, but one day we have to give up the Atman also, or else the journey cannot be completed. Then we will have to put aside the Atman and jump into the source itself. The way of the kundalini is comparatively easier, though long, and it is often the case that the longer path is easier than a short one. This is always so, and there are reasons for it.

Now if I want to come close to myself, I can only do so through some thing else. If I want to look at my face I cannot do so directly. I have to view it through a mirror. Now this is a long process. First my face will be reflected in the mirror, and then I will be able to see it. But though it would be quicker to see my face directly, it is very difficult—almost impossible.

So the method of raising the energy of the kundalini, though a long journey, takes us through the entire world of the senses and ultimately up to the Atman. Then the jump has to be taken from there, but then it becomes easy. He who has experienced the bliss of it, then hears the call of this *ananda* (bliss) to come and lose himself in order to attain the Ultimate Bliss. It is one kind of joy to know oneself; attaining oneself is one kind of joy. But losing oneself is the Supreme Bliss. When you have known yourself, you will have only one anguish left—the anguish of your own being. All other sufferings and sorrows will be no more.

Then you will be seized with a questioning of your own being. You will ask, "Why, oh why, do I exist at all ?" It seems superfluous and unnecessary. So you will take the jump. One day you will decide, "I have known my being; now I want to know 'Non-Being'. I have known light; now I want to know darkness also." However vast the light, it has its limits, whereas darkness is limitless. However significant the being, it has its limitations. But Non-Being has no limitations.

Therefore, Buddha was not understood by people for when they asked, "Shall we be liberated ?" he answered, "How can YOU be liberated ? You have to liberate yourself from your own Self." And yet they questioned, "When desires and sorrows and sins leave us, will not our being at least remain ?" "No," said Buddha, "When desires and sins and sorrows vanish, the anguish of your being will still remain." Now it is interesting that as long as desires remain, your being does not disturb you. You employ your being in satisfying your desires. If you have earned riches, you have involved your being in the work of gaining riches. If you have built up status for yourself, you have employed your being in that direction. When there is no desire for wealth or position or sex, when there is no doing, then what will you do with your being ? Then the being will begin to cause you anguish; it will make you restless.

Therefore, Buddha says, "No, no ! 'Nothing' will remain. When a flame is blown out, where does it go ?" Until his dying day people asked, "What will happen to Buddha when he dies ? What will happen when you die ?" Buddha replied, "When I myself am no more, what remains to happen ? Nothing is left over. It is just like a flame that goes out. You never ask what happens to the flame after it is extinguished. When the flame is gone, it is gone."

The attainment of the Atman is just a stage, just a preparation toward the losing of the Atman. But in one sense it is easy, because if you tell a person who has not parted from his desires to part from his being and plunge right into the kunda, he could not possibly do so. He will say that he still has a lot to do. Why are we so afraid of losing ourselves ? It is because there is so much to be done, and if I lose myself who will do the work ? I have started to build a house, but it is only half complete. Let me complete it, and then I shall be ready to lose myself. But in the meantime, several other things will be in a half-finished state. Actually, desire is a longing to complete something, and that is what goads us on. Therefore, as long as desires persist, it is impossible to lose the Atman. If desires are annihilated in someone, then one day he may be ready to lose the Atman—for then what use is the Atman ?

What I mean is that if you tell a person who has not given up sorrow to give up bliss, he will say, "Are you mad ?" But the moment sorrow is abolished and bliss alone remains, then you will also wonder what to do with bliss. Then you will be ready to give up bliss too. And the moment a person is ready to give up *ananda* (bliss), the happening takes place. Anybody can volunteer to do away with sorrow, but a moment does come when we are prepared to give up bliss as well. It is then that one is absorbed and immersed in the Universal Existence.

So one can enter suddenly by plunging directly into the kunda, but it is very difficult for a person to do this. We can, however, reach the state of preparation for this gradually. By and by desires leave us, our instinctual tendencies vanish, and all actions cease. All that supported your being becomes lost. What remains is oneself alone, the being, without any foundation and without support. Then you feel, "What is the use of salvaging this ? Then you plunge into the kunda, and to plunge into the kunda is Nirvana.

If you wish to go directly to the source, the kundalini does not come in the way. This is why some methods do not talk about kundalini, for it was not required. According to my knowledge and experience, these direct methods are rarely possible. They could be effective for a very, very few, but that does not solve our problem. Therefore, the longer route is useful. Many a time one has to knock at the doors of other people in order to reach one's own house. One has to recognize countless faces in order to recognize one's own, and one has to love God knows how many others before one begins to love one's own Self. However, the best and the most direct way is to love one's own Self. What is the difficulty or the hindrance ? It is best to come straight to one's own house, but it does not happen so. In fact, it is difficult to find one's own dwelling place before one has rambled about to other people's dwellings. And until we give and receive love from others, we do not come to know that the basic question is one of loving one's own Self.

This kundalini sadhana (spiritual practice) which I speak about is a preparation of the body to enter the bodiless state—to reach to the Atman. You cannot reach the Atman with the amount of energy that is currently awakened in you, for that is just enough to pull you through your daily tasks. In fact, it is not even enough for this either, and that is why the body experiences fatigue. The flame burns very low; thus, it cannot reach to the Atman.

The concept of Sannyas evolved with the very idea of conserving that energy which we already possess so that it can be used for a different purpose. In this way, one's ordinary day-to-day work like running a shop or serving somewhere was stopped. To my mind, this attitude is wrong, for in the effort to save this energy we have to consume a great deal of energy. Many a time, the energy required to be angry is not half as much as energy required to curb anger. More energy is utilized in prevention than in the actual act. Therefore, I am not in favour of this method. This is the way of a miser. This kind of sannyasin tries to scrounge and scrimp on the meagre amount of energy that he happens to have. Awaken more energy : that is what I say. There is an infinite storehouse to draw from within. There is much that you cannot possibly consume it all. Then why worry about conserving it ?

Now if a man feels, "How can I love the Divine after having loved my wife ?" the little energy that he has will be totally consumed in loving his wife. So he tries to save it, but this very act of saving requires twice the energy one would normally use. The energy will be spent in fighting with oneself. Besides, with this little of energy you are not even able to reach up to your wife fully, so how can you expect to reach the Divine ? The small bridge you had constructed was not even enough to reach to your wife. You missed many a step in between, and you failed to reach up to her heart. How is it then that with this same energy you wish to build a bridge that reaches up to the Infinite ? This is pure madness.

There is no question of conserving this energy. Infinite

energy lies dormant within you. The question is simply one of activating this energy. Once the stream of energy begins to pour forth, it is infinite. You can never settle its account. In other words, there is never a moment in your life when you can say there is no more left within to be awakened.

The capacity waiting to be awakened is immense and infinite. As the energy awakens, your ability to awaken more and more energy increases. When the amount of Divine energy within is in excess of what it normally is, then only can you utilize it for unknown paths. In the world also, we use excess reserve wealth to discover unknown paths. An over-affluent country decides to go to the moon. Going to the moon is not utilitarian, and one is not going to profit by it. Yet one loses nothing when he has more than enough to lose. As long as you have just enough or perhaps less, you have to keep a strict account of your expenses. Then you will not step out of the known, familiar world. To venture into the unknown you need an abundance of energy. Thus, you have to build up your kundalini from extra energy, to the extent that you have such an abundance of energy that the question of "how to use it" arises.

Remember, those who have abundant energy suddenly feel that all the old doors have become inoperative, for they are incapable of withstanding the influx of the extra energy. It is like the ocean falling into the river : the river will be completely wiped out; it will lose all track of itself. In a similar way, the track where your energy previously flowed is wiped out, the track of sex is wiped out, all at once. The moment this influx takes place, all of the old shores will be instantly annihilated. Then you will wonder where all which you used to scrimp and scrounge over has disappeared. All your puny efforts—such as to practise "brahmacharya" (celibacy), to subdue anger—where have they all vanished ? The rivers and channels are all washed away and only the ocean remains. Now that you have no known means of spending this new energy, you will find that you have set out on a new journey, for the energy has to flow : it must flow.

It is only a matter of awakening it but once. Then, as the energy pounds at new outlets and begins to push through the crevices and openings, your usual day-to-day interests begin to become meaningless. Then you begin to have extrasensory experiences. No sooner do these doors open when you begin to gain the knowledge of that extension of the body which is bodiless—of the Atman. Thus, kundalini is a preparation for your entry into the Bodiless.

Questioner : *In kundalini sadhana, the question arises of the ascent and descent of energy. Does it ascend first and then go down? And is this going down a plunge into the kunda, or something else? Kindly explain this.*

Bhagwan : Actually, the merging into the kunda is neither an ascent nor a descent. There is going up or coming down, but only a passing into extinction, into nothingness. When the drop falls into the ocean, it neither ascends nor descends. Of course, when it dries up under the rays of the sun, then it rises up toward the sky. And when it cools in the cold air of the clouds, it falls to the ground. In the ocean, the drop just drowns, dies, becomes extinct. So the reference to descent and ascent is in quite a different manner altogether. Now many a time, the power we awaken has to be sent back to the kunda, for the main reason that the body is not prepared to bear such a high voltage. Thus, the extra voltage has to be returned to its source.

We have our limited capacities when it comes to the capacity to bear joy, the capacity to bear pain, the capacity to bear the powers of our own energy. If the impact is greater than our ability to be in control of it, the integration of the personality is destroyed and the personality is broken into fragments. That would be quite harmful. Thus, many a time the extra energy must be sent back. The experiment that I tell of, however, does not bring about such a condition. The release of the energy depends entirely on the type of experiment. There are experiments which awaken the energy all at once. These are called experiments of "sudden Enlightenment". These are very dangerous, for as I said before the voltage may be so high that you may be unable to bear it. This situation is like that of a bulb that bursts with heavy voltage or a fuse that is blown or a fan that burns or a car that catches fire. The experiment I give you to follow first creates in you an ability, a capacity, and does not awaken the full energy right away.

We can also compare these two types of methods in this way : if a big dam gives way due to being overfilled, it can cause a great deal of damage. But if proper channels are constructed and if the water is released in a systematic manner, the same water could prove very useful.

A strange event took place in the life of Krishnamurti. In his childhood, he was made to go through all of the kundalini sadhanas by the Theosophists. All kinds of experiments were carried out on him which he does not now recall. He has no knowledge of all this. Knowledge came to him only when the ocean flooded the channels. Now he is unaware of all the practices he was made to undergo in order to prepare him. Therefore, he does not believe that any preparation is necessary. He was made to undergo many sadhanas, and perhaps this situation in which a person is prepared very intensively by others is a very unique kind of experimentation in this world. Many a person has gone through such preparations, but only for himself.

This kind of experimentation is possible, for the other is not the other in the depths of the being. All who are here are "others" only superficially. Deep within, we are all one. So these "others" carried out this experiment on Krishnamurti for the purpose of a very great happening, but the experiment misfired. They were trying to create conditions within Krishnamurti for the descent of a great soul, and he was to be a mere vehicle. The channels within were dug and the energy awakened, but this was the preliminary work. The main task was yet to be performed. Krishnamurti was not the goal. He was to be a means for a greater event. Some other soul was to descend into him. But this happening could not be brought about, because as soon as the waters rushed into the channels Krishnamurti refused to be the medium. This is the only reason why such experiments do not succeed, for when a person reaches the state when he himself becomes the power, why should he be an instrument for another ? Thus, at the critical moment he refused.

It is like this : I give you the key to my house and tell you to get the house ready tomorrow for a guest. If I leave the house in your care and go away when the guest arrives the next day, you can turn around and say that the house belongs to you—that you are the Master—for the key is with you. And though the key is with you, you have no knowledge how the key was prepared or how the house was made. The fact that the key is with you and you know how to open the house settles the question.

So this is what happened to Krishnamurti. Some people can be prepared; some come prepared from their previous lives. But these are extraordinary cases. Ordinarily, each one of us has to prepare himself. It is in the fitness of things that the experiment should be such that it prepares you first and the happening then takes place later. As your capacity increases, the energy increases. Care is taken that the energy awakens only in proportion to your preparedness. Many harsh experiments lead to insanity and madness. This is a major cause of why people recoil from religion. So experiments can be of two kinds.

Now I shall tell you how many a time it happens that our plans backfire. In America, the distribution of electric supply is so designed that excess power in one place can be automatically transferred to another place where it may be needed. For instance, if a town for some reason or the other uses less energy than the quota allotted to it, the excess energy automatically flows to another town which might require more. Now it can happen that a factory is closed because of labour trouble. Then the energy lying idle can be directed to another town where another factory may be facing difficulties due to lack of electric power. So things were arranged so that the electric power of a particular zone could carry out the task of supply and demand automatically.

But it so happened some three to four years ago that all the electric power in America (along the East coast) was cut off for ten to twelve hours, and this happened on account of this automatic system. As it happened, there was a power failure in a small town. This created a lack of supply. Now the excess energy in the power network immediately rushed into the lines of this town. But the sudden impact of the rushing energy caused a major breakdown that affected not only this town:

the complete zone (along the East coast) was plunged into darkness and all work came to a standstill.

It was then realized that the arrangements we make for our comfort and efficiency can boomerang back on us also. If each town had its own circuit, this would not have happened. Such a thing can never happen in India. It can only happen in America where everything is interconnected. The energy in these systems are flowing continuously from one place to another, and there is always the danger of a major catastrophy.

Within man also there is a complete electrical circuit, and if this energy flows toward you in a greater quantity than you are able to bear, it can be very dangerous. There are methods of increasing the load of the energy. If there are fifty people here, there are methods by which, if you wish, you can cause the current from all the fifty to flow toward you. These fifty will lie unconscious, and you will become the center of energy. But there are many, many hazards. It can happen that the energy thus released may be too much for you to take. Also, the opposite can happen. All your energy can flow toward them just as theirs flowed toward you. All these experiments have been carried out.

There are methods of sending back the extra energy, but with the method I speak of these are not necessary. The energy will rise according to how much your potentiality increases. The energy will come only after due preparation is made. Therefore, it will never happen that you will have to send back anything. One day, you yourself will turn back, one day you yourself, having known it all, will jump into the kunda. That is a different thing.

These words (up and down) have been used in a different way also. The meaning which Sri Aurobindo attached to his experiment is entirely different. We can think of the Divine energy in two ways : either we can think of it as being above us in the skies, or as being deep below us in the underworld. As far as the earth is situated, the words "up" and "down" hold no meaning. They only represent a way of thinking and observing. We take this roof to be above us, but it is not above us. If we were to dig into the ground beneath us and go on digging (from India), we might come out in America. Now if someone were to view things from there, he would see the roof as being below us—under our heads. We would look topsy turvy to him—as if standing on our heads. Even now things are like that. Everything depends on how and from where we view it.

Our East and West is also false. What is East and what is West ? If you walk from the East and keep on walking, you will reach the West. In the same way, if you walk from the West you will reach the East. Now if the West takes you along itself to the East, why should it be called the West ? Everything is relative, and all that is relative has no meaning in itself. Calling this East and that West is due to our makeshift boundary line. Otherwise, how could we work ? But where does the East start from ? From Calcutta ? Rangoon ? Tokyo ? Where does the West begin and where does it end ? These demarcations are only for our convenience. They are a means for us to distribute ourselves. In the same manner, the concept of "up and down" is in a different dimension. "East and West" is a horizontal concept and "up and down" is an imaginary, vertical division. There is nothing up and nothing down, for there is no roof to the world and no floor. All this is meaningless, but these concepts penetrate into religion as well.

Some people experience God as above. So when the energy comes it will DESCEND toward them. Some conceive of God as below—in the roots. So when the energy comes, it will rise from below and spread through them. But, actually, this has no meaning. Where we place God—above or below—is a matter of our own convenience. But in this makeshift arrangement of ours we have to make a choice.

I would say that it is aetter for the energy to rise up from below than to descend from above. There are reasons for this. When you begin with the concept of the energy rising from within YOU, YOU will have to raise the energy, you will have to work for it. When it is a question of the energy descending, there can only be prayer on your part; you cannot do anything. When the energy has to descend from above, all you have to do is to wait with folded hands. Therefore, two types of religion evolved in the world—one that favoured meditation and another that fovoured prayer and supplication (to God).

The religions that advocate prayer are those that believe God to be above. Now what is to be done ? WE cannot bring HIM down, because to bring Him down we will have to raise ourselves. And how can we raise ourselves so high ? Then we will ourselves become God. We cannot go up; we have to stand where we are. Then the only way is to call out to Him to come down.

Now those religions that believed that we have to rise up within ourselves, that there is something lying dormant within our roots which will awaken only by our own efforts, turned away from prayer and toward meditation. So between prayer and meditation there is this difference in concept of "above" and "below". The prayerful religions believe God to be above and the meditating religions believe Him to be the root of all Existence.

Note that the religions based on prayer are slowly dying out. There is no future for them, whereas those advocating meditation are gaining ground every day. There is a great future ahead for meditation.

I would like you to understand that the spiritual journey is from lower to higher. This will have other meanings also. All of these concepts are equal, so it does not matter to me if you hold one concept above the other. But I feel that this will be difficult for you.

As I said before, if we want to go West we are bound to reach by walking eastwards. Yet we never do that. If we want to go West we travel toward the West, And even though concepts are meaningless in themselves, even though by walking eastward we can reach the West, it is an unnecessarily long way. Do you understand what I mean to say ? Therefore, for the "sadhak" (meditator) and the "bhakta" (devotee) there are two different ways. The bhakta's God is above, and so he will fold his hands and wait. The sadhak's God is hidden in his very roots, so he will gird up his loins and get busy awakening Him.

There are other meanings too which we should take note of. When we believe God to be below, he becomes present in our "baser" characteristics also. Then nothing is base or low to our minds—for if God Himself is in the region below, He is present in the lowest rung of our beings and He will begin to awaken from there also. He will awaken from sex also. In other words, no place will be devoid of Him. In the lowest of hells, if anyone is there it is He. Now if we consider Him to be above, then what is below is automatically condemned, for it is not the Divine. Hence, unknowingly the feeling of one's own lowliness takes root. We then consider Him above and ourselves below. This produces drastic psychological results.

If you mean to stand firmly and strongly, it is but proper that the energy should rise from below, for that will strengthen your legs. When the power comes from above, it will first come in contact with your head—and from there it has to come down to the roots. Besides, if it comes from above, it will always seem foreign to you. This is why those who have attained through prayer have never agreed that God and we are one. Moslems have always opposed the concept of God and man being one, for He is up high and we are down below. Therefore, when one such as Mansoor or Sarmat declares, "I am God", it is but natural that they will cut his throat. For them, there is no greater *kafir* (infidel) than the one who proclaims himself to be God. How dare we, who are but worms wriggling on the earth, identify ourselves with the deity on high ?

The reason for this belief lies in the fact that when we consider God to be above and ourselves to be below, we become two. Therefore, the Sufis were always disliked by Mohammedans, for they always declared their identity with God. Now this can only be if the energy rises from below, for we are below. When the power comes from the earth itself and not from the skies above, then only can He and I be one.

When we install God above us, our earthly lives are condemned. Then birth will be the result of a past sin. When we regard Him as being below, our lives on earth becomes a thing of joy. Then it will become the grace of God and not the fruit of sin. Then everything, no matter how dark it may appear, can be a living experience of a ray of His light. Then no matter how bad a person may be, even if he is the most condemned criminal, his innermost depths will reveal a glimpse of His presence.

Therefore, I would advise that we follow the method of raising the Divine power from below. Those who know are aware that these two methods are not different, for the goal is the same and the matter of above or below holds no meaning. But if we do not know and we want to set out on this path, it is better that we opt for the path that can easily be traversed. Therefore, what I feel is proper for the sadhak is that he should understand that the energy will rise from below—that the journey is upwards from below.

This is the reason why those who have accepted the upward journey have taken fire as a symbol of God, for fire always rises upwards. That is why, deep within us, we use fire to symbolize God. The only reason was that the flames of the fire always rise upwards, and by rising upwards they are lost in space. Similarly, the sadhak will also rise upwards and become lost after some time. This is why I prefer to stress the ascent and not the descent.

Questioner : *In the Nargol meditation camp held at Nargol, you said that we have to exhaust the body completely by intense and deep breathing and by asking "Who am I?" in order to go into meditation. Excess reserve energy is required to enter meditation, but how is this possible with a tired body and mind?*

Bhagwan : Meditation does not mean the lack of energy. You tire yourself, but what is meant by yours "self"? It means those "doors" through which the energy flows out to maintain your day-to-day activities. I am not talking about the Self that you can be, but about the self that you are. So when you tire yourself out, a double action takes place. You tire your body so that all your senses, your mind and your body refuse to be a vehicle for the energy.

In the normal course of life, when we are tired, we stop all activities and say we cannot work any more. So this experiment will, on the one hand, exhaust your mind, your body and all your senses, and, on the other, it will knock at the source of your energy, the kundalini. On one side you are exhausted and on the other the energy awakens. Both these take place simultaneously. On one side you are exhausted and on the other the energy rises, but you are in no position to use it. Your eyes wish to see, but you are too weary to oblige. You want to think, but the mind is too tired ; the feet refuse to walk a step. Now, if you want to walk, you will have to do so without the help of the feet. If you want to see, you shall have to find other means of looking.

So the entire arrangement of your being is put out of gear. It refuses to cooperate with the newly awakened energy which then has to knock on doors that are as yet closed and unused. These virgin centers were always ready to function, but they never had the chance because you preferred to use up all your energy through the outgoing senses. Tired from this meditation, these "doors" will say, "Excuse us, please. Do not come in our direction." So to the energy that is arising, these "doors" will say, "No, we have no desire to see." Then, when the eyes refuse to see and the mind abdicates from all desires to see, what will the energy that has arisen do ? Then you will begin to see in a different dimension. A completely new part of your being will begin to work. Some psychic centers of sight within you will then begin to open, and you will begin to see things you have never seen before. It is not that these things were not there before : you had never given them an opportunity. So now they have a chance to manifest themselves.

Therefore, I emphasize exhaustion. The mind, the body and all that is you has to be completely exhausted. Then, that which is you even now—and of which you are completely unaware—can come into action. When the energy is roused it demands work, and your being will have to provide work for it. Also it will find work for itself. If your ears are too tired and the energy wishes to hear, it will hear the "nada" (inner sound) which does not require the services of the ears ; it will see light for which eyes are not necessary ; it will smell fragrance, but not through the nose. Thus, the subtle sensory organs—the extrasensory faculties or whatever we prefer to call them—will become active.

Each sense organ is connected with a corresponding extrasensory center. There is one ear that catches the sounds of the outside world and there is another that catches the sounds within. It is only that this ear has not had a chance to function. Now when the outer ear is tired, when the awakened energy comes to it when it refuses to cooperate, then this energy will activate the inner ear that has been lying neglected. So you will see and hear such things that if you tell another about them he will say, "You have gone mad. How can such things happen? You are under an illusion and you are dreaming." But to you the strains of the *veena* (sitar) within will be more clear than any *veena* music of the outside world ever was, and you will say, "If this is false then the outside *veena* that I hear must be completely false."

So in the beginning it is necessary that you exhaust your senses in order to open new doors within yourself. Once they are opened there is no fear, for then you can always compare by yourself. Then you will say, "If you must see, see within, for it is so exalting and blissful." Right now you cannot compare, for you have only one alternative—that of external perception. Once the inner eyes open, the alternative will be clear. Whenever you wish to see, you will prefer to see what is within. You will not miss a single opportunity. Then outer looking will have no meaning.

There is a story in the life of St. Rabiya. One evening the sun was setting and she was sitting inside her hut. A fakir named Hassan came to visit her, and he was witnessing the beautiful sunset. He called out to her, "What are you doing inside, Rabiya? The evening with the glorious sunset is so beautiful. Come out quickly. Such a beautiful scene we may not see again." To this Rabiya replied, "You foolish fellow. How long will you gaze at the outer sun? Come on in, for I see within He who has made the sun, and I see suns that are still in the making and suns that will be. It will be better if you step within."

Hassan did not follow what Rabiya said. Now this woman was really a wonderful person. She is one of the few significant women in the world's history. But Hassan did not understand her. Still he called out, "See? You are missing a wonderful sight." And Rabiya replied, "You fool! You view the sunset outside and miss the splendour within. How much you are losing!"

Now this conversation took place from two different levels of consciousness, for each is talking from a different plane. But if you are not aware of the inner senses, they hold no meaning.

Then only the outer ones are meaningful. To this end I have said that it is better if the outer senses are exhausted.

Questioner : *So in your dynamic meditation experiment, exhausting the faculties does not mean loss of energy?*

Bhagwan : No, No ! Not at all. The energy is rising all the time. And all this is done in order to awaken the energy. The sense organs become tired, but these are only the instruments that the energy works through and not the energy. And these outlets are not "me". "I" am something else; I merely go in and out of these doors. When the door is tired, it wishes not to be used; otherwise it will have to work. The eyes refuse to work, and so do the ears and the rest of the outer senses. Their complete exhaustion is very helpful in the initial stages.

Questioner : *If the energy is awakening there should be no feeling of exhaustion, but ordinarily this the feeling of exhaustion is there. What is the reason?*

Bhagwan : In the beginning you will feel tired, but gradually you will feel the freshness—such exhilaration as you have never felt before ! In the beginning you are bound to be exhausted. This is because you identify yourself with the senses : you take yourself TO BE the senses. When the sense faculties tire, we say, "I am tired." This association with the senses must be broken.

You are riding a horse and the horse becomes tired. Now you identify yourself so much with the horse that you think YOU are tired. We only know the fatigue of that with which we identify ourselves. The moment you realize that you are not the horse, a unique kind of freshness will begin to happen. Then you will know that it is the various organs that are tired and not you. On the contrary, when the body is tired to the point of exhaustion, a great deal of energy which would otherwise have been frittered away uselessly by the body is saved, and thus it accumulates within. Then you will begin to feel the conservation of energy within which is your treasure. And since this energy has not flowed out, it spreads into every pore of the body. But this you will only come to know when you break your identity with the body.

So by and by, with meditation, you will begin to feel extraordinarily fresh. In fact, it is wrong to say that you will feel fresh. Rather, you will become freshness itself—but, remember, *only* after the breaking of identifications.

Right now you take yourself to be the horse. Throughout life you have thought in this way. That you are the rider will take a long time to be understood. Perhaps if the horse drops with exhaustion, it will become easier to understand.

When you have to walk on your own feet, you will realize that you are separate from the horse. By riding on horseback, you have completely forgotten that you can also walk. Therefore, it is best that the horse drops with fatigue.

[*Text of a discourse given on July* 1, 1970, *evening, in Bombay, India*].

8

THE ALCHEMY OF BREATH

Questioner :

Bhagwan, the great mystic and spiritualist of Russia George Gurdjieff has written his reminiscences of his journey toward truth in the book "Meetings with Remarkable Men". In that he has given an account of his talks with a Sufi dervish in detail. He was very much impressed by the Sufi's talks on "pranayam" and "asanas" (yogic breathing and physical exercises). The dervish warned him not to indulge in any breathing experiments. He was of the opinion that tampering with the natural arrangement of the breathing system breaks up the person's being, and the results are disastrous. What is your opinion on this ?

Bhagwan Shree Rajneesh :

What the dervish says about pranayam and special breathing exercises is true to some extent. In fact, there is no falsehood without some truth in it. The case is never otherwise, and it is the truth within a falsehood that makes a falsehood credible. Then the falsehood manages to pass with the truth.

Now it is very true that as far as possible we should not obstruct natural functioning, or else there will be confusion. So it would be good if you do not interfere with the normal arrangements of the body's functions of breathing, sitting, standing or walking, for as soon as you begin to create hindrances, mutation begins to take place.

So, remember, loss means change and profit also means change. Both mean change. If you want to stay as you are, then it is not proper to tamper with the workings of the body. But if you want to reach somewhere, if you want to bring about a transformation within yourself, you have to take the risk. And the risk is that if you give a greater field and a different dimension to your breath, it will bring about a marked difference in your personality. If you are satisfied with being as you are, then you should not venture. But if you feel that your present personality is not enough, then you will have to take the step.

Then changing the breath is a priceless matter. If you cause a change in breathing to happen, many things within will begin to explode and new things will come into being. After thousands of experiments it is now known what things explode and what new things take shape through breathing exercises. In fact, these things are known thoroughly. A few things are known to all from their every-day experience. For instance, when we are angry we breathe differently; when we are silent the breath changes. In both the cases there will be a change in our normal breathing. Now if you note the quality of the breath in silence, you can bring about a state of tranquillity just by breathing in that same manner, for tranquillity and that particular way of breathing are both interconnected.

When the mind is filled with sex, the rate of breathing changes. However, if you do not allow the rate of breathing to change, you will find that the feeling of sex is gone. The desire will disappear; it will not last. In the body mechanism, a harmonious relationship must exist among all the other parts; otherwise no activity is possible. If you are filled with anger and you then begin to breathe slowly, anger cannot remain. It CANNOT remain at that particular rate of breathing.

So the rate of breath is very important, for the difference in breath brings about a difference in the mind. And now the relationship between the condition of the mind and the rate of breathing has been scientifically proven. So there is no danger. However, there were many hazards for those who began these experiments, and there is always danger in any new venture which we undertake in life. When everything becomes clear after experimentation, it is scientific.

For instance, it is impossible for a man to keep his breathing regular and yet be angry. These two things do not go together.

The opposite is also possible : if you begin to breathe as you do in anger, after a while you will find anger rising within you. Through the discovery of many laws about breathing, pranayam has evolved many ways of bringing about a change in your mind.

Another thing we must know is the difference between natural breathing and unnatural breathing. What we call natural breathing is not entirely natural breathing. If this is properly understood one will know that that too is an artificial way of breathing which we have become used to since childhood. You do not know actually what natural breathing is, and, therefore, your breathing in the day is different from your breathing in the night. Your breathing in the daytime is artificial, and your breathing at night is natural because it has nothing to do with the habitual pattern you have formed. So the breathing process of the night is more natural than the breathing process of the day.

We have formed a particular way of breathing in the day, and there are many reasons for it. Note your breathing when you are in a crowd and when you are alone by yourself. In a crowd you are tense : the breath becomes short and quick and does not go deep. When there are people all around you, the breath is shortened : it returns quickly without going deep. When you are all alone by yourself, it will be full and deep. Therefore, it is full and deep at night when you are asleep.

So what we call natural breathing is not natural but conditioned breathing, habituated breathing. Children breathe differently. Watch them when they are asleep and you will find that they breathe through their stomachs. We breathe from the chest. The child breathes naturally. If you begin to breathe the way children breathe, your mind will develop just like the mind of a child: it will become as innocent. Conversely, if your mind becomes innocent you will begin to breathe like a child.

That is why the images of Buddha in Japan and China are different from those in India: In India the stomach of Buddha is small, whereas in the images of Buddha in Japan and China he is depicted as having a big stomach and a small chest. It may look odd to us and we might think that it is very ugly, but it is proper. When a person so tranquil and serene and innocent breathes, he will breathe through his stomach and never through the chest. So the big stomach is a symbol of his serenity and innocence. It does not necessarily mean that Buddha had a big stomach. The big stomach depicts his serenity: he has become like a child. When this becomes clear in our minds, we will be able to take steps toward natural breathing.

Our breathing is artificial. The dervish is wrong when he says do not make your breathing unnatural. We already breathe the unnaturally. As our understanding increases and we begin to breathe naturally, the greater possibilities of life will begin to reveal themselves from within.

It is good to know also that sometimes sudden artificial breathing is beneficial. One thing is very clear: where there are many gains there are many losses also. A man runs a shop: he runs the same risk of loss as of profit. A man gambles: he also runs the same risk. The ratio of profit and loss is the same everywhere. So it is true that there are many hazards, but what the dervish says is only half the truth. There are great possibilities also, and it is a gamble. So if we practise a little "unnatural" breathing—unnatural in the sense that we have never done it before—we begin to experience new conditions within ourselves.

In these conditions we can go mad and in these conditions we can be liberated also. The chances for insanity are as much as the chances for liberation. Now because we ourselves create these conditions we can also stop whenever we please. Therefore, there is no danger. The possibility of danger is there only when you cannot stop yourself. But when you yourself have brought about the condition, you are capable of putting an immediate stop. You are also all the time fully conscious of all that happens. You know whether you are going toward joy or toward pain, whether you are going into peace or into chaos. You will be conscious of every inch of your progress.

When the rate of breathing changes suddenly and unexpectedly, the arrangement within undergoes a complete change. We can never know our separate identity from the body through our habitual patterns of breathing. Our manner of breathing has formed a bridge between the body and the soul, and we are so habituated to it that we take it for granted. For example, each day when you drive in past your gate you turn the wheel of your car in one particular direction. Now you do not have to think about this process every day when you enter through the gate. You turn your wheel in a certain direction, the car turns accordingly, and you find yourself at the door of your house.

But suppose that suddenly the wheels of the car do not obey the steering wheel, and they turn in the opposite direction: the entire direction of your daily drive will change. You will be thrown into the strangeness and wonder of a completely new situation, and this happening will immediately fill you with awareness. The strangeness of a situation at once breaks the mind's unconsciousness. In a regulated life where everthing happens as scheduled, your unconsciousness is not disturbed. It only breaks when something happens suddenly.

Now, for instance, I am talking : this will not disturb your torpor. But if suddenly this table starts speaking, not a single person will remain unconscious. He cannot ! My thousand words will not shake you out of your torpor, but a single word from the table will make you jump into awareness as this will be a strange happening. Anything new or unfamiliar breaks the established pattern. So when these experiences that happen as a result of changing the breath take you through the unknown, the new, the strange. They fill you with awareness, and you see the vast possibilities opening up within yourself. And if a man can go mad consciously, no experience is more priceless.

In my experiment you are completely conscious inwardly while you are completely mad outwardly. Within yourself, you are fully aware that you are dancing. You know also that if you had seen someone else dancing in this way you would have called him mad—but now you can call yourself mad. However, both things are simultaneous—your going "mad" and your calling yourself "mad". Therefore, since you know what you are doing you are not really mad. You are completely conscious within even though that which is happening to you externally is happening to a madman.

In this condition, a strange moment comes when you can separate yourself from the body. You do not separate yourself consciously, but you find that YOU HAVE BECOME separated from the body. All the inner workings are upset, all the old bridges are broken, all the day-to-day routines are shattered, everything becomes disorganized. The hand that used to move only at your bidding does not await your orders any more. The tears that you did not wish to shed stream down in spite of you. The laughter you wished to control cannot be restrained.

Such strange moments are unique for creating awareness, and these moments are brought about more quickly by the breathing experiment I give you than by any other practice. Other practices take years whereas the breathing experiment takes only ten minutes. This is because the breath is so intimately connected with our being that the slightest hammering reverberates in all directions.

Experiments on breath were very valuable, but I do not greatly recommend disciplined methods of pranayam. The more a practice becomes regulated, the more its strangeness wears off. A person breathes through one nostril, then holds the breath for a certain time, then lets it out through the other : He can practise this, and as a result of his practice it becomes mechanical. It is no longer a leap into the unknown, but a bridge which crosses it, a causeway which by-passes it. Now the method I talk about is absolutely non-methodical, non-regulated and absurd. There is no question of holding the breath or leaving it. It aims only at creating a strange and sudden unknown feeling within you. It plunges you into such an instant confusion that the mind finds it difficult to adjust itself to the new situation.

Remember that the mind is very clever if you allow it time to adjust itself. It will quickly agree to the new situation. If you regulate the breath methodically, the mind will have nothing against your new system of breathing and the experiment will become meaningless—for no newness, no strangeness will be created.

What I want is that all your roots, all your familiarities with yourself, should snap in a moment. One fine day, you should suddenly find yourself confronted with the fact that you have no roots anywhere. You have no mother, no father, no brother, no one and nothing to call your own—not even your own body. You will find yourself in such an absurd, senseless situation that you will go "mad". If you have not brought this situation on yourself, but it has come upon you sudddenly, you will really become mad. But if you find yourself in this situation by your own doing, you cannot go mad, for the matter is completely in your hands and you can retrace your steps at any moment.

This experiment is worth carrying out. I believe that if those who are mad are made to practise this breathing experiment, there is every possibility of their gaining sanity. If such a person can once see that he is capable of creating madness, he will know that he can destroy it also. This method will show him a way out of the madness that came upon him without his knowledge. So there are hazards in this method, but there are an equal number of possibilities within this venture also.

I firmly believe that this practice will be useful in order to expel insanity and also that he who practises this method can never suffer from insanity. The sadhak (seeker) who practises this method will never go mad, for he has the secret of bringing about madness in himself. What he can switch on he can also switch off. You can never goad him on to insanity. He will always be able to hold his own, for what was up until now beyond his control is now well within it.

The method of breathing that I speak about is absolutely non-rhythmical, non-methodical—so much so that it will not be the same today as it was yesterday, for there is no method to show how to go about it. Even throughout the experiment you will not be breathing in the same manner. The idea behind it is to loosen the hold of the mind's long embedded habits.

What the dervish says is correct: many nuts and bolts will loosen. They have to be loosened ! They are so jammed and rusted within that because of them the body and the soul cannot be made to go apart. No sooner do they loosen when you at once feel that there is something else within that has been joined to the body, which can be made to separate from it. But since this loosening happens by irregular breathing, the nuts and bolts become readjusted by themselves at the end of the experiment. We do not have to do anything to readjust them.

If the breathing becomes obsessive and continues for 24 hours and gets out of your control, then your condition will become precarious. But if someone practises for an hour a day, he finds that as soon as he ends the experiment everything falls back into place. Only the remembrance of the experiment remains. You remember that you had been apart from the body for a time although now all is settled as usual. But now, after settling down, you know that YOU are separate from the body. You are joined to the body, you are connected with the body—but, still, you are separate from it. Thus, without the use of the breath the work cannot be done.

So the dervish is not wrong: the hazards are great. But we should be prepared to take on so great a hazard as the height of existence which we want to reach. There is a difference in that we cannot escape from those hazards which fall on us without our knowledge, but we can easily extricate ourselves from the hazards which we knowingly bring upon ourselves.

Many processes take place within the body : some persons dance, some cry, some shriek, and the moment you say "stop !" everything ceases immediately, because this has been brought on by themselves. Now if this happens to a person without his knowing and without his will, he cannot stop it—for then it is beyond his control. I firmly believe that if not today, then in the near future this method will become a great therapy to cure the mentally ill. Also, if children are made to practise this method in school, there will be no chance for them to go insane later in life. The child will become immune to insanity, for he will be his own master. He will be well in control of all that goes on within him.

The dervish who met Gurdjieff is a follower of a different path. This man has not practised this breathing method. He has created a novel situation by a different method. This is the trouble: that someone who knows one way at once denounces other ways as wrong. Any particular thing can be wrong or right in context with a certain method. Now a man driving a car may say that a pin in the wheel of a bullock-cart is insignificant—useless. It is useless as far as a car is concerned, but it is as useful to the bullock-cart as the axle is to the car. So to call anything useful or useless has no absolute meaning, but this error is always committed.

This Sufi fakir has reached from a different path; his method is different. A Sufi normally hammers upon his sleep and not on his breath, so the practising of night vigils hold a deep meaning for him. He will keep awake for months, and this creates the same novel situation as breathing. If you do not sleep for a month at a stretch, you will reach the same point of madness that you reach with intense breathing.

The Sufi will work on the natural arrangement of his sleep. By hammering at his sleep many disturbances begin to occur, and in this there are also dangers—perhaps more dangers than the breathing exercise, for this technique is lengthier. One night's vigil will not do the trick. You have to give up sleep for a month or two months.

If something happens by this prolonged sleeplessness, you cannot stop it quickly. But in the ten-minute breathing exercise, you can control anything that happens. Besides, you cannot make up two months sleep in a night or two. Most probably, he who has not slept for two months may later find it difficult to sleep at night. He has started from a dangerous point. So the night vigil has its own uses. The fakir remains awake nights and awaits the happening.

Another Sufi way is dancing. Dance is another method used for separating from the body. But if you learn dancing specially for the experiment, then the happening does not take place. Then, as with pranayam, this also will become methodical. A man who knows dancing becomes one with the body—but if I tell those of you who do not know dancing to dance, and you begin to throw your legs and arms around, then the happening will happen. This will create such a novel situation that you will not be able to identify yourself with the dancing. You will not be able to say that "I am dancing". So these are two methods that the Sufis use—of sleeplessness and dance.

Other methods have also been used—for example, using woollen clothes in the middle of the hot desert. This too is going against the body. Some fast, some stand or lie down on beds of thorns : these are all practices to create a novel situation by going against the body.

It is natural, however, that one who treads on a particular path should not know the efficacy of another, for he has not tread upon it. So the Gurdjieff's dervish knows nothing of pranayam. Also, if he practises pranayam he might harm himself.

The hazard is great; it will be like fixing the pin of bullock-cart wheel into the wheel of a car. Then one could say the pin is a dangerous thing, for it spoils the car.

Now if a man who keeps awake all night practises pranayam, he will at once go mad. The reason is that a person's being cannot withstand hammering from two sides at a time. Therefore, Jains did not use pranayam. They created a novel situation by fasting. If you practise pranayam while fasting, you will find yourself in trouble. It is very dangerous. Therefore, the Jains had no use for pranayam. In fact, the Jain sadhu will say that pranayam is not required. He is not aware that he is denying not pranayam, but its relevancy in his situation. This is also why Jains did not concern themselves with yogasanas and such practices, for in their long fasts these would be very harmful. They require very mild food—butter, milk and other high-protein foods.

Long fasts dry up everything inside. The heat within the stomach becomes so much that the stomach seems to be on fire. In these circumstances any asana would be harmful. This fire can ascend to the brain and derange a person. So the Jain sannyasin will say that asanas and such things are worthless.

But for those on a particular path, practices like asanas are extremely valuable. If proper food is taken, asanas can work wonders. But for this, the body should be smooth and supple. In other words, it should be well lubricated, for each bone, each nerve, each fibre, has to undergo change. The slightest dryness, and these can snap.

Now through these asanas also we try to create novel body positions which we normally do not adopt. We are not aware that all body postures are tied to the consciousness. When a man is worried he scratches his head. Now what does the scratching of the head have to do with his worrying? But if you stop his hand from reaching the head he will not be able to worry. In order for his worry to be activated an association is required : it is necessary for his hand to be brought to his head. In this manner, all our actions are connected with our mental states. This is known as a result of experience and experiment.

As I told you this morning, in our meditation the body will assume many mudras (body gestures that happen as a result of inner psychic states) and asanas. As a result of endless experimentation it has been discovered which body posture is associated with which state of mind. And the reverse can also be brought about : If you assume a particular posture, the possibility of inducing the corresponding state of mind becomes greater.

Now if you sit in the posture of Buddha and if your body is exactly in the same condition, you will find it easier to enter the mental state of Buddha. This is because mental states are related to bodily states. If you walk as Buddha walked, if you breathe as Buddha breathed, if you lie down as Buddha did, it will be easier for you to attain the mental state of Buddha. Conversely, if you attain the mental state of Buddha, your walking, your sitting and your various body postures will resemble those of Buddha. Both of these are parallel.

Now people like Gurdjieff, who are uprooted in the sense that they do not have the backing of thousands of years of experience, are not properly informed. Gurdjieff gathered his knowledge from ten to twenty persons of different paths and put it together. He took parts from different machines. All of these were all right in their own place, but put together they made strange combinations.

These methods yielded results on a very small number of people, but they did not work completely in any case. Therefore, not a single follower of Gurdjieff reached to absolute fulfilment. They could not because the system taught by Gurdjieff was a multi-system : that is, it had a little bit of many systems. When one thing from among these many systems began to work on a seeker, it aroused his enthusiasm and he would even advance a little. But then the other systems which he simultaneously practised worked against him because Gurdjieff's was not a unified system. He took much from many systems and was completely unaware of still other systems.

Gurdjieff draws his information mainly from Sufi dervishes. He knows nothing of Tibetan yoga and not much of hatha yoga. Whatever he has heard of these two is from the dervishes who are against these. Therefore, his information in connection with hatha yoga or kundalini from followers of opposite paths causes his statements to be wide off the mark and irrelevant at times. For instance, he has made a very stupid statement in connection with kundalini. He insists on calling it "Kunda buffer". He says that kundalini is the reason why one does not attain knowledge—because it acts like a buffer and therefore has to be completely destroyed and transcended. According to him we have not to worry about awakening the kundalini at all. That is what he says, and he does not know what he is saying.

There are buffers in our personality, and because of them we are able to bear many shocks. The kundalini is not a buffer: it is a very big shock. But Gurdjieff was not aware that kundalini is the greatest shock in itself. When the kundalini awakens, your individuality experiences the greatest possible shock. There are buffers, shock absorbers within, and they need to be destroyed. But Gurdjieff has no experience of the kundalini ; he has not had the opportunity to sit among those who had experienced the kundalini. Thus, many a time strange situations are created.

Strange conditions have been created in the cases of persons like Gurdjieff and Krishnamurti, because they have no systematic knowledge of the secrets behind their words and powers. Such knowledge is very difficult to obtain also. In fact, it is almost impossible in one life time. It is possible only for the rare individual who has developed amidst a variety of different methods during the course of ten to twenty lives ; otherwise it is impossible. Then in the final birth he can strike a synthesis among the various systems ; otherwise not. Normally, it happens that a person reaches through one method. Then why should he take birth again? His goal is reached, his work is done. Therefore, no synthesis is possible.

On my part I feel that we should strive to form a synthesis between the various systems of the world. This work is worth doing. For this we shall have to work from different ends. The happenings are the same ; only the methods differ.

Now a Zen Master would pick a man up and throw him out of the window. This is only to create a novel situation; nothing else. But this same Master will say that there is no need for pranayam. "What ever can be attained out of this method of 'bhastrika' (bellows) breathing !" he would say. But then what can be attained by throwing a man out of the window? one may ask. If Buddha or Mahavir were told that a person had attained knowledge by being thrown out of a window, they would say it is impossible. People fall from housetops: do they become wise?

But falling is one thing and to be thrown down is quite another. Now when a man falls from a housetop, it is just like a man turning mad. But when a man is picked up by four people and he knows he is being thrown out of the window, then a situation is created : he experiences something unique. Throughout the process he is completely aware of what is happening, and this causes him to separate from the body.

Now if you go to a Zen Master he might pick up his staff and hit you on the head. It is strange! You fold your hands and say, "I want peace," and he picks up his staff and strikes you on the head. What a strange situation is created ! But this cannot happen in India where the seeker might turn around and give back blow for blow. In Japan, however, this method is known. There people know that there is a meaning behind such strange behaviour on the part of the Zen Master.

If you go to a Zen Master, he will abuse your mother and sister. He is creating a disturbing situation. You have gone to one who knows the Cosmos, the Brahman, and he abuses your mother and sister. If you know what is going on it is good, otherwise you will fall into difficulty. You might feel that he is the wrong man, for he indulges in abuses. You may never go to him again. But this method too has its usefulness. By uttering abuses he creates a novel situation.

There is a Master in a small village called Sai Kheda near Gadarwada. You could never tell what he would do. Not only would he let out abuses, but he would also stand up and urinate in the midst of a gathering. People would stand up in shock. The atmosphere in that room would suddenly become very disturbed, and people would wonder what had happened. He used to abuse and he used to beat. Sometimes he would run for miles behind the questioner.

Those who went to him and understood him gained a lot from him; those who did not understand him dismissed him as a madman. But what had he to do with them? Those who understood him definitely gained something from him. Now the man he pursued for miles would be thrown into a unique predicament. He runs for his life, the Master runs after him, and a big crowd runs after the Master. Thus, a strange atmosphere is created.

Many methods are employed to create such a unique situation, but those who know only one method refuse to concede that there is any other. There is another difficulty also. Sometimes if someone knows other methods to be effective, as I know for instance, even then, when I am talking of a particular method, I have to talk about it in extremes, or else it will not be effective. I will say, "This method and this method alone is capable of yielding results and no other."

There is a reason for doing this. Normally, people do not have that much intelligence to understand. If I say, "All methods lead to the same goal," you might feel that no method is particularly effective. Besides, all the methods are so contradictory that you will be confused. This is why those who are wise, those who know, have to use the language of the ignorant. To drive their point home they have to say, "This is the way and no other," knowing fully well that all methods are workable. Thus, I find myself in a great predicament at times.

[Text of a discourse given on July 2, 1970, morning, in Bombay, India].

9

KUNDALINI AND FACTS ABOUT INNER TRANSFORMATION

Questioner:

Bhagwan, yesterday you said that the "kunda"—the reservoir of energy—is not something separate and set apart in each person. But in the awakening of the kundalini, the "sadhak" (seeker) has to work on the kunda WITHIN HIMSELF in order to make the Divine energy rise. So is there a separate kunda for each person, or is there only one "kunda" for all? Please explain.

Bhagwan Shree Rajneesh:

It is like this: you fill your water from your well. The well in your house is separate from the well in my house, but the springs deep below the wells are connected to the same ocean. If you follow the path of the spring of your well, you will come across the spring of my well as well as the springs of the wells of others. Then, ultimately, you reach there where there are no wells—only the ocean. There where the journey begins is the individual, and where it ends there is no individual, but the aggregate of all things. It starts with the individual and ends with the Cosmic Reality.

So the starting point is the individual. Therefore, you are separate, I am separate. But at the ultimate point there is no "you" and no "I". We are both parts of, fragments of, that which is. So when the kundalini unfolds within you, it will seem to be your own, as if belonging to you yourself individually. This is natural, for you are standing at your own well. But as the manifestation of kundalini rises higher, you will come to feel by and by that your well is not entirely your own: it is connected with other wells also. As your experience deepens, the well slowly begins to merge into the vast ocean. In the final experience you will be able to say that the well belonged not to you alone, but to all. I have spoken in this context.

As individuals we appear to be different entities. Or, it is like this: suppose a leaf on a tree suddenly gains consciousness. It will look upon the other leaves as apart from it. How can it feel another leaf hanging from another stem to be a part of its own self? But let alone another stem: the leaves on its own stem will not appear to be its own self. Even the leaf hanging next to it will seem apart, for the awareness of the leaf is the awareness of the individual.

Now if the leaf were to go within itself, it will soon come to know that it is joined to the same branch as the others beside it and that they all get their life energy from the same channel. If it travels further, it will soon know that not only its own branches, but the neighbouring branches also form a part of the same tree, and the source of their life energy is the same. If it goes a little further it will reach the roots, and then it will realize that all the leaves and stems and branches as well as itself are different parts of one whole.

If it goes yet deeper, from the roots into the ground, it will find the roots of other trees. It will then realize that all the neighbouring trees and the one to which it belongs are the offsprings of the same soil. If it continues its search in this way, the ultimate point of existence of this little leaf will be the whole universe. The tiny leaf forms one extreme of the greater Existence. If it becomes conscious of itself as a fragment, it develops individual consciousness. If it becomes conscious of itself as an ocean, it cannot remain an individual.

On the awakening of the kundalini, your first experience of yourself will be as the "Atman" (Self) and the final experience will be as "Paramatman" (the Supreme Self). If you stop at the very first awakening and draw a boundary around your own well, stopping all further search, then you will stagnate at the level of the Atman. This is why many religions have stagnated at the Atman. This is not the Ultimate Experience; it is only half of the experience Upon going further, you will experience that even the Atman fades and what remains is the Paramatman. Then, as I told you, if you go further from the Supreme Self, that too fades away and only the Void, the Nirvana, remains.

We should actually saythat NOTHING remains. So those who had the potential of reaching even beyond the Supreme Self reached Nirvana, and they talked of the Ultimate Void. They say that nothing remains there. In fact, when you experience the All, you will also have the experience of the Nothingness—the Void. That which is the Absolute is also the Nothingness.

Let us understand it this way: The Void and the Absolute are two names of the same thing. Therefore, they are convertible. Zero is a complete circle; there is nothing like a half zero. If you are told to halve a zero, you will say it is impossible. You can halve 1, you can halve 2, but not zero. Zero cannot be cut into pieces. When you make a zero (0) on paper, it is only a symbol. As soon as you draw it it ceases to be zero, because you draw a boundary around it. Therefore, when asked, Euclid used to say that zero is that which has no length and no breadth. All signs are symbolic, and hence the SIGN of zero, no matter how small, is symbolic, for it still has dimensions. It is not the actual zero.

In the actual zero (nothingness) there are no dimensions. As soon as there are dimensions, it ceases to be zero. Therefore, the Upanishads say that when you remove the Void from the Void, what remains behind is Void. This means that you cannot take anything from the Void. If you try to run away with the whole Void, even then what remains behind will be the full Void, and you will find your effort wasted. The Void cannot be removed; it remains exactly the same. The same goes also for the Absolute, however. In fact, the Absolute cannot be visualized except through the Void.

The Absolute means that in which there is no further expansion. The Void means that which cannot be broken down further. There is no way of going beyond the Absolute and there is no course for going deeper down than the Void. You cannot break the Absolute or the Void into parts. The Absolute has no boundary. As soon as there is a boundary, it ceases to be the Absolute, for then something remains outside the boundary. And if something remains behind, where is the absoluteness ? Then this will become "non-Absolute".

Where my house ends, your house starts. The boundary of my house is the beginning of yours. But if my house is the Absolute, your house cannot be outside of it, for there is no boundary to the Absolute. Who will set its limits ? To set a limit there must be a neighbour. The Absolute stands alone; it has no neighbour to set its boundary. It takes two to make a boundary. Where I end and another starts, there will be a boundary. If another does not start, it will be impossible for me to end. And If I cannot end, there can be no boundary set around me.

There is no limitation to the Absolute, for who will set its limits ? The Void has no limits, for that which has a boundary becomes "something" and is no longer "nothing". So if you understand this properly, you will come to know that the Absolute and the Void are two different ways of saying the same thing.

So religion can follow two paths: either it can lead to becoming the Absolute or to becoming the Void. In both the cases you will become THAT WHICH IS. So he who goes on the path of the Absolute prefers the term "Absolute": his approach is positive. He says, "I am the Brahman. Whatever is, is ME. There is no other but ME. I have enclosed all the others within the boundary of my "I". When this happens, the person will have attained. But in the ultimate step, the "I" too has to be given up—for when there is no other, to whom will you assert "I am the Brahman ? The assumption of "I" becomes meaningful only in the presence of a "thou". And when you are the Brahman, there is no sense in asserting "I am Brahman", for then again there is an acceptance of two—the Brahman and "I". So ultimately the "I" becomes redundant and so does the Brahman, and we have to become silent.

There is another way, and that is that you annihilate yourself to such an extent that you can say, "I am NOT." In one case you say, "I am the Brahman": that means, "I am everything." In this second way, you are able to say, "I am Nothing, I am Not. There is nothing but Void." This path will also lead you to the same point of attainment as the first one, but after reaching there you will not be able to say "I am NOT", for the presence of the "I" is necessary to state "I am NOT". So the "I" will be lost in the ultimate stage. Then you will not be able to say, "All is Void," for to say this the All and the Void are both necessary. Then the only course open to you is silence.

So let the journey be from any way. Whether it is from the Absolute or from the Void it will, in both cases, lead to the ultimate silence where there is nothing left to be said. Therefore, from where a person begins is not the basic question. What is to be ascertained is where he ultimately reaches. Where he ultimately reaches is the basic question. His ultimate destination can be grasped, recognized. If he has reached there, whatsoever path he has followed is good. No path is wrong and no path is right. Whichever way leads to the ultimate goal is the right way, and reach we must. In the initial experience, however, one will always start from the "I", because that is the state we are in. That is the given situation from where we have to make the beginning.

So whether we awaken the kundalini or we practise meditation or we become tranquil, all experiences will be individual. What happens will pertain to the individual, for we are still individuals. But as we begin to penetrate within, as we go deeper and deeper, the individual will begin to be annihilated. If we travel outwardly, the individual, the ego, will grow.

For instance, if a man standing by the side of a well begins to travel inside of the well, he will find that he has reached the ocean and there was no such thing as a well. After all, what is a well ? It is just a hole to peep into the ocean. What other meaning does a well have except that it is a hole through which the ocean can be seen ? If you think the water in the well to be the well, that is wrong. The water is a part of the ocean. The opening through which you have viewed the water is the well.

Now if the opening gets bigger and bigger, more and more of the ocean will come into view. If you do not go within the well, but, rather, you move away from it, you will gradually lose sight of the water within. Then all that you will be able to see will be the opening in the ground and the encircling wall, and you will never be able to associate it with the ocean. Even when you go to the shores of the ocean, it will not occur to you that that which peeped out from within the well and this vast expanse of water are one and the same.

The journey within takes you to the One whereas the journey without takes you to the many. But the fact remains that the initial point of all experience is the individual—the well. The ultimate point will be the non-individual—the Supreme Self, the ocean. This is what I mean: if you go deep, your kunda will not remain yours any longer. Nothing at all will remain yours; it cannot.

Questioner: *Bhagwan, if all the wells (individuals) are one and joined to the same ocean, then there is the need to journey from within the well to the ocean. That is, where is the need for "sadhana" (spiritual practice) in order to become Void ?*

Bhagwan : You ask this question because by Void you understand "nothing". Therefore, you question the validity of sadhana in the absence of "Being". You understand Void as "Non-Being"; hence, according to you sadhana would be required if we were to become "SOMETHING". When there is "nothing" to become, where is the need for sadhana ? You do not know that Void MEANS "the Absolute". This "nothing" means "everything".

Right now, it will be difficult for you to understand how Void can mean everything. A well can also say, "If I have to journey toward the ocean just to discover that I do not exist, why should I set out on the journey at all ?" What it says is right, but that does not change the situation. The fact remains that you are not a well. You may not undertake the journey and you may stagnate as a well, but that will lead you nowhere, for it is a lie: you are not a well, no matter how much you deny being the ocean. This lie will keep tormenting you; it will tie you into bondage. With such a false situation there can be no bliss.

The well will destroy itself as it reaches the ocean. But together with it will die all its anxieties and woes, for these were all connected with its individuality, with the ego. To others it may seem that the well lost itself within the ocean, but ask the well and it will say, "Who says I am no more ? I have become the ocean." The neighbouring well might stop him and say, "Where are you going, you fool ? Why do you want to destroy yourself?" But the one that has gone will retort: "Who talks of extinction ? As a well I am no more, but I have become the vast ocean."

Therefore, the choice is always between remaining a well or becoming the ocean, between remaining tied to the finite or becoming one with the Infinite. All this is a matter of experience. If the well is afraid of losing its identity, it will have to break its connection with the ocean, for in this relationship there is always the fear of becoming aware that one is the ocean. Then the well will have to sever all connections with its streams, for they all lead to the ocean. And it will always have to take care to look without, for a slight peep within will bring back the knowledge of the ocean. Then again, the thinner the streams, the better it would be. If they dry up, even better, for then it would be easier to look without. But then the well will die, though it is under the illusion that it is saving itself.

Jesus has said, "Whosoever loses his life will save it, but whoever insists on keeping his life shall lose it." So the question invariably arises within us, "Why go and destroy oneself?" If extinction is the Ultimate Reality, then it is all right. And how, pray, will you save yourself? Granted that you cease to exist even after you become the vast ocean, how will you save the puny well—and for how long ? Soon its waters will dry up, its walls will crumble and the opening will be clogged with debris. How long will you save yourself?

This is where the fear of death is born. It is the fear of the well: it does not want to meet the ocean for fear of extinction. It, therefore, keeps far away from the ocean and remains a well. Then the fear of death grips, for as soon as it breaks away from the ocean death begins to draw near.

Joined with the ocean, there is life. Therefore, we are all afraid of death. We tremble with fear at the thought of death. But we shall have to die, and there are two kinds of deaths : either to jump into the ocean and die—and there is no greater bliss than this, for then you will become the ocean; or to hold fast to the well—and then you will dry up, rot, and ultimately be no more.

The mind always wants some sort of enticement. What will we get by falling into the ocean ? What is the gain for which we attempt Samadhi, for which we seek the Void ? Our first question is "What will we attain ?" We do not care to ponder over the fact that in this drive for attainment one loses one's own Self. We have attained all—a house to live in, wealth to spend : all is attained; only we are lost. We are totally absent—not a trace of ourselves anywhere. If you ask how one is to meet oneself, I will say, "Be ready to lose and you will find yourself." If you are not prepared to lose, if you try to save yourself, you will save everything else, but YOU will be lost completely. All else will remain; only you will not be there.

Questioner : *You have said that the ratio of oxygen and carbon dioxide changes during deep breathing. How is this connected with the awakening of the kundalini ?*

Bhagwan : There is a very close connection. Within us is the potential of both life and death. The oxygen is our life potential and the carbon dioxide is our death potential. When oxygen decreases and gradually becomes nil, carbon dioxide alone remains in the body and it then turns one into a corpse—just as wood burns as long as oxygen is freely available. There is life, there is warmth in the flame, but as soon as the oxygen is cut off the flame dies, and what remains is only carbon dioxide. Carbon is dead fire. So both these gases work within us.

The greater the proportion of carbon dioxide within us, the more lethargy there will be. This is why it is not as easy to sleep in the daytime as it is at night, for the proportion of oxygen decreases and that of carbon dioxide increases in the night. With the rising of the sun the ratio of oxygen rises, and it falls as soon as the sun sets. Therefore, darkness and night have become a symbol of laziness, lethargy, ignorance and sin. The sun is a symbol of brilliance, for with it comes life. Everything withers at night. Flowers close their petals, leaves drop, man sleeps. The whole world passes into a temporary death, so to speak.

With the crack of dawn, the flowers open once more, the leaves become erect, the branches begin to sway, the birds begin to sing, and people awaken. All around us the earth wakes up. The temporary death of eight to ten hours passes and life returns.

The same happening takes place within you. When the ratio of oxygen rises sharply within you, the energies lying dormant within you awaken. Oxygen is always required to awaken any sleeping energy. We can keep a dying man alive a little longer by giving him oxygen. We can manage to keep him going even for a year or two by supplying extra oxygen to his enfeebled energies. Then, even though they are at death's door, they are unable to ebb away because of the extra oxygen.

In Europe and America, thousands of people are kept lingering on in this way with oxygen. The greatest issue in these countries today is the right for a man to die when he must. Now the doctor's problem is that if he does not administer oxygen and allows a person to die, he will be charged with murder. So an eighty-year-old man will be kept going with oxygen. In this way, a low ratio of carbon dioxide is maintained, and his ebbing energies are not allowed to fade away. Now the exact opposite condition is brought about by "pranayam" (yogic breathing exercises), "bhastrika" (bellows breathing) and the deep breathing method I talk of.

In this method you take in so much of the life breath that all the dormant elements within you develop the strength to rise. They begin to rise immediately, and the tendency to sleep begins to break.

I shall tell you an interesting case. A Buddhist *bhikkhu* (monk) came to me about four years ago He was unable to sleep for three years. All treatment had failed, and it had to because he was practising "Anapansati Yoga". He was concentrating on deep breathing all the 24 hours of the day. Now the one who had initiated him into this did not know that by incessant concentration on deep breathing sleep is not possible—that it is impossible to bring on sleep. So on one hand he was being given intense treatment for insomnia, and on the other he continued his sadhana. This put him in a terrible plight, and there rose a conflict within his body. The drugs were inducing sleep within him, whereas his sadhana was keeping his energies awake. It was just as if the accelerator and the brake of a car are pressed simultaneously. So the poor man was in great trouble when he came to me.

I knew what was the matter with him, so I told him to stop his sadhana. But he could not see why. Then I explained to him that the ratio of oxygen he worked up by constant deep breathing exercises was so great that the body could not sleep. He should either give up his sadhana or give up the idea of sleep. If he continued his sadhana he would not be able to sleep, but this would not be harmful to him. He stopped his sadhana for eight days and sleep returned. There was no need for medicines.

So the possibility of sleep increases with the rise of carbon dioxide within us. Hence, all things that increase the proportion of carbon dioxide within us help to keep the dormant energies asleep, thus increasing our insensitivity. Now, as the human population upon the earth increases, the factor of insensitivity will also increase, for the oxygen will then be proportionately less for the growing number of people. A stage might come when human beings may find it difficult to keep awake.

This is exactly the reason why we feel so fresh in the morning or when we go to a forest or to the seashore. The crowds in the market bring listlessness and gloom, for there the carbon dioxide is more. And though oxygen is formed continuously, our habit of crowding together sucks it all away. This is why you feel fresh and cheerful wherever the oxygen is more. Then you feel more healthy. In crowded places, be they cinema houses or temples, you will find yourself becoming listless and insensitive.

So there is a method to increase oxygen within you, by which your inner balance changes. Instead of looking forward to sleep, you will now be eager to keep awake. And if this is carried out with added vigour, there will be a very great difference within. It will be like one side of the scales suddenly coming up and the other going down. If the balance within you can be made to change with a sharp jolt, you will be able to feel and experience the change at once. If the scales descend or ascend slowly, you will not know when it had taken place. This is why I advocate the method of deep breathing. It brings about the change with such vigour that in ten minutes you pass from one stage to another, and you also feel the change taking place. Only a swift change can be noticeable.

Now we all know that from infancy we pass on to youth and from youth to old age, but we can never tell when we passed from one stage to the other. We cannot set the date when the change took place. So an old man can never tell when he became old. Between his youth and old age there is no interval, nor is there a sharp change. A child never knows when it has reached adolescence, and so he keeps to his childish ways. To others he looks grown up, but he does not know it. The parents may feel that he should now feel responsible as a grown-up, but the child does not feel this way. This is because there was no sudden change to shock him into awareness.

The same goes for an old man who takes too long to realize that he is no longer young. How is he to know ? A quick and sharp motion is required to be conscious of the transition. If it were the case that on a particular day, at a given hour, a man passes from youth into old age, there would be no need for anyone to remind him that he is old. Similarly, if it were the case that at the completion of twenty years a boy turns suddenly into a youth, no father will have to remind his son to shed his childishness. He will himself know of the happening; he will know that he is a different person altogether.

I aim at a change so sharp that you can make out the difference between your sleeping consciousness and your expanded consciousness. It should happen that at a stroke, at a jump, you feel and know the difference. This knowing will prove useful; it is of great value. Therefore, I am in favour of such a method that brings about a sharp transformation. A long drawn out process will never make you aware of what is going on within. And where is there danger in it ? If you have no knowledge of what is happening within you, then even if some transformation has taken place it will not deepen your understanding.

It happens this way many a time: that a seeker, in his search, may without conscious effort reach very near a spiritual experience. But since it has happened by and by and not by a sharp change, he cannot grasp what has happened. And the explanations he puts forward are never correct, for there has not been a sufficient gap. Many a time it happens that you are on the brink of a new experience, but you put it off. You will interpret it with your old theories, for the change has been so gradual as to be unnoticeable.

I know of a man who can pick up a buffalo with ease. His father had kept some buffaloes, and from childhood he would pick up a small buffalo and carry it about on his shoulders. The buffalo would grow heavier day by day, and his strength also increased accordingly. Then he could carry a full grown buffalo without any effort. But now it seems like a miracle. For him it is no miracle, but for the onlookers it is. For him it was a gradual process. He could not feel the increase in the buffalo's weight from day to day, but those who witness his feat are taken by surprise. It seems to be a marvel that a single person can pick up and carry a full grown buffalo. No man can just pick up a huge animal like a buffalo. It is an impossible task, and hence the wonder.

This is why I advocate this sharp and dynamic method. And the life-giving oxygen is of great importance. The more speedily you fill yourself with oxygen, the quicker you will pass from the experience of the body into the experience of the Self. If you understand this well, you will know that your body is your dead end. It is that part of you which is dead, which has solidified, and which is no longer fluid; hence, it is visible. The soul, on the other hand, is that part of you which is liquid, unsolidified, which is like the air, beyond your grasp. The greater the strength of the life energy, the greater the awakening, then the more life there will be. Also, the clearer will be the difference between the body and soul. The distinction will become very clear to you. The body is one part and the soul is the other part, and the distinction will be very clear.

Therefore, the use of breath has a profound meaning in the awakening of the kundalini. Kundalini is your sleeping energy. It cannot be awakened with the help of carbon dioxide: that will deepen its slumber. Oxygen alone awakens it, and, therefore, all efforts are toward supplying more oxygen—by any method. This is why morning meditation is supposed to be very useful. The reason behind this is that in the morning even a small breath carries a lot of oxygen into you. The earth is in a very unique state for an hour after sunrise. This is why morning has been chosen as the time for meditation all over the world. The awakening of the kundalini depends entirely on the strength of the impact of the breath.

We see a lamp burning. We see the lamp, the oil in the lamp, the wick, the flame, but we do not see the oxygen which is actually burning. Neither the oil nor the wick nor the match-stick are of much importance, but all these form the visible part —the body that is visible. The actual cause, the oxygen, remains invisible.

A little boy was told by his father to mind the lamp that was lighted in the worship room and see that it did not go off. A strong wind arose. Now the lamp was to be kept lit all the twenty-four hours. What could the child do ? He brought a glass cover and put it over the lamp. But the flame died immediately. In his effort to save the flame from the strong wind, the child shut off all the air—and that was the end of the flame. This air is not visible; all the same, it is the life of the flame. What we call life within us, is also a process of oxygenation, just like the burning of the flame.

Really speaking, if we were to explain life in technical terms it is an oxygenation of the vital energy. Whether in man or trees or lamps or the sun, wherever the life energy burns, there is life. So the more you cause your vital energy to burn, the more profound and intense will your flame of existence become. The flame of your existence is nothing but the kundalini. The harder the breath strikes, the faster and greater will be the flow of the kundalini.

Questioner : *But many yogis make use of caves, where there is very little air. How does this help in the practice to attain Samadhi ?*

Bhagwan : Actually, this depends on many things. Those who meditate in caves will merely pass into unconsciousness, and not Samadhi, if other conditions necessary to meditate in caves are not fulfilled. That which they mistake for Samadhi will be profound sleep, a state of unconsciousness.

Only that person can make use of a cave who has oxygenated himself through pranayam to the extent that the cave poses no problem to him. If a man oxygenates each and every drop of his blood, every fibre of his body, each pore of his skin, he can remain alive for a week even if buried underground. The reason is simply this: he has enough oxygen in reserve to last him for that period. We have no surplus oxygen within us. If you tried to lie side by side with the yogi without any knowledge of pranayam or any accumulation of extra oxygen, you will be dead by the end of eight days whereas he will come out alive. Such a man can make use of a cave for his meditation. And it will be profitable for him, for he has no problem of oxygen. He has stored it within himself.

The cave is used because it gives many kinds of protection and security in sadhana. Not only does it keep out the general noise and disturbances, but it also keeps out many vibrations from outside. A particular kind of stone in the cave may have a special purpose. Particular stones, like marble, prevent many vibrations from penetrating within. This is why marble is so widely used in temples. Certain vibrations cannot penetrate within the temple because of marble. So marble is not used for ornamentation as generally understood, but because of the profound experience behind its use.

Some stones attract particular kinds of vibrations, and hence they cannot be used within temples. Yet others deflect or repel these vibrations. Some stones attract particular kinds of vibrations, so certain caves were carved in a particular manner, for the shape of the caves is also important and this also helps in attracting and repelling the different vibrations. When a science is lost, it is difficult to understand all this.

When we make a car, we make it in a certain shape. The shape should be such that the car tears through the air and does not fight with it. If the car is flat up front, it will fight with the wind, and the car's motion will be impeded. If it cuts through the air in a non-resisting manner like an arrow, then the air does not resist the car's motion. Rather, because the car is cutting through the air, the air rushes into the vacuum created behind the car and helps to accelerate its motion.

You might have seen the bridge on the river Ganges at

Allahabad. It was constructed with great difficulty, for the Ganges would not allow the pillars to stand within it. When at last the bridge was constructed, the Ganges still swept away one particular pillar. After a great deal of work, the engineers hit upon the plan of making this pillar in the shape of a shoe. This shape was able to withstand the force of the current. The shape of the shoe helps humans to walk. It cuts the air; it does not resist it. With this thought in mind, the pillar was constructed in the shape of a shoe. Thus, the pillar is now able to take the impact of the Ganges which was previously inimical to it.

So caves having special shapes, and special places for meditation are constructed out of special stones. A person can impose his personality up to a particular limit. For a person who has experience in these matters, the road is very clear. If I can fill a four-sided room eight feet long by eight feet wide with my personality—that is, if I just sit in one place but the vibrations emerging from my personality flood a circular area—then that place will be well protected. So such a person will try to see that there are as few openings as possible. There will be only a single entrance, and it will have its special shape. And this will have its own special function : it will not allow any outside vibrations to enter within and will prevent the vibrations being created within from going out.

When many sadhaks have carried out their practice in the same cave, the results are wonderful and that particular cave becomes very valuable. The cave retains those special vibrations created within it and becomes helpful to a new sadhak. Thus, particular caves were used for thousands of years for sadhana.

When Ajanta was first discovered, all of its caves were found covered with mud. There was a reason behind this. For hundreds of years there was no sign of these caves. Trees grew on the earth that covered them; no one suspected their existence. And the caves were filled up and covered in order to save the special vibrations within them, in the absence of worthy sadhaks. There was no other way to save them. Thus, they were enclosed with earth so that whenever a worthy sadhak came in search for them, they may yet be useful to him. These caves were never meant for spectators. Now they have destroyed all that was valuable in these caves and rendered them useless.

So though there was a lack of oxygen in the caves, they were useful and important for other reasons. There are many other advantages to this, and sadhana is a very intricate matter. The caves were helpful to those who were well advanced in sadhana. Besides, the sadhak did not remain within his cave all the time. From time to time he came out of the cave. Certain practices were to be carried out outside the caves whereas others had to be performed within the caves.

Temples and mosques were designed in order to hold in special tremors and vibrations, and these were utilized by sadhaks. Sometimes you find, upon reaching a place, that your thoughts have changed all of a sudden. You will think that a change has occurred within you. At times you notice that you have become a different person altogether in the presence of a particular person. Some other part of you has risen to the surface for a little while. You might attribute this to your whimsical mood, but such is not the case; it is not so easy.

Now a lot of research is afoot to find out why the pyramids were built and what they are. What was the motive behind the construction of those massive structures in the desert wasteland ? So much wealth and labour could not have been spent merely to entomb a few corpses. They are, in actuality, special places constructed for sadhana, and for this very reason the corpses of special people have been embalmed and kept there.

In Tibet, there are preserved corpses of sadhaks that are a thousand or two thousand years old, and they are heavily guarded. That body with which the soul of Buddha was connected for eighty years cannot remain an ordinary body. That body has absorbed vibrations which are absolutely unique and unsurpassed. Who knows whether such a phenomenon will ever occur again on this earth.

After his death, the body of Jesus was kept in a cave. The next morning it was to be buried, but it disappeared. This is a great mystery for Christianity. Where could it have gone ? What could have happened to it ? Then there is the story of his resurrection, and some people saw him. Then, afterwards, there is no account of the life of Jesus in Christian writings. The fact is that Jesus's body was so priceless that it had to be taken away immediately to a safe place where it could be preserved for a long time to come. Such a man is rare in the world. So these pyramids, these temples and caves and their particular shapes and forms, hold a deep meaning.

Questioner : *Bhagwan, when we enter into deep meditation, the body becomes inert (lifeless), and gradually the breath begins to abate and almost becomes extinct. With this lessening of breath, the ratio of oxygen also falls. What is the connection between the inertia of the body and the diminishing of oxygen in meditation and Samadhi (Cosmic Consciousness)?*

Bhagwan : Actually, when the breath awakens with full intensity and a gap is created between you and the body, the sleeping part of you and the awakened part of you will appear different due to the speed and sharpness of the change. As soon as you start to proceed toward the awakened part, the body will no longer need the oxygen. It is as it should be that the body should remain asleep, inert, as if in death, for now the vital energy has started to flow toward the soul.

The oxygen is needed for the body; it is not the need of the Atman. Therefore, when the vital energy begins to flow toward the Atman, the body requires a minimum quantity of oxygen—just enough to keep it alive and no more. If the body gets more oxygen, it will create a hindrance. Therefore, the breath will diminish as you proceed in sadhana. It is only useful to awaken the slumbering energies within. Once these are awakened, the breath is no more needed. Now the body requires the most minimum amount of breathing. In fact, there will be moments when the breath stops completely.

Actually, when you reach the exact point of balance which is called Samadhi, the breath will stop. We have no idea whatsoever of this stopping of breath or what it means. We have only two experiences of breath—the breath going in and the breath coming out. At the most we can stop the breath for a moment, but that would be a routine practice. A time comes when the breath is half in, half out, and everything is at a standstill. So there will be some moments in the course of sadhana when you will wonder whether the breath has stopped—whether it has ceased altogether—or even whether you will die. This is exactly what you will feel.

The deeper you go within, the fainter will be the trembling of the breath, because at that depth you do not need oxygen at all. Oxygen was required for the very initial impact. It is just as if I fit a key to open a lock. The lock opens; the key will have done its work. Now I will not go on applying the key to the lock: its work is done. The key will now be useless for the lock, and I will go in. There is no question of applying the key any longer. It served its purpose by opening the door.

As long as the kundalini has not awakened within, you will have to use the key of breath with all your might. But no sooner does it awaken, when the breath is no longer needed and you will have started your journey within. Your body will demand very little oxygen now. You have not to stop the breath forcibly. It will begin to slow down gradually. Then a moment will come in the course of this sadhana when everything will seem to stop—to be at a standstill.

That moment of ultimate balance, when the breath is absolutely still, it neither goes in nor comes out, is the moment of Samadhi. That moment you will know not life but Existence. Understand this difference well. The knowledge of life is interconnected with breath. Life is oxygenation, and hence a component of breathing. But in the moment of Samadhi, you will know that Existence where breath is unnecessary—where there is only Being; where the rocks and mountains, moon and stars are all motionless and still; where there is not the slightest tremor. The breath has no access to this state because life also has no approach there. What is there is beyond life.

Remember, that which is beyond death is also beyond life. This is why we cannot call God a living entity, for it is meaningless to call He who is beyond the possibility of death living. The Supreme Self has no life—only Existence. We have life : when we come out of the Existence we have life; when we step back into the Existence it is death. It is just like when a wave rises in the ocean: that rising becomes the life of the wave. Before this there was only the ocean—without any movement, without any waves. Life started when the wave rose. Then the wave fell, and that was its death. The rising of the wave was the life of the wave, and its falling, its death. But the ocean's Being is motionless, waveless. It is that which was when the wave arose and that which remained after it fell.

The experience of this tranquillity, this Existence, is the experience of Samadhi. So Samadhi is an experiencing of the Existence and not life. It is existential. There is no necessity of breath there. Breath has no meaning there; there is no question of breath in Samadhi. Everything there is still, tranquil, motionless.

This is why many a time, when a sadhak goes very deep in Samadhi, others are required to bring him back to life; otherwise there is the possibility of his being no more. He may not return from the Existence. Ramakrishna used to fall into this state many, many times. Many times it took more than six days to bring him back. Ramakrishna is greatly revered, but nothing is known of the man who saved Ramakrishna for the world.

He had a nephew by the name Hridyaram. It was he who kept a constant vigil over Ramakrishna. He would keep awake nights, pouring water into his mouth, forcing water and milk down his throat, massaging him when he seemed to be suffocating. Time and again he brought him back to life. Vivekananda talked to the world about Ramakrishna, but the man who saved him for the world remains unknown. Ramakrishna could have gone at anytime. The experience of Existence is so blissful, where is the need to return ? So it is possible to become lost at that moment into the Existence.

The line from where you go beyond is very thin. So schools and ashrams were developed to bring sadhaks back to life. Sannyasins did not make ashrams, and therefore they could not go deep into Samadhi. Theirs was a wandering Sannyas in which they went from place to place. They could not go deep, because this requires groups of people; a school of people, who knew how to help each other to return to life; otherwise a person is bound to be lost.

These sannyasins developed a method by which they did not

stay in any one place too long so that they would not develop any attachments. But he who can develop attachments over a long period can easily develop it over a short period also. What is the difference? In three months, the attachment could be a little more; in three days it will be a little less. There will only be a difference in proportion, and nothing else. So to all those cults where the Sannyasins merely go from place to place, yoga and Samadhi will be lost—for Samadhi requires a group of sadhaks. The individual can lose himself in Samadhi, but to bring him back is a different matter altogether.

So up to the stage of meditation, there is no difficulty. But after the event of Samadhi, great care is required. And from these moments of Samadhi a person who is brought back can give us some news of the other world where he has peeped momentarily. All the tidings we have received of this "other world" are entirely from such persons who have come back from Samadhi; otherwise we would not have known of it at all. We would have had no knowledge of it, we could never have thought about it, for there is no other way to know about it. And it has always been the case that those who reach Samadhi find it difficult to come back. They can be lost. This is the point of no return. It is that place from which the jump is taken into the abyss, from where the path breaks and no way is seen to return.

Great caution is necessary at such times. That is why I always wish that the moment I make you ready for Samadhi, there should be schools which can take care of you—or else you will be lost. Your individual effort will be insufficient. There should be people who can bring you back so that your experience is saved for posterity; otherwise the experience will also be lost with you.

Questioner: *What is the condition of breath in the case of a person who remains in "Sahaj (spontaneous) Samadhi"* ?

Bhagwan: The breath of such a one becomes dissolved, rhythmical, and harmonious. There are many other factors. For he who is twenty-four hours in Samadhi, whose mind does not waver and is always steady, who lives in Existence and not in life, the breath develops a rhythm of its own. And when he is not engaged in any activity, when he is neither speaking nor eating nor walking, breathing is a blissful experience. Then just to be, just the movement of the breath, gives so much bliss that nothing can compare with it. It becomes very musical; it is filled with "*nada*" (the uncreated inner sound).

This experience can be brought about to some extent by developing breathing. This is why breathing methods have been developed. If a person breathes according to the manner in which a person living in Sahaj Samadhi breathes, according to the rhythm in which such a person's breath moves, he will experience a sort of peace. This is how such methods like pranayam have been developed—by observing the rhythm of the breath of persons in Samadhi. This yields a few results and is helpful.

The breath of a person in Samadhi becomes minimal, for now life does not hold so much significance as Existence. A new dimension has opened within this individual where functions like breath are not necessary. He lives where he is; he stays where he is. He makes use of his body only in connection with us; otherwise he does not use the body at all. He eats, wears clothes, he sleeps, he bathes, but these are all means for him to maintain his relationship with us. In themselves, these acts have no meaning for him. And he breathes only to the extent of the amount of life energy which he requires for these actions. His breath becomes very slow. Therefore, such people can stay in places with very little oxygen.

This is why, in ancient temples and caves, there are minimum openings. This would be a matter of great concern in the modern world, for it seems to be against all rules of health and hygiene. In all these ancient caves and temples, we find no means for air currents to move, and this was because the one who lived within did not require air very much. He did not wish more air to come in, for the vibrations of air currents destroy the astral vibrations within; their impact sets them afire. Therefore, the sadhak protects the astral vibrations by shutting out air currents. Today this is not possible, for a long and extensive sadhana of the breath is required for the state of Sahaj Samadhi.

Questioner : *How does the Buddhist sadhana of "Anapansati"—the observing of the breath—affect the ratio of oxygen ?*

Bhagwan: It has a great effect. It is very interesting and worthy to note that when your attention is diverted to any activity in life, the momentum of that activity increases. All the vital processes of the body are involuntary. For instance, your pulse: when the doctor checks your pulse, it is a little faster than what it normally was, for your attention as well as the doctor's is directed toward it. And if the doctor happens to be a lady doctor, the rate is faster. This is because your attention is drawn even more toward your pulse. You might carry out an experiment: check your pulse rate; then concentrate for ten minutes on your pulse; then check it again. You will find it has increased. The act of concentration acts as a catalytic agent to increase the pulse rate.

"Anapansati" is a very valuable method. It is the method of concentrating on the breath. The breath has not to be increased or decreased. It has only to be observed as it comes and goes. But as soon as you begin to observe it, its rate increases. As an observer, you have seen how the rate increases. This increase in the breath rate is inevitable and will yield results. The main aim of Anapansati, however, is simply to observe the breath. By thus observing it continuously, you will gradually begin to feel the breath separating from you. In your deepest depth, you become separate from that which becomes your object of observation. In fact, the observer and the object can never be one. Therefore, whatever becomes your object of observation begins to separate from you.

So if you make your breath the object of observation and you begin observing it all the 24 hours—while sitting standing, walking, if you spend your whole time observing it going in and out, soon you wlll see it separating from you. One day you will suddenly find yourself standing apart and the breath working on its own, quite a distance away from you. Then the happening will take place. You will then gain the experience of standing outside your body.

In this way, you can observe any activity of the body and keep your attention centered upon it. For instance, if you observe your legs walking and for fifteen days you concentrate as one leg rises and then the other, then you will suddenly find yourself apart from your legs. Now you will find your legs working outside of YOU, and you will be a mere spectator. You will feel your own legs working mechanically, whereas you are absolutely apart from them. Hence, such a man can say that even while walking HE is not walking, even while talking HE is not talking, even while sleeping HE is not sleeping, while eating HE is not eating.

Such a man can assert this, and his claim is not wrong. But it is difficult to understand what such a man means. If he is witness to the act of eating, then he feels that even as he eats he does not eat. If he is witness to the act of walking, he feels he does not walk even though he is walking. So "Anapansati" has its usefulness, but it is a journey from another direction.

Questioner : *By deep and intense breathing, will not the lungs be harmed as a result of taking in more oxygen than is necessary for the body* ?

Bhagwan: Actually, no man breathes to the full capacity of his lungs. There are roughly about 6,000 air sacs in the lungs, out of which only about a 1,000 or 1,500 are filled with oxygen in the case of a healthy man. The rest of the air sacs are filled with carbon dioxide. Therefore, it is difficult to come upon a man who takes in more oxygen than required. A great part of the lungs remains useless in this way.

If you could manage to fill the complete lungs with oxygen, it would yield wonderful results. Your consciousness will expand immediately. You will experience life in proportion to the amount of oxygen you take in, and that will be the limit of your life. As the oxygen increases in the lungs, your life expands accordingly. So if the lungs were filled completely with oxygen, we would have the maximum experience of life.

This alone is the difference between a healthy and an unhealthy man. A sick person manages to fill his lungs with very little oxygen. A very sick man may not be able to take in any oxygen at all, and so he is supplied oxygen by external means or else he will die. We can judge a sick or healthy man by the proportion of oxygen that goes within him. This is why running and other exercises are good for health, because they increase the ratio of oxygen within the body. Anything you do that increases the proportion of oxygen is conducive to good health. Anything you do to bring down the ratio of oxygen helps to bring ill health. But it is a fact that you never take in as much oxygen as you are capable of, so the question of taking more does not arise. You cannot take more than the lungs can hold, and even that much is a very difficult task.

Questioner : *We do not only breathe in oxygen. We also take in nitrogen, hydrogen, etc. Are all these conducive to meditation ?*

Bhagwan: All that we breathe in is helpful for meditation. Whatever is in the air is conducive to life; therefore, you are alive. On these planets where the atmosphere does not hold the proper requisites in the right proportions, life is not possible. Our atmosphere has the possibilities of holding life; therefore, there is no need to worry. The harder you breathe, the more beneficial it is, for then more and more oxygen will quickly enter within you and become a part of you. Those things other than oxygen will be thrown out. The ratio of gases in the atmosphere is adjusted so as to be conducive to life. Therefore, there is no cause for alarm.

Questioner : *Bhagwan, why does the body begin to feel light after deep breathing ?*

Bhagwan: You are bound to feel light because body consciousness in itself is the cause of heaviness. What we call heaviness is brought about by the body consciousness. A person who is ill, no matter how thin he is, feels this sense of heaviness, whereas a healthy, fat person never feels the weight of the body. The consciousness of the body is the weight factor, and this consciousness is proportionate to the trouble within the body. If there is pain in the foot, we become conscious of the foot. If there is pain in the head, we become conscious of the head. If there is no pain anywhere at all, we do not feel the body at all.

Therefore, the definition of a healthy person is "one who experiences bodilessness". One who feels, "I am not the body" is a healthy man. If he feels any part of his body to be himself, then know that that particular part of the body is ill. So you will begin to have experiences that are of the Atman and not of the body to that extent which the oxygen increases within and the kundalini begins to rise. Due to these you will feel a lightness. Many will feel as if they have levitated from the ground. Usually this does not actually happen. Although it can happen to one in a hundred that the body may rise a little above the ground, generally one only FEELS as if he has risen from the ground. If you open your eyes, you will find yourself where you were.

How does this feeling come ? Actually, the mind, in its deepest depths, speaks not in language but in pictures. So it does not say in words that "I have become light and weightless". Rather, it conjures up a picture within the body of having risen above the ground.

The depths of our mind, the unconscious mind, knows only pictures. Therefore, at night, our dreams are pictures and pictures and not words. Everything in a dream has to be changed into images and illustrations. Therefore, they are difficult to decipher upon awakening in the morning, as then we turn the language of dreams into the language of words. For instance, how will a very ambitious man experience ambition in dreams ? He will become a bird and fly higher and higher into the skies, leaving everything and everyone below him. So ambition always takes the shape of flying in a dream. But on awakening in the morning, the mind's language changes and the man wonders what could be behind this dream of flying ? His ambition becomes the act of flying.

So also, in the depths of meditation there is this pictorial language. When you experience the feeling of lightness, this lightness will be translated into the picture of the body rising from the ground. Sometimes, in a state where much lightness is experienced, the body may actually rise from the ground; this is possible.

Questioner : *Sometimes it feels as if something has broken within and we feel frightened.*

Bhagwan : Yes, you may feel this—certainly.

Questioner : *Should we not feel afraid* ?

Bhagwan : There is no need to, though it is but natural that you should feel afraid.

Questioner : *A lot of heat is also created.*

Bhagwan : This too is possible, for your total system within undergoes a change. The points where we are attached to the body begin to lessen, and new connections are formed; old bridges break and new ones are constructed; old doors close and new ones open. So the whole house undergoes alteration. Therefore, when we feel many things breaking we feel much fear. The whole system is thrown into chaos. This is bound to occur in the period of transition, but ultimately a new order arises which is wonderful and unsurpassed in comparison to the old arrangement. Then you will not even remember the breaking of the old order, or even whether there was such an order before, and you will wonder how you ever tolerated the old state of things. All this will happen.

Questioner : *Is it necessary to continue deep breathing and the asking of "Who am I ?" even after the transmission of energy ? Should not the asking happen naturally* ?

Bhagwan : When it becomes natural, the question does not arise. Then the question becomes unnatural. But until this happens, many a time the mind will lure you into not asking any more. It will say, "Now stop! You have asked enough. How long will you keep asking ?" As long as the mind goads you to stop, continue unflinchingly, for the mind still is. Then, one day, suddenly you will find that it is no more necessary. Then even if you want to, you will not be able to ask. You can only ask, "Who am I ?" as long as you do not know. The moment you know, there is no need to ask again. Now you KNOW.

As long as I do not know, I will ask where the door is. But once I come to know, will I continue to ask, "Where is the door ?" Then I will not even inquire whether I should ask such a question, for it has no meaning. We only ask as long as we do not know. The moment we know, the matter ends. So as soon as the realization of "Who am I?" falls on you, you have passed the stage of questioning. And as you jump into this new dimension, there is nothing left to be done. Then whatever you do will be an act of meditation. You will walk in meditation, you will sit in meditation, you will speak in meditation; also, you will be in meditation when you are silent. Even if you wage a war, it will be in meditation. What you do, makes no difference.

Questioner : *When the influence of Shaktipat (transmission of energy) begins to work, the breath maintains its momentum. But at times the body becomes tranquil and so does the breath. Is it necessary to continue the exercise even at this time ?*

Bhagwan : If you do, it will be fruitful. The question is not whether the breath works or not. If it does not, there is no harm. The question is whether you have made the effort. If it does not work, let it not work. What will you do in the meantime ? You will continue with your effort; you will not leave it. The effort alone is meaningful. Again, I repeat : the question is not so much one of the result. What is of great importance is your effort. Have you staked your all ? Perhaps you have kept back a little of yourself. The mind tries its very best to hold you back. It says, "Nothing is happening; stop for the time being." The mind finds a thousand and one excuses to discourage you. It cries out aloud "No more ! No more ! Stop ! You are suffocating ! You will die !"

Do not listen to the mind. You should reply, "You are suffocating ? Very good." If the breath does not come of its own, it is not in your hands, but you, on your part, keep up deep breathing. You put in your strongest effort. Do not even spare an iota of yourself, for many a time this little bit keeps everything back. No one knows which is the last piece of straw that will cause the camel to sit down. You load the camel with hay—one maund (82. 28 pounds), two maunds : the camel can bear it. You go on and on, until you put one last small wisp of straw and the camel can hold out no longer. The balance is always decided by the last small bit and not by the first load.

You load the first maund: nothing happens. You add the second maund: the camel still holds on. Then as you go on adding bit by bit, when the last wisp is added the camel sits down. Or, take it this way: you hammer a lock fifty times, but nothing seems to happen. You are tired, and the fifty-first stroke is rather mild. But the lock breaks with this stroke. The balance is always struck by the last fraction. One tenth of an inch, one wisp of straw, is the deciding factor. Therefore, let it not be that you make your utmost effort and miss by a fraction. Just make this little extra effort, for without it you could lose all.

It happened in one case recently. One friend was taking part in meditation in Amritsar. He is an educated person—a doctor, but nothing was happening to him. I knew nothing about him; I had not met him. Then on the last day in the course of my talk, I said, "Water changes into vapour only when it reaches 100 degrees centrigrade. Even at 99 degrees it is still water, and even at 99½ degrees it is still water. Only when it crosses over the 100 degree mark does it turn into vapour. This point cannot be changed."

That very evening he came to me. He said, "I was thinking that little by little I will make progress. Today, when you gave the example of water turning into vapour, I realized I was wrong. Water turns into vapour only at 100 degrees, and even at 98 degrees the water could not be partly water and partly vapour. Every drop has to reach the 100th degree if it wishes to become vapour. Not until then can it give up its form as water. Your words opened my eyes today, and I put in all my effort in meditation. I am surprised. These three days I strived in vain, and I used to get so tired and nothing used to happen. Today I am not even tired, and something has taken place. All throughout the experiment your illustration of 100 degrees stuck in my mind and I did not spare an inch of myself." I told him, "That is exactly what is required—not to spare yourself and to make an all-out effort."

There is no other difference between those who are experiencing and those who are not; this is the only difference. There is one more thing to be kept in mind : many a time it seems that the man next to you is making a greater effort, but not making any headway. His 100th degree is different from your 100th degree. It is just as a man has 500 rupees and he makes a bet of 300 rupees, while you have 5 rupees and you stake 4. Then you will reach further than him. It is not the 300 or the 4, but the ratio that matters. You stake your all, and you will reach the 100th degree. Remember, the degree of each person is different. The question is of how much you wager. If you stake your whole you will win, whereas if the other person wagers even 400 rupees he will lose. He must stake all of his 500 rupees.

So in the final stage, it is very necessary to remember one basic thing, and that is, do not spare yourself in the least. Do not ever think, "It is enough for today; I shall try tomorrow." The moment you start thinking on these lines, you will fall back. And this happens always on the point where the happening takes place. Now the mind says, "Enough ! You have boiled enough. Water is turning into fire. What is the use ? Come back ! Come back !" This moment is very significant. This is the moment of consequence when the mind clamours to turn back, for the mind sees danger : it sees disintegration ahead; now it knows it must die.

As long as there was no danger in sight it encouraged you, but as soon as the boiling point is reached it will do all it can to stop you from going any further. It will say, "There is no more strength left; I can do no more." Be very cautious at that crucial moment. That is the moment when you should not spare yourself, for to lose that moment may be equal to losing many years. It takes ages to reach the 99th degree, and sometimes we do miss the opportunity of reaching the 100th degree mark. A small excuse, and we lose for a life time. Therefore, do not spare yourselves.

Questioner : *Can the blood vessels snap by too much pressure* ?

Bhagwan : Let them snap ! What will you gain by keeping them intact ?

Questioner : *We do not want to die in ignorance.*

Bhagwan : If you save your blood vessels, you WILL die in ignorance. What will you do ? Our problem has always been that we are worried about the safety of things that do not matter.

Questioner : *What little we have is all that we have. How can we lose even that* ?

Bhagwan : If you had something worth saving, it would be a different matter, for then you would not fear losing it. But even that you do not have. It is generally the naked man who is afraid of losing clothes, for with this comes the satisfying feeling that he too possesses clothes. There is a sense of pleasure—the feeling that he is not without clothes. He who has clothes is never obssessed with the idea of losing them, for they are, after all, mere clothes. If they are lost, they are lost. Get rid of this fear.

This does not mean that your blood vessels are bound to break. They can break out of fear, not through meditation. Out of fear, anxiety and tension, we are afraid that we will break down. We are afraid of meditation when there is no question of breaking. There all broken ends are joined. But we nurture our fears, and they provide us ready excuses : "This might happen, that might happen." And so we make all the necessary arrangements to be able to turn back. Then I say—why go on this path at all ! This uncertainty is dangerous. I say—do not go on this path ! Let the matter go; do not worry about it.

But we remain ambivalent. We want to go and we also do not want to go. Our vitality becomes weakened by this dilemma. Then we find ourselves overcome with uncalled for distress. Hundreds and thousands of people find themselves in this plight. They want to seek God and they are also afraid lest they should meet Him. Now this is a double difficulty. All our troubles are due to the fact that whatsoever we want to do, on another plane of mind we do not want to do it. Doubt and uncertainty are our very life. It is never the case that we want to do something with a total mind. The day this happens, there will be no more hindrances. Then life will flow with a smooth momentum. But our condition is such that we take one step forward and then immediately we take one step backward.

We put one brick into our house and remove another. We take pleasure in making the house and also in crying that it cannot be built. All day long you make the walls, and all night you feel that you cannot build it. All day long you make the walls, and you spend all night removing them brick by brick. Then by morning, the wall is just as it used to be. Then you sit and wail over how difficult it is to build a house. We must try and understand this difficulty within ourselves. And this you will only understand when you make up your mind and say, "Well, if it breaks it breaks." What will you do by saving it for thirty or forty years ? At the most you will work in an office; you will eat and sleep each day and produce a few children. There will be a wife, there will be a husband, there will be this and that, and such and such things. And then the day comes when all these have to be left behind.

These are the poor people who are busy protecting their blood vessels. After all, what will you do with them ? If you have even a slight inkling that life as we seek to make it has nothing in it worth saving, then only can you be prepared to stake your all. The worthlessness of all that we try to save should be absolutely clear to us. And what do you manage to save after all ? Then you will not be concerned whether your blood vessels break or not. No blood vessels have ever broken in this way. If they do, it will be a new happening.

[Text of a discourse given on July 2, 1970, evening, in Bombay, India]

10

THE NATURE OF A KUNDALINI MASTER

Questioner :

Bhagwan, in the Nargol meditation camp you said that the meaning of "Shaktipat" (transmission of the Divine energy) is that the power of the Divine descends into one. Later on you said that there is a difference between Shaktipat and grace. These two statements seem contradictory. Kindly explain.

Bhagwan Shri Rajneesh :

There is a slight difference between the two and there is a slight similarity between the two also. Actually, the field of each extends into the other. Shaktipat is also the power of the Divine. In fact, there is no other power except the power of the Divine. In Shaktipat, however, a person acts as a medium. Ultimately, that too is the Divine working, but in the initial stages an individual provides the means for this power to work.

It is just like the lightning that flashes across the sky and the electric light that lights the house: Both are the same, but the light that burns in the house is brought about through a medium and the hand of man is clearly evident behind it.

The lightning that flashes in the rain is the same power of the Divine, but it is not brought about by man. If man becomes extinct from the earth, the lightning will still flash across the sky, but the electric bulb will no longer work. Shaktipat is like the electric bulb in which man is the medium; grace is like the lightning in the sky that comes without the help of a medium.

A person who has attained this power and who, in a way, is united with the Divine can act as a medium, because he is a better vehicle than you for the purpose. He is familiar with the energy and its workings. The power can descend within you quicker through him. You are absolutely unacquainted, immature; this man is a well-matured vehicle. If the energy enters you through him it comes about easily, as he is an efficient medium. And another thing: that person is a very narrow opening from which you will attain energy—but only according to your capacity. You can sit under the light in the house and read, as it is a regulated light. You cannot sit under the lightning in the skies, for it follows no regulations.

So if by chance a person reaches the state of grace, if a situation of sudden Shaktipat happens around him, there is every possibility of such a person becoming insane. The energy that has descended on him may be too much and his capacity to hold it too little, and hence he is thrown completely out of gear. Then, unknown, unfamiliar experiences of joy become painful and unbearable.

If a man used to staying in darkness for years is suddenly brought out into the daylight, his darkness will deepen all the more, and he will not yet be able to see the light of the sun. His eyes were accustomed to seeing in the darkness, so they cannot bear the glare of light. So sometimes it happens that such conditions come about within you in which grace descends unknowingly on you, but its effect can be fatal—destructive, for you are not ready. You have been caught unawares, so the happening can turn into a disaster. Yes, grace can also become a violent misadventure.

In the case of Shaktipat the chances of accident are very very few—almost nil. This is because there is a person who is a medium. Then, through a narrow medium the flow of the energy becomes very narrow, and also the medium can control the energy. He can allow only that amount of energy to flow into you which you can hold. Remember, the medium is only a vehicle and not the generator of this power. Therefore, if any person says he brings about Shaktipat, he is wrong. It would be just like the bulb declaring that it is the giver of light. Because light is always emitted through the bulb, the bulb may be deluded that it is the creator of light. This is not so. It is not the primal source of light, but merely a medium for its manifestation. So a person who declares that he can perform Shaktipat is under the same illusion as the bulb.

The energy that is transmitted is always the energy of the Divine. If a person becomes a medium, we can call it Shaktipat. If there is no medium and this energy descends, it can be harmful. But if a man has waited infinitely, if a man has meditated with infinite patience, then Shaktipat too can take place in the form of grace. Then there will be no medium, but then there will be no mishap. His infinite awaiting, his boundless patience, his unflinching devotion, his everlasting resolve, develop his ability to endure the Infinite. So then there is no mishap, and the happening can take place both ways (with or without a medium). But in the absence of a medium he will feel it not as Shaktipat, but as grace from above.

So there are similarities as well as differences between the two. I am in favour of grace as far as it is possible. As far as possible, there should not be a medium. But in certain cases this is possible and in certain cases it is not. So instead of the latter category of people wandering for endless lives, some person can be made a medium, to bring down the vital energy to them. Only that person can be a medium, however, who is no more an individual. Then the hazards are less. Only that person can act as a medium who has no ego, no pride left in him. Then the hazard is almost nil, because such a person, while becoming the medium, does not become a guru: there is no person left to become a guru. Understand this difference well.

When a person becomes a guru, he becomes a guru vis-a-vis you; when a person becomes a medium, he does so in relationship to the Universal Being. Then there is no give and take with you; he has nothing to do with you. Do you understand the difference? Ego cannot stand in any state brought about in relation to the Divine, but it can exist when the state is brought about in relationship to you. So the real Guru is one who does not become a guru. The definition of a "Sadguru" (perfect Master) is one who does not become a guru. This means that all who call themselves "guru" do not have the potential to be a Guru. There is no greater disqualification than a declaration of "guru-ship", for that shows the presence of ego within such a person, and that is dangerous.

If a person unmistakably reaches the state of Void where ego has completely disappeared, he can become a medium. It is wrong even to say "he can become". Rather, one should say "he is" the medium. Then Shaktipat can take place in his presence, and there is no chance of any hazard. There is no hazard either to your individuality or to that of the medium. And yet, basically, I am in favour of grace. Then, when the condition that the individual is no more and the ego has died is fulfilled, Shaktipat almost becomes grace.

If the individual (who is the medium) is totally unaware of his state, then Shaktipat is very, very near to grace. Then, just being near him can bring about the happening. This person appears as a person to you, but in actuality he is one with the Universal Being. It would be better to say that he has become the "hand of the Divine" extended toward you. Now such a man is wholly instrumental. If that person speaks in the first person under SUCH conditions, we tend to misunderstand him—for when such a person says "I", he means "the Supreme Self". But it is difficult for us to understand his language.

Therefore, Krishna can say to Arjuna, "Leave all else and surrender unto me." For thousands of years we pondered, "What sort of a person is this who says "Surrender unto me"? His statement seems to confirm the presence of an ego. But he has said this only because "he" is not. Now his "I" is the outstretched hand of someone else, and it is He who is behind him who says, "Surrender unto me." These words, "··*mam ekam* (the only ONE)," are priceless words. Krishna says, "Surrender unto ME, the only ONE." The "I" is never "only One" : it is many. Krishna speaks from a place where the "I" is "the only ONE", and this is not the language of ego.

But we understand only the language of ego; therefore, we feel that Krishna has made an egoistic statement by telling Arjuna to come unto him. But this is a mistake. We always have two ways of looking at things : one is through our own point of view from where we are invariably deluded, and the other is from the point of view of the Divine from where there is no question of delusion. So the happening can take place through a person like Krishna in whom his own individuality plays no part.

Both the happenings (Shaktipat and grace) are very contrary at the periphery; both are very close to one another at the center. I am in favour of that place where it is difficult to distinguish between Shaktipat and grace. That alone is useful; that alone is valuable.

A sannyasin of China was observing the birthday of his guru with great éclat. People asked him whose birthday he was celebrating, for he always said that he had no guru, and that there was no need for a guru. Then what was all this about ? He begged them not to question him, but they kept on insisting, "Today is the 'day of the guru'. Have you a guru ?"

The sannyasin had no choice but to satisfy their curiosity. "If you insist, I will have to tell you," he said. "Today I remember the man who refused to be my guru, for if he had accepted me as a disciple I would have gone astray. That day when he refused me I was very angry with him, but today I want to thank him most gratefully. Had he wished, he could have been my guru, for it was I who had begged him to accept me. But he did not agree."

So the people asked, "Then what do you thank him for when he refused you ?" The sannyasin said, "It is enough to say that by not becoming my guru, this man did for me what no guru could do. Therefore, my obligation is doubled. If he had been my guru, there would have been some give and take on both sides. I would have touched his feet, offered my veneration and respects, and the matter would have been concluded. But this man asked for no respect, no *pranams* (salutations). Therefore, my obligation to him is double. This has been absolutely one-sided : He gave and I could not even thank him, for he left no place even for that."

Now Shaktipat in such a condition and grace are not different. If there is a difference, you should keep away from it. The lesser the difference, the better it is. Therefore, I lay stress on grace. The day you cannot distinguish between Shaktipat and grace, know that the right happening has taken place. When the electricity of your house becomes a part of the unrestricted, natural, infinite energy of the skies, when your bulb no longer makes any declarations, that moment you should know that Shaktipat is also grace. Remember what I have said.

Questioner : *In the Nargol meditation camp you have said that either the power rises from within and reaches up to the Divine or the power of the Divine descends and merges within. You explained that the first is the rising of the kundalini and the second is the grace of God. Then later on you said that when the sleeping energy within meets the enormous energy of the Infinite, an explosion takes place which is Samadhi. Is the union of the kundalini and grace absolutely necessary for Samadhi ? Or, is the evolution of the kundalini up to the "sahasrar" (the seventh or highest "chakra" or center) and Divine grace one and the same thing ?*

Bhagwan : Explosion never takes place with only one energy. Explosion is the union of two energies. If it were not so, the explosion would have taken place long ago. You have a matchbox and you place a matchstick near it. They can lie like this infinitely and no flame will result. No matter how small the distance between the two—be it half an inch or a quarter of an inch—there will be no result. For that explosion, the friction of the two is necessary; then only will you get light. Fire is hidden in both of them, but there is no way of producing it with only one of the two.

The explosion is the possibility of the union of two energies. Thus, the sleeping energy within the individual must rise up to the sahasrar, and then only is the explosion possible. No union is possible except at the point of the sahasrar. It is just as if your doors are closed and the sun is shining outside. Its light stands at your door. You proceed from within your house up to the door, but still you will not meet the light of the sun. Only when the door opens can you come face to face with the sun.

So the ultimate point of the kundalini is the sahasrar. That is the door where grace awaits us. The Divine forever awaits us at this door. It is you who are not at your door : you are away within somewhere. You have to come to the door ! There the union will take place, and that union will be in the form of an explosion. It is called an "explosion" because then YOU will immediately vanish: YOU will no longer be. The matchstick will have been burnt down in the explosion though the matchbox will still be. The matchstick that is you turns into ashes and merges into the Formless.

In the happening you will be no more. You will be lost; you will be broken and scattered; you will no longer be. You will not be what you were behind the closed door. All that was yours will be lost. Only He who waits outside the door will remain, and you will be a part of Him. This cannot happen to you alone by yourself. For this explosion, it is very necessary for you to reach up to the infinite Cosmic Energy. The sleeping energy within has to be awakened and made to rise upwards to the sahasrar where the Cosmic Power forever awaits. So the journey of the kundalini starts from your sleeping center and ends at the place, at the boundary, where you are not.

So there is one boundary which is of the physical body, which we have recognised. But this is not the larger boundary. If my hand is cut, it does not make much difference to me. If the feet are cut, the body will not suffer much, for I still remain. In other words, I still remain in spite of the changes within these limits. Even if the eyes and ears are not, I still remain. So your actual boundary is not the boundary of the body. Your actual boundary is the sahasrar center after which you no longer are. No sooner do you encroach on this boundary, when you are gone: you cannot remain.

Your kundalini is your sleeping energy. Its boundaries extend from the sex center to the brain. This is why we may be able to disidentify ourselves with the other parts of the body, but we cannot break our identity with the face. It is easy not to recognize other parts of the body as one's own, but to dissociate oneself with one's face is very difficult. This is the limit. Therefore, a man is ready to lose everything, but not his intellect.

Someone asked Socrates whether he would prefer to be a discontented Socrates or a contented pig. This question was asked when Socrates was talking about contentment, and he said that contentment was the greatest of possessions. Socrates replied, "I would prefer to be a dissatisfied Socrates than a contented pig, for the contented pig has no knowledge of his contentment. A dissatisfied Socrates will at least be conscious of his dissatisfaction." This man Socrates proves that man is willing to lose all, but not his intellect, even if it is a dissatisfied intellect.

The intellect is also very near the center of sahasrar. To put it correctly, we have two boundaries. One is the sex center below where the world of nature begins. At the center of sex there is no difference between trees, birds, animals and ourselves. This is the ultimate limit for these, whereas for man it is the first boundary. When we are based in the sex center, we too are animals. Our other limit is the intellect. It is near our second line of boundary beyond which is the Supreme Self. Beyond this point we are no longer ourselves. Then we are the Supreme Self. These are our two frontier lines, and between these two our energy moves.

Now the reservoir where the vital energy lies asleep is next to the sex center. This is why 99% of man's thoughts, dreams and imagination—99% of his life—is spent around this reservoir. No matter how much culture many display, whatever the false pretexts society may bring out, man lives there and there alone : he lives in sex only. If he earns money, it is for sex; if he builds castles it is for sex; whatever he does, at the root of it all we will find sex.

Those who understood talked of two goals—sex and liberation—and wealth and religion are the two resources of these. Wealth is a resource of sex. The more sexual the era, the more wealth motivated it will be. The more in search of liberation an age is, the more it will be thirsty for religion. Religion is a means just as wealth is a means. If you desire liberation, religion becomes the means. If you wish sexual satisfaction, wealth is the means. So there are two goals and two means, for we have two frontiers.

What is most interesting is the fact that between these two extremes you cannot rest anywhere, you cannot pause anywhere. Many people find themselves in great difficulty, as they have no desire for liberation. And if for some reason they become antagonistic towards sex, they find themselves in a terrible predicament. They stay far away from the sex center, but they won't go anywhere near the center of liberation. Instead, they fall into doubt and uncertainty, and that is very difficult, very painful and a veritable hell. Their lives are filled with inner turmoil.

To tarry in the middle is neither proper, nor natural, nor meaningful. It is as if a man climbs a ladder and stops halfway. To him we would say, "Do one of the two : either go up or come down, because the ladder is not the house and to stop in between is meaningless." There cannot be a more useless person than one who stops halfway up the ladder. Whatever he has to do he can do either at the top of the ladder or at the bottom of the ladder.

So the spine is the "ladder", so to speak. In this, ladder, each vertebra is a step. The kundalini starts from the lowest center and reaches to the very top. If it reaches the highest center, explosion is inevitable. If it remains at the lowest center, it is sure to take the form of sexual discharge. The explosion is inevitable in the first case and the discharge in the second case. These two things should be understood well.

If the kundalini is at the lowest center, a discharge of sexual energy is inevitable. If it reaches the highest point, explosion is certain. Both are explosions and both require the agency of another. In the discharge of sex, "the other" is necessary, even if it is an imaginary other. From there also your energy is diffused. But ALL your energy does not become scattered from here, because this is only the beginning point of your being. You are MUCH MORE than that and you have progressed much from there. The animal is fully satisfied at this point, and, therefore, it does not seek liberation.

If animals could write scriptures there will be written in them only two goals worth striving for : wealth and sex. Wealth will be also in forms suitable to the animal world. The animal that has more flesh, more strength, will be the richer one. He will win over the others in the competition of sex, he will gather ten females around him. And this also is a form of wealth. The extra "fat" within his body is his wealth.

A man too has a treasure which can be converted into "fat" at anytime. A king can keep a thousand queens. There was a time when a man's wealth was measured by the number of wives he possessed. If a man is poor, how can he afford four wives ? Today's criteria of education and a bank balance are a much later development. In the olden days, women were the only criterion of wealth. This is why, in extolling the affluence of our ancient heroes, we have had to inflate the number of their women, and this was many a time false.

For instance, the 16,000 queens of Krishna : In Krishna's days there was no other way of expressing his greatness : "If Krishna is a great man, then how many wives did he have ?" And so we had to conjure up the colossal figure of 16,000 which was an impressive number then, though today it might not seem so due to the population explosion. In those days there were not so many people. In Africa, even now there are communities that consist of only three people. So if they are told that a man has four wives, it would be an impossible figure, for they do not know anything beyond the figure of three.

Even on the plane of sex, the presence of "the other" is required. If the other person is not present, even imagining the other produces the necessary effect. This is why it was thought that if God is present even in imagination, the explosion can take place. Therefore, the long tradition of "Bhakti" (the path of devotion) developed in which imagination was used as the means for explosion. If ejaculation is possible by imagination, why cannot the energy explosion take place in the same way at the sahasrar ? This ejaculation by imagining the other's presence gave rise to the possibility of meeting God in the mind through the use of imagination. But this was not really possible. Ejaculation is possible in imagination because it has actually been experienced; therefore, it can be imagined. But we have had no meeting with God; therefore, He cannot be visualized.

We can only imagine that which HAS been experienced by us. If the experience was had, we can then use the imagination to have the same experience again. If a man has experienced a certain kind of pleasure, he can always sit back, recall the experience and enjoy it again. But if he has not actually experienced that pleasure, how can he recall it ? A deaf person cannot hear in his dreams no matter how hard he tries; he cannot even imagine sound. Similarly, a blind man cannot envisage light. But if a man has lost his eyes, he can always dream of light. Rather, now he can only see light in his dreams, for he no longer has eyes to see it.

So we can envisage our experiences, but there is no way to imagine what has never been experienced. Explosion is not our experience; therefore, imagination does not work here. There we shall actually have to go within, and then the actual happening takes place. So the sahasrar chakra is your ultimate boundary where YOU end.

As I said before, man is a ladder. Nietzsche's words in this context are very precious. He said, "Man is a bridge between two eternities." There is one eternity—that of nature which has no end—and there is the other, of God, which is also infinite, limitless. Man is a bridge swaying between these two. Therefore, man is not the "halting place". One either goes forwards or backwards. There is no place to build a house on this bridge. Whoever tries to settle on it repents, for a bridge is not a place where to have a house. It is only meant to cross over from one end to the other.

In Fatehpur-Sikri, Akbar tried to build a temple of all religions. He dreamed of one religion which he named "Din-e-Ilahi" —the essence of all religions. So he had the words of Jesus Christ inscribed on the entrance door: "This place is only a resting place and not a permanent house. You may halt here for sometime, but you cannot stop here forever." This is not the end of the journey. This is only a place of rest on your journey. It is a camping ground, a traveller's bungalow, where one can stay the night and resume travel in the morning. And we halt here only so that we may rest the night and start again at day-break. There is no other reason. We do not stop here for all time.

The human being is a ladder that has to be climbed. Therefore, he is always tense. It is not correct to say that man is tense : rather, man is tension. A bridge is always tense. It is a bridge BECAUSE it is tense: It is that which lies between two extremes. Man is an inevitable tension. Therefore, he is never at peace, never tranquil. Only when he is an animal does he experience a little peace, or else he attains perfect peace when he becomes the Divine. The tension loosens when he becomes an animal, for then he has climbed down the steps of the ladder to stand on the ground, the place with which he has been familiar since infinite lives. He has relieved himself of all botheration about tension. Therefore, man seeks freedom from tension in sex, or in other experiences related to sex such as alcohol, drugs, etc. that can take him into temporary unconsciousness. But you can be there for a short while only, for even if you wish you cannot stay in the animal state permanently. The worst example of a man can only be in the animal state for a very short period.

The man who commits murder does so only in the moment when he becomes an animal. Had he waited a moment longer, perhaps he might have been unable to do it. Our becoming like animals is somewhat like a man jumping. For a moment he is in the air, and back he comes on the ground. So the worst of men is not bad forever: he cannot be. He is so only during certain moments; otherwise he is normal like any other person. For one moment he derives comfort, then he falls back into known grounds where there are no tensions. Therefore, we find no tension in animals. Look into their eyes: there is no tension there. An animal never goes mad or commits suicide; he suffers no heart disease. All these belong to man, but all this is possible for an animal who is caught in the grip of man —when he draws man's cart or pulls his carriage or becomes his domestic pet. This is a different thing altogether. When man tries to pull him across the bridge, the complications start.

Now if a stray dog enters this room he will move about as he pleases, but if a pet dog enters he will go and sit where he is ordered. Now this pet dog has entered the world of man and left his animal world behind. He is bound to land himself in trouble, for he is an animal that has been made to undergo the tensions of a human being. Thus, he is forever in distress. He eagerly awaits the order when he could run out.

Man can fall back into the animal state only momentarily. Therefore, we say that all our joys are short-lived. Joy can be eternal, but where we look for it, it is but a transitory state. We try to find happiness in the animal state, and this can be only for a very short while. We cannot remain in the animal state for long. It is difficult to go back into our previous state of existence. If you want to go back to yesterday, you can close your eyes and visualize. But for how long ? When you open your eyes, you will find yourself where you are.

You CANNOT go back ! You can commit this excess for a moment or so, but then you always repent. Therefore, all momentary pleasures bring repentence in their course. One feeling is that your efforts have gone in vain, but after a few days you forget again and fall into the same error. Momentary joy can be obtained on the animal level, but eternal joy is attained only upon merging into the Supreme Soul. This journey has to be completed within your own self. You have to cross from one end of your bridge to the other. Then only does the second happening take place.

Therefore, I consider sex and Samadhi equivalent. There is a reason for this. In fact, these are the only two happenings that are equivalent. In sex we are at one end of the bridge, the lowest rung of the ladder where we are one with nature. In Samadhi we are at the other end of the bridge, the topmost rung of the ladder where we are one with the Universal Self. Both are unions; both are explosions in a certain sense. In both cases you lose yourself in a particular sense : In sex you lose yourself for a moment and in Samadhi, forever. In both cases YOU cease to exist. The former is a very momentary explosion, and after it you recrystallize because where you had gone was a lower state to which you cannot revert. But once you merge into the Divine you cannot recrystallize.

This reversal is as impossible as the one into the animal state. It is entirely impossible ! It is just like expecting an adult man to get into his baby clothes. You have become one with the Absolute, so you can no longer revert back to the individual. Now the individual self has become such a narrow and insignificant place, you can no longer enter there. Now you cannot even imagine how you could not have been in it always, or what you must have been like when you were there in that insignificant place.

The matter of the individual ends here; your journey within must reach the point of the sahasrar. Why we call this center "sahasrar" needs to be explained.

These names are not coincidental, though languages always develop accidentally and by constant use. Now we use the word "door". Any other name could have been easily used to denote the same thing. There are thousands of languages in the world and there must be thousands of words that mean "door", and they all are capable of conveying the same meaning. But when a thing is not accidental, it strikes a similarity in all languages. So the meaning of "door" or "*dwara*" conveys the meaning of that through which we pass—in and out. So in all languages, the word used for door will convey this meaning, because this is a part of an experience and not a coincidental arrangement. The idea of the space through which entrance and exit are possible is conveyed by this word (door).

Thus, the word "sahasra-dal-kamal" (thousand-petalled lotus) is only as a result of experiencing and is not accidental. No sooner do you attain the experience, when you feel as if a thousand flower-buds have bloomed within you all of a sudden. We say "a thousand" to mean "infinite", and we liken it to flowers because the experience is like a flowering. Something within that was closed like a bud has opened. The word "flower" is used in the context of flowering, of blossoming. Something which was closed has now opened. Something which was like a bud has now become a flower. And not only have one or two things blossomed: infinitely many things have blossomed.

So the term "sahasra-dal-kamal" is used to convey the meaning of a thousand-petalled lotus, and this comparison comes naturally to the mind—very naturally. Have you ever seen a lotus opening in the rays of the sun? Watch carefully. Go very near a lotus pond and observe silently as each flower opens little by little. Then you can visualize what the feelings would be if a thousand-petalled lotus opened in this way within the mind. Then you will be able to imagine the experience somewhat.

There is another wonderful experience: that of sex. Those who go deep into the experience of sex also feel this flowering, but it is a very fleeting experience. Something within blossoms, but it closes again almost immediately. Also, there is a difference between the two experiences. In the sex experience, the flower is felt to be hanging downwards, whereas in Samadhi the flowers are felt to be blooming upwards. Now this differentiation can only be made by passing through both experiences. It is natural that the flowers that bloom downwards join you to a lower realm, while the flowers that bloom upwards join you to a higher realm. In fact, this blooming is an opening that makes you vulnerable to another realm It is a door that opens—a door through which something enters within you for the explosion to take place.

Thus, both these things are required. You will travel up to the sahasrar and there someone is always awaiting you. It is not correct to say that someone will come there when you reach: That someone is already there waiting for the happening to take place in you.

Questioner : *Does the kundalini unfold toward the sahasrar only by Shaktipat ? Does the explosion take place only then ? If this is so, then does it follow that Samadhi is obtained through another person ?*

Bhagwan : This has to be understood properly. In this world, in this life, there is no happening so simple that you can understand it just by one aspect of it. It has to be viewed from all sides. Now If I strike a door with a hammer and the door opens, I can say that the door opened with the blow of my hammer. This is also correct in the sense that had I not struck the door, the door would not have opened. Now with the same hammer I strike another door, but the hammer breaks and the door does not open. Then the other side of the action comes to your mind. When I struck at the first door and it opened, it was not entirely because of the hammer. The door was fully ready to open. It may have been old, it may have been weak, but whatever the case it was ready to open.

So the door had as much a hand as the hammer in this happening. In one instance, the hammer struck and the door opened; in another, the hammer broke and the door did not open. So when the happening takes place in Shaktipat, it is not entirely due to Shaktipat. At the other end, the sadhak in such a case is inwardly prepared and ready, so a slight push becomes effective. If this push had not been effected by Shaktipat, the door may have taken a little longer to open. So the kundalini is not pushed up by Shaktipat: it is the time element that is decreased by it—nothing more. The sadhak would have reached in any case.

Suppose I had not hammered at the door, but this door is old and about to collapse. Then it could fall with a single gust of wind. And even if there is no wind, in the course of time it will collapse on its own. Then it will be difficult to explain why and how it fell, for it is all the time preparing to fall. So at the most, the difference will be of the time gap only.

So if Ramakrishna alone was responsible for the happening in Vivekananda, then it could have also happened to all the others who came to him. He had hundreds of disciples. If Vivekananda alone was responsible, it could have happened to him long before. He had gone to many before he came to Ramakrishna, but the happening did not take place. So Vivekananda was ready in his own way and Ramakrishna was capable in his own way. When this readiness and capability meet at a particular point, the time gap of the happening is reduced. It could be that if Vivekananda had not met Ramakrishna at that particular moment, the happening may have taken place one year later, two years later, or may be in his next birth, or perhaps after ten more births. But what is important is not when the happening will take place: it is the preparedness of the sadhak that decides this point.

The time gap is shortened, but time is fictitious so it does not have much importance; time is illusory and hence is not of any value. You can take a short nap and hardly a minute may pass, but in that short period you might see a dream from your childhood right up to your old age, with all the happenings. But in the waking state it will be hard to believe that such a long dream lasted not more than a minute. Actually, the time dimension in the dream state is very different. Dream time is capable of many, many incidents in a very short span; hence, the illusion.

Now there are insects that are born in the morning and are dead by the evening. We say, "The poor things!" But we do not know that in that span of time such an insect lives out life in its entirety, and it experiences all that we experience in seventy years. There is no difference: such an insect builds a house, finds a wife, breeds the young ones, fights with others, and even reaches the state of Sannyas—all within twelve hours. But their knowledge of time is different. We pity them for the short life granted to them, and they must be pitying us that we take seventy years to do all that they can do within a period of twelve hours. How dull we must be according to them!

Time is a mental concept. The time ratio changes according to our mental state. When we are happy, time becomes short. When we are in trouble or pain, time does not seem to end. If you are sitting at the deathbed of some relative, the night never seems to finish. It seems as if the sun will never rise. It seems as if it is the last night of the world and it will never end. Sorrow prolongs time: in sorrow you want time to pass quickly. The faster you expect the time to pass, the slower it seems to creep, for this is a relative experience. When your expectation is keen, time seems to crawl at a snail's pace, though it is actually moving at its normal speed. When a lover awaits his beloved, he feels she is taking too long to come, when actually she is walking at her normal pace. He would want her to acquire the speed of a jet.

So time appears slow in sorrow. When you are happy, when you meet your friends or loved ones, you spend the night talking, and at daybreak you wonder how the night passed so quickly. When you are happy, your experience of time is different; when you are unhappy your experience of time is different.

Time is a mind-oriented unit; therefore, changes can be brought about in it. Your mind can be worked upon by an outside source. If I hit you with a stick on your head, it is natural that your head is hurt; there is no question about it. So your body responds to an outside source and so does your mind, but YOU cannot be worked upon in a similar way, for you are neither the body nor the mind. However, you take yourself to be the body, you take yourself to be the mind.

So these two can be worked upon, and if one strikes at these your time interval can be reduced. Centuries can be reduced into moments, and vice versa.

The moment you are Awakened you will be struck with wonder. It is now 2,000 years since Jesus, 5,000 since Krishna, and a great deal of time has elapsed since Zarathustra and Moses. But you will be surprised that the moment you Awaken you will say, "My goodness, they too have just Awakened !" The time gap ceases completely then. Now these 2,000 and 5,000 years belong to a dream period. So when one Awakens, all Awaken. There is not even the difference of a single moment. This is difficult to understand. The moment you Awaken, you become the contemporary of Buddha, Christ and Mahavir. They will be around you as if they too have just Awakened with you. There is not a moment's difference: there cannot be.

Now if we were to make a circle and draw many lines from the center to the circumference, we would find that at the circumference the distance between any two lines will be the most. Then, as you proceed along these lines toward the center, the distance becomes less and less, until at the center point there is no distance: all the lines become one at that point. So when a person reaches the center of that profound experience, the distances that were present at the circumference—of 2,500 years, of 5,000 years—vanish. But it is difficult for such a person to explain such an experience, for his listeners are at the periphery. This is why there is the possibility of misunderstanding.

A man came to me. He was a devotee of Jesus. He asked me, "What do you think of Jesus ?" I replied, "It is not proper to give opinion about oneself." He looked at me in surprise. "Perhaps you did not hear," he said. "I asked your opinion on Christ." I said, "I also feel you have not heard. I said, it is not proper to give an opinion of oneself." He looked perplexed. Then I explained to him thus: "You can theorize about Jesus only so long as you do not know him. The moment you know him, what differentiation will you make between you and he ? How will you think ?"

An artist once made a picture of Ramakrishna and showed it to Ramakrishna. He asked him how he liked the picture he had made of him, but he found Ramakrishna bending down in obeisance to the picture. Those present thought there was some mistake, some confusion. Perhaps he did not hear that it was his own picture. So the artist reminded him that it was his own picture that he was bowing to. "I forgot about that," Ramakrishna replied. "This picture is so lost in Samadhi, how can it be mine? In Samadhi, where is 'I' and where is 'you'? So I bowed to 'Samadhi'. It is well you reminded me or people would have laughed." But the people had already laughed.

The language of the circumference is different from the language of the center. So when Krishna says, "It was I who was Ram," and when Jesus says, "I had come before also and had told you," and when Buddha says, "I will come again," they speak the language of the center, and this is difficult for us to understand. The Buddhists are waiting for Buddha's advent again on earth. The truth is that he has come many a time. If he were to come every day he would not be recognized, for there is no way of coming in the same form again. The original form has passed into a dream form that is now lost for ever.

So at the center there is no time gap. This is why any variation of speed can be brought about in your time state. This much can be done by Shaktipat.

As for the last part of your question, "the other" that you mention is the other because of your clinging hard to your own boundary. So Vivekananda will think that the happening took place because of Ramakrishna. If Ramakrishna thought the same way, it would be foolishness. For Ramakrishna the happening took place in a different way. It was as if the right hand is hurt and the left hand applies the medicine. Now the right hand might think that someone else is treating it and it might offer thanks or refuse the treatment. But then it does not know that the same power is working through the left hand that works through the right. So when a person is helped by another, it is not actually "another". It is your own readiness that calls out to this help from the other part of your very own self.

There is an ancient book of Egypt in which it is said, "Never go looking for the Guru. He will appear at your door the moment you are ready." It says further, "Even if you set out in search of him, how will you search? How will you recognize him? If you have become qualified enough to recognize the Guru, then what else is wanting in you?" Therefore, it is the

Guru who recognizes the disciple. The disciple never can recognize the Guru. There is no remedy. Since you still cannot recognize your Self, how will you recognize the Guru ? But it is a fact that the day you are ready, some "hand" that is really your own will present itself as your guide. That hand is the hand of another so long as you do not know. The day you know, you will not even wait to offer thanks.

There is a certain custom in a Zen monastery in Japan: When the sadhak comes to the monastery to learn meditation, he brings his mat along, spreads it on the ground and sits upon it. Every day he meditates on the mat and leaves it as it is. The day his sadhana (spiritual practice) is complete, he rolls up the mat and leaves. The Master then understands that his meditation is complete. He expects no thanks, for where is the necessity ? And who is to thank whom ? The Master does not say a word. He sees the sadhak rolling up his mat and he understands. The time has come to roll up the mat. It is good ! There is no necessity of even observing the formality of thanking. Who is to be thanked ? And if the sadhak commits this error, the Master might go after him with a stick and order him to unroll the mat. His sadhana is still incomplete then.

So the concept of the other is due to our ignorance; otherwise, where is the other ? It is oneself alone in myriad forms; it is only oneself on numerous journeys; it is oneself alone in innumerable mirrors. It is definitely oneself alone who is in the mirror, though what one sees is other than oneself.

There is a Sufi story. A dog lost his way in a palace room. The walls and the ceiling of this room were made of mirrors, so the dog was in a dilemma. Wherever he looked there were dogs, dogs and only dogs. He found himself alone and yet surrounded by so many dogs. There was no way to get out, for the doors were also of mirrors. Thus, he saw dogs there too. Then he began to bark, but all the dogs in the mirrors began to bark with him. And when his bark filled the room, he was sure his fears were not unfounded. He ran here and there to fight them. The dogs in the mirrors did likewise. All night he exhausted himself barking and fighting the dogs in the mirrors, and in the morning he was found dead inside the room by the palace guard. And all this happened without there being anyone except the dog in the room. When he died, all noise abated, all confusion came to an end.

There are many mirrors, and when we see the other it is our own reflection in different mirrors. Therefore, "the other" is a fallacy. The notion that we are helping others is an illusion, and the notion that we are receiving help from "the other" is also an illusion. "The other" is actually a delusion.

Once this is known, life becomes simple and honest. When all your actions cease to be other-oriented, then whether you do something for another person or for yourself only you remain. Then if you give a helping hand to someone on the road, you will have helped your own self. If someone else has given you a helping hand, then he too has only helped himself. But this comes within our understanding only after the Ultimate Experience. Before that the other is definitely the other.

Questioner : *You had once mentioned that Vivekananda did not stand to gain by Shaktipat.*

Bhagwan : It was not the Shaktipat that was harmful for Vivekananda, but what followed afterwards. But the idea of gain and loss also pertains to the dream state, and not to the happening. With the help of Ramakrishna, he had a glimpse of Samadhi which he would have had on the basis of his own strength—but much later. Now it is like this: I struck the hammer and the door fell, but I can make the door stand again by fixing nails into it with the same hammer. The hammer that can bring down the door can refix it also. But it is the same hammer working in both the cases.

Ramarkrishna had some difficulties, for which he had to make use of Vivekananda. Ramakrishna was a complete rustic—unlearned and uneducated. His experience was profound, but he had no means of delivering it. It was necessary for him to use the medium of another person to make his experience known. If this had not been so, you would never have heard of Ramakrishna. It was out of his supreme compassion that he tried to convey to you his experiences through another person. If I have come upon some treasure in my house, and if I am lame and I climb upon the shoulders of another man to deliver the treasure to your house, I would be making use of this man's shoulders. He would be put to a little inconvenience and trouble by carrying me, but my intention was only to deliver the goods to you—for I am lame and the treasure may be unclaimed for all time, I cannot even go out and give the news.

This difficulty was with Ramakrishna; it was not so with Buddha. In Buddha's personality, Ramakrishna and Vivekananda were both present together. Buddha could express what he knew; Ramakrishna could not express what he knew. He needed another person to deliver his message who could be his vehicle of expression. So he showed Vivekananda a glimpse of the treasure, but at the same time he told him that he himself would keep the key. He said he would give him the key only three days before his death. Vivekananda begged of him not to take away what he had given him, but Ramakrishna told him, "You have other work to do. If you go into Samadhi, you will be lost for ever and my work will suffer. It is well that you do not experience Samadhi before my work is over." Ramakrishna did not know that people have worked after attaining Samadhi also. He could not have known it, for he himself was unable to do anything after Samadhi.

Normally, we are guided by our own experiences. After his experience of Samadhi, Ramakrishna could not do a thing. If someone came along and said, "Jai Ram !" he promptly went into Samadhi. For him, it was difficult to retain consciousness even at the mention of Ram. It at once reminded him of the other world. Someone would say, "Allah !" and he would be gone. If he saw a mosque, he would be lost in Samadhi. He could not move from there. He would hear *kīrtan* (devotional chanting) while walking along the road, and he would swoon immediately. His difficulty was that the slightest remembrance of the bliss of Samadhi was very overpowering for him. So according to his own experience, he was right in thinking that the same could happen to Vivekananda. Therefore, he told Vivekananda, "You have a great task to perform, and after that you can go into Samadhi." Thus, Vivekananda's whole life passed without attaining Samadhi, and this caused him great pain.

But, remember, the pain belonged to the dream world. It was

like a man dreaming a bad dream. Three days before his death he was given the key, but until then there was great pain. The letters he wrote seven days before his death are full of pain and anguish, and the agony increased more and more with his restless longing for that of which he had only a glimpse.

Your longing is not yet that intense, for you have no idea of what it is. One fleeting glimpse, and the longing will begin. You can take it this way: You were standing in the dark with pebbles in your hands. You were happy with your treasure. Then along comes a flash of lightning, and you find out that there are mines of diamonds ahead of you while you are only holding pebbles in your hand. Then the lightning is gone, but it leaves a message behind that you have to inform others who stand holding pebbles in their hands that a priceless treasure awaits them. So now the lightning will flash no more, for you have to carry out your task. Thus, a particular work was given to Vivekananda which was necessary for Ramakrishna's task. What could not be performed through Ramakrishna's own personality was performed through another.

It happens like this many a time. If a single person is unable to perform a particular task, three or four other persons are required. Sometimes even five to ten persons are required to help spread the message of a single person.

Therefore, I say avoid Shaktipat. As far as possible, strive for grace. Only that Shaktipat is useful which is as good as grace, which has no strings attached, which has no conditions along with it, which is absolutely unconditional. Shaktipat should take place without the medium even inquiring what happened. If you want to thank him, you should not even know where to find him; then it would be easy for you. But at times, when someone like Ramakrishna needs the help of another, there is no other way of obtaining it than this: otherwise Ramakrishna's knowledge would have passed unknown. He needed a means for expression, and this Vivekananda provided.

This is why Vivekananda always said, "Whatever I say is not mine." When he was honoured in America, he said that he was very much pained because the honour belonged to one of whom they had no idea. And when someone called him a great man he said, "I do not even deserve to be the dust of the feet of that great personality who is my Master." But the fact remains that had Ramakrishna gone to America he would have been locked up in a lunatic asylum. He would have been put under psychotherapeutic treatment; he would definitely have been pronounced as mad.

We have yet not been able to differentiate religious madness from non-religious "madness", so in America both of these types of cases are put in the same asylum. Ramakrishna would have been kept under treatment, whereas Vivekananda would be given all the honour—because what Vivekananda says is intelligible. He himself was not in "that" condition: he was not "mad". He was only a messenger—a postman who carried the letter of Ramakrishna and read it to the people abroad. But he could read it well.

Mulla Nasrudin was the only literate person in his village, and you can imagine how literate he could be in that case. So everyone in the village looked to him to write their letters. One man went to him to get his letter written. Nasrudin said he would not write as his foot pained badly. The man said, "What has your foot got to do with writing a letter ? You write with your hand, don't you ?" Nasrudin said, "You do not know. When I write a letter, they call me to the other village (where it is to be sent) to read it also. I will write the letter, but who will read it ? My foot is in bad shape. As long as I cannot walk, I shall not do any letter writing."

So if people like Ramakrishna write a letter, they alone can read it, for they have forgotten your language. They have no knowledge of your language, and the language they speak is meaningless to you. We would call such people mad. So such people have to look for and choose a messenger from among us who can write in our language. Such a person is no more than a postman. Therefore, beware of Vivekananda. He has no experience of his own. What he says is another's experience It goes without saying that he is proficient in his art, he is an expert in his delivery. All the same, it is not his own experience.

Therefore, we find an overconfident strain in the talks of Vivekananda. He stresses his points more than is required, and this is to make up for the deficiency. He himself is aware of the fact that what he says is not out of his own experience. The wise one, however, always hesitates: he is afraid; he may not be able to put forth his experience as clearly as he feels it. He will contemplate a thousand ways in his mind before he speaks, and yet he will be afraid that what he says may not be quite what he wants to express. One who does not know goes ahead and says what he has to say. He feels no hesitation, for he knows exactly all that he has to say.

But this was very difficult for an Enlightened One like Buddha. He did not give answers to certain questions. He used to say, "There is difficulty in answering these questions." So people used to say, "There are better people than Buddha in our village who answer all our questions. They are wiser than Buddha. We ask them whether God is, and they reply either yes or no confidently. Buddha does not answer because he does not know." But for Buddha, it was very difficult to answer yes or no, so he hesitated and said, "Ask something else, not this." It was but natural for people to say that he did not know and that he should admit his ignorance. But this also Buddha could not say, for he knew. It is the fact that he speaks a different language from us that causes the difficulty.

Thus, it has happened time and again that many people like Ramakrishna left this world without giving their message. They could not ! It is a very rare combination for a person to know and also be able to convey. When this rare combination takes place, we call such a person a Teerthanker (a World Teacher of the Jains), an avatar, a prophet, etc. This does not restrict the number of Enlightened Ones only to those who have spoken. There have been many others, but they could not deliver their message.

Someone asked Buddha, "You have 10,000 *bhikkhus* (monks), and for the last forty years you have been teaching the people. How many have reached to your state ?" Buddha said, "Many, but we cannot make them out. They all look the same as before. The only difference is that I can speak and they cannot. If I too keep silent, you will not know me. You recognize only words; you cannot recognize pure knowledge. It is only a matter of coincidence that I know and can also speak about it."

So there was some difficulty for Vivekananda which he must rectify in his subsequent lives to come. This difficulty was inevitable. Therefore, Ramakrishna, out of sheer necessity, brought it upon him. He felt a loss, but his loss belonged to the world of dreams. But even then, why should one undergo loss even in a dream state ? If dream we must, then why not a good dream ?

There is a fable of Aesop: Once a cat was lying under a tree dreaming. A dog comes along and he too rests under the tree. The cat seemed to be dreaming a lovely dream, and the dog was curious to find out what it was all about. When she awoke, the dog asked her what she dreamt. The cat said, "Oh, it was a lovely dream. The sky was pouring mice." The dog looked down in disdain and said, "Fool ! Does it ever rain mice ? We also dream, and in our pleasant dreams we see bones pouring. And our scriptures say that whenever the gods are merciful it rains bones—not mice, as you say. If you must dream, dream of bones." For the dog, bones are everything. Why should he dream of mice ? But for the cat bones have no meaning, so the dog rebukes her. According to him, she is dreaming, which in itself is a useless occupation, and on top of that she is dreaming of mice, which is even more useless.

So I say to you if you must dream, why dream a bad dream ? And if you are to awaken, then make full use of your own ability, your own energy, your own resolve, and do not depend upon another person at all—not in the least bit. If help comes, it is a different matter. But do not expect any help, for the more you expect, the weaker your resolve will become. Stop thinking on those lines altogether. Expect no help and put in your full effort, accepting fully that you are all alone. Help will come your way from many directions, but that is a different matter altogether.

Therefore, all my stress is on your own willpower so that no other hindrance is created for you. And when you get something from someone, it will always be unasked for and unexpected by you. It should be like the wind that comes and goes.

This is why I said that Vivekananda suffered a loss, and as long as he lived he was acutely aware of it. His listeners sat up when he spoke; they even got a glimpse of what he said. But Vivekananda knew for himself that it was not happening to him. It would be a terrible thing for me to bring you the news of something savoury and have no knowledge of its taste myself, for me to bring it to you after having just once tasted it in a dream that then broke. And imagine if then I am told, "Now you will no more dream of it, but go and tell the others." So was it with Vivekananda. He had his own hardships, but he was a strong man; he was able to bear these hardships. This also is a part of compassion, but this does not mean that you too should bear such hardships.

Questioner : *Was Vivekananda's experience of Samadhi through Ramakrishna's contact authentic or non-authentic ?*

Bhagwan : You can call it "elementary", It would not be proper to call it authentic. It was elementary—absolutely elementary. It was a situation in which there is only a glimpse. This glimpse cannot be very deep or spiritual. This happening takes place at the borderline where the mind ends and the "Atman" (soul) begins. At its depths, it is only psychic; therefore, the glimpse was lost. But in Vivekananda's case it was not allowed to go deep, for Ramakrishna was afraid. He did not allow it to go too deep; otherwise this man would be of no use to him. He was so worried about his mission that it never occurred to him that his concept about the experience leaving a man useless for the world was not 100% certain.

Buddha spoke for forty years after attaining Samadhi; similar was the case with Jesus and Mahavir. They had no difficulty. But with Ramakrishna it was different, and his fear was justified. His own drawback was always in his mind. Therefore, he gave Vivekananda just a fleeting glimpse. It was authentic as far as it went, but it was elementary. It did not go deep enough; otherwise he would have found it difficult to come back.

Questioner : *Bhagwan, can there be an experience of partial Samadhi ?*

Bhagwan : Not partial, but elementary. There is a difference between the two. The experience of Samadhi cannot be partial, but there can be a mental glimpse of Samadhi. The experience is spiritual; the glimpse is mental. If I stand on the top of a mountain and see the sea, I will definitely see the sea, but from a distance. I will not have stood at the shore, I will not have touched or tasted of its waters, I will not have waded into it or bathed in it. If I am at once to climb down after having seen the sea from the mountain, would you call my experience a partial experience ? No ! And in spite of the fact that I did not touch even a drop of the ocean, you cannot call my experience inauthentic. I have seen the ocean from the top of a mountain even though I have not become one with it. So you can see the Atman from the topmost peak of your body.

The body too has its peaks—its peak experiences. If you have a deep and intense experience of the body, you can get a glimpse of the soul. If you are perfectly healthy and experience a feeling of well being, if the body is overflowing with good health, you can reach a height of the body from where you can get a glimpse of the Atman. Then also you will experience that you are not the body and that you are something else. You will not have known what the Atman is, but you will have reached the ultimate height of the body.

The mind too has its heights : for example, when you are deeply in love—not in sex, for sex is only the possibility of the body. But even in sex, if you reach the peak of sex experience you get a glimpse of the Atman. However, it will be a faraway glimpse. You will get it from the end that is the farthest away from the Atman. But if you have a deep experience of love, if you sit next to your loved one for a moment with not a word to break the silence, with only love moving between you two, without any transaction or expectation but only currents of love moving from one to the other, in that peak moment of love you will reach the height from where you will have a glimpse of the Atman. So lovers too get a glimpse of the soul.

An artist paints a picture: He is so engrossed in making it that for a moment he becomes God the Creator, for he experiences the same experience that God must have felt when he made the world. But this is the height of the mind. For a moment this man feels like the Creator, with his one glimpse of the soul. Many a time such a man commits the error of thinking that this experience is enough. This experience can be had from music, from poetry, from scenic beauty and other such things. But all these are far-off peaks. In Samadhi you must first immerse yourself completely; then Realization happens. So from the outside, you are able to peep into the Atman from any of these peaks. Vivekananda's experience was also at the level of the mind, for, as I said, another person can rouse you at the level of mind and you can be lifted up to a certain peak.

Look at it this way: I take a small child on my shoulders and he glances all around. Then I put him down. Now this small child could only see what he saw from the top of my shoulders, for as yet there is a long time to go for him to come up to my height. But now he can say that he has seen something. Normally, this is not possible, but it is possible to climb the shoulder of another and have a view. All this is the possibility of the mind, and hence it is not spiritual.

All the same, it is not inauthentic: it is elementary. The elementary experience can take place either in the body or the mind. And it is not partial: it is complete. It is an experience of the mind and not of the Atman, for in the experience of the Atman there is no coming back. There no one can keep back your key. Here no one can tell you here, "When I give back the key, only then it will happen." No one has a say there. If a person is to be given some special work, and if he is not allowed to proceed beyond the level of the mind as a result, there will be difficulty.

So Vivekananda's experience was an authentic experience, but its authenticity is psychic and not spiritual. This too, however, is not a small happening, for it does not happen to all. It requires a very powerful mind.

Questioner : *Could we say that Ramakrishna "exploited" Vivekananda ?*

Bhagwan : It could be said so, but it should not, for the word conveys an idea of condemnation behind it. He did not exploit him in the sense of trying to gain something selfish for himself. His idea was that through Vivekananda others will gain. He exploited him only in the sense that he made use of him. There is a great difference between exploitation and utilization. When I am grasping something or using something for the sake of my ego, it becomes "exploitation". But when I am doing something for the world, for the universe, for all, there is no question of exploitation.

Besides, where is the certainty that if Ramakrishna had not given him the experience Vivekananda would have got it all the same ? This point can only be settled by those who know. I feel that would have been the case, but we cannot show any proof in such matters. When Ramakrishna told Vivekananda that three days before his death he would get the key, it could only mean that, according to Ramakrishna, Vivekananda would reach Samadhi three days before his death as a result of his own efforts. Now as far as the return of the key is concerned, Ramakrishna was already dead, but the key was returned as promised.

This is possible, for you do not know your personality as much as another person who has gone deep within the Self. From his own depths, he can know your potential. He can even tell when you will reach if you walk at your own pace. For instance, you have started on a journey and there is a mountain in your path. Now I know the path and the steps of this mountain, how long it takes to cross it and what difficulties you will encounter. I see you climbing the mountain, and I can say that you will take, for example, three months to cross it. I can tell from the rate of your walking and the manner in which you are travelling that you will take that much time. If I were to pick you up on the way and give you a glimpse of the top, then leave you again where you were, promising you that within three months you will find your way, this cannot basically be looked upon as my making use of you. Everything within is so subtle and complex that you cannot know it outwardly.

Now, for instance, Nirmala (*a disciple in the audience*) went home yesterday and someone told her she will die at the age of 53. Now I have given her a guarantee that she will not die at 53. Now it is not I who will carry out the guarantee: it will fulfil itself on its own. But if she passes the age of 53, she will attribute it to me. Vivekananda would say that the key was to be returned three days before his death. But who was to return it ?

Questioner : *Could it be that Ramakrishna knew that Vivekananda had to go through a vain journey of sadhana in which he would encounter many doubts and disappointments, and so, out of compassion, he gave him a glimpse to keep up his hopes* ?

Bhagwan : Never think in terms of this language that "It could be. . .", for this has no end and there is no meaning to it. In this way you will go on thinking irrelevantly. It is enough to think in terms of what exactly is possible and no more, for otherwise these are meaningless paths that may lead you astray. There is also the possibility that by thinking in this manner you will lose sight of the facts as they occurred. Therefore, always see a fact as it is. And if you want to know a thing as it is, cut out all the "it-could-have-been's". If you do not know the exact facts, then know that you do not know, but do not try to cover your ignorance with wise assumptions of "it could be". This is how we cover up many of our short-comings. It is better to refrain from this.

[Text of a discourse given on July 4, 1970, evening, in Bombay, India].

11

KUNDALINI SADHANA : A JOURNEY TOWARD TOTAL FREEDOM

Questioner :

Bhagwan, in one of your previous discourses you said, a sudden and direct descent of grace can become a disaster sometimes. The person might harm himself or become schizophrenic or he may die. Thus, if grace is not always a blessing and not always beneficial, doubt naturally arises. Does grace not keep its own equilibrium ?

The mishap can also be due to the fact that the recipient was unfit. In that case, how can grace descend on an unqualified person ?

Bhagwan Shree Rajneesh :

God is not a person but an energy, a force, and the meaning of "force" is that whatsoever happens to each individual happens impartially. The tree on a river-bank receives its nutrition from the passing current; it will bear flowers and fruits and will grow tall and strong. But the tree that falls into the same current will be carried away broken with the swift tide. Now the river has nothing to do with either of these trees. It is neither interested in feeding the former nor in destroying the latter. The river merely flows. The river is a flowing energy: it is not a person. But we have always committed the error of looking upon God as a person. Therefore, all our thinking regarding God is as if He were a person.

We say He is very kind; we say He is merciful; we say He always blesses us. These are our own expectations and desires that we place upon Him. This "placing upon Him" can only be done to a person who can also be held responsible, but we cannot do this to a force. Whenever we take a force to be a person and deal with as though it were a person, we stand to lose, for then we lose ourselves in dreams. If we deal with energy as energy, the results will be entirely different.

For instance, the force of gravity: you are able to walk on the earth because of this force, but this force is not for your convenience. Even if you do not walk, the force of gravity continues to work. So do not be under the illusion that the force of gravity is because of you. It was there when you were not on the earth and it will be there even after you are no more. Also, if you walk in a wrong manner you might fall and break your leg. This will also be due to gravity, but for this you will not be able to sue anyone as there is no person to blame. Gravity is a current of energy. You will have to be careful how you deal with it, for it follows its own rules.

God's energy does not work out of consideration for anyone. In fact, it is not proper to say "God's energy": rather, we should say God is energy, and this energy has its own eternal law, and this eternal law is religion. "Religion" means the laws of behaviour of the energy that is God. If you behave discriminatingly, knowingly and in conformity with this energy, it becomes grace for you—not on its own, but because of you. If you do the opposite, if you go against the rules of the energy, and it becomes non-grace-yielding toward you. God does not withhold grace. Rather, YOU make it appear as if He does.

So it will be an error to look upon God as a person. God is not a person, but a force. Therefore, prayer and *pooja* (Hindu worship ritual) hold no meaning. It is meaningless to expect anything of God. Whatsoever needs to be done in order to make this force yield its grace unto you is to be done to your own self. Hence, "sadhana" (spiritual practice) has meaning, prayer does not. Meditation has meaning, worship does not. Understand the difference.

In prayer, you are doing something with God: you beg, you insist, you expect. In meditation, you do something with your own self. In worship you are saying something to God; in sadhana you are saying something to yourself. The meaning of sadhana is to see that you do not make yourself unfavourable to religion—to see that when the tide flows you are not swept away by the current. Instead, you are on the bank where the waters of the river strengthen your roots rather than washing them away. The moment we look upon God as a force, all our rules of religion change. Therefore, I say that if the happening is accidental it can prove detrimental.

Questioner : *Can an unfit person be the recipient of grace ?*

Bhagwan : Grace never descends on a person unqualified for it. It always descends on the person who is prepared for it. But sometimes an unfit person suddenly develops the necessary qualifications, and he himself is unaware of this. The happening always takes place under the right conditions, just as light is visible only to those with eyes and not to the blind. If a blind man is treated so that he can see, he will still have to put on dark glasses for a month or two before he can see the light directly. If an unreceptive person suddenly becomes receptive, there is bound to be a mishap. The sun cannot be blamed in the case of the blind man. He has to develop the strength of his eyes to bear the rays of the light, or else there is a danger that he can become totally blind. The first blindness was curable, but now it will be difficult to cure his second blindness.

Understand this well: the experience comes only to those who are deserving. But there is always the possibility of an undeserving person suddenly developing the necessary qualifications due to circumstances of which he himself is not aware. Then there is always a fear of disaster, for the power descends suddenly and you are not in a condition to bear it.

Acquisition of something should not bring on any mishap, but we usually find that if a man suddenly acquires, say wealth, it brings misfortune in its wake. Happiness that comes suddenly to a person brings a lot of unhappiness, for we need the power to bear it. We can bear happiness only if it comes upon us gradually. If bliss comes gradually the situation is similar: only then are we prepared for it. This preparedness, the capacity to bear, depends on so many factors. The nerves in the brain, one's physical fitness, one's mental capacity: all have their limitations, and the energy we are talking about is limitless. It is like the ocean falling into the drop : if the drop is not capable of holding the ocean, it will merely die; it will be destroyed and it will attain nothing.

So really speaking, there is double action in sadhana. We have to get ourselves on the path of this power and become in tune with it. But before that we have to develop our ability to contain it. These two tasks belong to sadhana. On one hand we have to open the door and improve our eyesight, and on the other we have to wait even after the sight is improved in order for the eye to be able to bear the brightness of light. Otherwise too much light proves darker than darkness. This is a one-sided transaction; the light has nothing to do with it. The responsibility is entirely ours, and we cannot blame anyone for it.

Man's journey is spread over a number of births, and he does many things during each birth. Many a time it happens that he gives up the body just as he is about to attain Samadhi. Then he loses all possibility of recalling his past lives; he dies knowing nothing about them. If you happened to have practised sadhana and you have reached the 99th degree, you have no knowledge of it, for you have forgotten all your past lives and all the events that took place within them. But your state of 99 degrees remains with you. Now there is another man sitting next to you who is still at the first degree of sadhana, but he too is unaware of his condition. Now both of you sit for the same meditation, but you are two different persons altogether. If the other man's progress advances one degree, nothing substantial is going to happen. At the most he will have advanced two degrees. But if your graph rises by one degree, the happening will take place. This will be sudden for you, for you have no idea that you are at the 99th degree. And so heaven can drop into you all of a sudden, and proper arrangements should be made for this.

When I say "mishap" I am only referring to a happening for which we are not prepared. "Mishap" does not necessarily mean a bad or painful event. It means only the occurrence of that event for which we are not yet ready. Now if a man wins a lottery of 1,00,000 rupees, it is not a bad happening. But he can die. A hundred thousand rupees ! It can stop the beating of his heart. So "mishap" means the occurrence of an event for which we are not prepared.

The opposite may also take place. If a man is prepared for

his death and it comes, it is not necessary that his death is a bad event. If a man such as Socrates is prepared to meet death and welcomes it with open arms, then for such a person death becomes Samadhi. He accepts death with such love and joy that he will see that Reality which never dies. We approach death with so much distress that we become unconscious before death. We do not experience death consciously. This is why, even though we have died many times, we are unaware of the process of death. Once you know what death is, then the concept of death will leave you. Then you will say, "I ? How can 'I' die ?" Then the event of death will take place, and you will be standing aside watching it. But this must happen with full consciousness.

So death can be a good fortune for one person and grace can be a misfortune to another. Therefore, sadhana is twofold. We have to call, to invoke, to search and to proceed, and at the same time we have to prepare ourselves for the event so that when light reaches our door we are not blinded by it. If you remember what I have told you there won't be any difficulty. If you take God to be a person, you will find yourself in great difficulty; if you take Him to be power, there won't be any difficulty.

This concept of God as a person has caused a great deal of difficulty. The mind desires Him to be a person so that we can transfer all responsibility onto Him. And having made Him responsible, we proceed to place the burden of every small thing onto Him. If a man finds a job, he thanks God; if he loses his job, he becomes angry with God. If a man gets a blister, he suspects it as the doing of God; if it heals, he thanks God. We never consider how we are employing God; we do not even think how egocentric is this attitude in which we assume that God should worry even about our blisters. If we drop a rupee on the road and happen to find it, we say, "By God's grace I found it." We expect God to keep our accounts to the last rupee. This thought is satisfying, for then we can stand at the center of the world. Then our dealings with God are akin to that of a servant before a master. We expect Him to stand guard at our door and take care of our possessions to the last paisa (pence).

The advantage of considering God as a person is that responsibility can easily be placed upon Him. But the sadhak takes responsibility upon himself. In fact, to be a sadhak means to hold no one but oneself responsible for everything. If there is sorrow in my life I am responsible, and if there is happiness in my life I am responsible. If I am tranquil it is I who am responsible; if I am restless it is my own making. There is no one but myself who is responsible for whatever state I am in. If I fall and break my leg it is my own fault, and I cannot blame gravity. If this is the attitude of the mind, then you will have understood rightly. Then the meaning of a "mishap" will be different. Therefore, I say that grace is beneficial and is a blessing to a person who is well prepared for it. In fact, there is a time for everything : there is a special moment for each happening, and to miss this moment is a great tragedy.

Questioner : *In one of your talks you said that the effect of Shaktipat diminishes gradually. Thus, must one maintain regular contact with the medium ? Does this not mean dependency upon some person in the form of a guru ?*

Bhagwan : This dependency can happen. If someone is eager to be a guru and if someone is eager to acquire a guru, this state of dependency will come about. Therefore, do not make the mistake of becoming a disciple or a guru. But if there is no question of guru or disciple, there is no fear of dependency. Then the person from whom you take help becomes only your own form that has travelled ahead of you. Then who is the guru and who the disciple ?

I often tell the story that Buddha told of one of his previous lives. He said, "I was an ignorant person in my previous life. A wise person had attained Enlightenment, so I went to see him and I bent down to touch his feet in salutation. But no sooner had I lifted myself up, when I found to my consternation that the old man had bent to touch my feet. 'What is this you have done !' I cried out. 'That I should touch your feet is right and proper, but it is not fitting that you should touch mine.' "

The old man smiled (at Buddha) and said, "If you touch my feet and if I do not touch yours it would be a grave error, for I am nothing but your own form two steps ahead of you. And when I bow at your feet, I remind you that you did well to touch mine. But do not be under the misconception that you and I are two. Also, do not make the mistake of thinking that I am wise and you are ignorant. It is a matter of time. A few hours more and you too will be Enlightened—for example, just as when my right foot comes forward the left remains behind to follow. Actually, the left foot remains behind in order that the right may go forward."

The relationship of guru and disciple is harmful. However, a "non-related" relationship between a guru and the disciple is very useful. "Non-related" means there are not two; relationship is where there are two. Now we can understand if the disciple feels the guru to be a separate entity from him, for the disciple is ignorant. But if the guru also feels the same, that is too much. Then it means that the blind is leading the blind—and the blind man who is leading is more dangerous, for the second blind man has full trust in him.

There is no spiritual meaning to a guru-disciple relationship. Actually, all relationships are the relationships of power. They are all relations of power politics. Someone is a father, someone a son. If this were a relationship of love, it would be a different matter. Then the father would not be conscious of his being the father, nor the son of being the son. Then the son would be the subsequent form of the father and the father would be the preceding form of the son. The natural relationship is only this.

We sow a seed and a tree grows. Then this tree gives rise to thousands of seeds. What is the relationship between these seeds and the first seed ? One came first, the others followed later. It is the journey of the same seed that fell to the ground and disintegrated in the soil. The father is the first link and the son the second, in the same chain. But then there is a chain, not individual persons. Then if the son touches his father's feet, he is showing his respect for the previous link. He is showing his reverence to that which is going out, for without him he could not have come into the world. He has issued forth from him. And if the father is bringing up his son, feeding him and clothing him, he is not taking pains for someone else : it is his own form he is nurturing. If we say that the father becomes a youth once more in his son, we would not be wrong. Then the matter is not one of relationship. It is a different matter. Where there are no relationships, there is love.

Generally, we find the relationship between father and son to be a political relationship. The father is strong and the son is weak, so the father dominates the son. He tries to make him feel, "You are nothing; I am everything." Little does he realize that a time will come when the son will be the strong one. Then he will override him in the same way.

These relationships between the master and the disciple, the wife and the husband, are perversions. Otherwise, why should there be any relationship between a husband and a wife ? Two individuals must feel they are one, and, therefore, they are together. But no, this is not so. The husband suppresses the wife in his own way; the wife suppresses the husband in her own way. Both are playing their own power games upon each other. The same is the case with the guru and the disciple. The guru oppresses the disciple, and the latter waits for him to die so that he may become the guru. If the guru would refuse to die, there would be plotting and scheming against him. So it is difficult to find a guru whose disciples do not rebel against him. The chief disciple is bound to be the enemy of the guru. So one must be careful in choosing the chief disciple, for the pressure of power is always met with rebellion. Self-knowledge has nothing to do with it.

I can understand a father pressuring the son. It is a case of two ignorant people, and they could be forgiven. It is not good, but it can be condoned. The husband oppressing the wife can likewise be excused for the same reason, even though this is not right. But when the guru suppresses his disciple, it becomes difficult. This place at least should be free of any claims that "I know and you do not".

What is the relationship between a guru and a disciple ? One is a claimant: he says "I know; you do not know. You are ignorant; I am wise. Therefore, the ignorant must bow to the wise." But we do not know what sort of a wise man is he who says, "You must bow in obeisance." He is the most ignorant person. He knows a few inherited formulas, and he has learned them by heart. There is nothing more to him than this.

Perhaps you have not heard this story: There was a cat that became all-knowing. She became famous among cats—so much so, that she came to be looked upon as a Teerthanker (a World Teacher). And the reason for her gaining such wide esteem was that she had found a way of sneaking into a library. She knew everything about this library. By "everything" I mean the means of entrance and exit from the library, which set of books was the most comfortable to snuggle against, which books gave warmth in the winter and which were cool in summer, etc. So the word went around among the cats that if anybody wanted any knowledge about the library, this all-knowing cat could provide the answer.

Naturally, there was no doubt about such a one who knew everything about the library being all-wise. This cat even had followers. But the fact remained that she knew nothing. All she knew about books was whether she could sit behind them comfortably, which books had cloth bindings and which ones did not. More than this she did not know. She had not the least inkling of what was inside the books. And how could a cat know what is inside a book?

There are such all-knowing cats among men too who know how to shield themselves with books. You attack them, and they will at once take refuse in the Ramayana and try to strangle you with its verses. Or, they will say, "So says the Gita." Now who is to fight with the Gita? If I were to say, "This is what 'I' say," you can debate with me. But if I bring the Gita in, I am safe. I take refuge behind the Gita. The Gita gives warmth in the cold; it gives me a vocation and becomes a protective shield against enemies. It even becomes an ornament, and the Gita can be played with, but a person who does this only knows as much about the Gita as the cat in the library; he knows no more than she does.

It may be possible that by long association the cat might come to know what is inside the books, but these book-knowing gurus will not know at all. The more they learn the book by heart, the less need there will be for them to know. They will then be under the illusion that they know all there is to know.

Whenever a man claims the authority of knowing, know that it is only ignorance that has become garrulous, for assertion is ignorance. But when a man hesitates even to mention that he knows, then know that he has begun to receive a glimpse, a ray of knowledge. Such a man, however, cannot become a guru. He cannot dream of becoming one, for with gurudom comes the authority of knowledge. The meaning of "guru" is one who knows and who is ready to impart his knowledge. So claim and the authority kill the sense of quest and inquiry in others. Authority cannot exist without suppression, for he who wields authority is always afraid of your finding out the truth. Then what would become of his power? So he will stop you from finding out. He will gather followers and disciples around him, and within the disciples also there will be a hierarchy of chief disciples and lesser disciples. This is again a political web, and it has nothing to do with Self-Knowledge.

When I say that a happening like Shaktipat (transmission of the life force)—which is the descent of the power of the Divine, the electricity, the vital energy—takes place easily in the presence of some special person, I do not mean that you should stop at this person; nor do I say that you should be dependent upon him or make him into a guru. I also do not say you should stop your search. On the contrary, whenever this event takes place through a medium, you will feel that if this experience through an indirect source could bring so much joy, how much more blissful it would be to experience a direct descent of the vital power. After all, when a thing comes through someone it does lose some of its freshness; it does become a little stale. I go to a garden and I am filled with the fragrance of the flowers, and then you arrive and you feel the fragrance of the flowers through me: you will find that it will also be mingled with my body odour, and it will also have become faint by then.

So when I say that initially Shaktipat is very useful, what I mean is that first you should get the news that there is a garden and there are flowers so that you may be encouraged to set out on the journey. But if you acquire a guru you will stagnate, so do not stop at milestones. The milestones tell us much more than the ones we call gurus. They tell us exactly how many miles more are left for the destination. No guru can give such precise information. And yet we do not worship the stones or sit near them. If we did, we would prove ourselves to be lesser than stones, for the stone is there only to indicate how much more of the journey is left. It is not there to stop you; that has no meaning.

Now if a stone could speak, it too would call out, "Where are you going? I have given you the necessary information. You have travelled ten miles and you have twenty more to go. Now you know, so you have no need to go further. Be my disciple; follow me." The stone cannot speak; therefore, it cannot become a guru. Man speaks; therefore, he becomes a guru. He says, "I have shown you so much; be grateful to me. You must show your gratitude, your indebtedness to me." Remember, he who demands gratitude has nothing to give you. He is like a milestone. A milestone does not know anything about the journey. There is only one intimation engraved on it which it gives to all who pass by.

Likewise, if gratitude is extracted from you, beware. You have not to stop at an individual. You have to travel toward the "non-individual"—the Formless, toward where there is no form, no boundary. However, a glimpse is possible through a person, for ultimately the individual also belongs to Him (the Divine). Just as I said that the ocean can be known through the well, so can the Infinite be known through the individual. If you can have a glimpse you shall see, but you have not to depend on anybody or be enslaved by anything. All relationships are binding, whether they be that of husband and wife, father and son, or guru and disciple. Where there is relationship there is slavery.

So the seeker of the Self has not to form relationships. If he keeps the relationship of husband and wife, there is no harm, for this relationship is irrelevant. But the irony lies in the fact that he breaks husband-wife, father-son relationships to form a guru-disciple relationship. This is very dangerous. The idea of a "spiritual relationship" has no meaning. All relationships belong to the mundane world. Relationship in itself is worldly. If we say that relationship alone is the mudane existence, it would not be wrong.

Alone, unassociated, YOU ARE! This is not an egotistical statement, for others too are alone and unassociated. There are some two steps ahead of you, and if you locate their foot-falls you can know the direction of your journey that far. There are some two steps behind you and there are some others travelling along with you. Thus, an infinite number of souls are travelling on the path to the Infinite. In this journey you are all fellow travellers. The difference is only of the distance to and fro. Take advantage of those ahead of you, but do not turn it into servility. Servility begins with relationships.

Therefore, keep away from dependence and relationships, and especially from "spiritual" relationships—always. Worldly relations are not half as dangerous, for worldliness means relationship. Get the message wherever you can, and I do not say not to be grateful for the message. This should not create any complication in your mind. What I say is that if gratitude is demanded it is wrong, but if you are not grateful it is equally wrong. One should thank the milestone also for giving us information, whether it hears or not.

When we say that the guru should not ask or expect gratitude, it deludes the listener and feeds his ego. He thinks it is absolutely correct. Where is the need to thank ? There we make a mistake, for then we grasp the statement from the opposite side. That you should not be grateful is not at all what I mean. What I mean is that the guru should not demand gratitude. So if you are not grateful, it will be equally wrong on your part. You must be grateful, but then this gratitude will not bind—for that which is never asked for never binds. If I thank you without your asking it is not binding. But if you demand thanks, whether I thank you or not it will cause binding.

Take the hint from wherever you get it : it will disappear time and again. It cannot be permanent, for it comes from another. Only that will be lasting which is yours. So you will have to undergo Shaktipat time and again. If you are afraid of losing your freedom, seek your own experience. It is no use being afraid of bondage—for if I bind myself to you it is bondage, and if I run away from you with the fear of being bound, then also I am linked and, hence, bound to you.

Therefore, take what you get silently, be grateful, and move on. And if you feel that something had come but became lost again, then seek the source within from which it can never be lost. There is no way of losing then, for our own treasure is infinite. That which is bestowed by another stands the chance of becoming lost. Do not be a beggar who keeps asking from others. That which you receive from another should start you on your own search. This is only possible when you do not strike any relationships. Offer your thanks and move on.

Questioner : *You said that God is a power which has no interest in man's existence and which does not have anything to do with man. In the Kathopanishad there is a sutra which means, "God meets only him whom He likes." What is the basis and reasons for His preference ?*

Bhagwan : The fact is that I did not say that God is not interested in you: if He was not, you would not have been. Nor did I say He was indifferent toward you: He cannot be, for you are not apart from Him. You are an extension of Him. What I said was that He does not have any SPECIAL interest in you. There is a difference between these statements.

The power that is God has no special interest in you in the sense that it will not violate its laws for your sake. If you hit your head with a stone you are bound to bleed; nature will take no SPECIAL interest in you. But nature has its own interest in you : that is why you bleed when the stone hits. It has taken a full part in your doing. When you drown in the river, then too nature is playing its part—that of drowning you. But there is no special interest in the sense that it will save you when its law was to drown you. The law is that if you fall from the roof your head will break. Nature has no special interest that it shouldn't.

Those who believe God to be a person have fabricated many stories of Divine favours—for instance, that Prahlad was neither burnt by fire nor hurt when he was thrown down the mountain. These stories are our wishful thinking: we wish that it should be so. We wish that God should have a special interest in us, that we should be the center of His attention. I do not say that God is not interested in human beings. I say that His interest is in accordance with His law. The workings of energy are always in accordance with His law. Man's interest can be special, man can be partial. But energy is always impartial. Impartiality is its only interest. Therefore, it will do what is within its law and never what falls outside of it. There are no miracles on the part of God.

Now about the Kathopanishad sutra : Its meaning is very different. It says, "He meets only those of His choice, with whom He is happy, whom He likes." Naturally, you will say this means that He has a special interest in some people. This is not so. In truth, there is great difficulty in explaining such things, for when a truth is to be explained it has to be dealt with from its manifold aspects. Those who have attained God have invariably said, "Who are we and of what value are our efforts ? We are no one and our worth is not even equal to a grain of sand; yet we attained Him. And if we meditated awhile, of what great value was that compared to the priceless treasure we attained ? There is no comparison between our efforts and our gain." So those who have attained Samadhi have maintained that it was not the result of their effort. "It was His grace, it was His wish to bless us. Otherwise, could we ever have found Him ?" they always ask.

This is the statement of an egoless person who realizes the magnificence and magnitude of his attainment. It is something beyond the scope of human attainment. However, if this should become the way of thinking of those who have not attained, it would be very dangerous. When this comes from those who have attained, this statement is fitting, and it carries a distinct mark of refinement of feeling. Such persons maintain, "Who are we that we should have attained Him ? What was our strength, our ability ? What was our right ? What claim did we have on Him ? Yet, in His utter compassion, He allowed us to stand before Him." For those who have attained, this statement is proper.

What they mean is that they do not consider their attainment to be the outcome of their labour. It is not the achievement of the ego; the ego only made the effort. What they say is correct, but reading the Kathopanishad or, for that matter, any scripture, is perplexing, for this is the statement of those who know and it is being read by those who do not. Then those who do not know take it according to their understanding and say, "Well and good. If He meets only him whom He wishes to meet, according to His own will, why should we bother ? Why should we do anything ?" Then the declaration of the egoless person becomes a shield for our lethargy. There is a vast difference between the two—like between the sky and the earth. This sense of emptiness, of nothingness, becomes the saving grace of the one who is merely indolent. Then he says, "Well, He meets only him whom He wants to meet and He doesn't meet those whom He does not want to."

There is a statement of St. Augustine which runs something like this : "Those whom He wished He made good; those whom He wished He made bad." This seems a very dangerous statement. If this is so—that He makes some bad and He makes some good as it suits His fancy—the matter ends there, and He apparently must be an insane God. When a layman reads this, it can prove dangerous for him. But what St. Augustine means is very different. He tells the good man, "Do not be conceited that you are good, for those whom He wished He made good." And to the bad man he says, "Do not be distressed, do not worry. Those whom He wished He made evil."

He is pulling out the pride from the good man's ego and he is pulling out the sting of the bad man's remorse. This statement comes from one who knows, but the bad man hears it and he says, "If that is so, I have no hand in it—for those whom He wants to be evil are evil." The good man's journey also slackens, for he says, "What is there to do ? Those whom he chooses to make good he makes good and those whom He chooses not to, He does not." Then life becomes stagnant, and this is what scriptures have done to the whole world. The scriptures are the words of those who are Enlightened. However, those who know do not find the need to refer to scriptures. Those who do not know read the scriptures; then the difference in understanding is poles apart.

The meaning we give to their words is our very own and not the actual meaning. To my mind, there should be two kinds of scriptures—one to be read by those with knowledge and one to be read by those without knowledge. Those scriptures that are written for the wise should be hidden from the ignorant man—for he is bound to deduce his own meanings, and then everything becomes twisted and contorted. In this way, all our knowledge has become contorted. You understand what I am saying ?

Questioner : *You have said the transmission of vital energy takes place through the medium of a desireless, egoless medium and that he who says "I can transfer energy" is for sure a phoney. But I know many such people who practise Shaktipat, and the kundalini processes take place as written in the scriptures. Are these false processes ? If so, how and why ?*

Bhagwan : This is also a matter that needs explaining. There is nothing in this world which cannot be reproduced artificially. Everything has its false side, its false aspect. And it is always the case that the counterfeit coin is brighter in appearance than the genuine one. It has to be, for it is its polish that will carry it : it has no authenticness to go by. A true coin works even if it is not bright; a false coin makes loud claims to hide its falseness. And because of its worthlessness, it is easily obtainable.

So all spiritual achievements have their counterparts, and there is no experience without a counterfeit counterpart. If there is a real kundalini, there is an imitation kundalini too. If there are genuine chakras (centers), there are false chakras also. If there are true methods of yoga, there are fake methods as well. The difference between the two is that the genuine experiences occur on the spiritual plane, whereas the false occur on the psychic plane.

Now, for example, if a person is able to enter deep into his mind, he will begin to experience many things. He can experience such fragrances as he has never known before; he can hear music that is out of this world; he can see colours that are not seen on earth. All these things can be brought by hypnosis in no time and without difficulty. Colours can be produced; melodies can be produced; tastes and fragrances can be produced. And for all this there is no need to go through any sadhana. All you need is to become unconscious; then whatever is suggested from without takes place within. This is like a false coin.

Whatever happenings take place in meditation take place in hypnosis also, but that is not spiritual. It is just put on and is like a dream. Now if you love a woman in your waking state you can love her in your dreams also, and it is not necessarily the case that the woman in the dream is less beautiful than the real one. Actually, she is usually more beautiful. Now if the man does not wake up and keeps on dreaming, he will never know whether the dream girl is real or illusory. How will he know ? Only when the dream is broken will he know that it was a dream.

So there are methods by which these dream conditions can be produced within you. A dream of kundalini can be created and so also of the chakras. Their experiences can also be brought about in the dream state. You will love to revel in these dreams, for they are so enjoyable. And they are such dreams that it is difficult to call them dreams, for they happen while you are awake, while you are walking. They are daydreams. They can be indulged in and you can pass all your life in them, but in the end you will find you have reached nowhere : you have only been through one long dream. There are means and methods for inducing these dreams. Another person can induce them in you and you will never be able to distinguish any difference, for you have no idea of the real experience.

If a man has always dealt with false coins, how will he know that his coins are false ? To know the false, the genuine must be known. So only the moment the kundalini unfolds itself can one find how far apart the two experiences are. It (the real) is a different experience altogether.

Remember, the kundalini of the scriptures is false, and there are reasons for this. Now I will tell you a secret of the scriptures. The sages and seers have purposely left some basic errors in each scripture for the purpose of judging the progress and authenticity of the pupil. Now, for instance, I may tell you from outside this house that there are five rooms within, but I know there are six. One day you might come and say, "I have seen the house from inside and there are five rooms only, as you say." Then I will know that you have seen some other place—an illusory one—and not the house I mentioned. There are six rooms there. So in this way a room is left out, and this gives the information whether you have really experienced or not: whether your experience is genuine or not. In the scriptures something is always left out, and it is very necessary to do so.

So if your experiences tally with the books, know that it is the book that is projected. The moment your experiences come in a different manner, a manner in which they might coincide with the scriptures in some places and not in others, then know that you are on the right track—that things are happening authentically and that you are not merely treading through the experiences of the scriptures in your imagination.

So when the kundalini awakens properly you will know where in the scriptures things have been devised to judge the authenticity of the sandhak's experiences. But before this you cannot know. Every scripture necessarily had to drop some information; otherwise it would be difficult to judge the sadhak's progress.

There was a teacher of mine. He was a professor in the university. Whatever book I mentioned, he would say he has read it. One day I mentioned a fictitious book and author. I said," Have you read the book of so-and-so ? It is a wonderful book. "He said, "Yes, I have." "Now all your previous claims of having read books is nullified," I told him. "There is no such book and no such author." He was surprised. "What do you mean there is no such book ?" he said. "No !" I said. "There was no other way to judge." Those who know will at once find you out. If your experience is exactly as laid down in the scriptures you will be caught, for there are gaps left in the scriptures: something wrong has been added, something correct has been left out, and all this was absolutely necessary—for otherwise it would be difficult to tell what is happening to whom.

Happenings similar to those in the scriptures can be brought about by following them. Anything can be brought about, for the capability of the human mind is such. And before one enters into the Atman (the self), the mind deceives him in a thousand ways. And if he too wants to deceive himself, then it is very easy So I say the question is not so much one of measures and methods or of claims and rules. The question is very different. There are many ways of discovering the authenticity of your experience.

A man drinks water in the daytime and his thirst is quenched. He drinks water in a dream, but his thirst is not quenched. In the morning he finds his throat parched and his lips dry. Thirst is quenched not in dream: it is the actual water that quenches the thirst. So whether the water was real or unreal can be found out from your thirst—whether it is quenched or not. So those whom you are talking about who claim to have awakened the kundalini are still searching. They claim they have experienced many things, and yet their search continues. They maintain they have found water, and yet they have no inkling of the lake.

It was only the day before yesterday that a friend came and said that he had reached the no-mind state, and he had come to ask me for a method of meditation. What is to be said to such a person ? His mind is tranquil, he has "reached the thoughtless state", and yet he wants to know how to meditate. What does this mean ? One man says his kundalini has awakened, but his mind is restless. Another says that the kundalini has awakened, but he is still tortured by sex. There are intermediate devices to discover the authenticity of your experience.

If the experience is real, the search ends. Then even if God comes and offers tranquillity or bliss, the person will refuse politely and ask Him to keep it for Himself; he no longer needs it. So in order to find out one must observe the personality of the sadhak, for that gives a clue to the inner happening.

Now one man says he goes into Samadhi (Cosmic Consciousness). He buries himself underground for six days and comes out alive. But if you leave money in the house, this man will steal. If he finds the opportunity he will indulge in drinking, and if you did not know about his claim of Samadhi you will not find anything of value in him. There is no fragrance, no lustre, no dignity in his personality. He appears very ordinary. He does not go into Samadhi: he has learned the trick of Samadhi. He has mastered the trick of staying underground for six days by pranayama (yogic breathing practices); he has learned how to control his breath so that within the given area of his resting place he can use the minimum amount of oxygen. Thus he can last for six days.

He is almost in the same state as the Siberian bear that hybernates beneath the snow for six months: he is not in Samadhi by any means. After the rains, the frogs lie underground for eight months: they are not in Samadhi. This man has learned the same; nothing more. Now it is quite likely that if you bury a man who has attained Samadhi underground for six days, he is likely to die, for Samadhi has nothing to do with being buried underground. If Mahavir or Buddha were made to lie underground in this way, there is little possibility of their coming out alive. But this man will come out alive, for this has nothing to do with Samadhi. Samadhi is a different matter altogether. But this man will come out hale and hearty, and Mahavir could not manage to do so. Then this man will be looked upon as the genuine Teerthanker (World Teacher) and not Mahavir.

So these false psychic coins have their own false claims, and methods have been evolved for "proving" them. Thus, a separate world has been created around them which has nothing to do with the Reality. Persons involved with them have left the genuine paths from where the real transformation comes. Staying six days beneath the ground has nothing to do with Self-Realization. You must mark the behaviour of such a man—how tranquil is his mind, what has happened in regard to his bliss. If he loses a coin he will not sleep at night, but he can stay comfortably underground for six days. All this has to be considered and the real meaning behind it has to be found.

So those who claim Shaktipat can do so, but it is not Shaktipat. It is intrinsically a kind of hypnosis. Some magnetic forces are brought into play deep within the psyche, and these persons have learned the art of mastering them. It is also not necessary for them to know the full science of this, nor is it necessary for them to be conscious of the falsity of their claim that they can do authentic Shaktipat. It is all such a subtle enmeshment.

Now you see a magician by the roadside (*common in India*). He spreads a cloth and bids a boy to lie on it. He keeps a charm on his chest. Then he asks the boy, "What is the number of the note in so-and-so's pocket?" The boy will tell the number. "What is the time on the watch of the person standing there?" The boy will tell the exact time. "What is the name of this man?" The boy will tell you the name. Everyone watching is convinced of the magic of the charm. Then he removes the charm from the boy's chest and repeats the questions. The boy lies silent: he cannot answer. Now this magician makes a brisk sale of the charm—fifty paisa or so each. You take the charm home. You can put it on your chest for the rest of your life, but nothing is going to happen. Now it is not that the boy has been taught by the magician to speak when the charm is on his chest and to be silent when it is removed, nor is there any special quality in the charm itself. The trick is more deep rooted, and you will be shocked when you know it.

This trick is called "post-hypnotic suggestion". A person is made unconscious, and in this state of unconsciousness he is told to have a good look at the charm. He is also told that as soon as this charm is placed on his chest, he must become unconscious. Then, in this state of unconsciousness, he can be made to read the number on the note or tell the time in the watch; there is no doubt about this. As soon as the boy is made to lie on the sheet and the charm is placed on his chest, he goes into a hypnotic trance. This makes it possible for him to answer the magician's questions.

The boy does not know what is happening to him, nor does the magician know what is happening inside of him. This man has learned a trick. He knows that when a man is made unconscious and shown a thing, and if he is then told, "Whenever this thing is placed on you, become unconscious," he will then become unconscious whenever it is placed upon him. This is all the man knows. What the internal mechanism, the internal dynamics are, both of them do not know, for if they were to know they would not be performing tricks by the roadside. To know the dynamics is a great thing, even though it is only psychic. Even Freud or Jung or any other great psychologist of the world did not know the dynamics fully. This magician, however, has stumbled on a trick which he utilizes to earn a living.

To press a button, it is not necessary for you to know what electricity is and how it is produced or what its mechanism is. You press a button: the current comes. So this is a trick. Any man can do this, and so also can any man learn the trick of the charm. He learns the necessary rudiments and succeeds in fooling you. Now this charm that you take home is absolutely impotent. It is useful only for the one who has been previously worked upon. You place it on your chest and nothing happens.

Then you feel that YOU are wrong somewhere, for you have seen the charm working.

So many false and pseudo conditions can be created. They are false and pseudo not in the sense that they are nothing, but in the sense that they are not spiritual: they are merely psychic happenings. Everything has its psychic parallel. Therefore, these conditions can be created by one who is false. Also, the one who makes claims can bring these about, but he who does not claim anything can bring them about better and more strongly.

A non-claimer means one who does not claim that he is performing Shaktipat; he does not claim to produce results in you. If I am the "doer", you will be tied to me when the happening takes place. But all this is immaterial to the authentic person, for he is like a Void. Even when you merely approach him something begins to happen, though he himself is not aware of it.

There is an ancient Roman story: once upon a time, there was a great saint in Rome. The fragrance of his actions and the rays of his knowledge reached up to the "devas" (gods) in heaven. They came to him and said, "Ask a boon. We are prepared to do anything you wish". The saint replied, "What was to happen, happened. There is nothing more to desire. Please do not embarrass me with your offer. It would be the height of bad manners if I do not ask, and the fact is that there is nothing left for me to ask." The devas were impressed even more by his words, for his fragrance became stronger with the fact that he was beyond desire. "You must ask something," the devas insisted. "We shall not leave without conferring a boon upon you."

The saint was in a fix. "What shall I ask for? I cannot think of anything," he told the devas. "You give whatever you like. I will take it." "We shall give you a power that will bring the dead back to life and the sick back to health," they told him. "This is good," he said, "but what about me? I shall be in a dilemma, for if I begin to feel that 'I' am healing the sick, 'I' am bringing the dead back to life, I shall die. Do not kill me like this. Do something that I may not know of these miracles."

So the devas agreed. They said, "Wherever your shadow falls it will bring back the dead to life." "That is good," said the saint. Now do me a last favour. Please grant that my neck becomes stiff so that I cannot look back to see the working of my shadow." The boon was granted. The saint's neck became stiff. He went about from town to town. Wherever his shadow fell withered flowers began to bloom, but by then he would have gone past it; his neck did not allow him to look back. He never came to know. When he died, he asked the devas whether their boon was productive or not, for he never came to know about it. I feel this story to be a very lovely story.

When the happening takes place, it takes place just like this. It happens with the shadow, and the neck is stiff. The medium must be a complete Void or else, the neck may turn. If there is even a trace of the ego, there will be the urge to look back and see whether the happening has come about or not. If it has, then the feeling of "I have done it" comes in. It will be difficult to avoid this feeling.

So wherever the Void occurs, Shaktipat happens with great ease around it, just as the sun comes out and the flowers open, or as the river flows and the trees are nourished. The river never claims it has watered so many trees, and so many trees are blooming because of it. The river does not even know all this. By the time the flowers bloom, the waters that nourished the trees will have reached the ocean. Where is there time for it to wait and see? There is no way of turning the head. When the happening takes place amidst such conditions it has spiritual value. But where there is the ego, the doer, what someone says that "I am the doer," then it is a psychic phenomenon and it is nothing more than hypnosis.

Questioner : *Is there not a possibility of hypnosis and illusion in your new method of meditation? With many participants nothing is happening: Are they not on the right track? There are others in whom there are a lot of reactions : Are they on the right path? Could some of these be just putting on an act ?*

Bhagwan : There are two or three things which have to be properly understood. Hypnosis is a science and it can be easily used for deception. However, hypnosis can also be used to help you. Besides, science is always a two-edged sword. Atomic energy can produce wheat in the fields; it can also wipe out the whole world at a stroke. The electric current that moves the fans in your house can also kill you, but you will not hold electricity responsible for this. If an egoist makes use of hypnosis, he will do so to suppress, destroy and delude the other. But the opposite of this can also be brought about.

Hypnosis is a neutral energy; it is a science. It can be used to break the dreams that go on inside of you, and your deep-rooted illusions can also be eradicated by it.

So the method I use is hypnosis in its initial step, but with this is joined a fundamental element which will protect you and which will keep you from being hypnotized—and that is the witness state. This is the only difference between hypnosis and meditation, but this is a very great difference. When you are hypnotized, you are made to become unconscious. Only then can you be worked upon. However, I say that in meditation hypnosis is useful, but only when you become the observer. Then you are awake and alert, and you know what is happening all the time. Then nothing can be done against your will; you are always present. In hypnosis, the same directions can be used to make you unconscious and the same directions can be used to break your unconsciousness.

So the initial steps of what I call meditation are all hypnotic, and they are bound to be—because any journey toward the Atman starts only from the mind. This is because you live in the mind; that is the place where you are. So the journey starts from there. But this journey can be of two kinds; either it can take you on a circular route within the mind where you will keep going around and around like an ox at an oil mill who is never able to come out, or it can take you to the edge of the mind from where you can jump out of the mind. In both the cases, the initial steps will be within your mind.

So the initial form of hypnosis is the same as that of meditation, but the final form is different and so is the goal. And in both the processes, there is only basic element that is different. Hypnosis immediately requires unconsciousness, sleep. Therefore, all its directions start with sleep, drowsiness, and then the rest follows. In meditation, the direction starts with wakefulness, and later the stress is on the "witness state". The witness in you is awake, so no outside agency can affect you. And also, remember that what is happening within you is well within your knowledge.

Now the difference between those to whom things are happening and those to whom they are not happening is only this: that the latter's resolve is weak—a little less than what it should be. These persons are fearful, frightened. They are afraid that the happening will take place. How strange man is! These persons come to practise meditation; they have come for meditation to take place. But at the same time they are afraid that it may take place. And when they see things happening to others, they wonder if it is all put on. This is a defense mechanism. They say, "We are not so weak as to become affected. These are weak people." This way they satisfy their egos, little knowing that this happening cannot happen to a weak person. They also do not know that this happens only to those who are strong of mind and not to the weak-minded.

An idiot cannot be hypnotized, nor can he be taken into meditation. Both are impossible. Similarly, an insane person cannot be worked upon. The sharper the intellect, the quicker is the response in hypnosis. The duller the intellect, the longer it will take to be hypnotized. So those of weak resolve and of weak minds will say in their defense, "It seems that these people are merely acting. They are weak-minded and are influenced from the outside."

Recently, in Amritsar, a person came to meet me. He is an old learned person—a retired doctor. He came on the third day of the experiment. He said, "I have come to ask your forgiveness for a sinful thought that came to my mind. "What happened ?" I asked him. He replied, "The first day when I came for meditation, I felt you had organized your own people to dress up and put on this show, and that there were some weak-minded people who were following them blindly. Then I said, 'Let me see for a second time.' The second day I saw two or three of my friends who are also doctors taking full part in the experiment. I went to their houses to inquire. I told them, 'It cannot be that YOU had been prepared for this. Was it really happening to you or were you pretending ?' They replied, 'Where is the need to make anything up? Until yesterday we too thought the same, but today it has happened to us."

Then on the third day, when it happened to him, he came to apologize. He said, "Today it happened to ME, and now my illusions are all gone. Otherwise I would not have believed it. I also suspected my doctor friends. You can never say these days what a person will do. I know them, but who can tell? They might have come under your hypnotic spell. But today it has happened to me. When I reached home, my younger brother, who is also a doctor, asked, 'How was the show?' I told him 'Forgive me, brother. I can call it a show no longer. And I am not angry with you, for I too thought the same way'." This man again asked my pardon for his "evil" thoughts.

These are our defense measures. Those who find nothing happening to them will find ways and means of protecting their egos. But there is only a distance of an inch between the one to whom it happens and the one to whom it does not happen. There is only the lack of a little more resolve. If one gathers courage, makes a strong resolve and drops all inhibitions, the happening will take place.

Now today a lady came and told me that her friend called her up and told her that "In these experiments of Rajneeshji, some people become naked, some do something else, and so how can ladies of decent families take part in them? And then what will happen to these girls of good repute?" Now some people have the illusion of belonging to 'decent families'. Are there indecent families as well? So the girls from lesser families will gain and the decent ones will lag behind. These are all defense measures. A decent girl will think of her decent family and will hold herself back at home. She will wonder what sort of a person she is. If she is troubled by another person becoming naked, then she is NOT of a decent family. What has she to do with him?

So our mind creates strange devices. It says, "This is all a muddle and a mess, and it cannot happen to me. I am not a weak person: I am strong of mind." If this were so, if you had been strong of mind and intellect, the happening would have taken place. The sign of an intelligent person is that he makes no decisions before trying out a thing. He will not even say that the other is false. He will say, "Who am I to comment on him?" To brand another as false is deplorable. Who are you to decide that someone else is wrong? Such wrong decisions have caused a lot of difficulty.

Did people believe that Jesus had attained anything? If they did, why would they have hung him on the cross? They said, "This man is dangerous: he says anything." People would not have stoned Mahavir if they had not thought that he was causing confusion by becoming naked. On what authority can we decide what is happening inwardly to another person? So the qualification of an intelligent person is not to express an opinion until he has tried a thing out for himself. If nothing is happening to me, I must find out whether I am carrying out the instructions of the experiment fully. If I am not doing it fully, how will anything happen?

In Porbandar, I said on the last day, "If a person has not exerted himself up to the 100th degree, even if he has come up to the 99th he will fail. One friend came and said, "I was going along leisurely thinking that it will happen after some time. But today I realized that it will never happen this way. So I exerted myself fully today, and it has happened."

If you must have this attitude of doing the experiment slowly, why do it at all? In this way we want to sail in two boats at a time, but he who puts his feet in different boats finds himself in great difficulty. One boat is best. Then even if it goes to hell, at least it is in one boat. One foot in heaven, one in hell—that cannot be! In truth, the mind is doubtful where it should go. It is afraid and undecided whether it will be happy in heaven or in hell. But in this way neither heaven is attained nor hell, and there is every possibility of falling into the river. Such is the working of the mind—all the time. We will make an effort to go and then stop ourselves too. This is harmful.

Go through the experiment fully, and do not form any opinions of others. He who goes through the full experiment will surely attains. Now I talk scientifically and not religiously. It is a scientific fact that with a full effort the result is bound to take place. There is no other way, for God is power and this power is impartial. Here, no prayers or worship, or the fact of having been born into a high-caste family or on the soil of India, will work. This is purely a scientific matter.

If a person goes through this faithfully, even God cannot stop him from attaining. And even if there is no God, it does not matter. Concentrate your thoughts on completing the experiment. And always make your decisions according to your inner experiences, not from without; otherwise you can go wrong.

[Text of a discourse given on July 5, 1970, evening, in Bombay, India].

12

KUNDALINI SADHANA : FROM BONDAGE TO LIBERATION

Questioner :

In yesterday's talk, you said that false experiences of kundalini sadhana (practice) can be projected which you believe to be not spiritual but psychic. In your initial talk, however, you had said that kundalini is only psychic. This means, according to you, that there are two states of the kundalini—psychic and spiritual. Kindly explain this.

Bhagwan Shree Rajneesh:

In order for you to understand this, the structure of the various subtle bodies must be fully elaborated upon. The individual can be divided into seven bodies. The first body is the physical body which we all know. The second is the etheric body and the third which is beyond this second is the astral body. The fourth which is beyond this is the mental or psychic body and the fifth which is beyond this is the spiritual body. The sixth is beyond the fifth and it is called the Cosmic body. Then the seventh and the last is the "Nirvana Sharir" or the Nirvanic body. A little more information about these seven bodies will make it possible for you to understand the kundalini fully.

In the first seven years of life, the "sthul sharir"—alone is formed—the physical body. The other bodies are in seed form. They have a potential for development, but they lie dormant in the beginning of life. Therefore, the first seven years are years of limitation. There is no development of intellect, emotion or desire during these years. Only the physical body develops within this period. Some people do not develop beyond seven years. They stagnate at this stage and are no more than animals. Animals develop only in the physical body ; the other bodies remain untouched within them. In the next seven years, that is from seven years to fourteen years, the "bhawa sharir"—the etheric body (the second body)—develops. These seven years are years of emotional development of the individual. This is why sexual maturity, which is the most intense form of emotion is reached at the age of fourteen. Now some people stagnate at this stage. Such people develop only the first two bodies.

In the third seven-year period, between the ages of fourteen and twenty-one, the "akash sharir"—the astral body—develops. In the second body, emotion is developed; in the third body, reasoning, thinking and intellect are developed. This is why no court of law holds a child responsible for his actions up to the age of seven, for the child has only the physical body. We treat the child the same way as we would treat an animal; we cannot hold him responsible. Even if a child commits a crime, it is assumed that he has committed it under the guidance of someone—that the real criminal is someone else.

After the development of the second body, a person reaches adulthood. But this is the adulthood of sex. Nature's work is complete with this development, and this is why nature gives its full cooperation up to this stage. But at this stage man is not man in the full sense of the word. The third body, where, reason, intellect and the thinking power develop, is an outcome of civilization and culture. This is why the right of suffrage is granted to a person when he is twenty-one years of age. Though this is prevalent all over the world, some countries are debating whether to allow an eighteen-year old the right to vote. This is natural, for as man is becoming more and more evolved the usual span of seven years for the development of each body is becoming less and less.

All over the world, girls reach puberty at the age of thirteen to fourteen years. Since the last thirty years, the age for this is becoming less and less. Even a girl of eleven reaches puberty. The lowering of the age of franchise to eighteen is an indication that man now completes the work of twenty-one years in eighteen. Normally, however, twenty-one years are required for the development of the third body, and the majority of people do not develop further than this. Their growth stops short with the development of the third body, and there is no further development for the rest of their lives.

What I call "the psyche" is the fourth body—the "manas sharir." This body has its own wonderful experiences. Now a person whose intellect is not developed may not be able to take interest in or enjoy mathematics, for instance. Mathematics has its own charm, and only an Einstein can be absorbed in it as a musician is in music or a painter is in colours. For Einstein, mathematics was not work but play, but the intellect must reach this peak of development in order to turn mathematics into play.

With each body that develops, infinite possibilities open before us. One whose etheric body does not develop, who stagnates after the first seven years of development, does not have any interest in life beyond eating and drinking. So the cultures of those civilizations where the majority of people have developed only up to the first body revolve entirely around their taste buds. The civilization where the majority of people have stagnated at the second body will be sex centered. Their personalities, their literature, their music, their films and books, their poetry and paintings, even their houses and vehicles, will all be sex centered : all these things will be completely filled with sex.

In the civilization in which the third body develops fully, people will be intellectual and imaginative. Whenever the development of the third body becomes very important in a society or in a nation, many intellectual revolutions take place. In Bihar, the majority of people were of this calibre at the time of Buddha and Mahavir. This is why eight persons of the stature of Buddha and Mahavir were born in the small province of Bihar. Besides, there were thousands of others at the time who were endowed with genius. Such was the condition of Greece at the time of Socrates and Plato; such also was the condition of China at the time of Lao Tse and Confucius. What is yet more wonderful to note is the fact that all these luminaries existed within a period of 500 years. Within those 500 years, the develompent of the third body in man reached its peak, whereas generally man halts at the third body. The majority of people do not develop after twenty-one years.

There are unusual experiences of the fourth body. Hypnotism telepathy, clairvoyance, are all the potential of the fourth body. Persons can have contact with one another without hindrances from time or place; they can read the thoughts of another without asking or project thoughts into another. Without any external help, one can instill a seed of thought into another. A person can travel outside of his body; he can do astral projection and know himself apart from the physical body.

There are great possibilities in the fourth body, but we do not normally develop this body as there are many hazards as well as a great deal of deception. As things begin to get more and more subtle, the possibilities of deception increases. Now it is difficult to find out whether a man has actually stepped out of his body or not. He can dream that he stepped out of his body and he can actually do so too, and in both the cases there is no other witness than himself. So there is every possibility of deception.

The world that starts from the fourth body is subjective, whereas the world before that is objective. If I have a rupee in my hand, I can see it, you can see it, fifty others can also see it. This is a common reality in which we can all take part, and it can be investigated whether the rupee is or is not. But in the realm of your thoughts you cannot be a partner, nor can I be a partner in the realm of your thoughts. From here the personal world begins with all its hazards, for none of our external rules of validity can be used here. So the real world of deception starts from the fourth body. All the deceptions of the preceding three can be apprehended.

The greatest danger is that it is not necessarily the case that the deceiver is aware of the fact that he is deceiving. He can deceive unknowingly—himself as well as others. Things are so subtle, so rare, and personal on this plane, that one has no means to test the validity of his experiences. So he cannot tell whether he is imagining things or whether they are really happening to him.

So we have always tried to save humanity from this fourth body, and those who made use of this body were always condemned and slandered. Hundreds of women were branded as witches and burnt in Europe, for they used the fourth body. Hundreds of those who practised Tantra were killed in India because of the fourth body. They knew some secrets that seemed dangerous to human beings. They knew what was taking place in your mind; they knew where things were placed in your house without ever having stepped into it. So the realm of the fourth body was looked upon as "black art" all over the world, as one never knew what might happen. We have always tried our level best to stop progress from going any further than the third body, as the fourth has always seemed very dangerous.

There are hazards, but together with these there are wondrous gains. Thus, instead of stopping, research was necessary. Then we could have found ways of testing the validity of our experiences. Now there are scientific instruments, and also man's power of understanding has increased. So ways can be found just as in the case of many other new discoveries that have been made in science.

Now it is not known whether animals dream or not. How could this be ascertained unless an animal speaks ? We know that we dream because we get up in the morning and say that we have dreamt. After great perseverance and effort, now the way has been found. One man has worked for years on monkeys in order to find out about this, and the measures he took for this experiment are worth noting. He started by showing a film to the monkeys. As soon as the film started, the monkey being experimented upon experienced an electric shock. A button was provided on the monkey's chair, and he was taught to press this button whenever he felt the shock. So every day he was made to sit on the chair, and when the film began he felt the shock. Then he pressed the button to turn it off.

This went on for some days; then he was made to sleep in this chair. Now when he began to dream he would begin feeling uncomfortable, for to him the film on the screen and the film in his dream were one and the same. He at once pressed the button. Time and again he would press the button, and this proved that he was dreaming about the film. Thus, man is now able to penetrate into the inner dream-world of dumb animals.

Sadhaks too have found ways of testing the experiences of the fourth body from outside, and now it can be proved whether what happens is valid or not. Now the experiences of the kundalini on the fourth body can be psychic too, but that does not make them false. There are authentic psychic stages and false psychic stages. When I say that kundalini it could be only a mental experience, it does not necessarily mean that it is a false experience. Mental experiences can be false as well as authentic.

You see a dream at night. Now this is a fact, for dreams are a fact. But on waking in the morning, you might recollect some dream that you did not actually dream; yet you can insist that that is what you dreamt. Then this is false. A man might get up in the morning and say he never dreams. Many people believe they do not dream. They do dream: all night long they dream, and this has been proved scientifically. But in the morning they assert they never dreamt. So what they say is absolutely false, though they are not aware of it. Really speaking, they do not remember the dreams. Quite the opposite also takes place: you remember dreams you never dreamt. This will also be false.

Dreams are not false; they have their own reality. But dreams can be real as well as unreal. Real dreams are those which have been actually dreamt. The trouble also is that you cannot narrate your dream precisely upon awakening. Therefore, in the olden days any man who could narrate his dream clearly and precisely was held in high esteem. It is very, very difficult to report a dream correctly. The sequence of the dream is one thing when you dream it, and just the opposite when you remember it. It is like a film. When we see a film, the story unwinds from the beginning of the film. Similarly, the reel of the dream drama winds in one direction in sleep and begins to unwind in the opposite direction in the waking state. Thus, we remember the last part of the dream first and go backwards in recollection. Therefore, what we dreamt first becomes last in recollection.

This would be just like someone who tries to read a book from the wrong end; the topsyturvy words would cause just such a chaos. So to remember a dream and give a true representation of it is a matter of great art. Generally, when we recall a dream we recollect happenings we never dreamt of. We drop a good portion of the actual dream and alter most of the rest.

Dreams are a happening of the fourth body, and the fourth body has a great potential. Whatever *siddhis* (psychic powers) are mentioned in the yogas are attained in this body. Yoga has incessantly warned the sadhak not to go into them. The greatest hazard here is of going astray upon the wrong path. Even if you go into a psychic state, it has no value in the spiritual field.

So when I said that the kundalini is psychic, what I meant was that it is actually a happpening of the fourth body. This is why physiologists cannot discover the kundalini within the human body. So it is but natural that they deny the existence of kundalini and the chakras (centers) and call them imaginary. They constitute an arrangement of the fourth body. The fourth body exists, but it is very subtle; it cannot come within our grasp. Only the physical body can be grasped. Yet there are points between the first body and the fourth body which interlink and which are synonymous.

If we were to place seven sheets of paper one on top of the other, and if we were to prick a hole through them with a paper pin so that all the papers are pierced, then even if the hole disappears from the first sheet it will still carry a mark that corresponds to the holes in the rest of the sheets. Then although the first paper does not have the hole, it has the point which will correspond directly with the pinholes on the other sheets when it is placed upon them. So chakras, kundalini, etc. do not belong to the first body as such, but there are corresponding points in the first body. Therefore, a physiologists is not wrong if he denies them. The chakras and the kundalini are in other bodies, but points corresponding to them can be found on the physical body.

So kundalini is the happening of the fourth body, and it is psychic. And when I say that this psychic happening is of two kinds—one true and one false — then you will understand what I mean. It will be false when it is a product of your imagination, for imagination is also a condition of the fourth body. Animals do not have the power of imagination, so they have very little memory of the past and no idea of future. Therefore, animals are free from anxiety as anxiety is always of the future. Animals see many deaths taking place, but they never imagine that they can die also. Therefore, they have no fear of death. Among men also, there are many who are not bothered by the fear of death. Such a man always associates death with others and not with himself. The reason is that the power of imagination in the fourth body has not developed fully enough to see into the future.

This means that imagination can also be true or false. True imagination means that we are capable of seeing further ahead, that we can visualize that which has not yet come to pass. But to imagine that something will happen that cannot be, which does not exist, is false imagination. Therefore, when imagination is used in its right perspective it becomes science, for science, primarily, is only imagination.

Since thousands of years, man has dreamed of flying in the air. The men who had dreamed in this way must have been very imaginative. If man had never dreamt about flying, it would have been impossible for the Wright Brothers to make the first plane. They made man's desire to fly something concrete. This desire took some time to take shape, then experiments were carried out, and finally man succeeded in flying in the air.

Also, for thousands of years, man has wanted to reach the moon. First it was only in his imagination, slowly it gained ground, and now it has been fulfilled. Now these imaginations were authentic: that is, they were not on of a false path. These imaginations were on the path of a reality which could be discovered at a later date. So a scientist also imagines, and so does a person who is schizophrenic.

Now if I say that science is imagination and schizophrenia is also imagination, do not think they are one and the same thing. A madman imagines things which do not exist and which have no relationship with the physical world. The scientist also imagines: he imagines things which are directly related with the physical world. And if it does not seem so at first, there is a complete possibility of their being so in the future.

Among the possibilities of the fourth body, there is always a chance of going wrong. Then the false world begins. This is why it is best if we do not harbour any expectations before entering this body. This fourth body is the psychic body. Now, for instance, if I want to go down to the ground floor of this house, I shall have to look for a lift or a staircase in order to do so. But if I want to go down in my thoughts, there is no need for a lift or a staircase. I can sit right here and go down.

The hazard of imagination and thoughts is that one has to do nothing except to imagine or think, and so anyone can do it. Moreover, if anyone enters this realm with preconceived ideas and expectations, then he immediately goes down only into these, for then the mind will be only too willing to cooperate. It will say, "You want to awaken the kundalini ? All right ! It is rising; it has risen." Then you will begin to imagine the kundalini rising, and the mind will encourage you in this false feeling until ultimately you will feel that it is fully awakened and that the chakras are fully activated. But there is a way of testing the validity of it, and that is with the opening of each chakra there will be a distinct change in your personality. This change you cannot imagine or preconceive, for this change takes place in the world of matter.

Now, for instance, when the kundalini awakens you cannot take intoxicants; it is impossible. The mental body gets influenced by alcohol very quickly, for it is very delicate. This is why (and you will be surprised to know this) when a woman consumes alcohol she becomes more dangerous than a man who does so. This is because her mental body is still more delicate, and it gets affected so quickly that things get out of her control. This is why women have protected themselves from this hazard by certain regulations in society. This is one place where women did not seek equality with men, though unfortunately, of late, she is trying to. The day she asserts her equality in this matter and tries to outdo men in it, she will cause such harm to herself as has never been caused by any action by men.

In the fourth body, the awakening of the kundalini cannot be proven by your telling about the experience, for, as I said before, you can falsely imagine the awakening and experiencing of the kundalini also. It can only be judged by your physical traits: whether any sizable transformation has taken place in your personality. No sooner does the "*shakti*" (power) awaken when there will be immediate signs of change in you. This is why I always say that behaviour is the criterion and not the medium. It is a criterion of what has happened within. With each attempt, some things inevitably begin to happen. When the energy awakens, it becomes impossible for the sadhak to take any intoxicants. If he does indulge in drugs and alcohol, then know that his experiences are all imaginary, for it is absolutely impossible.

Now after the awakening of the kundalini, the tendency to war and violence disappears completely. Not only does the sadhak not commit violence, but he has no feeling of violence within himself. The urge to commit violence, the urge to harm others, can only exist when the vital energy is dormant. The moment it awakens, the other ceases to be the other, and so you cannot wish to harm him. Then you will not have to repress violence within yourself, for then you cannot be violent.

If you find that you have to repress the feeling of violence, then know that the kundalini has not awakened. If after the eyes open you still feel your way about with a stick, then know that the eyes cannot see yet, no matter how much you claim otherwise—for you have not as yet given up your stick. Whether an outsider can find out whether you can see or not is dependent upon your actions. Your stick, your stumblings and your unstable walk prove that the eyes have not yet opened.

So there will be a radical change in your behaviour with the awakening, and all the religious vows like those of the '*mahavrata*' (non-violence, non-stealing, non-possession, celibacy and full awareness) will become natural and easy for you. Then know that your experience is authentic. It is psychic, however, but authentic all the same. Now you can proceed further. You can proceed ahead if your path is authentic, but not otherwise. You cannot stay for ever in the fourth body, for it is not the goal. There are yet other bodies that have to be crossed.

We find, as I said, that very few are able to develop the fourth body. That is why there are miracle performers in the world today. If the fourth body in everyone were developed, miracles would vanish from the earth at once. If there were a society of people whose development had stagnated after the fourteenth year of age, then the one who had developed a little further, who could add or subtract, would be considered to be one who was performing miracles.

A thousand years ago, when a person declared the date of the eclipse of the sun, it was considered a miracle that only the very wise could perform. Today we know that even a machine can give us this information. It is a matter of calculation and does not require an astronomer or a prophet or a very learned person. A computer can give the information not of a single eclipse, but of millions of eclipses. It can even forecast the day when the sun will get cold, for these are all calculations. The machine can calculate from the data provided that the rate of the energy the sun emits per day, divided by the aggregate energy of the sun, gives the number of years the sun will last.

But all this does not look like a miracle to us now, for now we are all developed up to the third body. A thousand years ago, it was a great miracle if a man prophesied that next year, in this month, on this night, there would be an eclipse of the moon. He would be considered superhuman. The "miracles" that take place nowadays—the magic charms, the ash dropping from picture frames—are all ordinary happenings of the fourth body. But since we do not know, it is a miracle for us.

It is just as if you are standing under a tree and I am sitting on the tree, and we two are talking. Now I see a cart coming from afar and I tell you that in an hour's time a cart will come and halt under the tree. You will say : "Are you a prophet ? You talk in riddles. There is no cart anywhere around. I do not believe what you say." But in an hour's time the cart rolls up to the tree, and then of necessity you have to touch my feet and say, "Gurudev, my salutations. You are a prophet." The difference was only this, that I was sitting on a little higher level than you—on the tree—from where the cart became visible an hour before it did for you. I was not talking of the future. I was talking very much in the present. But there is a distance of one hour between your present and my present because I am at a higher level. For you, it will become the present after one hour, but for me it is present now.

The deeper a man stands within his inner self, the greater a miracle he becomes for those who are still on the surface layers. Then all his doings will become miraculous for us, for we have no way to gauge these happenings as we do not know the laws of the fourth body. This is how magic and miracles take place: they are a slight development of the fourth body. So if we want miracles to end in this world, it will not happen by preaching to the masses. Just as we have given man the education of the third body and made him understand languages and mathematics, we must now give him training for the fourth body. Each man has to be qualified accordingly, for only then will miracles cease. Otherwise, someone or the other will always take advantage of this. The fourth body develops until the 28th year—that is, for seven years more. But very few people are able to develop it.

The "Atma sharir"—the fifth body (which is called the spiritual body)—is of great value. If development in life continues in the proper manner, then by the age of 35 this body should be fully developed. But this is a far cry, for even the fourth body is hardly developed in but a few people. This is why the soul and such things are only a topic of discussion for us. There is no content behind the word. When we say "Atman" (Soul), it is merely a word; there is nothing behind it. When we say "wall", there is not only the word but also the substance behind the word; we know what "wall" means. But there is no meaning behind the word "Atman", for we have no knowledge, no experience, of the Atman. This is our fifth body, and only if the kundalini awakens in the fourth body is entrance possible in the fifth; otherwise we cannot enter. We are not aware of the fourth body, so the fifth also remains unknown.

Very few people have discovered the fifth body; they are those whom we call "spiritualists". These people take this to be the journey's end and declare, "To attain the Atman is to attain all." But the journey is not yet over. However, these people who stop at the fifth body deny God. They say. "There is no Brahman; there is no Paramatman (Supreme Self)," just as he who stagnates on the first body would deny the existence of the Atman. Just as the materialist says, "The body is everything; when the body dies, everything dies," so does the spiritualist declare, "There is nothing beyond the Atman: the Atman is everything; it is the highest state of Being." But this is only the fifth body.

The sixth body is the "Brahmasharir"—the Cosmic body. When a person evolves beyond his Atman, when he is willing to lose it, he enters the sixth body. If mankind develops scientifically, the natural development on the sixth body would ensue at the age of forty-two and that of the "Nirvana sharir"—the seventh body at the age of forty-nine. The seventh body is the Nirvanic body which is "no-body"—which is a state of bodilessness, an incorporeal state. This is the ultimate state where only the Void remains—not even the Brahman (the Cosmic Reality), but only the Emptiness.

Therefore, when anyone asked Buddha, "What happens there? he replied, "The flame dies out." "Then what happens?" he would be asked again. "When the flame is lost, you do not ask, 'Where has it gone? Where is the flame now?' It is lost, and that is all." The word "Nirvana" implies "the extinction of the flame." Therefore, Buddha said, "Nirvana takes place."

The knowledge of bliss remains until the fifth body, for its culmination is the ultimate liberation. So liberation is the experience of the fifth body. Heaven and hell pertain to the fourth body, and he who stagnates here will experience them. For those who stop at the first, second or third body, life between birth and death becomes everything; there is no life beyond death for them. If a person goes beyond into the fourth body, after this life he experiences heaven and hell where there are infinite possibilities of happiness and misery.

If he reaches up to the fifth body there is the door of liberation, and if he reaches up to the sixth there is the possibility of knowing the Brahman—and that is even beyond bliss. Then there is no question of liberation or no liberation: he becomes one with that which is. The potential of "*Aham Brahmasmi*" (I am the Brahman) is of this plane. But there is yet one step more, which is the last jump—where there is no "*Aham*" (I) and no "Brahman" (God), where "I" and "thou" are totally nonexistent, where there is simply nothing, where there is total and absolute Void. That is Nirvana.

These are the seven bodies which are developed within a

period of forty-nine years. This is why the midpoint of fifty years was known as the point of revolution. For the first twenty-five years, there was one system of life. Within this period efforts were made to develop the necessary "sharirs" (bodies); then one's education was supposed to be complete. Then one was supposed to search for his fifth body throughout the remainder of his life, and in the remaining twenty-five years he was expected to attain the seventh body. Therefore, the age of fifty was looked upon as a crucial year. At this time a man became a "*wanaprasth*" (one who has retired into spiritual life), which only meant that he should now turn his gaze toward the forest—that he should now turn eyes away from people, societies and crowds.

The age of seventy-five was yet another point of revolution when he was to become initiated into Sannyas. To turn toward the forest does not only mean to remove oneself from crowds and people, but also from one's own self. One had to turn himself away from his own self. In the forest, the "I" will necessarily be with him though he has renounced all else, but at the age of 75 this "I" too has to be renounced.

However, the condition was that in one's life as a householder one had to pass through and develop all the seven bodies so that the rest of the journey would become easy and joyful. If this is not done it is very difficult, for with every age limit a particular state of development is connected. If a child remains an invalid for the first seven years of his life, he will always be ailing throughout life from something or the other. At the most, we can see to it that he does not remain ill—but healthy he never will be, for his basic foundation for health that should have been formed in the first seven years has been shaken. That which should have become strong and firm was disturbed, and that was the time for its development.

It is just like laying the foundations for a house : if the foundations are weak, it would be difficult—nay, impossible—to repair it once the roof is reached. At the foundation stage only could it have been well laid. So in the first seven years, if proper conditions are available for the first body, the body develops properly. Now if the second body and the emotions do not develop fully over the next seven years, a number of sex perversions result. Then it is very difficult to remedy these. So the period of development for a particular body is most crucial.

On each step of life, each body has its predetermined period of development. There may be a slight difference here and there, but that is besides the point. If a child does not develop sexually within fourteen years of his life, his whole life becomes a long ordeal. If the intellect does not develop by the time he is twenty-one, there is very little chance of its developing at a later period. But so far we are in agreement: We take care of the first body, then we take care to send the child to school to develop his intellect also. But we forget that the rest of the bodies also have their apportioned time, which if lost, puts us in great difficulties.

A man takes fifty years to develop the body he should have developed in twenty-one years. It is obvious that he does not have as much strength at fifty as he had at twenty-one, so he has to put in a lot of effort. Then what would have been easier to accomplish at the age twenty-one becomes long and arduous.

There is yet another difficulty which he encounters: at the age of twenty-one he was right at the door, but he missed it. Now, over the following thirty years, he had been to so many places that he has lost sight of the right opening. His wandering now makes it impossible for him to locate the place where he stood at twenty-one and which then needed only a slight push to open.

Therefore, a well-organized situation is required for children until they reach the age of twenty-five. It should be so well planned that it takes them to the fourth body. After the fourth body the rest is easy. The foundation will then be well laid ; now only the fruits remain to blossom. The tree is formed up to the fourth body ; then fruits begin to appear from the fifth which culminate in the seventh. We may have to make a little allowance here and there, but we should be very mindful of the foundations.

In this respect a few more things should be kept in mind : There is a difference between man and woman throughout the first four bodies. For instance, if the individual is a man, his physical body is a male body. But his second body—the vital body which is behind the physical body—is female, because no negative or positive pole can exist by itself. A male body and a female body, in the terms of electricity, are positive and negative bodies.

The woman's physical body is negative; therefore, she is never aggressive in the matter of sex. She can bear the violence of man in this respect, but cannot be violent herself. She can do nothing to a man without his consent. Man's first body is positive—aggressive. He can, therefore, do something aggressive to a woman without her consent; he has an aggressive first body. But by "negative" is not meant "zero" or "absent". In terms of electricity, negative means "reservoir". In the woman's body, energy lies "in reserve"; much energy lies in reserve. But it is not active : it is inactive.

This is why a woman does not create anything. She does not compose poetry, nor does she create a great painting, nor does she carry out any scientific research. This is because it is necessary to be aggressive for research or for some work of creation. She can only wait; that is why she can only produce children.

Man has a positive body, but wherever there is a positive body there must be a negative body behind it, or else it cannot last. Both are present together; then the circle is complete. So the second body of a man is female, whereas the second body of a female is male. This is why (and this is an interesting fact), man looks and is, as far as his physical body goes, very strong. But behind this outward might stands a weak female body. This is why he manages to show his strength only for a few moments at a time. In the long run he loses at the hands of the female, for the body behind her weak female body is positive.

This is why a woman's power of resistance, her capacity to endure, is greater than a man's. If a man and a woman suffer from the same malady, the woman can endure it longer, whereas the man cannot. Women produce children. If men had to produce children, they would realize the ordeal that has to be passed through. Then perhaps there would be no need for family planning, for man cannot bear so much pain for so long a time. For a moment or two he can writhe in anger, throw a stone perhaps, but he cannot bear a child in his abdomen for nine months, nor bring him up patiently for years afterwards. If it cries all night long, he might choke it. He will not be able to bear the disturbance. He has extraordinary strength, but behind him is a frail, delicate body. Because of this he cannot bear pain or discomfort.

This is why women rarely suffer illness. Their life span is more than that of men. Therefore, we keep a difference of five years between a boy and a girl at the time of marriage, or else the world would be filled with widows. If the boy is twenty, we choose a girl of fifteen or sixteen for him. Man's life span is four or five years less, so this difference equalizes things and both synchronize each other.

A hundred and sixteen males are born as against every hundred females. The difference in number at time of birth is sixteen, but later on the number becomes equal. Sixteen males die by the time they reach the age of fourteen, and so the number becomes almost equal. More boys die early than girls. This is because the latter have a great power of resistance that comes to them through the second male body.

Now the third body of the male—that is the subtle body—will again be masculine, and the fourth or the psychic body will again be female. The opposite takes place in the female. This division of male and female exists only up to the fourth body ; the fifth body is beyond sex. Therefore, as soon as the Atman is attained, there is no male and no female—but not until then.

There is another thing that comes to mind in this connection: Since every male has a female body within him and every female has a male body within her, if by coincidence a woman gets a husband who is identical with the male body within her, or if a man marries a woman who is identical with the female body within him, then only is a marriage successful; otherwise not.

This is why 99% of every hundred marriages are failures : because the intrinsic rule of success is not known yet. As long as we are unable to ascertain the right alliance between the respective electrical bodies of two persons, marriages are bound to remain a failure no matter what steps we take in other directions. Successful marriages can only be possible if absolutely clear scientific arrangements concerning these various bodies are made. A boy or a girl who has reached up to the point of the awakening of the kundalini finds it very easy to choose the right partner in life. With the full knowledge of all his bodies within, one can make the right choice outwardly. Pricr to this it is very difficult.

Therefore, those who knew insisted that the child should be made to develop his first four bodies in the first twenty-five years by maintaining "brahmacharya" (celibacy), and then only could he marry—for, whom should he marry? With whom does he want to spend the rest of his life? Whom is he seeking? What man does a woman seek? She seeks the man WITHIN HER. If by coincidence the right connections are made, then both the man and woman are satisfied. Otherwise, dissatisfaction remains and a thousand perversions result from this. The man then goes to a prostitute or seeks the woman next door. His distress grows day by day, and this misery is bound to increase with the development of man's intellect.

If a person's development stops at fourteen, he will not suffer this agony, for all suffering starts from the development of the third body—the mind (the mental body). So there are two ways: either in the first twenty-five years, during the period of brahmacharya, we should develop the child up to the fourth body, or else encourage child marriages. Child marriage means marriage before the development of intellect so that the person stagnates at sex. Then there is no trouble as the relationship is entirely on the animal plane. The relationship of a child marriage is purely a sexual relationship; there is no possibility of love in it.

Now in places like America, where education has made great strides and where the third body has developed completely, marriages break. They are bound to, for the third body rebels at a wrong partnership. So divorce results, for it is not possible to drag such marriages along.

The correct form of education is that which develops the first four bodies. Right education is that which guides you up to the fourth body. There the work of education is complete. No education can help you enter the fifth; you have to go there by yourself. Right education can easily take you up to the fourth body. After this the development of the fifth body, which is very valuable and personal, begins. Kundalini is the potential of the fourth body; this is why kundalini is a psychic phenomenon. I hope this is now clear to you.

Questioner : *Is there a psychic binding between the sadhak and the medium in Shaktipat ? Can it be detrimental to the sadhak or is it helpful for him ?*

Bhagwan : Ties that bind can never be useful, for they are bad in themselves. The deeper the attachment, the worse it is. Psychic binding is a very bad thing. If someone ties me in chains, only my physical body is affected. But if someone ties me with the chain of love, it penetrates deeper and is more difficult to break. If someone binds me with the chain of *shraddha* (faith), it goes deeper still. Then to break this chain would be "unholy". So all bonds are bad, and psychic bonds even more so.

He who acts as a medium in Shaktipat should never want to bind you. If he does so, he is not worthy of being a medium. But it is quite likely that you may get tied to him. You may catch hold of his feet and vow never to leave him due to the great benefaction bestowed on you. It is necessary to be very alert at that moment. The sadhak should protect himself from attachment. However, if it becomes clear to the sadhak that all attachments prove to be heavy burdens on the spiritual journey, then instead of binding himself he will have an attitude of thanksgiving, and this will liberate. Now if I am thankful to you for something, where is there any question of attachment ? In fact, if I do not express my gratefulness, this fact will remain as a bondage within: that I did not even show my gratitude. But this thanksgiving ends the matter there.

Thanksgiving is not a bondage. On the contrary, it is the expression of ultimate independence. But the tendency to become bound is always within us. We are never sure whether we shall be able to stand by ourselves or not, and hence there is an urge to cling to someone. But let us not even consider clinging to another : When a man crosses a dark street in the night, he sings out loudly because the sound of HIS OWN voice alleviates fear. If it is the voice of another person, then too it would be something to cling to, but basically he musters strength and courage from his own voice. Man is frightened, so he holds on to anything. That is why if a drowning man comes across a piece of straw he will hold fast to it even though this does not protect him from drowning. Rather, the straw also sinks with him. So out of fear, the mind tends to hold on to someone, to something, be it a guru or anyone or anything else. By doing so we want to protect ourselves.

Sadhaks should always be wary of security. Security is the greatest web of attachment for a sadhak. If he seeks security for even a single moment, if he feels that he has the support of someone in whose protection he has nothing to fear and thus he will now not go astray, if he is thinking that he shall go nowhere and be under his guru forever, then he has already lost his way. For a sadhak there is no security; insecurity is a blessing, for a sadhak. The greater the insecurity, the greater is the opportunity for his Atman to expand and to become bold and fearless. The more the protection, the weaker he will become in the same proportion. To take assistance is one thing, but to keep on being dependent is quite another.

You are given support so that you can stand without support. It is given with the intention that you will need no more. A man teaches his child to walk. Have you noticed that when he is helping the child to walk the father holds the child's hand and not the child ? In a few days time he learns to walk, and then the father leaves his hand. But at first the child catches hold of the father's hand for confidence. So if the child takes hold of the father's hand, it means that although he has learned to walk he will not leave it. If the father holds the child's hand, then know that the child still does not know how to walk and it is dangerous to let him be on his own. The father will want that his hand should be relieved soon, for that is why he teaches him to walk. If some father allows his child to go on holding his hand out of the sheer pleasure he gets from it, he is his child's enemy.

Many fathers, many gurus, do this, but this is a mistake. The reason for which the support was given is defeated. Instead of giving rise to a strong healthy person who can walk on his own two feet, he has given rise to a cripple who will depend upon crutches all his life. This, however, is the pleasure that gives satisfaction to the father or the guru—that you cannot proceed without their support. Thus, their egos are then satisfied.

But such a guru is not a guru. So it is for the guru to shake off the sadhak's hand and tell him firmly to walk on his own two feet. And there is no harm if he falls a couple of times : he can get up again. After all, one has to fall in order to rise, and it is necessary to fall a few times in order to get over the fear of falling. Then one can take precautions in the future against falling.

The mind tries to catch hold of some support, and so the binding starts. This should not happen. The sadhak should always keep in mind the fact that he is not in search of security. He is in search of truth—not security. If he is earnest about his quest for truth, he must give up all ideas of safety and security. Falseness affords a lot of protection—and very quickly too. Thus, he who is in search of safety is quickly attracted toward it. The seeker of convenience never scales the heights of truth, for the journey is long. Then he fashions falsehoods out of fanciful ideas and begins to believe that he has attained, while he remains sitting just where he was.

Therefore, any type of attachment is dangerous—and even more so the attachment to a guru, for this is a spiritual attachment. The very term "spiritual attachment" is contradictory. "Spiritual independence" has a meaning, but "spiritual slavery" is meaningless. Yet, in this world other types of slaves are considerably less enslaved than are the slaves of spirituality. There is a reason for this: The fourth body from where the spirit of independence rises remains undeveloped. The majority of human beings have developed only up to the third body.

It is seen very often that a High Court judge or a Vice-Chancellor of a university is sitting at the feet of an absolute bumpkin. Seeing this, others follow suit thinking that if such high-placed people are sitting at this man's feet, we are nothing in comparison. They do not know that though this judge, this Vice-chancellor, has developed his third body to the full, that though he has developed his intellect to a very high level, he remains ignorant in so far as his fourth body is concerned. He is equally as ignorant as they are in matters of the fourth body.

And his third body—that which has developed intellect and reason—is thoroughly exhausted by constant thinking and debating and it is now at rest.

Now when intellect gets tired and relaxes, it indulges in very unintellectual pursuits. Anything that relaxes after extreme activity becomes opposite to its nature. This is the danger, and this is why you will invariably find High Court judges in ashrams. They are exhausted and they are distressed by their intellects, so they wish to be rid of them. In such a condition, they will do anything irrational. They will just close their eyes and put their faith in anything. Their contention is that all their learning and reasoning and discussions led them nowhere, so they drop these. And in order to sever all connection with them, they promptly catch hold of something that is completely contrary. Then the rest of the crowd, which gives credence to the intellects of such high-placed people, begins to imitate them. These people may be very intellectual, but in the matters of the fourth body they are just nothing. Therefore, a slight development of the fourth body in any individual will bring the greatest of intellectuals to his feet, for he has something that the intellectual lacks completely.

This sort of binding occurs when the fourth body is not developed. Then the minds wants to hold on to someone whose fourth body is developed, but this will not help you to develop YOUR fourth body. Only by understanding such a person can your fourth body develop. However, in order to escape the trouble of understanding him, you catch hold of his person. Then you will say, "Where is the need to understand? We shall hold on to your feet so that when you cross the river of hell we too shall cross with you. We shall bring you into our boat to cross the "Vaitarani" (In Hindu mythology, the counterpart to the River Styx in Greek mythology).

There is agony in understanding, for then one has to change oneself. To understand is an effort, a sadhana (spiritual practice). Understanding needs exertion, understanding is a revolution. A transformation takes place; everything changes. The old has to be changed into the new. Why go through all this bother? It is better to hold on to one who knows. But the fact is that no one can attain Truth by following someone. There one has to go alone. The road itself is unpopulated, lonely, for it is a private path meant for only one. Therefore any kind of attachment is a hindrance.

Learn, understand, accept the glimpse wherever you get it. But do not stop anywhere; do not make an abode out of any resting place; do not catch hold of the hand that is extended to you and take it as the destination. You will, however, find many who will say, "Go no further: Stay here; this is the other side." As I said before, some fearful people desire to be bound, and there are other fearful ones who want to bind them in order to feel fearless themselves. When a man sees a thousand people following him, he is bound to feel that he is wise—or else, why should these people follow him ? "Surely," he says to himself, "I know something, or else why should these people believe in me ?"

It is surprising that many a time gurudom is caused by a psychological inferiority complex that seeks to gather a crowd around itself. Thus, a guru gets busy increasing the number of his disciples—a thousand, ten thousand, twenty thousand. The greater the number, the more he is assured of his knowledge—or else, why should these people follow him ? This reasoning helps to boost his morale. If these disciples are lost, everything is lost. Then he would feel that all is lost and that he does not know.

Many psychic games go on, and it is better to be aware of them. And this game can be played from both sides. The disciple is bound to the guru, and he who is bound today will bind someone else tomorrow, for all this is a chain reaction. He who is a disciple today shall be a guru tomorrow. How long can he remain a disciple ? If he has caught hold of someone today, he will see that someone catches hold of him tomorrow. Slavery runs in a series, and the intrinsic reason for all this is the non-development of the fourth body. If you set about to develop this body, you can be indepedent. Then there is no bondage.

This does not mean that you become inhuman, that you will have no connection with people. Rather, the contrary will be the case. Really speaking, where there is bondage there is NO relationship. Between a husband and wife there is bondage. Do we not use the expression "To be tied in the marital bond" ? We send out invitations reading that "My son or my daughter is being joined by the thread of affection". Where there is servitude there is no relationship. How can there be? Perhaps, in some distant future, a father might send out an invitation saying that "My daughter is becoming independent in someone's love".

Where there is bondage, there is the agony of hell. Outside there are false appearances; inside everything is rotten. Be this the bondage of guru-disciple, father-son, husband-wife or even of two friends : where there is bondage relationship cannot be. If there is a relationship then the outer bondage is false And though it seems outwardly correct that where there is a bond there should be relationship, the fact is that we can have a relationship only with that person to whom we are not tied in any way. This is the reason why many times it happens that you tell a stranger things which you would never tell your son.

I was surprised to know that a woman talks more openly to a stranger whom she has met just an hour before and even tells things which she would not dream of telling her husband. In truth, when there is no bondage, relationship becomes easier. This is why we are always so nice to strangers and not so nice to those we know. With strangers there are no bonds, and hence there is relationship. Otherwise there are bonds, and hence no relationship. Then even if you wish "Good-day", it seems like a task. There can be a relationship between guru and disciple, however, and all relationships can be beautiful. But bondage can not be beautiful. Relationship means that which liberates.

There was a priceless custom among the Zen gurus. When a disciple finished his training, the guru ordered him to join the camp of his antagonist and study there. He would say, "You have gained knowledge from one side, now know it from the other." Then the sadhak would go from ashram to ashram for years and sit to learn at the feet of his guru's rivals. His guru would say, "It could be possible that what my opponent says is correct. Go and hear all that he has to say; then you decide for yourself. It may also be possible that you will be able to decide things better after hearing both of us. Or, perhaps what remains after discarding both of us may turn out to be the actual truth. Therefore, go and seek." This only happens when spiritual genius reaches its ultimate development. Then nothing can bind.

I believe that when the condition of this country (India) becomes such that gurus will send their disciples out into the world without binding them, then there will be wonderful results. And who knows what the final outcome would be ! Now such a man who sends you out to learn and hear others cannot be wrong, even if all that he himself has taught you turns out to be wrong. When such a man says to you, "Go seek elsewhere; perhaps I may be wrong," then even if all his teachings prove false, you will be grateful to him. He can never be wrong, for it is he who has sent you out.

Today what is happening is that everyone binds the sadhak and stops him from going out. One guru forbids his disciple from hearing another guru. The *shastras* (scriptures) say, "Never go to another temple. It is better to be trampled upon by a mad elephant than to take refuge in someone else's temple." The fear is always there that something might fall on the sadhak's ears. So even if the teachings of a guru who binds you are correct, still the man is wrong and you can never be grateful to him. Such a man has only made you a slave. He has crushed your spirit and killed your soul. If this is understood, there is no question of bondage.

Questioner : *You have said that if Shaktipat is authentic and pure, there is no bondage. Is that correct* ?

Bhagwan : Correct ! There will be no binding.

Questioner : *Is psychic exploitation possible in the name of Shaktipat? How is it possible and how is the sadhak to guard against it?*

Bhagwan : It is possible ! Much spiritual exploitation is possible in the name of Shaktipat. In fact, where there is a demand, a declaration, there is always exploitation. When a person declares that he will give, he will take something in return also, for giving and taking go together. Then be it in any form —in the form of wealth, in the form of reverence, in the form of faith—take he will. Where there is giving with insistance, then for sure there is taking. And he who claims to give is bound to take more in return, or else there was no need for him to shout in the marketplace.

A fisherman puts a worm on the hook of his rod, for the fish does not eat the hook. Perhaps someday the fish may be coaxed into swallowing the hook directly, but it is the worm that attracts the fish to the rod, and it swallows the hook with the intention of eating the worm. It is only after swallowing it that it comes to know that the hook was the main thing and the worm was only a bait. But by then it is caught.

So whenever you come across anyone who claims to do Shaktipat, who claims to give you knowledge and take you to Samadhi, who makes a thousand other claims, beware. Beware, for he that belongs to the realm of the beyond makes no claims for himself. If you tell such a one, "Because of you, I experienced grace," he will say, "How can it be ? I do not even know. You must be mistaken. It must be the doing of God." Thus, your thanks will not be acknowledged by such a one. He won't even acknowledge that he was a medium for the happening. He will insist that grace descended because you were worthy of it—that it was God's compassion falling on you. Who is he ? Where does he stand ? What is his worthiness ? He does not come in at all: that is what he will say.

Jesus was passing through a town. A sick man was brought to him. Jesus embraced him, and he was cured of all his ills. This man told Jesus, "How can I thank you ? You have rid me of all my woes," Jesus replied, "Do not speak thus. Give thanks where it is due. Who am I and where do I come in ?" The man said, "But there is no one else except you here." Jesus said, "You and I are not. You cannot see He who is, and all happens through HIM. He has healed you."

Now how can such a man exploit ? The hook has to be covered with the worm in order to exploit. He is not even ready to own the worm, leave aside the hook. He has no designs on you. So wherever a person claims results, be on your guard. When he claims to do this for you and that for you, he is only covering the hook with the worm. He is fomenting your expectations; he is inciting your hopes and raising your desires. And when you are seized with desire and you say, "Oh Master,

Give !" he will begin his demands. Very soon you will come to know of the worm on top and the hook within.

So watch your step wherever there are miraculous claims. It is dangerous territory. Shun the path where someone awaits to be your guru. There is fear of entanglement there. So how is the sadhak to guard himself? He should guard himself from those who make tall claims, and thus he will save himself from all evil. He should not seek those who claim wonderful results. Otherwise he will be in difficulty, for such men are also seeking: they are on the lookout for those who will fall into their trap. There are persons such as these going about everywhere. Do not ask for any spiritual gains and do not accept any spiritual claims.

What you have to do is entirely a different matter. You have to prepare yourself from within. And the day you are ready, the happening is bound to take place. Then it will happen via any medium. The medium is secondary; he is like a peg. The day you acquire a coat, the peg is ready to hang it by. Then the peg is not very important. If there is no peg, you can hang your coat on the door. If there is no door, you can hang it on the branch of a tree: any peg will work; the main question is of the coat. But we do not have the coat while the peg calls out: "Come here! I am the peg." You will be caught if you go. You do not have the coat, so what will you do by going to the peg? There is every danger of your hanging yourself on it. You have to seek your own worthiness, your own capability. You have to make yourself ready, in order to be able to receive grace when it comes.

You do not have to worry about the guru at all; that is not your concern. This is why what Krishna says to Arjuna is correct. He says, "Carry out your action and leave the fruits received thereof to the Divine." You have not to worry about the result of your action, for that will cause hindrance in your progress. Then all kinds of perplexities will arise: concerns over what your action will yield, over what will be the result. And in your anxiety about the result, your performance will go haywire. That is why the action itself should be our main concern.

We should be concerned about our own worthiness and receptivity. The moment when our effort is complete—just as when a seed has reached its point of bursting—that very moment all is achieved. The moment the bud is ready to burst and blossom into a flower, the sun is always ready, for it shines every day. The sun is always ready, but we do not have the bud that breaks into a flower. Then even if the sun shines brightly in the sky, it is of no use. Therefore, do not go seeking the sun. Get busy and develop your bud. The sun is there for ever and is always available.

No receptacle remains unfilled for even a moment in this world. Any kind of receptacle becomes filled immediately. Really speaking, to be receptive and to be filled are not two happenings. They are the two sides of the same happening. Now if we were to remove all air from this room, fresh air from outside would at once fill the vacuum. These are not two happenings, for as we remove the air in the room, the outside air rushes in: such are the laws of the physical world. We are hardly even ready on our side when the fulfilment of our efforts begins to descend. Our difficulty is, however, that our demands start long before our preparedness. Then there are always false supplies for false demands.

Some people really confound me. One man comes and says, "My mind is very restless; I want peace." He talks to me for half an hour, and in the course of his talk he confesses that the cause of his unrest is that his son is jobless. If he gets a job, his mind will be at rest. Now this man came with the excuse that he wanted peace of mind, but his actual requirement was absolutely different; it has nothing to do with peace of mind. He only wanted a job for his son. Thus, he had come to the wrong man.

Now he who has opened a shop in the market of religion will say, "You want a job? Come here. I will get you a job and I will give you peace of mind too. Whoever comes here gets a job; whoever comes here, his wealth increases and his business runs well." Now a few people will gather around the "shop" who will tell you, "My son got a job." Another will say, "My wife was saved from death." A third will say, "I won my lawsuit." A fourth will say, "Wealth is pouring on me." Now it is not that these people are telling untruths or that they are hirelings; nor are they the agents for this "shop": it is nothing like that. When a thousand men come asking for jobs, ten of them are bound to get employed in the normal course of things. Now these ten remain while the remaining 990 go away.

Then these ten slowly spread word of the "miracle", and the crowd around the "shop" increases. This is why every such "shop" has salesmen and advertisers. Those who say their son got a job are not telling an untruth; nor have they been bought over by the "shopkeeper". Such a man had also come seeking, and it happened that his son got a job. Those whose sons did not get a job left long ago to seek other gurus who would fulfil their desires. Now those whose desires are fulfilled begin to frequent the "shop" often. They come on each festival every year. The crowd increases day by day, and a group forms around such a so-called guru. Then what they tell becomes his indisputable testimony. If so-many people's wishes were fulfilled, why not yours? Now this is the worm; the hook which traps the man is within.

Never ask or else you are bound to be caught. Prepare yourself and leave all else to the Divine. Let the happening happen when the moment is ripe for it to happen. If it does not happen, we shall know we are yet not ready to receive.

Questioner : *Is it all right for a sadhak to receive Shaktipat from many individuals or is it harmful? What are the risks involved in being a medium and why should there be any?*

Bhagwan: The fact is that you will feel the need of obtaining Shaktipat again and again only when the happening has not yet taken place. And you will find the need to take from others only when your experience with the first has been in vain. If the first Shaktipat is successful, the matter ends there. It is like trying many doctors because the disease has not yet been cured. Naturally, the doctors have to be changed. But the patient who is cured never raises the question of changing doctors. The slightest experience of a glimpse due to Shaktipat makes this question irrelevant. Besides, once this glimpse is attained from someone it makes no difference if it is attained again from another. It is the same energy coming from the same source, only the medium is different. But this does not result in any difference. Whether it comes from the sun or an electric bulb or oil lamp, the light is the same.

It makes no difference and there is no harm, if the happening has taken place. But do not go seeking for the happening. If it comes to you along the way, accept it and go further—but do not seek it. If you seek there are hazards, for then only the confidence artists will come your way and not someone who can really give. He will appear only when you are not seeking, when you are preparing yourself. Therefore, to seek him is wrong, to ask is wrong. Let the happening take its own time and let the light come from a thousand paths. All roads will prove the authenticity of the same original source. It is the same; only it is appearing from all sides.

Someone was saying the other day that he went to a sadhu and said that knowledge should be one's own. The sadhu retorted that it cannot be—that knowledge "always pertains to another, and that such and such a *muni* (monk) gave it to such and such a *muni*, then he passed it on to another *muni*." Then I explained to this friend that Krishna's knowledge was his own. When he says that "so and so got it from so and so", he means that this knowledge that has revealed itself to him has not been revealed to him alone. It was revealed to so and so also, before him. Then this person had apprised another person of the happening, and this happening took place in him also. But what is to be noted here is that the revelation did not take place by mere telling. It was told AFTER the happening. So Krishna says to Arjuna, "This knowledge I am conveying to you is the same that has come to me. But my telling of it will not bring it about in you. When it happens to you, you will be able to tell others that it is like this.'

"Do not go begging for it," says Krishna, "For it is not attained from anyone. You prepare yourself for it, and it will begin to come from all directions. Then one day when the happening takes place, you will say, 'How blind I was that I could not see that which was coming to me from all sides.' "

A blind man may pass by a lamp or an electric light or go out in the sun, but he will never see light. Then one day his sight is restored and he is shocked to see that he was always surrounded by light.

So on the day of the happening, you will see it all around you. And until the time comes when it takes place, offer your respects wherever you get the glimpse of Truth. Take it from wherever you can get it, but please do not beg for it like a beggar—for Truth is never obtained by a beggar. Do not beg for Truth, or else some tradesman might lure you with lucrative suggestions. Then a spiritual exploitation will begin. Go along your way always preparing yourself, preparing yourself, and wherever you happen to find it, accept it. Offer your gratitude and proceed on; then on the moment of full attainment you will not be able to say that you got it from so and so. That moment you will say, "What a wonder of wonders ! I got from the All. Whosoever I approached, I got from him." Then the final thanksgiving will be to the "ALL" and not to anyone in particular.

Questioner : *This question had arisen because of the fact that the effect of Shaktipat wears off by and by.*

Bhagwan : Yes, it will get less and less. In fact, what is attained from another is bound to diminish. Besides, it is only a glimpse and you are not to depend on it. You have to awaken it within yourself : then only will it be permanent. The effect of all influences are foreign; they belong to the outside. I pick up a stone and I throw it in the air: it will fall according to the force exerted by me. The stone has no strength of its own, but it may well think, as it flies through the air, that it has strength to cut through the air and that there is no one to stop it. But then it does not know what influence has caused this; it does not know the push of the hand behind it. It will fall—if not at ten feet then at twenty, but fall it will. Actually, any effect that comes from another is always limited, and it is bound to diminish.

The only advantage of an outside influence is that in the momentary glimpse you experience you may be able to find your original source. Then it will be useful. It is like this: I light a matchstick to strike a light. How long will its flame last ? Now you can do two things: Firstly, you stay in the darkness and depend on the light of my matchstick. In a moment the light will go out, and it will become pitch dark. Secondly, in the light of the matchstick you locate the door and you run out; you no longer depend on my matchstick. You are out; now it makes no difference to you whether the match is burning or not. Now you have reached where the sun is. Now something has become lasting and stable.

All these happenings have only one use : that with an outside help you do something inner for yourself. But do not wait for these happenings, for the matchsticks will burn and extinguish time and again and you will become conditioned to these. Then you will become dependent on the matchstick, and you will wait in the dark for the match to light. And when it lights, you will keep on dreading the moment of extinguishment when once again you will be plunged into darkness. So this will become a vicious circle. No, you are not to stop at the matchstick. It is lit so that in its light you see the way and run out of the darkness as fast as possible.

This is all the advantage we can take from the other. It can never be a permanent gain; yet it is a sizeable gain and is not to be neglected. It is a wonder that we can get even so much from another. If the other is wise and understanding, he will never tell you to stay on. He will say, "The match has been lit, now run—for soon the match will burn out." But if the medium tells you to stay on, on the ground that he and no other has lit the match, if he tells you that you should be initiated by him and take vows of being loyal to him, then this relationship will remain; it cannot break. He will assert his right over you and forbid you to go elsewhere or listen to anyone else. This is very dangerous.

It would have been much better if such a one had not lit the matchstick at all, for he has done great harm. In the dark you would have felt your way out someday and reached the light. Now you have landed yourself in difficulty by holding on to his matchstick. Now where will you go ? And one thing is certain: this man has stolen this match from somewhere. It is not his own; otherwise he would have known its use : he would have known that it is meant to help a man to get out of darkness and that it is not meant to stop anyone or halt his progress.

Therefore, this is a stolen match that he is trading in. Now he proclaims that all who get a glimpse from his matches must stay with him and be devoted to him. This is the limit ! First darkness barred the way; now it is this guru. And darkness is better than a demanding guru, for it does not spread its hands to stop you. The obstruction of darkness is passive, it is quiet, but this guru obstructs actively. He will catch you by the hand and bar your way, saying, "This is treachery; this is deceit."

Recently, a girl came and told me that her guru objected to her coming to see me. The guru said, "Just as a husband or a wife belong to each other and not to anyone else, so also, if a disciple forsakes the guru it is a great sin." He is right, but his are stolen matchsticks. There is no difficulty in stealing matches; there are many available in the *shastras*.

Questioner : *Can stolen matches burn* ?

Bhagwan : The thing is that one who has not seen the light cannot tell what has been burned in order to show him the light. When he sees the actual light, only then will he know what was what. Not only will he know what had been lit, but he will even know whether anything was really lighted or whether he was only made to imagine that it was.

The moment the light is seen, 99% of the gurus will be proven to be friends of darkness and enemies of light. Then only will we know what dangerous enemies they are : they are the agents of Satan.

[Text of a discourse given on July 6, 1970, evening, in Bombay, India.]

13

KUNDALINI SADHANA AND THE SEVEN CHAKRAS

Questioner :

In yesterday's talk you said that the "sadhak" (seeker) should first worry about his own receptivity and should not go begging from door to door. But the very meaning of a sadhak is that there are obstacles on his path of "sadhana" (spiritual practice): He does not know how to be receptive. Is it so difficult to meet the right guide?

Bhagwan Shree Rajneesh :

To seek and to ask are two different things. Actually, only he who does not want to seek asks. To seek and to ask are not one and the same: rather, they are contradictory. He who wants to avoid seeking asks. The process of seeking and the process of begging are very different. In asking the attention is centered on the other—on the giver; in seeking the attention is centered on oneself—on the receiver. To say that there are obstacles in the path of sadhana means there are obstructions within the sadhak himself. The path too lies within, and it is not very difficult to understand one's own hindrances. It will have to be explained at length what obstructions are and how they can be removed. Yesterday I told you about the seven bodies. We shall talk in greater detail about these, and it will become clear to you.

As there are seven bodies, there are also seven "chakras" (centers), and each chakra is connected in a special way with its corresponding body. The chakra of the physical body is the "muladhar". This is the first chakra and it has an integral connection with the physical body. This muladhar chakra has two possibilities. Its first potentiality is a natural one that is given to us with birth; its other possibility is obtainable by sadhana.

The basic natural possibility of this chakra is the sex urge of the physical body. Now the very first question that arises in the mind of the sadhak is what to do in regard to this central principle. Now there is another possibility of this chakra, and that is "brahmacharya" (celibacy), which is attainable through sadhana. Sex is the natural possibility and brahmacharya is its transformation. The more the mind is focused upon and gripped by sexual desire, the more difficult it will be to reach its ultimate potential of brahmacharya.

Now this means that we can utilize the situation given to us by nature in two ways. We can live in the condition that nature has placed us in, but then sadhana cannot begin. Or, we transform this situation. The only danger in transformation is that there is the hazard that we may begin to fight with our natural center. What is the real danger in the path of a sadhak ? The first obstacle is that if the sadhak indulges only in nature's order of things, he cannot rise to the ultimate possibility of his physical bodv, and he stagnates at the starting point. On the one hand there is a demand; on the other hand there is a suppression which causes the sadhak to fight the sex urge. Suppression is an obstacle on the path of a sadhak. This is the obstruction of the first chakra. Transformation cannot come about with suppression.

If suppression is an obstruction, what is the solution ? Understanding will then solve the matter. Transformation takes place within as you begin to understand sex. There is a reason for this. All elements of nature lie blind and unconscious within us. If we become conscious of them, transformation begins. No sooner does something begin to awaken within us when these natural elements begin to change. Awakening is the alchemy; awareness is the chemistry of changing them, of transforming them. If a person becomes awake toward his sexual desires with his total feelings and his total understanding, then brahmacharya will begin to take birth within him in place of sex

Unless a person reaches brahmacharya in his first body, it is difficult to work on the potentiality of other centers.

The second body, as I said, is the emotional or the etheric body. The second body is connected to the second chakra—the svadhishthan chakra. This too has two possibilities. Basically, its natural potential is fear, hate, anger, and violence. All these are conditions obtained from the natural potential of the svadhishthan chakra. If a person stagnates at the second body, then the directly opposite conditions of transformation—love, compassion, fearlessness, friendliness—do not take place. The obstruction on the sadhak's path in the second chakra is hate, anger and violence, and the question is of their transformation.

Here too the same mistake is made: one person can give vent to his anger; another can suppress his fear and make a show of courage. But both of these will not lead to transformation. When there is fear, it shall have to be accepted; there is no use hiding or suppressing it. If there is violence within, there is no use in covering it with the mantle of non-violence. Shouting slogans of non-violence will bring no change in the state of violence within, for it remains violence. It is a condition given to us by nature in the second body. It has its uses, just as there is a meaning to sex. Through sex alone other physical bodies can come into being. Before one physical body falls, nature has made provisions for the birth of another.

Fear, violence, anger, are all necessary on the second plane, or else man could not survive, could not protect himself. Fear protects him, anger involves him in struggle against others and violence helps him to save himself from the violence of others. All these are the qualities of the second body and are necessary for survival, but generally we stop here and do not go any further. If a person understands the nature of fear he attains fearlessness, and if he understands the nature of violence he attains non-violence. Similarly, by understanding anger we develop the quality of forgiveness.

Actually, anger is one side of the coin, forgiveness is the other. They each hide behind the other, but the coin has to be turned over. If we come to know one side of the coin perfectly, we naturally become curious to know what is on the other side; and so the coin turns. If we hide the coin and pretend we have no fear, no violence within, we will never be able to know fearlessness and non-violence. He who accepts the presence of fear within himself and who has investigated it fully will soon reach a place where he will want to find out what is behind fear. His curiosity will encourage him to see the other side of the coin.

The moment he turns it over, he becomes fearless. Similarly, violence will turn into compassion. These are the potentials of the second body. Thus, the sadhak has to bring about a transformation in the qualities given to him by nature. And for this it is not necessary to go about asking others; one has to keep seeking and asking within oneself. We all know that anger and fear are impediments, for how can a coward seek Truth ? He will go begging for Truth; he will wish that someone should give it to him without his having to go into unknown lands.

Then third is the astral body. This also has two parts. Primarily, the third body revolves round uncertainty and thought. If these are transformed, doubt becomes faith and thought discretion. If doubts are repressed, you never attain "shraddha" (faith), though we are advised to suppress doubts and to believe what we hear. He who represses his doubts never attains faith, for doubt remains present within though repressed. It will creep within like a worm and eat up your vitals. Beliefs are implanted for fear of scepticism. We will have to understand the quality of doubt, we will have to live it and go along with it. Then one day we shall reach a point where we will begin to have misgivings about doubt itself. The moment we begin to doubt "doubt itself", faith begins.

We cannot reach discretion without thought. There are people who do not think and people who exhort them not to think. They say, "Do not think; leave all thoughts." He who stops thinking lands himself in ignorance and blind faith. This is not wisdom. The power of discretion is gained only after passing through the most subtle processes of thinking. What is the meaning of wisdom ? Doubt is always present in thoughts. It is always indecisive. Therefore, those who think a great deal never come to a decision. It is only when they step out of the revolution of thoughts that they can decide. Decision is possible only outside the confusion of thoughts.

Thoughts have no connection with decision. He who is always engrossed in thoughts never reaches a decision. That is why it invariably happens that those bereft of thoughts are very resolute, whereas those who think a great deal lack determination. There is danger from both. Those who do not think go ahead and do whatever they are determined to do, for the simple reason that they have no thoughts to create doubt within.

The dogmatists and the fanatics of the world are very active and energetic people, for there is no question of doubting with them: they never think. If they feel that heaven is attained by killing one thousand people, they will rest only after killing one thousand and not before. They never stop to think what they are doing, so there is never any indecision on their part. A man who thinks, on the contrary, will keep on thinking instead of taking any decision. If we close our doors for fear of thoughts, we shall be left with blind faith only. This is very dangerous and is a great obstacle in the path of the sadhak. What is needed is open-eyed discretion and thoughts that are clear, resolute and which allow us to make decisions. This is the meaning of "*vivek*" (wisdom). It means that the power of thinking is complete. It means we have passed through thoughts in such detail that all the doubts are cleared. Now only pure decision is left in its essence.

The chakra pertaining to the third body is "manipur": doubt and faith are its two forms. When doubt is transformed, faith is the result. But, remember, faith is not opposed or contrary to doubt. Faith is the purest and most ultimate development of it. It is the ultimate extreme of doubt, where even doubt becomes lost: because here doubt begins to doubt even itself, and in this way it commits suicide. Then faith is born.

The fourth plane is the mental body or the psyche, and the fourth chakra, the "anahat", is connected with the fourth body. The natural qualities of this plane are imagination and dreaming. This is what the mind is always doing: imagining and dreaming. It dreams in the night and in the daytime: it daydreams. If imagination is fully developed, that is to say, if it is developed to its fullest extent, in a complete way, it becomes determination, will. If dreaming develops fully, it is transformed into vision—psychic vision. If a man's ability to dream is fully developed, he has only to close his eyes and he can see things. He can then see even through a wall. At first he dreams of seeing beyond the wall; later he actually sees beyond it. Now he can only guess what you are thinking, but after the transformation he SEES what you think. Vision means seeing (and hearing) things without the use of the usual sense organs. The distances of time and space are no more for a person who develops vision. In dreams you travel far. If you are in Bombay, you reach Calcutta. Thus, in vision also you can travel distances. But there will be a difference: in dreams you imagine you have gone, whereas in vision you actually go. The fourth, psychic body can actually be present there (in dreams). As we have no idea of the ultimate possibility of this fourth body, we have discarded the ancient concept of dreams in today's world. The ancient experience was that in dream one of the bodies of man comes out of him and goes on a journey.

There was a man of Swedenberg. People knew him as a dreamer. He used to talk of heaven and hell, and they can only exist in dreams. But one day in the afternoon, as he slept, he began to shout, "Help! Help! My house is on fire." People came running, but there was no fire there. They awoke him to assure him that it was only a dream and there was no danger of fire. He insisted, however, that his house was on fire. His house was 300 miles away, and it had caught fire at that time. On the second or third day, news came of this disaster: His house was burnt to ashes, and it was actually burning when he cried out in his sleep. Now this is no longer a dream, but a vision. The distance of 300 miles was no longer there. This man witnessed what was happening 300 miles away.

Now the scientists also agree that there are great psychic possibilities (of the fourth body). Now that man has set out in space, research in this direction has become all the more important. The fact remains that no matter how reliable the instruments at man's disposal, these cannot be relied upon completely. If the radio in a spaceship goes out of commission, the astronauts lose contact with the world for all time. They will not be able to tell us where they are or what has happened to them. So today scientists are keen to develop telepathy and vision of the psychic body to overcome this risk. If the spacemen were able to communicate directly with the world by telepathy, it would be a part of the development of the fourth body. Then interspace travel can be safe. A lot of work has been carried out in this direction.

Thirty years ago, a man set out to explore the North Pole. He was equipped with all that was necessary for wireless communication. One more arrangement was also made which has not made known up until now : A psychic person whose fourth body qualities were functioning was also made to receive the transmission from the explorer. The most surprising thing was that when there was bad weather the wireless failed, but this psychic received the news without any difficulty. When the diaries were compared later on, it was found that 80-95% of the signals received by the psychic were correct, whereas the news relayed by the radio was not more than 72% correct, for there were many break downs in between. Now Russia and America are both very eager, and a great deal of work is afoot in the field of telepathy, clairvoyance and thought reading. All these are the possibilities of the fourth body. To dream is its natural quality; to see the Truth, to see the Real, is its ultimate possibility. The chakra of this fourth body is "anahat".

The fifth chakra is the "vishuddhi chakra": it is located in the throat. The fifth body is the spiritual body. The vishudhi chakra is connected to the spiritual body. The first four bodies and their chakras were split into two. The duality ends with the fifth body. As I said before, the male and the female difference lasts until the fourth body; after that it ends. If we observe very closely, all duality, belongs to the male and the female. Where the distance between male and female is no more, at that very point all duality ceases. The fifth body is undivided. It does not have two possibilities, but only one.

This is why there is not much effort for the sadhak to make : because here there is nothing contrary to develop; here one has only to enter. By the time we reach the fourth body, we develop so much competence and strength that it is very easy to enter the fifth body. In that case, how can we tell the difference between a person who has entered the fifth body and one who has not ? The difference will be that he who has entered the fifth body is completely rid of all unconsciousness.

He will not actually sleep at night. That is, he sleeps, but his body alone sleeps; someone within is forever awake. If he turns in sleep he knows it; if he does not he knows it. If he has covered himself with a blanket he knows it; if he has not then also he knows it. His awareness does not slacken in sleep : he is awake all the 24 hours. For the one who has not entered the fifth body, his state is just the opposite. In sleep, HE is asleep, and in the waking hours also one part of him will be asleep.

People "appear" to be working. When you come home every evening, the car turns left into your gate; you apply the brake when you reach the porch. Do not be under the illusion that you are doing all this knowingly. It happens unconsciously by sheer force of habit. It is only in certain moments, moments of danger, that we really come into awareness. When the danger is so much that it will not do to go about lacking unawareness, we awaken. For instance, if a man points a dagger at your chest, you spring into consciousness. The point of the dagger takes you right up to the fifth body. With the exception of these few moments in our lives, we live in a somnolent state.

Neither has the wife seen the husband's face properly nor has the husband seen the wife's face. If the husband tries to visualize the wife's face, he will not be able to do so. If the lines of her face change in the slightest degree, it will be difficult to say whether it was the same face he has seen for the last thirty years. You have never seen, for there must be an awakened person within you to see.

A sleeping man appears to be seeing, but actually he is not—for he is asleep within, dreaming, and everything is going on in this dream state. You get angry, then you say, "I do not know how I got angry; I did not want to," as if you are talking of someone else. You say, "Forgive me ! I did not want to be rude: it was a slip of the tongue." You have used uncivil language, and it is you who deny the intention of its use. The criminal always says, "I did not want to kill. It happened in spite of me." This proves that we are going about like an "automaton": We say what we do not want to do this or that, but we do what we do not want to do.

In the evening, we vow to be up at four in the morning.

When it is four a.m. and the alarm goes off, we turn over saying there is no need to be up so early. Then you get up at six and are filled with remorse for having overslept. Then you again vow to keep the same vow of yesterday. It is strange that a man decides on one thing in the evening and goes back on it in the morning ! Then what he decides at four in the morning changes again before it is six a.m., and what he decides at six changes long before it is evening, and in between he changes a thousand times. These decisions, these thoughts, come to us in our sleepy state. They are like dreams: they expand and burst like bubbles. There is no wakeful person behind them—no one who is alert and filled with consciousness.

So sleep is the innate condition before the beginning of the spiritual plane. Man is somnolent before he enters the fifth body, and there the quality is wakefulness. Therefore, after the development of the fourth body, we can call the individual, a "Buddha" (an Awakened One). Now such a man is awake. "Buddha" is not the name of Gautam Siddharth, but the epithet bestowed upon him after his attainment of the fifth plane. "Gautam the Buddha" means Gautam who has Awakened. His name remained Gautam, but that was the name of the sleeping person. So gradually it fell off and only Buddha remained.

This difference comes with the attainment of the fifth body. Before we enter into it, whatever we do is a somnolent action which cannot be trusted. We cannot put our faith in such actions. One moment a man vows to love and cherish his loved one the whole life long and the next moment he is quite capable of strangling her to death. The alliance which he vowed for a lifetime does not last long. This poor man is not to be blamed. What is the value of promises given in sleep ? In a dream I may promise, "This is a life-long relationship." What value is this promise ? In the morning I will deny it because it was only a dream.

A sleeping man cannot be trusted. This world of ours is entirely a world of sleeping people. Hence, so much of confusion, so much of conflicts, so many quarrels, so much of chaos. It is all the making of sleeping men.

There is another important difference between a sleeping

man and a wakeful man which we should bear in mind. A sleeping man does not know who he is, so he is always striving to show others that he is this or he is that. This is his life-long endeavour. He tries in a thousand ways to prove himself. Sometimes he climbs the rungs of politics and declares, "I am so and so." At times he builds a house and displays his wealth, or he climbs a mountain and displays his strength. He tries in all manners to prove himself. And in all these efforts he is, in truth, unknowingly trying to find out for himself who he is. He knows not who he is.

Before crossing the fourth plane we cannot find the answer. The fifth body is called the "*Atman sharir*" (the spiritual body) because there you get the answer to the quest for "Who am I?" The call of the "I" stops once for all on this plane; the claim to be someone special vanishes immediately. If you say to such a person, "You are so and so," he will laugh. All claims from his side will now stop, for now he knows. There is no longer any need to prove himself, for "Who I am" is now a proven fact.

The conflicts and problems of the individual end on the fifth plane. But this plane has its own hazards. You have come to know yourself, and this knowing is so blissful and fulfilling that you may want to terminate your journey here. You may not feel like resuming your journey. The hazards up to now were all of pain and agony; now the hazards that begin are of bliss. The fifth plane is so blissful that you will not have the heart to leave it and proceed further. Therefore, the individual who enters this plane has to be very alert about clinging to bliss so that it does not impede him from going further. Here bliss is supreme and at the pinnacle of its glory; it is in its profoundest depths. A very great change comes about within one who has known himself. But this is not all; there is further to go also.

It happens that distress and suffering do not obstruct our way as much as joy. Bliss is very obstructive. It was difficult enough to leave the crowd and confusion of the marketplace, but oh ! it is a thousand times more difficult to leave the soft strains of the *veena* (sitar) in the temple. This is why many sadhaks stop at "*Atma Jnan*" (Knowledge of the Self) and do not go up to "*Brahma Jnan*" (Knowledge of the Brahman—the Cosmic Reality).

We shall have to be alert toward this bliss. Here our effort should be not to get lost in this bliss. Bliss draws us toward itself; it drowns us; we get immersed in it completely. Do not become immersed in "*ananda*" (bliss). Know that this too is an experience. Stand outside of it; be a witness. As long as there is experience, there is an obstacle : the ultimate end has not been reached. At the ultimate state, all experiences end. Joy and sorrow come to an end, so also does *ananda* (bliss). Our language, however, does not go beyond this point. This is why we have described God as "*Sat-chit-ananda*" (Truth-consciousness-bliss). This is not the form of the Supreme Self, but this is the ultimate that words can express. Bliss is the ultimate expression of man. In fact, words cannot go beyond the fifth plane. But about the fifth plane we can say, "There is bliss there; there is perfect awakening; there is knowledge of the Self there." All this can be described.

Therefore, there will be no mystery about those who stop at the fifth plane. Their talk will sound very scientific, for the realm of mystery lies beyond this plane. Things are very clear up to the fifth plane. I believe that science will sooner or later absorb those religions that go up to the fifth body, for science will be able to reach up to the Atman.

When a sadhak sets out on this path, his search is mainly of bliss and not Truth, though he says he has set out to discover Truth. Frustrated by suffering and restlessness, he sets out in search of bliss. Therefore, he who seeks bliss will definitely stop at the fifth plane. Therefore, I must tell you to seek not bliss, but Truth. Then you will not tarry long here.

Then a question arises : "There is *ananda* : this is well and good. I know myself : this too is well and good. But these are only the leaves and the flowers. Where are the roots ? That I know myself, that I am blissful, I know, but from where do I arise ? Where are my roots ? From where have I come ? Where are the depths of my existence ? From which ocean has this wave that I am arisen ?" If your quest is for Truth, you will go ahead of the fifth body. From the very beginning, therefore, your quest should be for Truth and not bliss. Otherwise your journey up to the fifth plane will be easy, but you will stop there. If the quest is for Truth, there is no question of stopping there.

So the greatest obstacle on the fifth plane is the peerless joy we experience—and more so because we come from a world where there is nothing but pain, suffering, anxiety and tension. Then, when we reach this temple of bliss, there is an overriding desire to dance with ecstasy, to be drowned, to be lost in this bliss. This is not the place to be lost. That place will come, and then you will not have to lose yourself : You will simply be lost. There is a great difference between losing yourself and being lost. In other words, you will reach a place where, even if you wish, you cannot save yourself. You will see yourself becoming lost; there is no remedy. Yet, here also you can lose yourself. Your effort, your endeavour, still works here—and even though the ego is intrinsically dead on the fifth plane, pride still persists. It is necessary, therefore, to understand the difference between ego and pride.

The ego, the feeling of "I", will die, but the feeling of "am" will not die. There are two things in "I am", the "I" is the ego and the "am" is the pride— the feeling of being. So the "I" will die on the fifth plane, but the "being" the "am", will remain: the pride will remain. Standing on this plane, a sadhak will declare, "There are infinite souls, and each soul is different and apart from the other." On this plane the sadhak will experience the existence of infinite souls, because he still has the feeling of "am", the knowledge of being which makes him feel apart from others. If the quest for Truth grips the mind the obstacle of bliss can be crossed, for incessant bliss becomes tedious. A single strain of a melody can become irksome.

Bertrand Russell said once jokingly, "I would not prefer salvation, for I hear there is nothing but bliss there. Bliss alone would be very monotonous— bliss and bliss and nothing else. If there is not a single trace of unhappiness— no anxiety, no tension in it— how long can one bear such bliss ?"

To be lost in *ananda* is the hazard of the fifth plane. It is very difficult to overcome. Sometimes it takes many births to do so.

The first four steps are not so hard to cross, but the fifth is very difficult. Many births have to be taken to be tired of bliss, to be tired of the Self, to be tired of the Atman.

So the quest up to the fifth body is to be rid of pain, hatred, violence and desires. After the fifth, the search is in order to be rid of the Self. So there are two things: the first is freedom from something. This is one thing, and it is completed at the fifth plane. The second thing is freedom from the Self, and so a completely new world starts from here on.

The sixth is the "*Brahm sharira*" (the Cosmic body) and the sixth chakra is the "ajna chakra". Here there is no duality. The experience of bliss becomes intense on the fifth plane and the experience of Existence, of "Being", on the sixth. Pride will now be lost. "I am": the "I" in this is lost at the fifth plane and the "am" will go as soon as you transcend the fifth. The "is-ness" will be felt as "*tathata*"—suchness. Nowhere will there be the feeling of "I" or of "am": only THAT WHICH IS remains, So here will be the perception of Truth, of Being: the perception of Consciousness. But here the mind is free of "me". It is no longer "my consciousness": it is only Consciousness; no longer "my existence", but only Existence.

Some sadhaks stop after reaching the "*Brahm sharira*"—the Cosmic body, for the state of "I am the Brahman" has come—of "*Aham Brahmasmi*", when "I" am not and only the Brahman is. Now what more is there to seek? What is to be sought? Nothing remains to be sought. Now everything is attained. "The Brahman" means "the Total". He who stands at this point says, "The Brahman is the Ultimate Truth, the Brahman is the Cosmic Reality. There is nothing beyond."

It is possible to stop here, and sadhaks do stop at this stage for millions of births, for there seems to be nothing ahead. So the "*Brahm Jnani*" (the one who has attained Knowledge of the Brahman) will stagnate here; he will go no further. This is so difficult to cross, for there is nothing to cross to. Everything has been encircled. Does not one need a space to cross into? If I want to go outside of this room there must be some place where to go. But the room has now become so enormous, so beginningless and endless, so infinite, so boundless, that there is nowhere to go. So where shall we go to search? Nothing remains to be found; everything has been covered. So the journey may halt at this stage for infinite births.

So the Brahman is the ultimate obstacle—the last barrier in the ultimate quest of the sadhak. Now only the Being remains, and the "Non-being" remains also. The Being, the "IS-NESS", is known, but the Non-Being, that which IS NOT, still remains to be known. Therefore, the seventh plane is the "*Nirvana kaya*" (Nirvanic body), and its chakra is the "sahasrar." Nothing can be said in connection with this chakra. We can only continue talking at the most up to the Brahman (the sixth)—and that too with great difficulty: most of it will turn out to be wrong.

Until the fifth body, the search progresses within a very scientific method. Everything can be explained. On the sixth plane, the horizon begins to fade; everything seems meaningless. Hints can still be given, but, ultimately, the pointing finger breaks and the hints too are no more, for one's own Being is eliminated. So the Absolute Being is known from the sixth body and the sixth chakra.

Therefore, those who seek the Brahman will meditate on the ajna chakra which is between the eyes. This chakra is connected to the "*Brahm sharir*". Those who work completely on this chakra will begin to call the vast infinite expanse that they witness "the third eye". This is the third eye from where they can now view the Cosmic, the Infinite.

One more journey yet remains—the journey to Non-Being, Non-Existence. Existence is only half the story: there is also Non-Existence. Light is, but on the other side there is darkness. Life is one part, but there is also death. Therefore, it is necessary also to know the remaining Non-Existence, the Void, for the Ultimate Truth can only be known when both are known—the Existence and the Non-Existence. "Being" is known in its entirety and "Non-Being" is known in its entirety: then the knowing is complete. Existence is known in its entirety and Non-Existence is known in its entirety: then we know the whole; otherwise our knowledge is incomplete. There is an imperfection in "*Brahm Jnan*", which is that it has not been able to know the Non-Being. Therefore, the *Brahm Jnani* denies that there is such a thing as Non-Existence and calls it an illusion. He says that it does not exist. He says that "To be is the Truth, and 'not to be' is a falsity. There simply is no such thing, so the question of knowing it does not arise."

"*Nirvana kaya*" means the "*Shunya kaya*" (the Void) from where we jump from the Being into the Non-Being. In the Cosmic body something yet remains unknown. That too has to be known—what it is "NOT TO BE", to be completely erased. Therefore, the seventh plane, in a sense, is an ultimate death. Nirvana, as I told you previously, means the "extinction of the flame". That which was "I" is extinct; that which was "am" is extinct. But now we have again come into being by being one with the ALL. Now we are the Brahman, and this too will have to be left. He who is ready to take the jump knows the Existence and also the Non-Existence.

So these are the seven bodies and the seven chakras, and within them lie all the means as well as the barriers. There are no barriers outside. Therefore, there is not much reason to inquire outside. If you have gone to ask someone or to understand from someone, then do not beg. To understand is one thing, to beg is another. Your search should always continue. Whatever you have heard and understood should also be made your search. Do not make it your belief or else it will be begging.

You asked me something; I gave you an answer. If you have come for alms, you will put this in your bag and store it away as your treasure. Then you are not a sadhak but a beggar. No, what I told you should become your quest. It should accelerate your search; it should stimulate and motivate your curiosity. It should put you into greater difficulty, make you more restless and pose new questions before you, new dimensions, so that you will set out on a new path of discovery. Then you have not taken alms from me. Then you have understood what I said. And if this helps you to comprehend yourself, then this is not begging.

So go forth to know and comprehend; go forth to search. You are not the only one in quest: many others are searching also. Many have searched, many have attained. Try to know, to grasp, what has happened to such people and also what has not happened; try and understand all this. But while understanding this, do not stop trying to understand your own self. Do not think that by understanding others your knowledge is complete. Do not put faith in their experiences; do not believe them blindly. Rather, turn everything into questions. Turn them into problems and not answers; then your journey will continue. Then it will not be begging: it will be your quest.

It is your search that will carry you to the last. As you penetrate within yourself, you will find the two sides of each chakra. As I told you, one is given to you by nature and one you have to discover. Anger is given to you; forgiveness you have to find. Sex is given to you; brahmacharya you have to develop. Dreams you have; vision has to evolve.

Your search for the opposite will continue up to four planes. From the fifth will start your search for the undivided One. Try to continue your search for that which is different from what has come to you in the fifth body. When you attain it, try to find out what there is besides this. On the sixth plane you attain the Brahman, but keep inquiring, "What is there besides the Brahman?" Then one day you will step into the seventh body where Being and Non-Being, light and darkness, life and death, occur together. That is the attainment of the Ultimate, and there are no means of communicating this state.

This is why our *shastras* (scriptures) end with the fifth body, or at the most they go up to the sixth body. Those with a completely scientific bent of mind do not talk about what is after the fifth body. The Cosmic world, which is boundless and unlimited, begins from there, but mystics like the Sufis talk of the planes beyond the fifth. It is very difficult to talk of these planes, for one has to contradict oneself again and again. If you go through the text of all that one Sufi has said—say Kabir—you will say, "This person is mad, for sometimes he says one thing and sometimes something else. He says, 'God is' and he also says, 'God is not.' He says, 'I have seen him' and in the same breath he says, 'How can you see Him? He is not an object that the eyes can see!" These mystics raise such questions that you will wonder if they are asking others or asking themselves.

Mysticism starts with the sixth plane. Therefore, where there is no mysticism in a religion, know that it has finished on the fifth body. But mysticism also is not the final stage. The ultimate is the Void—Nothingness. The religion that ends with mysticism ends with the sixth body. Void is the Ultimate, for after it there is nothing more to be said.

So the search for "*Adwait*" (the Non-dual) starts with the fifth body. All search of the opposites end with the fourth body. All barriers are within us and they are useful, for these very obstacles, when transformed, become your means to go ahead.

A stone is lying on the road. As long as you do not understand, it will remain an obstacle for you. The day you understand it will become a ladder for you. The stone is lying on the road. As long as you did not understand, you shouted, "The stone is in my way. How can I go ahead ?" When you have understood, you will climb over the stone and proceed ahead, thanking the stone with the words, "You have blessed me very much, because after climbing over you, I have found myself on a higher plane. Now I am proceeding along on a higher level. You were a means and I took you to be a barrier," you will say. The road is blocked by this boulder. What will happen ? Cross it and know. In this way, overcome anger, cross over it and reach forgiveness which is on a different level. Cross over sex and attain brahmacharya which is an entirely different plane. Then you will thank sex and anger for being the stepping-stones.

Every stone in the way can be a barrier as well as a medium. It depends entirely on you what you do with it. One thing is certain: Do not fight with the stone, for then you will only break your head and the stone will not be helpful. If you fight with the stone the stone will bar your way, for wherever we fight we stop. We have to stop near the person or thing we fight with; we cannot possibly fight from a distance. That is why, if someone fights sex, he has to be in and around sex just as much as another who indulges in it. In fact, many a time he is closer to sex, for the one who indulges in it can get out of it someday, can transcend it. But the one who fights cannot get out of it; he keeps going around and around.

If you fight anger, you will become anger yourself. Your whole personality will be filled with anger and each fibre of your body will vibrate with it. You will emanate anger all around you. The stories we read of *rishis* (sages) and *munis* (ascetics) like Durwasa being very wrathful happen because they fought with anger. Thus, they could think of nothing but cursing. The personality of such a person turns into fire. These are people who have fought with stones and who are now in difficulty. They have become what they battled against.

You will read of another *rishi* that a celestial maiden descended from heaven and corrupted him in a moment. How strange ! This is only possible if this man has fought with sex; not otherwise. He has fought and fought and thus weakened himself. Then sex is secure in its own place: it is just waiting for him to break down. This sex can now burst from anywhere. There is less possibility of an *apsara* (a celestial maiden) actually coming down from heaven, for are such maidens on contract to harass *rishis* and *munis* ? When sex is unduly suppressed with a heavy hand, an ordinary woman becomes a celestial being. The mind projects the dreams we dream at night and becomes completely filled with these thoughts. Then a thing which is not at all fascinating becomes bewitching.

So the sadhak has to beware of the tendency to fight. He should try his utmost to understand, and by "trying to understand" is meant understanding that which is given to him by nature. Through that which has been given to you, you will attain that which is yet to be attained, for this is the starting point. If you run away from that which is the very beginning, it is impossible to reach the goal. If you run away from sex in fright, how will you ever reach brahmacharya ? Sex was the opening given by nature and brahmacharya is the quest that has to be undertaken through this very opening. If you see in this perspective, there is no need to beg from anywhere; understanding is what is required. All of life is there for the purpose of understanding. Grasp knowledge from anybody, hear everyone and, finally, understand your own self within.

Questioner: *You have just enlightened us about the seven bodies. Could you tell us the names of some individuals—ancient or modern—who have attained the Nirvana body, the Cosmic body and the Spiritual body ?*

Bhagwan : Do not bother about this. It serves no purpose; it is meaningless. Even if I tell you, you have no means to verify it. As much as possible, avoid comparing and contrasting individuals, for it serves no purpose; it has no meaning. Leave it alone.

Questioner : *Do those who reach the fifth and following bodies again assume physical forms after death ?*

Bhagwan : One who attains the fifth or the sixth body before death is reborn in the highest celestial realm, and there he lives on the plane of the "*devas*" (gods). He can stay in this realm as long as he likes, but to attain Nirvana he has to come back to the human form. After attaining the fifth, there is no birth in the physical body, but there are other bodies. In fact, what we call "*devatas*" (*devas*) or gods signifies the kind of body that is obtained. This type of body is obtained after reaching the fifth body. After the sixth body, even these will not be there. Then we shall obtain the form of what we call "*Ishwar*" (the Supreme Being). But all these are still bodies. What type is a secondary matter. After the seventh, there are no bodies. From the fifth onwards, the bodies become more and more subtle until they reach the bodiless state after the seventh.

Questioner : *In a previous talk, you said you prefer "Shaktipat" (transmission of energy) to be as close to grace as possible--that it is better if it is so. Does this mean that there is a possibility of gradual progress and development in the process of Shaktipat ? In other words, is there a likelihood of qualitative progress in Shaktipat ?*

Bhagwan : There is every likelihood : many things are possible. In reality, the difference between Shaktipat and grace is a wide difference. Fundamentally, only grace is useful, and without a medium it is at its purest, for there will be no one in between to make it impure. It is just like when I see you directly with my own eyes : your image will be the clearest. Then I put on a pair of spectacles: the vision will not be that pure, for now a medium has come in between. Now there could be many kinds of mediums—some pure, some impure. A pair of spectacles could be coloured, another transparent and the quality of the lens itself will vary.

So when we obtain grace from a medium, there are bound to be impurities, and they will be of the medium. Therefore, the purest grace is that which is received directly when there is no medium. Now, for instance, if we could see without the eyes it would mean purer vision, for even the eyes are a medium and are bound to cause some hindrance. Now someone may have jaundice, someone may have weak eyesight, someone may have some other eye trouble: so these are the difficulties. Now one whose eyesight is weak will find the medium of a particular pair of glasses very helpful. It may perhaps give him a clearer vision than his unaided eyesight, and so the spectacles will have become one more medium. There are now two mediums, but the second medium compensates for the weakness of the first.

In exactly the same manner, the grace that reaches a person through another gathers impurities along the way. Now if these impurities are such that they have reverse effect upon the impurities within the sadhak, these both will offset each other. Then what will happen will be nearest to grace. But this will have to be decided separately in each case.

Therefore, I advocated direct grace. Do not bother about a medium. If at some time it is necessary in the course of life the glimpse can come through a medium also, but the sadhak should not worry or be anxious about this. Do not go begging, for, as I said, then the giver is bound to turn up. Then the more dense the medium, the more adulterated will be the effect. The giver should be such that he is not conscious of giving; then Shaktipat can be pure. Even then it is not grace. You will still require to attain directly without a medium. There should be no one between you and God; there should be no one between the power and you. And this should always be in your mind. This should be your vision and this should be your search. Many happenings will take place on the way, but you are not to stop anywhere; that is all that is required of you. And you will feel the difference. There are bound to be qualitative as well as quantitative differences, and the reasons will be many. That will be a very expansive situation.

Shaktipat can take place through a medium who has attained

the fifth body, but it will not be as pure as that which would come through a person of the sixth body, because his pride is still established. The "I" is dead, but the "am" still remains. Now this "am" will still feel pleasure. In a person of the sixth body, the "am" also is dead; there is only the Brahman. Then the Shaktipat will be purer. Yet some illusion remains, for the state of Non-Being has not yet been reached even though the state of "Being" has been. This "Being" is also a very subtle veil—very fragile, very transparent; all the same, it is there. So Shaktipat through a person of the sixth body will be better than that which comes through a person of the fifth body, and it will be very near to direct grace.

However close it may be, the slightest distance is, after all, a distance. And the more priceless a thing, the more even the slightest distance becomes a great distance. So invaluable is the realm of grace that even the most subtle veil of Being proves a barrier. Now the Shaktipat obtained from a person who has attained the seventh plane would be the purest; yet it will not be grace. The purest form of Shaktipat descends through the seventh body—the purest ! Here Shaktipat will reach its ultimate direction, for there is no veil as far as the medium is concerned: he is one with the Void. But as far as you are concerned, there are barriers. You will consider him as a human being all your life ; your veil will cause the ultimate barrier. He is one with the Void; he is without any barriers. But you will look upon him as an individual.

Now suppose I reach the seventh plane : I would know that I have attained Void, but what about you ? You will look upon me as a person, and this notion of an individual will become the final veil. You can only get rid of this notion when the happening occurs through the Formless. In other words, then you cannot point out from where and how the happening took place. When you will be unable to find the source, this notion will fall. The happening must be sourceless. If sunrays are coming you will think that the sun is a person. But when a ray comes from nowhere, when the rain falls without any cloud, then the final veil that is formed by personification falls.

As you proceed, the distances will become more and more subtle, and the final happening of grace will take place when there is no one in between. Your very thought that there is someone in between is a barrier enough. As long as there are two, there is a lot of obstruction : you are there and the other is there. Even when the other is no more, YOU are, and because you are the other's presence is also felt. The grace which descends without any source, without any origin anywhere, will be the best. The individual in you will flow away in this grace that comes from the Void. If another person is present, he serves the purpose of saving your individuality despite the fact that he is working for you.

If you go to the seashore you experience greater peace, if you go to the forest you experience greater peace, for "the other" is not present there and so your "I" remains firm and strong. If two men sit in a room, there are waves and counter waves of tension there even though these two may not be fighting or quarreling or even talking. So even when they are silent, the "I" of each is constantly working. There is aggression, and defense in full swing. These things can go on silently also, and there is no need for a direct encounter. The mere presence of two people, and a room is filled with tension.

If you were to gain full knowledge of all the currents that come out from you, you would see clearly that a room (containing two persons) has been divided into two, and each individual has become a center. The electric vibrations from both stand facing each other as armies on a battlefield. The presence of the other strengthens your "I". When the other leaves, the room will become a different place altogether: You relax. The "I" that was standing on edge will let itself go. It now leans against the cushion and rests, it now breathes freely, for the other is not there. Hence, the significance of solitude is to relax your ego and to help it to let go. Thus, you are more at ease near a tree than in the company of another person.

This is why, in countries where tensions between man and man are becoming deeper, people tend to live with pets. It is easier to live with animals than with men, for they have no "I". Tie a collar to a dog, and he goes about gaily. We cannot tie a collar to a man in this manner, though we try very hard. The wife ties the husband, the husband the wife, and they both go about merrily. But these collars are subtle and cannot be seen openly.

Yet, each tries to shake off the collar and be free. But the dog walks merrily along wagging his tail. So the pleasure the dog gives no other man can give, for another man at once brings your ego to your attention, and then the trouble starts.

Gradually, man tries to break his relationship with others and establish relationships with objects, for they are easier to handle. So the bulk of objects is increasing day by day. There are more articles in the house than people. People bring disorder and confusion; objects give no botheration. The chair remains where I place it. If I sit on it, it creates no trouble. The presence of trees, rivers, mountains, is not irksome; therefore, we feel at peace near them. The reason is only this : the "I" is not standing in full strength before us. Therefore, we too feel relaxed. When "the other" is not there, where is the need for the "I"? Then the "I" too is not. But the slightest inkling of "the other", and the "I" springs to attention. It is worried about its security, about its lack of information as to what the next moment may bring; hence, it has to be ready all the time.

The ego always remains alert until the very last moment. Even if you meet a person of the seventh plane, the ego is alert. Sometimes it becomes excessively alert before such a person. You are not so much afraid of the ordinary man, for even if he hurts you the injury is not very deep. But a man who has reached the fifth body or beyond can inflict deep wounds that reach up to the same body of yours that he has reached. Thus, your fear becomes more, for "God knows what He might do ?" You begin to feel something unknown, as if unfamiliar powers are peeping at you through him, so you become wary. You see an abyss all around him. You begin to feel the experience of the deep valley, and you are caught by the fear that if you go within him you will fall into this abyss.

That is why, when men like Jesus, Krishna and Socrates are born, we kill them: their very presence causes great confusion among us. To go near them is to go wilfully near danger. Then when they die we worship them, for now there is no fear. Now we can cast their image in gold and stand with folded hands before them calling them our "Lord God". But in their lifetime we treat them differently. Then we are terribly frightened of them, and this fear is of that which is unknown to us: you do not know for certain what is the matter. The deeper a man goes within himself, the more he becomes like an abyss to us. Then it is just like when someone is afraid to look down into a valley because it makes his head reel. Similarly, to look into the eyes of such a person will also create fear: our heads are sure to reel.

There is a wonderful story about "Moosa": After Hazrat Moosa had the vision of God, he never kept his face uncovered. All his life he went about with a veil drawn over his face, because to look at his face became dangerous. Whoever did so ran for his Life. There was an infinite abyss in his eyes. So Moosa moved about with his face covered, for people were frightened of his eyes. His eyes seemed to draw them on like a magnet toward that unknown abyss within themselves. They became struck with fear, for they did not know where his eyes would take them and what would happen to them.

The man who has reached the seventh and the last plane also exists so far as you are concerned, but you will try to protect yourself from him and a barrier will remain in between. Therefore, Shaktipat in this case also cannot be pure. It can be pure if you give up the thought of such a one being a person. But this can only happen when your "I" is lost. When you reach the stage where you are completely unaware of the ego, you will be able to obtain Shaktipat from anywhere, for then there is no question of its coming from anybody: it will have become sourceless, it will have become grace.

The greater the crowd, the harder and more condensed is your ego. Therefore, it has been a practice of old to get out of the crowd and try to drop the ego in solitude. But man is strange: if he stays under a tree for long, he will begin to talk to it and address it as "you". If he stays near the ocean, he will do the same. The "I" in us will go to any length to keep itself alive. It will create "the other" no matter where you go, and it will establish sentimental relationship even with inanimate objects and will begin to look upon them as individuals.

When a person approaches the last stage, he makes God "the other" so that he can save his "I". Therefore, the devotee always says, "How can we be one with God? He is He and we are we. We are at His feet, and He is God." The devotee is saying nothing but this, that if you want to be one with Him you will have to lose your ego. So he keeps God at a distance and he begins to rationalize. He says, "How can we be one with Him? He is great, He is Absolute. We are degenerated outcastes, so how can we be one with Him?" The devotee is saving the "you" in order to save his "I". Therefore, the *bhakta* (devotee) never rises above the fourth plane. He does not even go up to the fifth plane : he stagnates at the fourth. Instead of imagination, on the fourth plane visions come to him. He discovers all the best possibilities of the fourth body. So many happenings take place in a devotee's life that are miraculous, but the *bhakta* remains on the fourth plane all the same.

The "Atma sadhak" (one who is searching for the Self), the Hatha yogi (the yogi who goes through austerities) and many others who undergo similar practices, reach the fifth plane at the most. Such a sadhak's intrinsic desire is to attain bliss, to attain *Moksha* (liberation) and freedom from suffering. Behind all of these desires stands the "I": He says "I want liberation"—not liberation from the "I", but liberation of the "I". He says, "I want to be free, I want beatitude." His "I" stands condensed, so he only reaches up to the fifth plane.

The Raja yogi reaches up to the sixth plane. He says, "What is there in the 'I'? I am nothing ; He alone is—not I, but He: the Brahman is everything." He is ready to lose the ego, but he is not prepared to lose his Being. He says, "I shall remain as part of the Brahman; I am one with him. I am the Brahman. I shall let myself go, but my inner being within me will remain merged in Him." Such a seeker can go up to the sixth body.

A sadhak like Buddha reaches the seventh plane, for he is ready to give up all—even the Brahman, He is ready to lose himself and lose everything. He says, "Let what is remain, On my part I do not desire anything to remain: I am ready to lose my all." He who is prepared to lose everything is entitled to gain ALL.

The Nirvanic body is attained only when we are prepared to be "Nothing", when we have renounced all. Then there is a readiness to know even death. For knowing life we have many means. Therefore, he who knows life will stop at the sixth plane. But he who is ready to investigate death also will be able to know the seventh plane.

Questioner : *Why has the sadhak who has gained the capacity for vision and subtle sight on the fourth plane (and many have attained this stage) not been able to reveal the knowledge of the moon, the sun, the earth and their movements, as the scientists have done?*

Bhagwan : Three or four things have to be understood in connection with this. The first thing is that many of these facts HAVE been revealed by persons such as these, of the fourth plane. For instance, there is very little difference between the age of the earth as shown by these men and as shown by the scientists, and as yet it cannot be said that science is correct. Scientists do not themselves claim to be absolutely correct.

Secondly, there is even less difference in the information given by each of these two types of persons about the shape and measurement of the earth. Besides, even in connection with this matter it is not necessarily the case that those who have reached the fourth plane are wrong in their estimate. The shape of the earth is forever changing. The earth was never as far away from the sun as it is today and the moon also was never that far away from the earth as it is today. Africa is not where it used to be. Once upon a time it was joined with India. Thousands of happenings have occurred and are still occurring, and many changes take place constantly. Keeping in mind these constant changes, you will be surprised to know that people of the fourth plane have long ago revealed many of the discoveries that science is discovering today.

It should also be understood that there is a fundamental difference between the language of expression of the man of the fourth plane and the scientist. This is a very great difficulty. The man of the fourth plane has no language of words. He has the language of vision, images and symbols. He has the language of signs. As there is no language in dreams, in vision too there is no language. If we understand thoroughly, we will know that if we were to dream at night what we did throughout the day we would have to choose the medium of symbols and signs, for there is no language there.

If I am an ambitious person who wants to be above everybody else, I will dream I am a bird flying high in the skies over and above other birds. In dreams I will not be able to express verbally that I am ambitious, so the whole language changes in dreams. In the same manner, the language of vision is not of words but of pictures.

Dream interpretation began to develop after Freud, Jung and Adler. Now we can find out the meaning of a dream. In the same manner, whatever the persons of the fourth plane have said still awaits interpretation. As yet, we have not even been able to explain the phenomenon of dreams thoroughly. Thus, explaining the term "vision" is an altogether different matter. We must know the meaning of what has been seen in visions and of what people of the fourth plane are saying.

For example, when Darwin said, "Man has evolved from the animal," he spoke in a scientific language. But if we were to read the story of the Hindu Avatars, we would find that this is nothing but the same story told thousands of years ago in symbolic form. The first Avatar was not a man : he was a fish. Darwin also says that man's first form was that of a fish. Now when we say that the first Avatar was "*Matsya Avatar*"—a fish, this is symbolic. This is not the language of science: an Avatar and a fish. We denied this statement. But when Darwin said that the first element of life came in the form of the fish and then other forms followed, we readily agreed, for it seemed reasonable to us. Darwin's method and search is scientific.

Now those who saw visions saw the Divine first taking birth as a fish. The visionary speaks the language of parables. Then the second Avatar is a tortoise. Now this creature belongs both to the land and water. Obviously, the transition of life from water to land could not be sudden. There had to be an intermediary state. So whatever creature evolved must have belonged both to land and water. Then gradually, the descendants of the tortoise began to live on land, and then there must have been a marked separation from life in the water.

If you read through this story of the Avatars, you will be surprised to note that we had discovered long ago what Darwin discovered a thousand years later, and in the right chronological order. Then before the final metamorphosis, there is the half-man, half-animal Avatar—"*Narasinh Avatar*". After all, animals did not become human at one stroke. They too must have had to pass the intermediate phase where there were half men and half animals. It is impossible that an animal gave birth to a human being. There is a missing link between animal and man which could be "*narsinh*"—half man and half animal.

If we understand all these stories, we shall know that what Darwin said in scientific terms people of the fourth plane said long ago in the "Puranic" language (the language of symbol and legend). But to date, the Puranas (Hindu mythological scriptures) have not been properly explained. The reason for this is that the Puranas have fallen into the hands of ignorant, illiterate people. They are not in the hands of scientists.

Another difficulty is that we have lost the key to decipher the code of the Puranas. We do not have the deciphering code; hence, the difficulty. Now science says that man can exist on earth at the most for another 4,000 years. The forecast in many Puranas is that this world cannot last for more than 5,000 years. Science speaks a different language. It says the sun will cool down, its rays will diminish, its heat will diffuse, and in 4,000 years it will get cold. Then life on earth will cease together with it.

The Puranas speak a different language. And if the Puranas give a time of 5,000 years and not 4,000 as the scientists say, it should be kept in mind that it is yet not decided whether science is absolutely correct. It can be 5,000 and I believe it will be 5,000, for there can be a mistake in the calculation of science, but there is never a mistake in vision. Science, therefore improves upon itself day by day. It says one thing today and another tomorrow and yet another the day after. It has to change every day: Newton says one thing, Einstein says something else.

Every five years science changes its theories, for it comes upon better solutions. It cannot be decided whether the ultimate in science will be different from the visions of the fourth plane. And if these do not coincide with each other, it is not necessary to make hasty decisions on the grounds of what we know now through science and through what is told by the visionaries. Life is so profound that only an unscientific mind makes a hasty decision. If we examine the discoveries of science over the last hundred years, we will find that all discoveries that are a hundred years old read like Puranic tales. No one is ready to believe them any more, for other and better things are discovered in the course of time.

The code that revealed the truth in the Puranas is lost. Now, for example, if there is a third world war, the first outcome of it will be that all of the educated, civilized class of people will be destroyed. It is strange that only the uneducated, uncultured, people will remain. Some Adivasi, some Koal, some Bheel (Primitive tribes in India) in the far away mountains and jungles will go unscathed. No one will be spared in Bombay or New York. Whenever there is a world war, it is always the best communities that are destroyed, for it is they who are attacked. Some Bheel or Koal of Baster (India) might survive. He might tell his children of the planes in the skies though he will not be able to explain them. He had seen them flying and that is a truth, but he cannot explain the how and why of it as he does not have the code. The code was with the people of Bombay, but now they are dead.

For a generation or two the children might believe in their elders, but later on they will ask in doubt, "You have seen them?" And the elders will reply, "So we have heard, so our fathers said, and they in turn were told by their fathers that planes flew in the skies. Then came the big war and everything was destroyed." By and by the children will question, "Where are the planes? Show us some semblance, some sign." After 2,000 years, the children will say, "This is all the imagination of our forefathers. No one ever flew in the skies."

Such events have taken place. In this country the knowledge that was obtained by the psychic mind was destroyed in the battle of the Mahabharat (the great Indian war). It is now only a story. Now we are suspect of whether Ram could have flown in a plane from Lanka. It is all a matter of doubt because when not even a bicycle remains from that age, then the aeroplane seems to be an impossibility. And there is no mention of it in any book. In fact, the entire knowledge that existed before the Mahabharat was destroyed in this war. That which could be held in memory was all that could be saved. Therefore, the names of the ancient branches of knowledge were "*Smriti*" (traditionally remembered and written down later) and "*Shruti*" (traditionally heard and then written down). These are collections of knowledge which were remembered and which were told. They are not an account of proven and tested facts. Someone told someone, then he told someone else, and all these things we have gathered and kept in the form of these scriptures. But now we cannot claim to prove anything from them.

Remember also that the intelligentsia of the world consists of a very small number of people. If an Einstein dies, it will be difficult to find another to explain the theory of relativity. He himself said that there were not more than ten to twelve people who understood this theory. If these twelve die, we shall have books on relativity, but not a single man who understands it. Similarly, the Mahabharat destroyed all the proficient people of those times. Then what remained became just stories. Now, however, investigations are afoot for their verification, but we (in India) are unfortunate people, for we ourselves are doing nothing in this direction.

Recently, a place has been discovered that is about 4,000 to 5,000 years old and which seems to have been an airport. There is no other possible reason for such a big place. Such constructions have been found which could not have been possible without machines. For instance, the stones that were lifted up the pyramids are as yet beyond the capacity of our largest crane. These rocks have been placed there—that much is clear: and they have been lifted by men. Either these people had elaborate machinery at their disposal or they made use of the fourth body.

For example, I shall tell you an experiment which you may try. Let one man lie down on the ground. Now four others should gather around him. Two should place their fingers under his knees one on each side, and the other two, similarly, under his shoulders. Let them put only one finger each. Then each should make a firm resolve to lift him by his finger. They should breathe hard for five minutes, then hold the breath and lift the man. They can succeed in lifting this man by their mere fingers. So the boulders of the pyramids were either lifted by giant cranes or by some psychic force. The ancient Egyptians might have utilized some such method; there is no other way. The stones are there and they have been placed there: this cannot be denied.

Another thing to note is that psychic force has infinite dimensions. It is not absolutely necessary that a person who has attained the fourth plane should know about the moon. It is possible he is not interested to know; he may not consider it worth his while. Such persons were interested in knowing other things—things which were more valuable according to them—and they have completed their search in these directions. For instance, they were eager to know if spirits were an actuality or not, and they have known. Now science has discovered that spirits are there. These men of the fourth body were eager to know where people go after death and how.

Those who reach the fourth plane have hardly any interest in the material world. They could not care less what the dimensions of the earth are. To expect them to be interested in such matters is like children telling a grown-up, "We do not consider you wise because you cannot tell us how a doll is made. The boy next door knows all about it. He is all-knowing." They are right in their own way, for they are interested in knowing what is inside the doll, whereas the elders cannot be.

The inquiry of a man of the fourth plane changes dimensions. He wants to know other things. He wants to know where lies the path after death: where does a man go when he dies, what roads does he travel, what are the principles of the journey, how is he born again, and whether his birth and birthplace could be foretold. This man is not bent upon a man going to the moon: that is irrelevant for him. He is eager to find ways for man's liberation, for that alone is meaningful for him. Such a man was always anxious to know how the Atman entered the womb when a child was conceived, whether an Atman could be helped to choose the right conception, and how long it takes for an Atman to enter the embryo.

There is a book of Tibet called "The Tibetan Book of the

Dead". Every man in Tibet who attained the fourth body has laboured on one project: how a man can best be assisted after death. Suppose you are dead: I love you, but I cannot help you after death. But in Tibet there is a full arrangement to guide and assist a man and to encourage him to take a special birth and enter a special womb. Science will still take time to discover this, but it will discover it: there is no difficulty. And the Tibetans have found ways and means to test the validity of these happenings also.

When the Dalai (chief) Lama dies in Tibet, he tells beforehand where he will take birth next and how the others should recognize him. He leaves symbols behind for his recognition. Then after he dies, the search starts all over the country. The child that tells the secret of the symbol is taken to be the incarnation of the dead Lama, for he alone knows the secret. The present Dalai Lama was discovered in this manner. The Lama preceding him had left a symbol. A special saying was proclaimed in every village, and the child who could explain it was understood to be the one in whom the former Lama's soul had taken entry. The search took long, but ultimately the child was discovered who could explain the code. It was a very secret formula, and only the authentic Dalai Lama could know its meaning.

So the curiosity of a man of the fourth plane is entirely different. Infinite is the universe and infinite are its mysteries and secrets. Do not think that we have discovered all that is to be discovered by present-day scientific research. A thousand new sciences will come to light, for there are thousands of different directions and dimensions. And when these are revealed, people will call us non-scientific people, for we do not know what they will know. But we shall not call the ancient people non-scientific; it is only that their curiosity was of a different nature—different and beyond calculation.

Now we can very well ask that as we have found cures to many illnesses, why these ancient people of the fourth plane did not find them. You will be shocked to know the number of herbal remedies prescribed in Ayurveda and Yunani branches of medicine (Indian and Arabian systems of medicine). How could these people, without the aid of research in laboratories, discover the proper cures for every illness ? There is every possibility that this was brought about by the use of the fourth body.

There is a wellknown story about Vaidya Lukman (an ancient doctor) which tells that he would go up to each plant and ask what were its uses. Now this story has become meaningless in the world of today. It seems to be a logical fallacy to expect plants to talk. It is also a fact that until the last fifty years plants were not supposed to have life, but now science admits there is life in plants. Thirty years ago we did not believe that plants also breathe; now we admit that they do so. Fifteen years before we did not believe that plants could feel, but in the last fifteen years we have had to admit that they do. When you approach a plant in anger its psychic state changes, and when you approach it in love then again it changes. Therefore, it will not be out of place if we discover in the next fifty years that we can talk to plants also, but this will be a gradual development.

However, Lukman proved it long ago, but his mode of conversation could not have been the same as ours. To become one with plants is a quality of the fourth body. Then they can be questioned. I believe this story, for there is no mention of any laboratory huge enough in those days where Lukman could have carried out his research on the infinite herbs he brought into use. It is improbable, for each herb would require a lifetime to reveal its secret if done scientifically, whereas this man talked of unlimited herbs. Now science admits the efficiency of many of these herbal cures in illness, and they are still used. All of the research of the past is the research of the men of the fourth plane.

Now we treat thousands of illnesses, which is very unscientific. The man of the fourth piane will say, "There are no illnesses at all. Why are you treating them ?" Now science understands this and allopathy is now using new methods of treatment. In some hospitals of America, they are working on new methods. Suppose there are ten patients suffering from the same ailment. Five are given water injections and the other five are given the regular medicinal treatment. Then the findings show that the patients of each group respond to their treatment equally.

This proves that those treated with water were not really ill, but had an illusion of illness. Now if these people were given the regular treatment of this illness, it would have poisoned their systems and brought about contrary results. They required no treatment.

Many illnesses are born out of unnecessary treatment, and then they are difficult to cure. If you have no real illness—only a phantom illness—the medicine for that illness will have to act in some way, even though the necessary conditions of the illness are not within you. It will create poisons within for which you will have to undergo new treatments. The phantom illness will go on giving way to some actual malady. According to old science, 90% of illnesses are phantom maladies. Fifty years ago modern science refused to believe this, but now allopathy admits it 50%. I say they will have to admit to 40% more, for that is the reality.

There is no one to define what the man on the fourth plane (of the past) knew; no one has tried to interpret him. There is no man who can put his knowledge in the right perspective in today's scientific terms; this is the only hitch. Once this can be done, there will be no difficulty. But the language of parables is very different.

Today science says that the sun's rays pass through a prism and break into seven parts, and in this way they become distributed into seven colours. The *rishi* of the Vedas says, "The sun-god has seven horses of seven colours." Now this is the language of parables. "The sun has seven horses of different colours and he rides them" means the same as "the sun's rays break into seven parts". The former is a parable and the latter is the scientific version. We shall have to understand the language of parables just as we understand the language of science today. There should not be any difficulty.

People with psychic powers predict things much earlier and science understands them much later. But then predictions are all in a symbolic language. It is only when science proves the same facts that they are put down in the normal day-to-day language. Before that there is no language. Now you will be surprised to know, if you investigate in all directions, that science is just a recent arrival and language and mathematics came much earlier. Now those who discovered language and mathematics, what statistics could they have used? What means could they have had—what measure? How did they come to know that the earth goes around the sun once a year? It is this one revolution of the earth around the sun that has been taken as one year. Now this is a very old discovery—very much before science; the same is the case with the fact that there are 365 days in a year. But there does not seem to have been any scientific means behind the ancient seers. Therefore, psychic vision is the only alternative answer.

A very strange fact has come to light. A man in Arabia has in his possession a map of the world which is 700 years old. Now this is an aerial view of the world which could not possibly have been conceived of on land. There are only two solutions: either there were aeroplanes 700 years ago—and this does not seem possible, or some person lifted himself that high in his fourth body and then drew the map. Now one thing is certain: there were no aeroplanes then. But this aerial map of the world was made 700 years ago. What does this mean?

If we were to study Charak and Sushrut, we would be shocked to know that they have described everything about the human body which scientists came to know by dissection. There could be only two means of knowing. One possibility is that surgery had become so subtle that there could be no evidence of surgery being carried out—because no surgical instruments or books on surgery have been discovered. But there are descriptions of very minute parts of the human body—parts so minute that science could discover them only much later, parts which only twenty-five years ago scientists refused to accept as being present. But these have been described by these ancient physicians. There is second possible way by which they could have known: a person in a state of "vision" may have entered the human body and seen these things.

Today we know that x-rays can enter the human body. If a man said he could photograph our bones a hundred years ago, we would not have believed him. Today we have to believe, for he does.

But do you know that the eyes of a man in the fourth body can see even more deeply than an x-ray, and that a picture of your body can be made which is more complete than that which is made as a result of dissection? Surgery developed in the West because there they bury their dead. In a place like India where the body is burned, this was not possible. And you will be surprised to know that this research came about with the help of thieves.

The custom of cremation was also the idea of psychic persons, as they believed that the soul had difficulty in taking a new birth if the body of the previous life still remained. It then hovered around the old body. If the body is burned to ashes, the soul will be rid of this encumbrance—for once it sees the body turning to ashes, in the next body it will perhaps realize that what it considered to be its own was, after all, only a destructible thing.

So there was cremation in our country, and, hence, no way of dissecting the human body. In the West, thieves had stolen the bodies from burial grounds, and they sold them to scientists for their research. There were court cases and many other difficulties for these people, for stealing a corpse and dissecting it were both considered crimes.

So what we have come to know by countless dissections, books 3,000 years old reveal without them. This only proves that there is another method by which things can be known besides experimentation. Sometimes I shall talk in detail on this subject so that you may understand better.

[Text of a discourse given on July 7, 1970, evening, in Bombay, India].

14

THE PLUNGE OF SCIENCE INTO THE MYSTERIES OF RELIGION

Questioner :

In yesterday's talk you said that it is possible for science to enter the fifth or the spiritual body. Then you talked of the possibilities of science in the fourth body. Kindly tell us about the possibilities of science in the fifth body ?

Bhagwan Shree Rajneesh :

What we call the physical body and what we call the "Atman" (Soul) are not two things that are different and apart. There is no break between them; there are links. We have always been thinking that the body is separate and the soul is separate, and that there is nothing to connect them. Also, we have been thinking not only that they are apart, but that they are the opposite of each other. This idea separated religion from science. Religion was supposed to search for that which is other than the body, whereas science was that which discovered everything about the body — all except the Atman. So it is but natural that each should deny the other.

Science was engrossed in the physical body and so it asked, "Where is the body ?" Therefore, when religion reached its peak it described the body as an illusion, a fantasy, and said that in actuality it did not exist. It proclaimed the Atman as Truth and the body as illusion. When science reached its heights, it disclaimed the Atman. It said, "The concept of the soul is false; it is a lie. The body is everything." This error is the cause behind the concept that the body and the Atman are two opposite things.

I have talked the seven bodies. If the first body is the physical and the last is the spiritual, then if we do not consider the intervening five bodies there will be no bridge between these two. It would be just as if you were to climb a ladder and then discard all the intervening rungs between the last and the first. Then there is no connection between the first and the last steps.

If you see the full ladder, you will find that the first rung is connected with the last. And if you examine it more closely, you will find that the last rung is the last part of the first rung, and the first rung is the first part of the last one. Similarly, if we take all the seven bodies together we will find a connection between the first and the second bodies. The first body is the physical body; the second is the etheric body — the emotional body. It is only the subtle form of the physical and it is not non-material. It is just that it is so subtle that it has not yet been fully grasped by physical means. But now the physicists do not deny the fact that physical matter becomes more and more rarefied and non-physical in its subtle form.

For instance, modern science says that matter, when analyzed, is ultimately reduced to electrons which are not matter, but which are particles of electricity. Nothing like substance remains in the end—only energy. So science has made a wonderful discovery in the last thirty years. Though it had considered matter to be a reality, it has now come to the conclusion that matter does not exist, whereas energy is a fact. Science now says that matter is an illusion brought about by the revolution of energy at a high speed.

When a fan is made to rotate at great speed, we cannot see the three blades separately. What we see is a circle going around and around. Also, the spaces between the blades appear filled. Actually, the blades move so fast that before the reflection of one blade passes our eyes, the second blade is already there. Then the third blade comes just as swiftly, with the result that they follow one after the other so that we cannot see the vacant spaces between them. The fan can be made to revolve at such a speed that you can sit on it and never know that anything is moving underneath you. The space between two blades can become filled so swiftly, that after one blade passes under you the second will immediately replace it. Then you will not feel the empty space at all. It is entirely a matter of speed.

When energy revolves at a high speed, it looks like matter. The atomic energy on which our entire modern scientific research is based has never been perceived visually; only its effects are visible. The fundamental energy is invisible and the question of seeing it does not arise, but we can observe its effects.

So if we look upon the etheric body as the atomic body, it will not be wrong—for in this case also, we only see the effects and not the body itself. Because of the effects, we have to admit its existence. This second body is the subtle form of the first, and hence there is no difficulty in connecting the two. They are, in a way, joined to each other. One is gross, and so it can be seen; the other is subtle, and hence it cannot be seen.

Beyond the etheric is the astral body. It is a subtle form of "ether". Science has not yet reached there, but it has reached a conclusion that if we analyze matter, what ultimately remains is energy. This energy can be called ether. If ether is further broken up into more subtle components, what will remain is the astral—and this is subtler than the subtle. Science has not yet reached the astral, but it will. Until yesterday, science only accepted matter and denied the existence of the atom. Until yesterday, it said that matter is solid. Today it says that there is nothing like solid substance and everything is non-solid. Now they have proved that even a wall, which appears solid, is not so solid. It is porous, and things can pass back and forth through its holes. We may be inclined to say that at least that which is around the pores must be solid, but this too is not solid : each atom is porous.

If we magnify an atom we will find that there is as much distance between two components of an atom as there is between the earth and the moon or the sun and the stars. Then we might say that at least the two components at the two ends are solid, but science says that these too are not solid. They are particles of electricity. Now science is not even ready to accept the word "particle", for with that is joined the concept of matter. "Particle" means a portion of matter, but the atom's components are not matter, for matter is solid and keeps its shape whereas these components are continuously changing shape. They are like waves, not particles. When a wave arises in water, before you even say to yourself, "This is a wave," it has changed, for a wave is that which comes and goes continuously.

But a wave is also a material happening, so science has coined a new word which was not there thirty years ago. The word is "quanta". It is difficult to find a Hindi equivalent just as many Hindi words have no equivalents in English: for instance, the word "Brahman" (the Cosmic Reality). Words are formed because there is a necessity of expression on the part of those who have experienced. When the Brahman was experienced, it was necessary for those who experienced to coin a word to express it. Thus, the word "Brahman" was coined in the East. The West has not reached this stage yet, and hence they do not have any equivalent word, for they did not require it.

This is why many religious terms do not have any equivalents in English. For example, the word "AUM". This word cannot be translated in any language of the world. It is an expression of a deep spiritual experience. The West has no parallel word by which it can be expressed. In the same manner, "quanta" is a word coined to express the peak of scientific heights, and it has no parallel word in any other language. If we try to understand the meaning of "quanta", it means "a particle and a wave together". It will be difficult to conceive of it, however. It is something which behaves sometimes like a particle, sometimes like a wave, and whose behaviour is very unpredictable.

Until now, matter was most reliable; there was a certainty about matter. But the ultimate part of matter, the atomic energy that has been discovered, is very uncertain. Its behaviour cannot be foretold. First the science stood firmly by the certainty of matter. It said that everything is precise and definite. Now the scientist does not press this claim, for he knows that from where he has now reached in research this certainty is very superficial. There is a deep uncertainty within, and it would be interesting to know what this uncertainty means.

Where there is uncertainty there is bound to be consciousness; otherwise uncertainty cannot be. Uncertainty is a part of consciousness, certainty is a part of matter. If we leave a chair in a certain place in a room we will find it exactly there upon our return, but if we leave a child in the room we will never find it where we left it. There will always be a doubt, an uncertainty, where it will be and what it will be doing. We can be sure of the chair, we can be sure about matter—but never about consciousness. Therefore, when science accepted the uncertainty in behaviour on the part of the ultimate portion of the atom, it also accepted the possibility of consciousness in the ultimate part of matter.

Uncertainty is the quality of consciousness, but matter cannot be unpredictable. It is not that fire may burn when it chooses and not burn when it does not choose to, nor can water flow in whatever direction it pleases or boil at any temperature it fancies. The functions of matter are determined, but when we go within matter we find that ultimately it is undetermined.

You can take it this way: If we want to find out how many people die in Bombay, this is possible. If there are one crore of people, we can take the number of deaths in one year and find out approximately how many die per day, and this would be almost correct. If we calculate the mortality rate for this whole country of 500,000,000 in the same way, the figure would be closer to the exact number. If we calculate the mortality rate for the whole world, the certainty of the figure will be yet greater. But if we want to find out when a single person will die, our calculations will be most uncertain.

The greater the crowd, the more material things become. The more individual the phenomenon, the more we find consciousness. In fact, a single piece of matter is a crowd of millions of atoms; therefore, we can predict about it. But if we penetrate within the atom and catch hold of the electron, we find that it is individual: we cannot determine its course, and it seems as if it decides that on its own. So about a solid rock we can be certain: we will find it in a particular place, etc. But the structure of the individual atoms within will not be the same. By the time we return again to the rock, all the atoms within will have changed their positions and travelled from one place to another.

Uncertainty begins by going deep within matter. This is why science has changed its language from "certainty" to "probability" No longer does it say, "This is how this or that will be." Rather, it says, "It is more probable this way than that." It no longer says emphatically, "This is it." In the past, all the claims of science were in the language of certainty. Whatever it said was bound to be. But when the search of science went deeper, all its former concepts began to totter. The reason was that science had unknowingly stepped from the physical realm into the etheric, about which it has no understanding. Until it accepts the fact of stepping from the physical to the etheric plane, it cannot have any understanding. It has reached the second part of matter, the etheric body, and this has its own possibilities. There is no gap between the first and the second body.

The third or the astral body is even more subtle. It is the subtlest of the subtle. If we break the ether into atoms (which still seems improbable, for we have barely unfolded the physical atom; thus, to experiment with ether will still take a long time) when the ether atoms are known, we shall find that they are the particles of the body that comes next—namely, the astral body. When we broke the physical atom, its most subtle particles were found to be etheric. Similarly, if we break the etheric atom, the most subtle particles will be that of the astral body. So we shall find a connection between them. These three bodies are clearly joined to one another; therefore, photographs of ghosts have been taken.

A ghost does not have a physical body. Its veiling starts with the etheric body. It has been possible to photograph ghosts—for when the etheric body condenses, a sensitive camera can catch its reflection. Another thing about ether is that it is so subtle, it is easily influenced by the psyche. If the spirit of a dead person wishes to appear, it can condense its form so that the atoms that are spread out come closer and form an outline. This can be caught by a camera.

Thus, our second body that is etheric is much more influenced by the mind than the physical body. The latter too comes under the influence of the mind, but not to that extent. The more subtle the body, the more it is affected by the mind and the nearer it will be to the mind. The astral body is even more influenced by the mind. This is why astral travelling is possible. A man can be asleep in this room, but he can reach any part of the world with his astral body. You must have heard stories of a man being seen in two or three places at the same time. This is possible. His physical body will be in one place and his astral body in another. It is a matter of a little practice, and this can be brought about.

The powers of the mind develop more and more as we go inward, and they dissipate as we go outward. Going outward is just like burning a lamp and then putting glass encasements over the flame. After putting one, the flame will not appear very bright. Then we put another covering, and the flame becomes more dim. Then we put still another and yet another. In this way we place seven covers over it. After the seventh covering the light of the flame will be extremely dull and dim, for it has to pass through seven layers.

In this way, our life energy becomes very dim by the time it reaches the physical body. This is why we do not seem to have much control over the physical body. But if someone begins to travel within, his control over his physical body becomes more and more, exactly in proportion to the depth of his inner journey. The subtle form of the physical is the etheric and the still more subtle part of the etheric is the astral. Then comes the fourth body — the mental body.

Until now we were under the impression that mind is one thing and matter another. Mind and matter were considered as two separate things. In fact, there was no way of defining them. If we were to ask, "What is mind ?" We would be told, "That which is not matter," and vice versa. If we were to ask, "What is matter ?" there was no other definition. And this is how we have always been thinking about them — as being different and apart. Now, however, we know that mind also is a more subtle form of matter. Conversely, we can say that matter is the condensed form of mind.

When the atoms of the astral are broken, they become thought waves. Now there is a close proximity between "quanta" and thought waves. It was not considered. So far, thoughts were not considered to have a physical existence, but it is a fact that when you think a particular kind of thought the vibrations around you change accordingly. It is interesting to note that not only thoughts, but even words have their own vibrations. If you spread sand particles on a glass top and chant "Aum" loudly, the pattern caused by the vibration of the sound will be different from the pattern caused by chanting "Ram". If you were to utter an abuse, the pattern will again change.

You will be surprised to know that the more foul an abuse, the more ugly is the pattern formed, and the more beautiful a word, the more beautiful will be the pattern of its vibration. The abuse will form a chaotic pattern, whereas the lines of the beautiful words will be well formed and well balanced.

Therefore, for thousands of years research was carried out to find words that produced beautiful vibrations, and it was considered whether their weight was enough to strike the heart. Words are thoughts that are manifested. However, unmanifested words also carry a resonance, and we call them "thoughts". When you think about something, a particular kind of resonance is created around you, a particular kind of vibration surrounds you. This is why you find sometimes that when you go near a particular person, you feel sad for no apparent reason. It could be that the person has not uttered a single negative word, and perhaps he is even laughing and happy to meet you. Yet a sadness takes hold of you from within. On the other hand, in the company of someone else you may suddenly feel cheerful.

You enter a room and you may feel a sudden change inside yourself. Something holy or unholy takes hold of you. In some moments you are surrounded by peace and tranquillity, and in others by restlessness. You cannot understand and you wonder, "I was feeling very peaceful. Why has this restlessness suddenly arisen in my mind?" All around you there are thought waves, and they keep on entering within you all the 24 hours.

Recently, a French scientist developed an instrument which has succeeded in catching the thought waves. As soon as a man approaches this instrument, it begins to show what thoughts are within him. The instrument begins to catch the thought waves. If an idiot is made to stand before it, there will be very few waves reported, for such a person hardly thinks. If an intellectual is made to stand before it, the machine takes over, all the vibrations of his thoughts.

So what we know as the mind is the subtle form of the

astral. As we go more and more within, the layers get more and more subtle. Science has reached the etheric body, but even now it insists on calling it the atomic plane, or the plane of "atomic energy". But science has reached down to the second body of matter. It will not take long to reach the third plane, for now it has become necessary to do so.

Work is being done on the fourth plane also, but from a different dimension. As mind was considered to be apart from the body, some scientists are working only upon mind. They have left the body completely out. They have experienced a lot of things about the fourth body. For instance, we are all, in a way, transmitters. Our thoughts spread all around us. Even when I am not talking to you my thoughts reach you.

A lot of work is in progress in Russia in the field of telepathy. One scientist, Fiyadev, has been successful in transmitting thoughts to a person at a distance of a thousand miles just as is done in radio transmission. If we concentrate our attention with full willpower in a particular direction and transmit a thought, it reaches that particular destination. If the mind at the other end is equally open and ready to receive at that moment and is concentrated in the same direction, the thought is received.

You can try a simple experiment at home. Small children catch thought waves very quickly, for their receptivity is very sharp. Seat a child in a dark room in one corner and tell him to concentrate on you for five minutes. Tell him that you will tell him something in silence and he should try and listen. If he hears it, he should repeat what he heard. Then you choose a word, say "Ram". Now concentrate on the child and repeat this word within yourself until it resounds in you. Do not say it aloud. In two to three days time, you will find that the child has caught the word.

The reverse can also take place. Once the experiment succeeds, it will be easy to carry out further tests. Now you may tell the child to concentrate on you. He should think of a word and throw it in your direction in the same way. With the first part of the experiment, your doubt was cleared when the child caught your word. Thus, now you will be receptive and catch the child's word. When the experiment is successful you will stop doubting, and your receptivity will increase accordingly.

Between you and the child there is the physical world. This thought should be intrinsically physical in its content, or else it will not be able to cross the physical medium. You will be surprised to know that Mahavir has even defined karmas (actions) as material. If you are angry and you kill someone, it is an action of anger and of murder. Mahavir says that the subtle atoms of these actions cling to you as the scum of karmas and actions. So actions too are physical, and they also hold you like matter.

Mahavir calls becoming free of this filth of karmas as "*nirjara*". All the atoms of these karmas that have collected around you should fall off. The day you are rid of them all, what remains of you will be absolutely pure. "*Nirjara*" means the falling off of the atoms of actions. When you are angry, it is an action. Then this anger remains with you always, in its atomic form. That is why, when the physical body falls, these atoms do not disintegrate, for they are very subtle. They come along with you in the next birth.

So the mental body is the subtle form of the astral body. Thus, as you can see, there is no gap between these four bodies. Each is a more subtler form of the preceding body. A lot of work is being done on the mental body. Scientists are working in the field of psychology and, especially, n iparapsychology, and the strange and wonderful rules of mental energy are slowly coming within their grasp. Religion grasped them a long time ago, but now many things have become clear to science as well.

There are many people in Monte Carlo who cannot be defeated in the game of dice. Whatever dice they throw brings about the number they want. At first it was thought that perhaps the dice were specially designed to throw the number they desired. Then the dice were changed, but the result was the same. The dice fell exactly where these people wanted them. Several changes of dice yielded the same result.

Even when blindfolded, these people managed to throw the right number. This made the others sit up and take note. Investigations were begun to find out the reason. Actually, the keen determination of their thought influenced the dice. They threw the dice with a sharp resolve to get the number they wanted. Their thought waves then brought the dice to that very number. What does this mean ? If thought waves are capable of changing the direction of dice, they must also be material, or else this would not be possible.

Carry out a small experiment, and you will understand. Since you talk of science, I talk of experiments. Take a glass filled with water. Add a little glycerine, or any other greasy liquid, so as to form a thin film on the surface of the water. Place a straight pin lightly over this film, so that it floats on the surface. Close the room from all sides. With your palms flat on the ground, concentrate your attention fully on the pin. For five minutes look straight at the pin. Then tell the pin to turn to the left, and it will turn to left. Then tell it to turn to the right, and it will turn to right. Tell it to stop, and it will stop. Tell it to move, and it will move. If your thoughts can move a pin, it can move a mountain also; it is only a matter of proportion. Fundamentally, the principle is the same. If you have the ability to move a pin, the fundamentals are proven. It is a different matter that the mountain may be too massive a structure to move, but move it can.

Our thought waves touch matter and transform it. There are people who, when given your handkerchief, will be able to tell approximately as much about you as can be told by seeing you. This is because your handkerchief absorbs your thought waves. Also, your ornaments absorb your thought waves. These waves are so subtle, that a handkerchief which belonged to Alexander the Great will still carry the facts about his personality. The waves are so subtle that it takes them millions of years to come out of the object. This is why graves and "*samadhis*" (burial spots for saints) came to be constructed.

Yesterday I told you that (in India) we have the custom of burning our dead, but not our dead sannyasins. An ordinary man's body is burned so that his soul does not go on hovering round him. But the sannyasin is not cremated, for his soul had already stopped hovering around his body while he was still alive. Now there need be no fear of his soul having any attachment to his body. We wish to conserve his body, for the body of a man who has spent years in pure thoughts will diffuse the same thought waves for thousand and millions of years. His *samadhi* (burial spot) will be meaningful; it will yield results. The body is dead, but this body has been so close to this soul that it absorbed a great deal of the waves that had spread from it.

Thoughts have infinite possibilities, but they are physical all the same. Therefore, be very careful what you think, for the subtle thought waves will remain with you even after the body falls. Your physical age is quite short compared to the age of these subtle waves. Scientists have now come to the conclusion that if there have been people like Jesus and Krishna, in the near future they will be able to catch hold of the thought waves of these people. Then we shall be able to tell whether Krishna ever told the Gita, for the thought waves that emanated from Krishna are still present in the firmament, striking some planet, some asteroid.

It is just like when we throw a stone into the sea. When it falls, it forms a small circle. The stone will sink, for it cannot stay long on the surface of the water : it begins to sink as soon as it touches the water. The ripples caused by its impact on the water begin to increase. They become larger and larger, and endless is their extension. They may go beyond the horizon of your vision, and who knows what distant shores they have reached.

So thoughts, no matter when they were born — not only those that were spoken, but also those that were in the mind—also spread in the space of the universe, and they go on spreading. And they can be caught hold of. Someday, when the momentum of science increases and man progresses further, we shall be able to hear them once again. Now the news relayed from Delhi to Bombay takes some time to reach Bombay, for sound takes time to travel. By the time it reaches Bombay, it is no more in Delhi: the waves have left Delhi though the distance is only of a few moments duration. There is a time gap.

Now suppose we are seeing a man in New York on television. When his image is formed in New York, it is not at once visible to us. There is a gap between its formation and the time when it reaches us. It could be that in that interval the man may have died, but he will appear alive to us.

Thought waves from the earth, as well as the ripples of other happenings, go out to the infinite number of planets. If we were to go before them and catch them, they would still be alive in a sense. Man dies, but his thoughts do not die that quickly. Man's life is very short; the life of thoughts is very long. Remember also, the thoughts we do not express live longer than those we express, for they are more subtle. The more subtle a thing, the longer is its life; the more gross, the shorter is the life.

Thoughts influence the physical world in many ways. We have no idea how their effect is. Biologists have now experienced that if a loving type of music is played before a plant, it begins to flower soon — even out of season. If noisy, chaotic tunes are played before it, then it does not flower — not even in season. The vibrations of the tune touch the plant. Cows give more milk under the influence of certain music and stop giving milk under the influence of a different type of music. Thoughts produce a more subtle ether that produces an aura of ripples. Each man carries around him his own world of thoughts from which ripples go on spreading out continuously.

These thought waves are also physical. What we know as the mind is a very sublte form of physical energy. Therefore, it is not difficult for science to reach them, for these waves can be caught and investigated. For instance, we did not know until recently how deeply a man sleeps — at what depth his mind goes. Now we know; we have instruments to find out. As we have instruments to measure the pulse rate, we have instruments to measure sleep. A device is fixed to the head all night long, and from the graph formed on it we can tell exactly when the person's sleep became deep, how long he slept, how long he dreamt, what was the duration of good dreams, what was the duration of bad dreams, how long were the dreams, and whether, they were sexual or non-sexual. All this the graph shows. There are about ten laboratories in America where thousands of people are paid to come and sleep and whose sleep is closely examined. It is a matter of great concern that we should remain unacquainted with sleep.

One-third of a man's life passes in sleep. Sleep is not a small matter. If a man lives for sixty years, he sleeps for twenty of them. If this period of twenty years remains unknown, a third of his life will remain unknown to him. Now the interesting fact is that if he does not sleep for these twenty years, he will not live for forty years. Therefore, sleep is a basic necessity. A man can sleep without awakening for sixty years, but he cannot live without sleeping. Thus, sleep is a basic requirement.

In sleep we are somewhere else; the mind is somewhere else. But this mind can be measured. Now it can be known how deep it goes in sleep. There are many people who insist they do not dream. This is an absolute falsehood, and they say this because they do not know. It is very difficult to find a man who does not dream. It is VERY difficult ! Dreams occur all night long. You may be thinking that you only have a dream or two, but that is wrong. The machine says that dreams occur throughout the night, but we do not remember them. You are asleep, so remembrance is absent. The dream you remember is the very last that takes place when sleep is almost done. When you come back from sleep, the last dream remains in your thoughts. Its faint echo still lingers within as you wake up. But you do not at all remember all the dreams of deep sleep.

Now it has become necessary to investigate what dreams occur in deep sleep, for that which a man dreams in the depths of sleep reveals his authentic personality. In truth, we become inauthentic upon awakening. Ordinarily, we say, "What is there in dreams ! But dreams reveal more truth about ourselves than our waking state. In our conscious period, we cover ourselves with false mantles. If some day we should succeed in making a window in man's head from where we can observe all his thoughts, his last freedom will be gone. Then he will not be free even to dream. He will be afraid to dream, for there also morality with its laws and regulations will set up its policemen. It will say, "This dream is not proper; you are not dreaming right." At present, however, we do have this freedom. Man is free in his sleep — but his freedom will not be for long, for encroachment on sleep has already begun. For instance, now Russia has started its "education in sleep".

A lot of work is going on in sleep teaching. Also, in the waking hours more effort has to be made because the child resists. It is difficult to teach a child something, for basically he refuses to be taught. In fact, every man refuses to learn, for each man starts off with the basic thought that he knows already. The child also refuses, saying, "What are you teaching?" In no way is he ready to learn. Then we have to bribe him by giving prizes after examinations, gold medals, etc. We have to raise the fervor of ambitiousness within him; we have to go on driving him in order to educate him. This conflict takes too long a time. What the child can be made to learn in two hours we get through to him in two months.

So the method of sleep teaching has been evolved, and it has become as clear as day that a child can be taught very well in sleep. The reason is simple: there is no resistance in sleep. A recorded tape is played near the sleeping child which imparts whatever has to be put into the child— "2 and 2 is 4; 2 and 2 is 4" : the tape will go on repeating. Ask the child in the morning, and he will say, "2 and 2 is 4."

Now this thought that was imparted in sleep can also be made to penetrate the mind by means of thought waves, for now we know about thought waves. In the past we did not know, but now we know that words themselves are not imprinted on a phonograph record. Rather, the impact of the sound-waves are recorded on the record. When the needle touches the grooves that have been created, it repeats the same waves that caused the grooves to be imprinted.

As I said before, if you chant "Aum" a pattern will be formed on the sand. The pattern itself is not Aum — but if you know that this particular pattern is formed by Aum, then someday you will be able to convert this pattern back into Aum. Upon the formation of the pattern, the sound of Aum should occur. The pattern and Aum can be looked upon as the same thing. In the phonograph record there are no words — only the grooves created by the impact of the sound of words. When those grooves come in contact with the needle, they are converted into the corresponding sounds. In the very near future we shall be able to make thought records. As the impact of thoughts has been caught, it will not take long for man to record it.

Then a wonderful thing will happen. Then it will be possible that even though Einstein is dead, his full thought process will be recorded. Then what Einstein would have thought in the future, had he remained alive, will also be supplied by the machine, because the machine will catch the impact of his entire thought waves.

Sleep, dreams and unconsciousness have been fully investigated. Thus, all the scientific possibilities of the mind are now known to man. Therefore, it is well to understand them.

For instance, take a man who is angry. According to our old calculations we will advise him, "Do not give in to anger; you will go to hell." We have no other way. But if this man says he is willing to go to hell, then we are helpless; we cannot do a thing to him. And if the man further declares that he is eager to go to hell, all our morality becomes useless. We can have control over a man only if he is afraid of hell. This is why no sooner did the fear of hell leave the world when our morality went with it also. No one is now afraid of hell. "Where is hell ?" everyone wants to know.

So morality is completely finished, for the fear on which it was based is gone. But science says there is no need for morality, as it has developed another formula based on stopping certain bodily secretions. When we are in anger, a particular chemical process takes place within the body, for anger is a physical happening. When there is anger within, it is absolutely necessary for certain substances to be secreted within the body. Thus, the formula of science is this : these secretions can be stopped from forming, and then there will not be any anger. Then there is no need to stop anger directly. If these fluids are stopped, man will find it impossible to be angry. If we try to advise young boys or girls to abstain from sex, to practise "brahmacharya" (celibacy), they never listen. Science says, "Stop all this ! If we restrict the growth of certain glands, sexual maturity will not come before the age of 25."

This is very dangerous. The moment the mind comes fully within the grip of science, man will begin to misuse its knowledge. Science says that the chemical composition of a man who has a rebellious mind is different from that of a man with an orthodox mind. This finding contains dangerous possibilities. If the composition of these chemicals become known to man, we can make a rebellious man passive and an orthodox man rebellious. Once the compositions of the chemicals that bring about the urge to steal or kill are known, there will no longer be any need for jails and executions. All that will be required then is the necessary surgery or treatment to rid the person of these. The chemicals in question can be removed or other chemicals can be introduced to neutralize them or antidotes can be given. All this work is presently under investigation.

All this shows that there are no longer any difficulties in the path of science to reaching the fourth body. The only hitch is that a very large part of science is engaged in research for war purposes. That is why this kind of research is not given primary consideration. It remains a secondary matter. Yet there has been sizeable progress, and unusual results have been obtained.

Aldous Huxley has claimed that that which had happened to Meera or Kabeer can be brought about by injections. It is a very striking claim, though true to some extent. Mahavir would fast for a month and his mind would become tranquil. Fasting is a physical act. And if the mind can become peaceful by a physical act, then the mind too is physical. With a month's fasting, the whole chemical composition of the body changes; that is all there is to it. The nutrition that the body should have had is denied to it, and all of the body's reserve is used up. Fat melts, and the non-essential elements undergo destruction while the essential ones are saved. Thus, the whole chemical arrangement of the body undergoes a complete change.

Science says, "Where is the need to undergo such hardship for one long month ? The chemical ratio can be changed according to specifications here and now." If this chemical change is brought about by science you will experience the same peace that Mahavir experienced after a month's long fast in no time at all; a month's fasting will not be necessary.

Now I tell you during meditation to breathe hard and fast, but what is going to happen after a half hour of hard breathing? It is only that the ratio of carbon and oxygen within you will change, but this can be brought about by external means also. There is no need to make you labour for half an hour. The ratio of oxygen and carbon dioxide in this room can be changed, and all those sitting here will experience peace and calm and will feel joyous. Thus, science has entered the fourth body from all sorts of directions, and it is still penetrating into it further.

Now in meditation, various experiences happen to you. You smell all kinds of fragrances, you see colours. All this can now be brought about without meditation also, for science has found out which part of your brain becomes active during these experiences. If the back part of my brain is stimulated when I see beautiful colours, scientific investigation will show exactly the portion that becomes active and the length of the waves produced. Now you need not go into meditation. The same vibrations can be brought about within you with the help of electricity, and you will begin to see colours. These are all parallel happenings, because no matter which polarity we take hold of the other end at once becomes activated.

There are hazards in this, however. The more a new research by man penetrates within, the more its hazards increase. For example, we can now increase the age of man as much as we like. It is no longer in the hands of nature: it is in the hands of science. Thus, in Europe and America there are thousands of old people clamouring for the right to die of their own free will, but they are kept lingering on their deathbeds. They are given oxygen and can be made to live for long periods. Now a ninety-year-old man begs to die, but the doctors say, "We cannot be a party to it as it is against the law." Even if an old man's son feels that his father is suffering too much and he should now be allowed to die, he cannot say so openly. There are machines to keep a dying man alive, and the nearly dead are made to live on. Now this, in a way, is dangerous.

Our old laws were made when there were no means of keeping a person alive and when we could also kill a person. Now laws need to be revised, for we can keep a dying person alive and lingering on for so long that the man feels to cry out, "This is violence! This is an atrocity! I do not want to live any longer. What are you doing to me?" There was a time when we punished a man for his crime by hanging him. It will not be surprising if fifty years hence we may punish a man by not allowing him to die. And this punishment will be worse than the first, for dying is a matter of a few seconds whereas living on can be for decades. So whenever there is a new discovery in the inner world of man, there are two results : either mankind can suffer because of it or it can benefit. When power comes, it is always two-sided.

Science has reached the fourth plane within man. Within the next fifty years—rather, within the next thirty years —it will penetrate deeper into the fourth body. Perhaps you may not know that whatever has been undertaken during a particular century reaches its climax at the end of the century. Every century completes its work by the time it comes to its end. This century has taken very many works upon itself which will be completed in thirty years' time. Its greatest task is the entrance into man's psyche, and this will be completed.

The fifth—the spiritual body—is even more subtle than the fourth. Here there are not only vibrations of thought, but also vibrations of the being. If I sit absolutely silent without a single thought within, even then my being creates vibrations. If you come near me and there is no thought in me, you will still be within the field of my vibrations. And the most interesting thing is that the vibrations of my thoughts are not half as strong or half as penetrating as the vibrations of my being. Therefore, the one who reaches the "no-mind" state becomes very powerful. It is difficult to gauge the effect of his power, for the vibrations of Existence begin to arise within him. This man has knowledge of the most subtle vibrations of the spiritual body.

So it has happened, in many cases, as in the case of Mahavir (and this is as it should be) that he did not speak. That is, he either spoke very little or he did not speak at all; he just sat. People came, sat before him, understood him and went back. This was possible in his time, but not so now. It is very difficult now because you will only experience the deep waves of the spiritual body if you are ready to be in the no-thought state yourself, and not otherwise. If you are filled with the noise of your own thoughts, you will miss these subtle vibrations. They will just pass through you and you will not be able to grasp them.

If the vibrations of Existence come within one's grasp, if there is a no-thought state on both sides, then there is no need to talk. Then communication takes place on a very intimate level, and this communication goes straight to the heart. Then there is no explaining, for there is no way to explain. Then you also will not waver over whether this or that will be or will not be. Your being will directly know what has happened.

It is not necessarily the case that only human beings are reached by the vibrations of the fifth body. There is a wonderful phenomenon in the life of Mahavir: It is said that even animals attended his gatherings. Jain sadhus have been unable to explain this phenomenon and they never will. Now an animal does not understand human language, but it understands the language of "BEING" very well. If I sit in a no-thought condition near a cat, the cat is already in the state of no-thought. With you, however, I will have to talk, for to take you to the cat's state of no-thought is a very long journey. Animals, plants and even stones understand the vibrations that begin from the spiritual body; there is no difficulty in that. So this body is also accessible, but only after the fourth body. The fourth body has been penetrated from many fronts, and science will accept the spiritual state readily. But after this, there is some difficulty.

Therefore, I said that things can be made very scientifically clear up to the fifth body — but after the fifth body difficulties begin. There are reasons for this. If we understand science well, it is a specialization in a particular direction; it is a particular selection. Therefore, science can only go deeper when it restricts its search to as few things as possible and tries to know as much as possible only about them. The aim of science is to know more and more about less and less. Its work is twofold: it tries to know more about as small a thing as possible. It makes the subject of its inquiry as small as possible and increases its knowledge about it.

The doctors of old were knowledgeable about the whole body, but the doctor of today is not. The general practitioner of old is now hardly to be seen. In the world of today, he has become a relic; he is no longer reliable. He knows about too many things, and hence he cannot know about any one thing sufficiently well enough to be trusted. Now there are eye specialists and ear specialists, and they can be relied upon because they have acquired the maximum knowledge in a specialised field.

For instance, all the literature obtainable about the eye is so vast, that one life time is not enough to go through it. It is quite probable that in the near future there might be one eye specialist for the right eye and another for the left eye or perhaps one specialist for the pupil and one for the retina. As knowledge increases, the eye will be divided into many parts for special study, for each part is an important case in itself. The aim of science is to concentrate its focus of attention to such a pinpoint that it can penetrate to the greatest depth. This is how science can come to know a great deal.

So, as I said before, science will reach up to the fifth body, for up to the fifth the individual still exists, and hence he can come within its focus. From the sixth the Cosmic starts, and this is beyond the focus of science. The Cosmic body means "the Total". Science cannot enter there, for science goes from the small to the smallest. Therefore, it can only grasp the individual; it will find it very difficult to grasp the Cosmic. Religion alone can grasp the Cosmic.

Hence, up to the Atman, the Self, science will have no trouble. Difficulties start with the Brahman—the Cosmic Self. I do not think science will ever be able to grasp the Brahman, for then it will have to leave its specialization. And the moment it leaves specialization, it no longer remains science. It will then be as generalized and vague as religion. So with the help of science we can travel along to the fifth body. At the sixth, science will be lost, and the seventh is impossible for it because all of its search is focused only upon life.

Actually, our center of existence is life. We want to be less ill and more healthy; we want to live longer, more happily, more comfortably. The aim of science is to make life more deeply happy, satisfying, healthy and enjoyable. But the seventh body is the acceptance of death: it is the ultimate death. Here, the sadhak goes beyond the search for life. He says, "I want to know death also. I have known Existence and the mystery of Being; now I want to know Non-Existence, the Non-Being."

Science has no meaning in this area. Scientists like Freud will call this the "death wish" and say that this is not a healthy condition of the mind—that it is suicidal. According to Freud, liberation and Nirvana are not conducive to life and these concepts are a proof of your wish to die. He says that you wish to die, so you are ill. The scientist is against the desire for death, for science is based on the will to live and on an expansion of life.

The man who wishes to live is a healthy man, but a moment comes when the wish to die is equally healthy. If someone wishes to die before this moment comes, it is definitely unhealthy. However, a moment does come in life when a person wishes to die for the sake of death.

One may say it is healthy to be awake and unhealthy to sleep, and gradually we are giving more place to day than to night. At first night started at 6 p.m., now it begins at 2 a.m. We have given the night's time to the day. There are some modern thinkers who go so far as to feel that if night can be completely removed from man's life, a sizeable part of his life can be rescued from going to waste. Where is the need to sleep? It should be done away with they argue. But as there is a joy in waking, there is a joy in sleeping also. Just as the desire to awaken is natural and healthy, so also is the desire to sleep. If a man keeps alive his eagerness to live even up to his last breath he is not healthy, and if a man nurtures the desire to die from his very birth that too is unnatural and unhealthy. If a child longs for death, he is ill—abnormal, and he should be treated. If an old man longs for life, he too should be treated for he is ill also.

Life and death are the two limbs of Existence. If you accept only one, you are bound to be crippled. Until the time comes when you accept the other, this disability will remain. Both limbs are important—Being and Non-Being. He who embraces and accepts both Being and Non-Being equally can be called perfectly healthy. He who says, "I have known what it is 'to be'; now I wish to know what it is 'not to be'," is not afraid of "Non-Being".

The seventh plane is only for people of courage—who, having known life, are eager to know death, who are keen to explore death—the state of extinction. They are keen to know what it is not to be, what extinction is like, what is the Non-Being. They have tasted life; now they want to taste death.

At this point you should know that death descends from the seventh plane. What we normally know as death comes from the seventh plane and what we know as life comes from the first plane. Birth starts with the physical; birth means the beginning of the physical. This is why the physical body first comes into being in the mother's womb, and the other bodies follow later. So the first body is the beginning of life and the last body, the Nirvanic body, is from where death comes. Therefore, he who clutches fast to the physical body is very much afraid of death, and he who is afraid of death will never ever know the seventh body.

Thus, as we gradually become more and more detached from the physical body, a time comes when we accept death also. Then only do we know. And he who knows death is liberated in the true sense of the word, for then life and death become two parts of the same thing and one is beyond both. So there is no hope of science reaching to the seventh body, though there is a possibility of its going up to the sixth.

The doors of the fourth body have opened to science, and now there is actually no difficulty for it to go up to the fifth body. But such persons are required who have scientific minds and religious hearts. Once they appear, entry into the fifth will not be difficult. This combination is very difficult though, for the training of the scientist bars him from becoming religious from several directions. Also, in the same way, religious training prevents a man from becoming scientific. Nowhere do these two branches of training overlap, and this is the great difficulty. It happens sometimes, and whenever this happens in the world a new peak of knowledge comes into being. For example, take Patanjali: He was a man with a scientific mind, but he slipped into religion. He brought religion (yoga) to a height which has been difficult to surmount up to now. It is now a long time since Patanjali died, and a great deal more work could have been carried out in this field. But no man was found who had the intelligence of a scientist and an inner world of religious sadhana (spiritual practice). There has been no one to climb to higher peaks of yoga. Sri Aurobindo tried, but he did not succeed.

Sri Aurobindo had a scientific mind, perhaps more scientific than Patanjali, for he was educated in the West. His education was superb. When he was about six years old his father sent him out of India and forbad him to return until he was fully matured. Even on his deathbed, when others in the family talked of calling Aurobindo back, his father would not allow it. He said, "It is all right if I do not see him before my death. He must imbibe the Western culture completely. Let not the shadow of the East fall upon him. . Do not even let him know that I am dead." He must have been a very courageous father. Thus, Aurobindo drank deep of the Western culture. If there was ever a man who was Western in the real sense of the word, it was Aurobindo. He had to relearn his mother tongue after returning to India.

So the knowledge of science was complete in him, but religion was a later implantation and so it could not be expressed deeply; otherwise this man would have scaled greater heights than Patanjali. But this was not to be. The training of the West, in a deep way, became a barrier, because his thinking was entirely like that of a scientist. He brought the whole evolution theory of Darwin into religion. He introduced into religion thoughts that he brought from the West. As a result, he created a voluminous scientific literature in which religion is very superficial, because any effort to explain about the mysteries of the sixth and seventh plane is bound to be a failure as it cannot be expressed in scientific and logical terms.

Whenever a balance has been struck between a scientific intellect and a religious mind, great heights have been attained. But there is very little possibility of this coming about in the East, for the East has lost its religion and science it never had. There is more of a possibility in the West, for there science has become overbearingly excessive. Whenever there is an excess, the pendulum tends to swing toward the other extreme. That is why the very intellectual class in the West reads the Gita with a relish as is not seen anywhere in India.

The first time Schopenhauer read the Gita, he put it on his head and danced with joy. When people asked him what was the matter, what was the cause of this mad behaviour, he said, "The book is not only worth reading, but is worthy of being put upon the head and danced to. I never knew that there were once people on this earth who spoke this way. What I thought could never be bound into words has been expressed in this book." Now we shall not find a single man here (in India) who would put the Gita on his head and dance. We will only find people who will place the Gita on the seat of a carriage and ride sitting upon it, but this is meaningless.

By the end of this century a new height will be touched, for when the need arises many forces are activated in the world. Einstein became a religious man before he died. During his life he remained a scientist, but as his life drew to an end he became religious. That is why those who were essentially scientific said, "We should not take Einstein's last statements seriously. He was out of his mind." His last words were very meaningful. He said, "I thought I would know everything there is to know about the world, but the more I knew, the more I found this to be impossible, for there was a vast infinity still left to be known. I thought that one day I would solve the mystery of the world of science and reduce it to a mathematical equation, and that then it would be a mystery no longer. But the mathematical problem became bigger and bigger, and instead of solving the mystery of the world it became a mystery in itself. It is now impossible to solve this problem."

A few topmost scientists of modern times are hovering around the periphery of religion. Such possibilities now occur in science, for it has crossed the second body and is approaching the third, and as it nears the third body the echoes of religion become unavoidable. It is, of its own, entering into the unknown world of uncertainties and probabilities. Now, sometime, somewhere, it will have to admit the unknown. It will have to agree there is more besides that which can be seen with the naked eye. What cannot be seen exists ; what cannot be heard also exists. A hundred years ago we said that what cannot be heard or seen or touched does not exist. Now science says differently. It says that the range of touch is very small, but the range of the untouchable is very vast. The range of sound is very little, but that which cannot be heard is limitless. What is seen is but infinitesimal compared to the limitlessness of the unseen.

Actually, what our eyes behold is a very small part of what is. Our eyes catch a particular wavelength, our ears hear at a particular wavelength. Above and below these wavelengths there is an infinity of other wavelengths. Sometimes, by accident, these wavelengths are also caught by our senses.

Once a man fell from a mountain and his ear was hurt. Now his ear began to catch the air waves of the radio station of his town. When he was in the hospital, he was in a terrible predicament. In the beginning he could not understand what was happening. He thought, "Either I am going crazy or I cannot grasp that meaning of what is happening." Then things began to seem clear and he complained to the doctor. He asked the doctor, "Where is the radio kept in the hospital?" The doctor said, "Have you become superstitious? There is no radio." Still, he insisted that he was hearing the news and he related what he heard. The doctor ran to the office and put on the radio. To his consternation, he found exactly the same news being relayed. Then things became clear. It was discovered that his ears had become activated to hearing strange new wavelengths, and they had changed with his fall from the mountain. It is quite possible that in the near future we shall be able to catch wavelengths directly by fixing a small gadget to the ear.

Infinite sounds are passing by us and around us, but we cannot hear them because our field of hearing is very limited. Even many loud sounds cannot be heard. We cannot hear the sound below the hearing capacity of our ears and we cannot hear the sounds above the hearing capacity of our ears. When a star falls the tremendous sound of its falling spreads out all around us, but we cannot hear it. If the situation were otherwise, we would become deaf. Similarly, the range of our body heat is approximately between 98 degrees and 110 degrees. If it falls under 98 degrees or over 110 degrees, one dies. One's life flickers between ten to twelve degrees. Heat has a tremendous range. It can be lower than this twelve degree range, but we are not related to this.

In the same way, we have our limitations in everything. But we can know about things outside these limits, for they too exist. Science has begun to accept their existence. Once there is acceptance, the quest for where and what these things are begins. All this can be known, all this can be recognized. Therefore, I said it is possible for science to reach up to the fifth body.

Questioner : *Who knows Non-Being and on what basis can it be known?*

Bhagwan : The question itself is wrong. This question cannot arise and cannot be formed, for when we ask, "WHO knows the Non-Being? we take it that SOMEONE remains behind. Then it is not Non-Being.

Questioner : *How is the knowledge of it reported?*

Bhagwan : There is no reporting. For instance, when you sleep at night you are conscious of only that which occurs in your waking hours. Once you sleep you are oblivious of your surroundings. So you can only report about your waking hours—of the situation that existed up to the point you slept. But as a rule you do the opposite. You say, "I slept at 8 o'clock." This is wrong. You should have said, "I was awake until 8 o'clock." You cannot report sleep, for when you sleep who is to report? Reporting is possible from the other side: "I was awake until 8 o'clock or until 8 o'clock I knew I was awake, but I do not know anything after 8. Then I know of having awakened at 6 a. m. There is a gap between 8 p. m. and 6 a. m. during which time I was asleep."

This is by way of example. You will know what is until the sixth body. When you plunge into the seventh body and come out again into the sixth, you will be able to say "Oh! I have been elsewhere. I have experienced Non-Being." This account is given only in the sixth body, and so many did not speak after reaching the seventh plane. There was a reason: why tell those who cannot be told?

Recently, there was a man named Wittgenstein, and he had made some priceless statements. One of them is: "That which cannot be said must not be said." Many persons have said what cannot be said and have thus put us into difficulty, for they have also told us that it cannot be said. So this becomes negative reporting. This is the news flashed from the last boundary where one says, " 'I was' up to that point, but thereafter 'I was not'. After this point there was nothing left to know and no one there to know. There was no report and no reporter. But this happened after a particular boundary before which 'I was'." That line of boundary is the boundary of the sixth body.

The Vedas, the Bible, the Upanishads, the Gita, go up to the sixth body. The seventh is that which is inexpressible and cannot, in fact, be expressed. Up to the sixth there is not much difficulty and up to the fifth it is very easy to express. But at the seventh plane, neither the knower remains nor the knowledge. In fact, that which we imply to be the remainder does not remain. If we talk of this empty gap, we shall have to use the language of negation. Therefore, the Vedas and the Upanishads have to say, "Not this, not that." They say, "Do not ask what there is. We can only tell you what was not there; we can only say what is not. There was no father there, no wife, no matter, no experience, no knowledge. And 'I' too was not : the ego was not. Nor was there the world or its maker. There was nothing there." This is the boundary line of the sixth body. What was there ? You will remain silent, for it is inexpressible.

News about the Brahman has been reported, but what is conveyed thereafter is bound to be negative—as was that which was told by Buddha. Buddha tried his utmost to express the seventh plane. Therefore, all that he conveys is denial, all that he conveys is negation, and so it did not come within the grasp of the people of his land. Knowledge of the Brahman, being positive, was well grasped by the people. The Brahman was said to be *Sat-Chit-Ananda* (Truth, Consciousness, Bliss), and these positive assertions were well understood. One could say about it that this is, that is, but Buddha talked about that which is not. Perhaps he is the only one who laboured to make the seventh plane known.

Buddha was not accepted in this country (India), for the place he talked of is without roots, forms or shapes. People heard and thought it was useless. "What shall we do there where there is nothing ?" they said. "At least show us a place where we shall be." But Buddha said, "You will not be." So people of his land withdrew from him, for they wanted to save themselves to the very last.

Buddha and Mahavir belonged to the same age, but people understood Mahavir better as Mahavir talked of phenomena up to the fifth plane. But he did not even mention the sixth plane. This was because Mahavir had a scientific mind, and whenever he tried to explain about the sixth he felt that words seemed to become ambiguous, hazy and illogical. Up to the fifth everything is stable, and it is possible to give an account that this is or that is, because we find things similar to our experience up to the fifth plane.

Suppose there is a very small island in the middle of an ocean and only one kind of flower grows on this island. There are a few people inhabiting it and they have never stepped off the island. Then one day a passing ship takes one of them aboard and takes him to its land. Here he sees flowers of different kinds. For him "flower" meant one particular type of flower that grew on his island. Now, for the first time, the meaning of "flower" has expanded, and he realizes that the word "flower" does not pertain just to one flower but to thousands of them. He sees there are roses, lilies, lotuses and jasmine. Now he is worried. How will he go and explain to his people that "flower" does not stand for just one type of flower ? How will he explain that flowers have names, for on his island the flower, being just one, has no other name: it is merely a "flower". Now he wonders how he will speak to the others about lilies and the jasmine flowers.

He returns to his island, and in spite of his difficulty there is a way out for him. There is at least one flower to go by. Now he can elaborate on this one flower and try and explain the varieties of colours and shapes and scents of the others in order to convey some idea of his discovery. He can say, "Just as this one is white, there are others that are red, pink, yellow and many other colours. Just as this one is small, there are big flowers also like the lotus. In this way he can communicate, for one flower is already there to indicate something about the others.

But suppose that this man does not go to another land, but instead he goes to the moon where there are no flowers, no plants, where the atmosphere is unusual for him and the atmospheric pressure is different. When he goes back to his island and they ask him what he saw on the moon, it will be very difficult to explain, for there is nothing equivalent to his experience to explain by. There are no words or symbols in his language to convey the report.

This is exactly the situation. Until the fifth we find words to express, but it is the same as trying to express the difference between one flower and a thousand flowers. From the sixth plane language becomes confusing. There we reach a point where even the difference between the one and a thousand is not enough for explaining. It is very difficult. Even then, with the use of negation or totality some idea can be conveyed. We can say there is no limit there; it is boundless. We are familiar with boundaries, so with the help of this knowledge we can convey that there is no boundary there. This will give some idea, and though it is still vague we can assume that we understand. But it is not so.

So there is a lot of confusion. We feel we have followed what is told—that there are no boundaries there. But what is meant by "no boundaries" ? Our experience is that of the boundary. It is just as if those people of the island would say, "Yes, we have understood. It is 'flower' that you talk of." Then the man will say, "No, no ! Do not go by that flower. It has nothing to do with those flowers; such a flower is not found there at all." Then the people will say, "Why do you call them 'flower' if it is not like this flower? This alone is a flower."

We too are under the illusion that we understand. When we are told, "The Paramatman (Supreme Self) is infinite," we say, "Yes, we understand." But our experience is only of boundaries. We understand nothing; we only know the word "boundary". We fix the suffix "less" to it, and we feel that we know that there is no boundary there and we are sure that we have understood. But once you begin to conceive of that which has no limits, then it will be frightening. No matter how much you visualize, the boundary remains. You go further and further, even beyond millions and billions of miles beyond where light-years end. But wherever you stop, the boundary will appear.

The meaning of the boundless in our minds can at the most be the boundary of that which is very very far away. It is so far that it is beyond our grasp, but still it exists. Then again we shall have missed. So something can be said about the sixth plane and we might think we have understood, but we have not understood.

Now with the seventh, we will not even do so much as to say that we understand. The seventh cannot even be talked about. If someone tries, we will immediately say, "What absurd things you are saying !" Therefore, an absurd word was used to indicate the seventh plane—a word which has no meaning, which would mean nothing.

Take, for instance, the word "Aum": it has no meaning. It is a meaningless word, and we have used it in connection with the seventh body. Until the fifth body we can talk, but when someone insists on talking about the seventh, we say, "Aum". Therefore, when a scripture was completed, the words "Aum Shanti" (Aum peace) were written. You know what it means ? It means that the seventh is final; there is nothing further to be said. The scriptures end as soon as the seventh appears; the beginning of the seventh is the end of the scriptures. Therefore, at the end of each scripture we do not write "conclusion". We write "Aum Shanti". The "Aum" is the symbol of the seventh, and it is meant to convey that there cannot be any further discussion. It urges us to be tranquil and at peace thereafter.

We have conveyed an absurd word which has no meaning, no motive behind it. And if there is any motive behind it it is rendered useless, for we have created this word for that world where all motives end. It is a motiveless world, and, therefore, it does not exist in any other language of the world. Experiments have been carried out, but there is no meaning to "Aum". A Christian will pray, and at the end of his prayer he will say, "Amen". He is saying, "Enough ! Finished ! Peace thereafter. Now no more words." But this is not equivalent to "Aum". Aum cannot be translated. It is the symbol we have chosen for the seventh.

It was carved in temples to remind us not to halt at the sixth because there is also a seventh plane. It is placed in between the images of Ram and Krishna to suggest that "Aum" is greater than they are. Krishna peers out of it, but "Aum" is much greater. Aum is very vast. Everything peers out of it, everything merges into it. Therefore, we have not evaluated "Aum" with anything else in the world. It is the holiest of the holy in the sense that it is the Ultimate, the Beyond where everything loses its identity.

So nothing can be reported about the seventh plane. It can only be described in the language of negation : "It is not this; it cannot be that, etc." But this also holds meaning only up to the sixth plane. Therefore, many seers have remained silent about the seventh. Those who tried to talk about it raised many difficulties for themselves, for even while talking about it they had to repeat again and again that it is inexpressible. Time and again they had to warn their listeners : "We speak about it, but it indeed cannot be spoken about." Then we are perplexed. Why do they speak of a thing which cannot be spoken of ? They should not tell about it. But they say, "The seventh definitely is, but we have no words worth enough to describe it."

There is nothing in the world comparable to it; it is inexpressible. There is a lot that can be told about it, a lot that can be expressed, but the difficulty is that there is no means of conveying it in words. It can be known, but it cannot be expressed.

That is why those who were once very garrulous, those who were great orators, those who could explain everything under the sun, became suddenly mute when they returned from the seventh plane. When they are suddenly struck mute in this way, their muteness conveys a message: their silent eyes speak of the Unspoken. For example, in reference to what you are asking now, Buddha had made a rule that certain questions should not be put to him. He said, "Do not ask these questions. It is not proper to ask them; it is not proper that they should be known." He would say that a certain subject was indefinable and hence should not be discussed. It would be improper to discuss it.

Lao Tse said, "Please do not ask me to write, for whatever I write will become false. I will never be able to convey what I want to convey; I can only write that which I do not want to convey. But what is the use of that ?" So he did not write until the very end. When his countrymen forced him, he wrote a small booklet. The very first sentence he wrote was: "As soon as Truth is expressed it becomes a falsehood." But this is the Truth of the seventh plane. At the sixth plane it becomes not false, but ambiguous. At the fifth, the Truth expressed is indisputable. At the seventh only, its expression is impossible. Where we ourselves are no more, how can our speech and language remain ? They too end with us.

Questioner : *What are the distinctive characteristics of "Aum" for which it has been chosen to represent the seventh plane ?*

Bhagwan : There are two reasons for choosing Aum. One is that a word was sought which had no meaning, which cannot be given any meaning—for if it conveys any meaning it is reduced to the fifth plane. A word was, therefore, required which was, in a sense, "meaningless". All of our words are meaningful. We make words so that they will convey meaning. If they do not convey any meaning, why should they be used ? We use them to speak, and the purpose of speaking is to convey some thought.

When I utter a word, it should strike a certain meaning within you. So when people returned from the seventh plane, they felt that if they made any words to express the seventh plane which conveyed a meaning, they would at once be reverting to the fifth plane. Then those words would be added to the dictionary where people will read them and think that they have understood. But the seventh has no meaning. You can say either that it is "meaningless" or "beyond meaning". Both of these mean the same thing.

So in the context that all meaning is lost and no meaning remains, what sort of a word could be found for this and how was it to be formed ? This word was made with the help of great vision and foresight, and in a very scientific way. A root word was to be constructed, a basic word, which was to be made the foundation. So how was this word that should convey no meaning to be found, and in what manner was it to be formed ? In a deep way it would become a symbol for the original source.

The three basic sounds of our speech are A-U-M. All our developments of words are an expansion of these three sounds. They are the root sounds. Now the sounds of A-U-M in themselves carry no meaning, for it is their relationships that decide the meaning. When "A" becomes a word it carries a meaning; when "M" becomes a word it carries a meaning. But by themselves they are meaningless. Yet they are the roots, and all our speech developments are extensions and combinations of these three sounds.

So these three root sounds were taken and were joined to make the word "Aum". Now Aum could be written, but by writing it one could begin to think that it might have a meaning like the written words "now" or "today". People would think that "Aum" means that which is in the seventh plane. So no word was coined, but a picture of Aum was made. No letters were used for it. The three letters A-U-M are only sounds and not letters or words. So Aum came into being in a pictorial form in order that it would not be relegated to a dictionary and would instead strike the eye and become a question mark. It came into being in this way so that one would become eager to find out what it means.

Whenever a man reads Sanskrit or comes to study the ancient books, this word becomes difficult to explain. Words come within their grasp, for they have a meaning. But Aum (ॐ) is beyond comprehension. They always ask "What does 'Aum' mean? What is its significance? What does it mean and why is it not written in letters (like A-U-M)? Why this pictorial form? If you observe its picture carefully, you will see that it is made up of three parts which are the symbols A, U and M (in Sanskrit).

This picture requires deep research; it is not an ordinary picture. Research upon it has been carried out from the fourth body and not from the physical plane. Actually, when a person enters the fourth body and is in the "no-thought" state, the notes of A-U-M begin to resound within him, and their combination makes up the word "Aum". When there is perfect stillness within, when thoughts are completely lost, then the hum of Aum begins to resound within. This sound has been caught from the fourth plane where thought is no more and language is no more. Then what remains is the sound of "Aum". So in this way the sound was caught.

Now as I said before, each word has a pattern of its own. When we use a certain word a particular pattern forms within the mind. If someone concentrates on Aum, when it resounds on the fourth plane, the corresponding picture will begin to manifest within. This is how all "bija mantras" (seed mantras) were discovered. When the resonance of a particular chakra (center) is caught a sadhak in concentration, the seed mantra of that chakra is revealed. This is how these seed mantras have been formed, and Aum is the ultimate seed. It is not the seed of any particular chakra. Rather, it is the symbol of the seventh which is the Infinite or the Eternal.

So in this way the word "Aum" was hit upon. And when it tallied with the experiences of thousands of seekers who gave it their approval, this word was accepted. It did not come into existence with the approval of a single man or even of a group of men. When the same word reverberated in a number of sadhaks, when millions of them testified to its authenticity, then only was it chosen. Therefore, the word "Aum" is not the ancestral property of any religion or organization. Hence, the Buddhists and the Jainas make use of it freely without any apprehensions. It is not the property of the Hindu religion. The reason is that it has been attained by all sorts of sadhaks from various paths. Whatever equivalents we find in other countries are also, in a way, fragments of this very word.

Now if we examine the findings of Roman or Arabic sadhaks, we find that the note "M" is invariably mentioned. Some carry A along with M, but M is certain. This is because A and U are very subtle, and thus, they are difficult to catch. So the first part of the word slips from our attention, and only the latter part is heard. Therefore, when the sound of Aum begins to resound within, the M in it is easily caught. If you sit in a closed room and pronounce "Aum", the preceding sounds will give way to the sound of "M". Thus, A and U become completely inaudible, and it is the M that resounds everywhere. So sadhaks then came to the conclusion that the note M is certain, while that which precedes was not quite clear. The difference is only one of hearing, but wherever a search has been made in this direction something or the other of this word has been grasped by sadhaks. When an extensive research is carried out, for example, if a thousand scientists carry out the same experiment and get the same result, then its validity is proved.

This country is fortunate in that thousands of years have been spent here in the journey toward the Self. Nowhere in the world have the people of any country carried out this experiment on such a large scale and in such great numbers. Now 10,000 sadhaks sat around Buddha, 40,000 (both male and female) sat around Mahavir, and they carried out mass experimentation. In a small place like Bihar, 40,000 disciples of Mahavir were experimenting. Nowhere in the world has such an event taken place. Jesus, poor fellow, was all alone, and Mohammed had to spend all his time futilely battling with ignorant people.

In this country, a special situation had developed in which people are aware of the fact that these are not matters to fight over. Here things were clear. Mahavir would sit and 40,000 people would practise sadhana before him. This afforded a great opportunity to observe and verify the experiences of different sadhaks on different planes. There could be some error where there are only one or two practising, but when there are 40,000 there cannot be any error. Forty thousand persons were occupied in different sadhanas. Everything was properly thought out, everything was verified, everything was properly grasped.

Therefore, this country has made many more discoveries in the spiritual field than other countries, because in other countries the seeker was all alone. Just as the West is today carrying out scientific experiments on a large scale employing thousands of scientists, in the same way this country had at one time employed thousands of its brilliant intellectuals in the science of the Atman. The discoveries which they brought back from their journey into the Self are very useful, but on their sojourns to other lands this knowledge became fragmented and distorted.

For instance, the cross of Jesus: It is a remnant of the Swastika. On its long journey to distant lands, this is what has remained of the Swastika. The Swastika was a symbol like Aum Aum is the symbol of the seventh, the Swastika is the symbol of the first. Therefore, the picture of the Swastika is dynamic. Its branches spread out and give the effect of motion; it is rotating all the time. The ordinary world means that which is moving all the time. Thus, the Swastika was made the symbol of the first body, and "Aum" that of the last. There is no movement in Aum. It is absolutely still; there is dead silence; everything is at a standstill. With the swastika there is movement.

In its journey, the swastika became a cross by the time it reached Christianity. There is every possibility of Jesus having come to Egypt as well as India. He was in Nalanda (In India, an ancient Buddhist university and monastery for religious sciences) as well as Egypt, and thus he gathered a great deal of knowledge. One piece of knowledge was the knowledge of the swastika. But this knowledge turned out to be like the news brought back by a man who had seen many flowers to a place where only one flower existed. The message of Jesus was destroyed, and only the cross remained.

The upper portion of Aum (ॐ) reached Islam. The half moon that they revere is the upper fragment of Aum which was separated from the main part during its travel to Arabia. Words and symbols get badly distorted in their journey, and after thousands of years they get so worn out that it is difficult to recognize their original form. New sounds, new words, are added upon them as they travel from place to place, and different people with different languages use them. All kinds of changes take place, and then, when something separates from its original source, it is difficult to discern its place of origin, how it came to be and what happened to it.

The spiritual flow of the whole world is intrinsically connected with this country (India), for the basic, original source (of spirituality) was born here and it is from here that news of it spread far and wide. But the messengers who took the message to other lands and the people who received the message spoke a different language Therefore, clarity was lacking in the delivering and receiving of the message. Now no Christian wearing the cross around his neck could ever think that it is a part of the swastika. No Moslem can dream that the half moon he reveres is a fragment of Aum.

According to some Catholic erudites, "Amen" is only a corrupted form of Aum. At the end of all Christian prayers, the word "Amen" is used to offer obeisance to the Divine. It is also the belief of researchers that in the Bible, where it says, "In the beginning there was the word and the word was with God" (John 1 : 1), "Aum" is the word implied. "Amen" is referred to as the "Alpha and the Omega"—the beginning and the end (The Revelation of St. John the Divine, 1: 8). It is also said that Jesus had told the apostle John, "I am Amen". In other places, Amen has been used to mean "absolute Truth" or "So be it".

Many Latin words are utilized in the Catholic mode of worship, and in all of them a corrupted form of Aum is present. For instance, "per omni secula seculorum," etc. It is also in the English words omnipresent, omniscient and omnipotent.

Nowadays many churches in India have begun to use the word "Aum" in their prayers, and they have also carved it on their main doors. For instance, St. Mary's College in Darjeeling has the symbol of Aum (ॐ) carved on the entrance of the main library of its temple of worship.

[Text of a discourse given on July 8, 1970, evening, in Bombay, India.]

15

THE INTIMATE MYSTERIES OF SHAKTIPAT AND GRACE

Questioner :

In the context of the seventh body, we had a discussion on the word "Aum" yesterday. There is yet a small question on the same subject. Which "chakras" (centers) do A, U and M influence and how is this helpful to the "sadhak" (seeker) ?

Bhagwan Shree Rajneesh :

Yesterday I told you a few things about Aum. There are a few more things worth knowing in the same context. In the first place, Aum is the symbol of the seventh body, an indication of the seventh plane. It is a symbol of the seventh state which cannot be explained by any word. No word can be associated or utilized in connection with it. Thus, a meaningless word was found—a word which has no meaning. This I told you yesterday. The search for this word had been carried out through the experiencing of the fourth plane.

This was not an ordinary search. Actually, when the mind is empty in all respects without any clamour of words, without even a ripple of thought, even then the sound of the Void remains. The Void also speaks; the Void has its own stillness. Go and stand in a very secluded place where there is not a single sound, and you will find that emptiness has its own music. Seclusion has its own kind of solitude, its own kind of stillness, and in this stillness only the basic notes remain—A, U, M. All our melodies and tunes are developed by permutations and combinations of these basic notes. When all words, all sounds, are lost, these basic notes remain.

So Aum is the symbol of the seventh state, the seventh body, but this word has been grasped in the fourth plane. In the emptiness of the mental body, the resonance of Aum is captured. If the sadhak makes use of this Aum, there can be two results. As I told you before, all planes have two possibilities. The repetition of Aum can bring about a state of somnolence, and this the repetition of any word can bring about. The modulated repetition of any word has the same impact on the mind as gentle strokes on the head that produce drowsiness and sleep.

If this state is brought about by the repetition of Aum, you become lost in a word of dreams and imagery which is the natural potential of the fourth body. It will then be a hypnotic sleep in which you can see whatever you want to see. You can travel to heaven and to hell or have a vision of God, but all this will be in dreams. You can experience bliss, you can experience peace, but all in a dream; nothing will be real.

This usage of Aum happens more often than not, for this is easy. To produce the sound of Aum with great force and be lost in it is very easy and very enjoyable, like pleasant dreams. The form of the mental plane, as given by nature, is that of imagination and dreams. If the mind wishes to dream it can dream; this enjoyment is possible for it. The other possibility is that of resolve and vision.

If Aum is used only as repetition upon the mind, its impact brings hypnotic sleep. That which is called "*yoga-tandra*" (a hypnotic sleep that sometimes comes after a meditation practice) is brought about by the repetition of Aum. But if Aum is pronounced with the witness well established within; if you are fully awake and are listening to the sound without drowning in it, without getting lost in it; if the sound is on one plane and you are standing on another as the listener, the observer, the witness, if you are fully awake to the sound; then only can work on the second possibility of the fourth plane begin. Then you will not go into *yoga-tandra*, but into "*yoga-jagriti* (wakefulness).

I strive constantly to keep you from using words. I always advise you not to use any mantra or any word, for there are 99 chances out of 100 that you will go into a trance. There are reasons for this. The fourth plane is vulnerable to sleep; it knows only sleep. Its dream track is already there. It dreams every day. It is just as if we were to throw water into this room. After some time the water will dry up, but it will leave a mark on the floor. Then if we throw water again on the floor, this water will flow along the same previous tracks.

The greater possibility with words and mantras is that your mind with its tendency to dream will at once, by its very mechanical process, fall into dreâming. But if you are fully awake and witnessing inside, observing the sound of Aum without merging into it, without losing yourself in it, then it could do the same work as repeating "Who am I?" which I advocate. Now if you ask "Who am I?" in a sleepy state and are not a witness, the same error can take place here and you will merely be dreaming. But the possibility of this happening with "Who am I?" is less than with the repetition of Aum, and there is a reason for it.

With Aum, there is no question asked : it is only a gentle blow. With "Who am I?" there is a question, not a mere pat. There is a question mark after "Who am I?" and this will keep you awake. It is an interesting fact that when there is a question in the mind, it is impossible to sleep. If a difficult question revolves in your mind during the day, it spoils your sleep at night also. The question will not let you sleep. The question mark is a helpmate of sleeplessness. If there is any question, any anxiety, any curiosity in the mind, it is difficult to sleep.

I advocate "Who am I?" in place of Aum because, basically, it is a question. And since it is a question, it is an intrinsic search for an answer. Besides, you will have to keep awake for the answer. In Aum there is no question. It has no spikes, and hence it does not strike. It is absolutely round, and there is no question. Its continuous gentle strokes generally lead only to trance.

Besides, there is no melody in "Who am I?" whereas Aum is full of melody. The greater the melody, the more it will hasten you to sleep. "Who am I?" is disproportionate like the masculine form ; Aum is well proportioned like the feminine form: its gentle strokes quickly make you sleep. Words have forms, and their strokes are different, their resonance is different. "Who am I?" has no melody; it is difficult to sleep with it. If we repeat "Who am I? Who am I?" near a sleeping man, he will awaken.

If, however, we repeat "Aum-Aum" before a sleeping man, his sleep will become deeper because the impact is different. This does not mean that Aum is not workable. The possiblity is there for someone who stands behind the repetition as an observer, a witness. But I do not advocate the use of Aum for "sadhana" (spiritual practice). There are many reasons for this

If you utilize Aum for sadhana, then it will inevitably become associated with the fourth body. Aum is the symbol of the seventh plane, but its resonance is experienced on the fourth plane. Once you start the sadhana of Aum, this inevitable relationship of Aum with the fourth plane will come about which will prove a barrier to further progress. So there is this difficulty with the word. It is experienced on the fourth plane, but it is used for the seventh plane. We have no other word for the seventh body. Our experience of words ends after the fourth plane.

We use the last word on the fourth plane as the symbol for the seventh plane. There is no other remedy, for from the fifth starts the wordless state. Then the sixth is absolutely wordless and the seventh is the Void. On the last boundary line of words in the fourth state, where we leave all words, the last word heard will be "Aum". So Aum is the final word in the realm of speech and the primal word in the realm of "no-word". It is at the boundary line between the realm of words and the no-word state. This word is primarily of the fourth plane, but we have no other word nearer to the seventh plane; all others lag behind. Therefore, this word is used for the seventh.

So I prefer that you do not bind it to the fourth. It will be experienced in the fourth, but it should be kept as a symbol of the seventh. Therefore, there is no need to use it for sadhana. For sadhana we should use such devices which will fall off with the fourth plane. For example, "Who am I ?" this can be used in the fourth and can be discarded also.

The meaning of Aum should remain symbolic. There is yet another reason for not using it as a device. That which is the symbol of the Ultimate should not be made a means : it should remain the end. The symbol of the Absolute should remain only for the attainment. Aum is that which we have to attain;

therefore, I am against using it in any way as a means of sadhana. It has been used in the past with detrimental results.

The sadhak who uses the sadhana of Aum takes the fourth for the seventh plane, for the symbol of the seventh is experienced in the fourth. When it is experienced in the fourth, the sadhak becomes confident that he has reached the seventh plane. He takes this to be the journey's end; thus, great harm is done on the mental plane. The sadhak then stops here.

There are many sadhaks who take visions, colours and inner sounds (*nada*) to be the attainment. This is but natural, for the symbol of the Ultimate is felt on the boundary of this plane. Then they feel that they have reached the destination. Therefore, I am not in favour of prescribing the practice of Aum for persons in the fourth body, as this sadhana will have no effect on the first, second and third bodies. Its effect will be felt only in the fourth. This is why other words are used to cause the necessary impact on the first, second and third bodies.

It is necessary to take one more point into consideration regarding the basic notes of A-U-M. Just as an example, the Bible does not say that God made the world : He did not perform the act of creation. It says, "God said, 'Let there be light' and there was light." God pronounced the word. The Bible also says, "In the beginning there was the word." And many old scriptures testify to the same. At the very beginning there was the word, and all else followed afterwards. Now even in India we say, "The word is the Brahman," although this causes a great deal of misunderstanding. Many people tend to believe that the word is enough for the attainment of the Brahman. The Brahman is attained only in the wordless state. "The word is the Brahman" means only this, that from all the sounds we know the most subtle of sounds is that of the word "Aum" (ॐ).

If we go back, back and back toward the source of the universe until we come to the Void from where the world must have started, there also we shall hear the resonance of Aum. As we reach nearer to the Void by entering the fourth plane, the sound of Aum is heard. From here we begin to fall into that world which must have been in the beginning. From the fourth, we go to the spiritual body, from there to the Cosmic body and finally to the Nirvanic body. The last resonance, which is heard between the last two, is also that of Aum.

On one side is our individuality of four bodies which we call the corporeal world, and on the other side is our non-individuality which we may call the Brahman. The resonance that vibrates on the boundary line of these two is Aum. From this experience, we come to understand that when the world of matter took form from the Brahman, the resonance of Aum must have been ringing continuously. Hence, "There was the word." So the belief is that everything came into being through the WORD. If "the word" is broken into its basic components, we find the three basic notes of A-U-M in it. This combination is Aum.

Therefore, it is said that there was Aum in the beginning and there will be Aum in the end. The end means to revert to the beginning, and thus the circle is completed. Yet I always feel that Aum should be used only as a symbol and not for sadhana. Other things can be employed for sadhana. A pure word like Aum should not be made impure by using it for sadhana.

Many people fail to understand me. They come to me and say, "Why do you forbid the repetition of Aum?" Perhaps they think that I am an enemy of Aum, but in truth they themselves are. Such a pure word should not be used as a means of sadhana. In fact, our tongues are unworthy of pronouncing it : it is too pure to be uttered by the physical body. It is a word that begins where the tongue becomes meaningless, where the body becomes useless. Therein lies its resonance, and this resonance vibrates on its own. It can be known ; it cannot be created. Therefore, Aum has to be known and not pronounced.

There is another danger. If you use Aum as a means of sadhana, you will never know the basic sound of the word as it arises from the Existence, for you will impose your own articulation upon it. So you will never witness its purest manifestation. Whoever uses the sadhana of Aum never experiences Aum in reality. By continued practice, they will superimpose their own intonations upon the actual resonance when it comes. Then they will be unable to hear the pure reverberation of Aum. They fail to hear the direct resonance of the Void because they are filled with their own sound. This is natural, for that with which we are familiar becomes implanted in us. Therefore, I say that it is better not to be familiar with Aum ; it is better not to make use of Aum. Someday it will appear in the fourth body, and then it will have some meaning.

Its appearance in the fourth body will mean that you have reached the limits of the fourth body. Now you are about to step out of the psyche, out of the realm of words. The last word has come, and you now stand at the place where the word started ; you stand where the whole world stood at the beginning ; you stand at the threshold of creation. And then, when its own melody begins to flow, its charm is inexpressible. There is no way of describing it. Our best music cannot compare with its farthest echo. No matter how hard we try, we can never hear this music of silence with the outside ear. Therefore, it is better that we do not have any preconceived ideas about it. Let us not give any form or colour to it or else we will be caught by our own imagery, and this will be an obstacle.

Questioner : *The electrical difference between man and woman persists until the fourth body. Does this mean that the effect of a male medium or a female medium is different on the male and female sadhaks? Also, please explain why.*

Bhagwan : Many things will have to be clarified in this context. As I said before, the difference between male and female exists until the fourth body. After the fourth there is no difference. The fifth is beyond any difference in gender. But the difference is very fundamental up to the fourth body, and this basic dissimilarity will bring many kinds of results. Let us first understand the male body, then we shall go on to the female.

The first body of the male body is male, the second is female, the third again is male and the fourth female. In the female it is the opposite : her first body is female, the second male, the third is again female, and the fourth is male. There are radical differences because of this. It is these differences that have deeply influenced the whole history and religion of mankind and which have given man's culture a particular type of order.

There are some characteristics unique to the male body and some characteristics and specialities unique to the female body. These characteristics and specialities complement each other. Really speaking, the female body is incomplete and so is the male body. Therefore, in the act of creation they have to unite. This union is of two kinds. If male A unites with female B externally, a creation of nature takes place. If male A unites with female B "within himself", a creation takes place which is toward the Brahman. This is the journey toward God, whereas the external union is the journey toward nature. However sex is involved in both. If the male body unites externally with a female body, coitus takes place. If the male body unites with its own inner female body, then also sex takes place. In the first the energy is diffused outwardly, whereas in the second the energy begins to move inwardly. That which is known as the ascent of the energy is this very path : it is a union with the woman within.

The energy always flows from the male to the female regardless of whether it happens outside the body or inside the body. If the sex energy of the physical body of a male flows toward the etheric female within him, it is not diffused. The sadhana of "brahmacharya" (celibacy) is nothing but this. Then it flows up continuously; it reaches up to the fourth body. After the fourth body brahmacharya has no meaning, for there is nothing like male and female there.

That is why, after crossing the fourth plane, the sadhak is neither a male nor a female. Now the Concept of "*ardhanarishwar*" (Shiva as half man, half woman) came into being with the first and the second body in mind. But this merely remained a symbol and we never understood it. Shankara (another name for Shiva) is incomplete and so is Parvati (his female consort). Together they become one. So we drew a picture of Shiva as being half man, half woman, but in actual life this other half is not visible outwardly. It hides behind each of us. One side of you is male and the other female, and this is why very amusing incidents take place sometimes.

No matter how fearless a man is in the outside world, no matter how influential, whether he be Alexander the Great or Napoleon or Hitler, whether in the office, in the store or in the bazar, he lives haughtily as a man the whole day. But by evening all his swagger is lost before a simple woman in his house. This is very strange. What is the reason behind this ? The fact is that he uses his male body fourteen or twelve hours, and after that time his first body becomes tired. When he reaches home, the first body demands rest. Then the second body which is the female comes to the forefront, and the male body becomes secondary.

Now the wife has made use of her first body the whole day long, so by evening the male body behind her has the upperhand. Then the woman begins to behave like a man and the man like a woman. It should be remembered that the intercourse with one's own inner female body is the method for the upward flow of the life energy. This process has more inner details, but we shall not talk about that at present.

Another thing: the energy always flows from the male to the female. The most important quality of the male body is that it is not receptive; it is always aggressive. The male can give, but he cannot take. No current flows from the female to the male; it is always from the male to the female. The female is receptive. She can take, but she cannot give.

There are two results of this and both are worth knowing about. The first result is that since the female is receptive, she can never become the giver of Shaktipat; Shaktipat cannot take place through her. This is the reason why female teachers are not in great numbers in the world, nor are there any female gurus of the stature of Buddha and Mahavir. The reason is that no energy can be imparted to anyone through her. It is a fact though that women gathered in great numbers around Buddha, Mahavir and Krishna, but not a single woman of the stature of Krishna was ever born around whom millions of men would gather. The reason for this lies in the fact that women can only be recipients.

It is also an intersting fact that around a person like Krishna there will be very few men, but very many women. The same was the case with Mahavir : there were 10,000 male ascetics —monks, and 40,000 female ascetics—nuns. The ratio is 4 to 1 —always. If there is one man, there are always four women around him. Men could not be as affected by Mahavir as women could be, for both they and Mahavir are men. What was transmitted by Mahavir the women could absorb. But men are "non-absorbent"; their receptivity is very limited. Therefore, though it is man who is the harbinger of religion, it is woman who always protects and preserves it; it is woman who saves religion on earth. Men only pioneer religion.

Woman is receptive; the quality of her body is receptivity. She has this quality biologically also. She has to bear a child for nine months, and after that she also has to bring it up. Thus, she has to be receptive. So such work is assigned to man by nature. He becomes a father for a moment and then he is out of the picture. The woman receives the semen and then retains it. This fact works in Shaktipat also. Therefore, in Shaktipat a man cannot receive from a woman. This is speaking generally; there can be exceptions. Of these rare cases I shall talk later. Sometimes this can happen, but the reasons are different.

Ordinarily, Shaktipat does not take place through a female body. You can call this a weakness of the female body. But she has a complementary quality—the strength and power to take Shaktipat quickly. Man can conduct Shaktipat, but he is unable to receive it. Therefore, Shaktipat is also difficult from man to man because the male sadhak is not receptive, such is his personality. At the very first step, there where he has to begin, stands the male in him who is not receptive. Many methods have been evolved to make him receptive. There are cults in which a man performs his sadhana taking himself to be a woman. This is a method of making him receptive. Yet man does not become receptive. Woman becomes receptive without any difficulty because she is receptive by nature. Therefore, in Shaktipat a woman is always in need of a medium. Why she is not able to get grace directly, please understand well.

Shaktipat happens from the first body. If I hold Shaktipat, it happens to your first body. The power will emerge from my first body and strike at your second body. If you are a woman, this will happen quickly. If you are a man, then it will require more effort; it will be difficult. Somewhere deep within, somehow, you will have to acquire the state of complete surrender. Then only is it possible; otherwise not. Man does not surrender;

no matter how hard he tries he cannot surrender. Even if he says "I surrender," it will be in an aggressive manner. In other words, it is the ego that is proclaiming the act of surrender. It says, "Look ! I surrender." The "I" standing behind him does not leave him.

A woman does not have to surrender: she is already surrendered; it is in her nature. To yield is the quality of her first body. She is very receptive. Therefore, Shaktipat from a man takes place easily within her. From man to man it is very difficult and from woman to man nearly impossible. From man to man though difficult, it is possible. If there is a powerful man, he can reduce the other man to a near-female condition. Shaktipat through a woman is well-nigh impossible, for in the moment of the happening she tends to absorb the vital energy herself. Her first body is like a sponge and sucks everything in.

Until now we talked of Shaktipat. In the case of grace the conditions are the same. Grace comes from the fourth body. The fourth body of the male is female, so he receives grace very readily. Now the woman's fourth body is male, so she experiences the same difficulty with regard to grace: she cannot receive grace directly. The fourth body of the male is female; therefore, Mohammed, Moses, Jesus, established relationships with God instantaneously. As the fourth body was feminine in them, they were able to drink in the grace as soon as it descended upon them.

The female has the fourth body of the male. At this extreme is her male body, and this makes it impossssible for her ever to receive grace. Therefore, the female has no direct message; that is, no woman has been able to claim that she has known the Brahman. At her fourth body is the male that causes the hindrances. She cannot receive grace from that end.

Man receives grace directly. It is difficult for him to take it from someone such as happens in Shaktipat, for he himself is the barrier there. But not so for the woman. She can receive Shaktipat from any medium. Even very weak people are capable of performing Shaktipat on women. This is why even very ordinary mediums are successful in this. Shaktipat depends less on the medium himself and more on the receptivity of the recipient. But women always require a medium. It is very difficult for them without a medium, for then no happening can take place.

We have been talking of the ordinary state of things. Extraordinary conditions can also be created. It is because of the ordinary course of things that there have been fewer woman sadhaks. This does not mean that women have not experienced God. They have experienced God, but there was always a medium in between. However negligible, the medium has always been present; they had their experience through a medium. Another thing : there can be differences caused by unusual conditions. For example, it is more difficult for grace to happen in a young woman; it is a little easier in an older woman.

It is an interesting fact that throughout life our sex remains flexible; we do not remain in the same male-female ratio throughout life. There is a continuous change; the ratio keeps on changing. Therefore, it happens that a woman develop hair on the upperlip and chin in later years. Even her voice changes by the time she is fifty and it becomes heavy like a man's. The feminine voice will have gone. Her ratio changes: the male factors emerge and the female factors recede. Actually, her work as a woman is over. There was a biological binding up to the age of 45 which now is no more. She is no more bound to the female in her, so the possibility of grace is more in an old woman. This is so because the male element increases in her first body and the female element decreases in her second body. Also, the male element in her fourth body decreases, and the male element in her third body increases. So grace is possible in an old woman.

A very old woman, under certain conditions, can act as a medium for a young woman. A very old woman who has crossed the 100 mark, and who has no trace of sex left in her mind that she is a woman, can act as a medium for men also. But this will be a different thing altogether. It is the same for men: as a man gets older his female traits go on increasing. Old men generally behave like women. Many masculine traits fall from their personalities and feminine traits develop.

In this connection, it is necessary to know that the personality of whoever receives grace in the fourth body develops feminine traits. For instance, if we were to examine the body or the personality of Mahavir, or of Buddha, they appear more feminine than masculine. The soft tenderness and loveliness of a woman combined with feminine respectivity is increased in them. The quality of aggression leaves them, and, therefore, they are filled with non-violence, compassion and love; violence and anger are banished for ever.

Nietzsche has accused Jesus and Buddha of being effeminate, and he says, therefore, they should not be counted among men. They have no manly qualities and they have succeeded in making the whole world effeminate. There is a meaning to his complaint. You will be surprised to note that we have shown Buddha, Mahavir, Krishna and Ram without a beard or moustache. It is not that they did not have moustaches and beards, but by the time we made their pictures their personalities had become filled with feminine qualities. Thus, the beard and moustache would have looked out of place. We dropped them because they no longer suited their effeminate demeanour.

Such an incident had taken place in the case of Ramakrishna. His condition could have become a unique case for scientists. It was a very strange happening. Later on his followers tried to hide the facts, for how were they to talk about it? He developed breasts and began to menstruate. This was such a strange happening—a miracle we might say. His individuality became so effeminate that he walked like a woman and talked like a woman, and in such an exceptional case many other changes can occur. For instance, in such circumstances one cannot perform Shaktipat on anyone. His personality had become completely feminine.

With the help of the methods and the sadhanas of Buddha and Mahavir, millions of sadhaks attained the fourth body....As soon as they reached the fourth plane, their personalities became effeminate. By this I mean that the tender side of their nature developed. Violence and anger vanished as aggression took leave of them; affection, love, compassion and non-violence increased. Femininity took hold as the inherent nature of this whole country (India), and I feel that this was the cause for the great amount of aggression that occurred here. All the neighbouring masculine countries succeeded in subduing the feminine personality of India.

In one way, a very precious and memorable thing took place—that we experienced wonderful things on the fourth plane. But on the plane of the first body, we found ourselves in difficulty. Everything has to be compensated for. Those who were prepared to leave the treasures of the fourth plane attained the wealth and kingdoms of the first plane. Those who were not prepared to leave the pleasures of the fourth plane had to give up many things on the first.

After Buddha and Mahavir, India lost its aggressive instinct and became receptive. So with whoever came we got busy absorbing them within us. The question of segregating them never occurred to us, let alone attacking them. That question was lost for ever, for our personality had become effeminate. Bharat (India) became one large womb that harboured all who came to her. We denied no one; we never tried to remove any of these aggressors from among us, for the quality of warring that was required in order to fight was no longer within us. With the intelligentsia it became lost, and the ordinary masses followed the intellectual class. And the masses had to remain suppressed and controlled by them. The ordinary man heard intellectuals talk on non-violence, compassion, and saw them living accordingly, so he accepted their word and remained silent. He could have fought, but he had no leader.

If the history of the world is ever written from a spiritual point of view; when we no longer will consider only physical happenings as history but, instead, will begin to consider the happenings on the plane of consciousness as history (for that is the real history); then we shall understand that whenever a country turns spiritual it becomes feminine. And whenever it becomes feminine, lesser cultures, most ordinary cultures, will defeat it. It is a surprising fact that those who conquered India belonged to very backward cultures. In many ways they were wild barbarians, whether they were Turks or Mongols or the Moghuls. They had no culture, but in a sense they were men—though wild men, and we were feminine, passive. We had no other way than to absorb them within us.

So the female body can absorb. Therefore, a woman needs a

medium, while the male body can transfer energy as well as receive grace. That is why men like Mahavir had to say that women will have to be reborn as men for the final attainment. This was one among many other reasons. She cannot receive grace directly. It is not necessary that she should die to become a man. There are methods in which a transformation of personality can be brought about. The second body can become your first body and the first body can be made to take the position of second. For this there are sadhanas of profound resolution by which in this very life, physical transformation is brought about.

There is an interesting story about one of the Jain Teerthankers (World Teachers). One of the Jain Teerthankers was a woman by the name of Mallibai. The Swetamber sect calls her Mallibai while the Digamber sect calls her Mallinath. They take her to be a man, for the Digamber Jains feel that women are not entitled to *moksha*—Liberation. Therefore, a Teerthanker cannot be a woman, and so they call Mallibai as Mallinath. Now nowhere else in the history of mankind is there such a controversy about a person. There have been all kinds of other controversies: over whether a man was 5′6″ or 5′5″, over when he was born, over when he died, but never was there a controversy where the sex of the individual became a matter of dispute. One sect believes Mallibai to be a man and the other, a woman.

What I feel is that when Mallibai began her sadhana, she must have been a woman. But there are such methods by which the first body can be changed into a masculine body, and it was after this took place that she became a Teerthanker. So the first sect who take her to be a woman revere her first state, and the second sect who take her to be a man worship her second state. Both are correct. She was a woman, but she must have turned into a man. Mahavir's sadhana is such that any woman who goes through it is bound to become a man. His complete sadhana is a sadhana not of "Bhakti" (path of devotion), but of "Jnan" (path of Knowledge), and so it is completely aggressive. His sadhana is not one of receptivity.

If any man begins to sing and dance like Meera for years on end, sleeping with the image of Krishna on his chest and considering himself his *sakhi* (beloved), he will remain a man in name only. His consciousness will undergo a complete transformation. The first body will recede and become the second, and the second will take its place. If the transformation is very deep, there will be physical changes in his body also. If not, the body will remain the same, but the mind will not be the same. He will develop a feminine consciousness. So in these special cases, things can happen : the happening of Shaktipat can take place; there is no difficulty. But this cannot be a general rule.

Shaktipat can happen through man and he can receive grace directly also, but it is difficult for a woman to attain direct grace. The door to grace can only open for her through Shaktipat. This is a fact and not an evaluation. There is no question of high and low, above or below : such is the fact. It is as much so as the fact that man ejaculates semen and woman receives it. If someone asks whether a woman can ejaculate semen into a man, we shall have to say no, for there is no natural law for this. There is no question of one being above or below. But all manner of evaluation arose out of this fact. Woman came to be looked upon as inferior, for she is the recipient. Then the value of the giver went up.

The difference in status between man and woman all over the world arose from the fact that man considers himself the giver, the provider, whereas woman considers herself the recipient. But who said that the receiver must necessarily be inferior ? And if there were no one to receive, what use will there be of the giver ? Conversely, if there is no giver, of what use the receiver ? There is nothing superior and inferior in it. In fact, these two are complementary to each other, and neither is independent of the other. They are tied to each other. These are not two separate entities, but, rather, two sides of the same entity in which one gives and the other receives. Normally, however, the very concept of the giver raises a picture of superiority within our minds. There is no reason why the receiver should be inferior. Many things are connected with this, however, and the status of women has been accepted as second in place to men. Not only men, but even women have accepted this position. In fact, both are first in their respective places—

he as a man and she as a woman. There is no second place; both are complementary.

Now this concept has had extensive consequences in matters both great and small, and it has permeated our entire civilization and culture. That is why man went hunting, for he was aggressive. And the woman sat at home waiting for him; she accepted him naturally. He went to the fields, he harvested the corn, he worked in his shop, he flew in the air, he went to the moon, he went out to do all these things because he was aggressive. The woman sat at home waiting for him. She also did a great many things, but because of her passive nature she did not make a fuss about it. She set up his house, she gathered things together, she kept everything in place. In all cultures, the principle of stability is due to women.

If the woman was not there, man would have been a wanderer —a vagabond; he could never set up a house. The woman acts as a peg. He wanders here and there, but has to return to the peg. If the situation were otherwise, he would never have settled down. Then there would have been no towns and cities. City culture came into being because woman wanted to stabilize her living in one place. She always pleads to the man, "Enough! Let us stop; let us halt. Let a little difficulty come, but let us not go any further." She catches hold of the soil and grows roots in it. Then man has to make a world around her. That is how towns and cities came into being. This is how all cultures and civilizations and homes, which woman beautified and sanctified, were made. No matter what the man earned or gathered in the outside world, she saved.

Man is never interested in saving. He earns, and there the matter ends; he is no longer intersted. He is eager and anxious as long as he is fighting with the world, challenging the world. His attention is always turning to other places for conquest. He goes, but in regard to the spoils he brings, there is someone else looking after it all, saving it all, and this individual has her own place, her own value. She is a complementary part of the whole situation, but as she does not go out to earn, as she does not accumulate, as she does not create, it seemed to her that she was lagging behind. This feeling entered even into very small things, and everywhere she began to feel a sense of inferiority, of lowliness, which is absolutely unfounded.

This inferiority brought evil results. As long as woman was uneducated she bore this inferiority, but now she will not. In order to break this sense of inferiority, she has gone about doing exactly what men do. This will prove very detrimental to her. She can violate her basic personality, and this can have destructive results deep within her consciousness. Now she wants to be at par with man, but she cannot be like a man completely. She will only succeed in making herself a second-rate man; she cannot be a first-rate man. She can, if she chooses, make herself first rate in her own class. There is no evaluation in this, but the facts are such about these four bodies; that is what I mean to say.

Questioner : *In that case there must be a difference in the sadhana of man and woman.*

Bhagwan : There will be a difference, and it will not be in sadhana so much as in the state of mind. For instance, when the method of sadhana is one and the same, even then a man will go about it aggressively, whereas a woman will go about in a passive way. The man will attack; the woman will surrender. The sadhana will be the same, but the attitudes will be different. When a man approaches sadhana, he catches it by the neck, so to speak, but when a woman goes to do sadhana she will place her head at its feet.

This difference in attitude is natural, and there is no more difference between the two than this. The woman's attitude will be that of surrender. When she reaches the last attainment, she will not say that she has attained God: rather, she will say that she is fortunate that God has taken her unto Him. When man reaches the Ultimate, he will not say that God has taken him unto Him. He feels that he has attained God. This is the difference in their comprehension. This difference is bound to be, but only up to the fourth body. After that there is no question of male and female.

Questioner : *You have said that the sadhana of Aum brings about the "nada" (uncreated inner sound). Does it come about automatically also ? Which is the proper "nada" ?*

Bhagwan : If it comes automatically, it is more valuable. If it comes with the repetition of Aum, it can be imaginary. That which comes of its own is authentic, valuable. If the nada begins you should become a witness. Do not be merged into it, for that is the state of the seventh plane. If you tend to get lost in the nada before reaching the seventh, you will halt there; it will act as a brake.

As these inner sounds become more and more subtle, our witnessing too will have to become more and more subtle. We will have to go on observing, until the last when the sound is completely lost.

Questioner : *On which plane does Shaktipat take place in the sadhak and on which plane does grace take place ? If the sadhak's first, second and third bodies are not fully awakened, what effect will Shaktipat and grace have on him ?*

Bhagwan : I have already told you that Shaktipat takes place in the first body and grace in the fourth. If Shaktipat takes place in the first body and the kundalini is not awakened, it will awaken—and with great speed. Then we shall have to be very careful, for with Shaktipat, what ordinarily happens in the course of months happens in a few seconds. Therefore, before Shaktipat there should be at least three months' minimum preparation of the first three bodies. A sudden Shaktipat on a person who is not at all prepared, say on a man on the road, can be harmful. Therefore, a little preparation is necessary before Shaktipat. No elaborate preparation is necessary; only enough to bring the three bodies in focus. That is the first thing.

The next is that there should be a line of connection between the three so that the energy does not become blocked anywhere. If Shaktipat gets caught on the first plane, it can be dangerous. If it spreads to all the three planes, it will not be harmful. If it stops at the first, it is very harmful.

It is just as if you receive an electric shock while you are standing on the ordinary ground. This is then harmful. But if you are standing on a wooden frame, it will be quite safe. The current of electricity then passes through your body and makes a circuit. If the circuit is formed, there is no danger. It is only dangerous if the circuit breaks. All energies follow the same rule: they go around in a circle. If the circuit breaks in between, you receive a shock. So if you stand on wood, you cannot receive any shock.

You will be surprised to know that the use of wooden platform for meditation had no other purpose than the fact that they were non-conductors. Deerskins and leopard skins were used for the same reason : so that the energy that is released by meditation should not give a shock. Therefore, these non-conductors were used as seats. A man can be killed by this electric shock. Therefore, the sadhak put on wooden sandals and slept on a wooden platform. He may not have known why he did all this; he merely followed the rules laid down by the "shastras" (scriptures). Perhaps the sadhak who practised this thought that he was torturing his body so that the body should not have any comfort. This was not the reason. The danger was quite different. Any moment the happening might take place within the sadhak from any unknown source. He must be fully prepared.

If his preparations for the first three bodies are completed, the energy he receives will form a circuit within him. If he is not ready and the energy is obstructed at the very first body, it is harmful. Therefore, this minimal preparation is necessary so that the sadhak is able to make a circuit. This preparation is easy and does not take long. It is not at all difficult.

Kundalini rises with great intensity through Shaktipat, but it can go only up to the fourth body. However, this much of a glimpse is more than sufficient. The journey after that is entirely individual. If a flash of lightning on a dark night reveals the path to you to some extent, it is more than enough. Once the road is seen, everything changes. Then you will no longer be the same person you were before. Thus, Shaktipat can be used to see a little of the distance that lies ahead. The initial preparation, however, is necessary. If given to the masses directly, it can be harmful.

And the most surprising thing is that it is the masses who are ever looking for Shaktipat and such things. The ordinary man for ever wants to get something for free, but nothing is ever obtained free. Many a time we come to know afterwards how expensive the free gift turned out to be. Never try to obtain anything for free. We should always be ready to pay the price, in fact. The more we show our readiness to pay the price, the more worthy we become. The greatest price we pay is by our sadhana.

Two days ago, a lady came to me and said, "I am well advanced in years and am nearing death. When will I attain Knowledge? Please hurry and do something lest I die." I told her to come for meditation for a few days; then we would see what is to be done. She said, "I do not want to be bothered with meditation. Do something so that I may attain knowledge." Now this lady is searching to get something without paying for it. Such a search is dangerous. You gain nothing by it. On the contrary, you lose. The sadhak should not harbour any such expectations. One receives what one is ready for. You should have faith in this.

You do get! In fact, a man never gets less than he deserves. This is a rule in the world; it is the justice of universal law. You get as much as we are prepared for, and if you do not get then know that it is not an injustice. Rather, you are lacking preparation. But our minds always lull us into the belief that injustice is being done to us. We are always very sure of our own worthiness and complain against fate.

We always get according to our own worthiness. Worthiness and attainment are two names of the same thing. But the mind expects a great deal and strives for very little. There is a great gap between our expectations and our effort. This gap is very self-defeating. It can be very harmful. Because of this we roam from place to place in the hope of getting something somewhere. Then, when the number of such persons has increased, it is certain that some clever person will come forward to exploit them. He will offer to give them what they seek for free. Such a person hardly knows anything. He comes upon some formula from somewhere which he can work upon them, and though its effect will not be very deep, it can still be harmful.

For instance, take a man who has no knowledge of Shaktipat: he too can practise a little bit of Shaktipat with the help of body magnetism. But he has no knowledge of the other six bodies within. The body has its own magnetic force. If arrangements are made through some situation, you can be made to receive "shocks" through it. This is why the ancient sadhak was careful about which direction he would face when sleeping. He would not put his head in a certain direction or his feet in a certain direction.

The earth has its magnetic force and the sadhak is always mindful to be properly aligned with it so that he is constantly magnetized by it. If you sleep at an angle to this force, your body magnetism becomes less. If you lie in the direction of the current, the force which gives the earth its magnetism and which forms the earth's axis will also magnetize your own body magnet. It fills your body with the magnetic force in the same way that a piece of iron is magnetized by placing it in front of a magnet. After becoming magnetized it will begin to draw smaller objects like pins and needles.

So the body has its own magnetic power. If it can be properly aligned with the magnetic power of the earth, it is very beneficial. The stars too have magnetic forces. On special occasions, certain stars are particularly magnetic. This can be verified, for we have all the necessary information. So if you are in a particular state seated in a particular posture at a certain special moment, a particular star will cause your body to become especially magnetized. Then you can give magnetic shocks to anyone, and they can take it for Shaktipat. But it is not Shaktipat. The body has its own electricity. If this is produced in a proper way, you can light a bulb of 5 to 10 candle power by merely holding it in your hand. These experiments have been successful. There are people who just hold the bulb in the palm of their hand and it is lighted. But the energy within the body is infinitely more.

Twenty years ago, a woman in Belgium became unexpectedly electrically charged. No one could touch her. Anyone who did got a shock. Her husband divorced her, and the reason given was that he got an electric shock whenever he touched her. The divorce created a sensation all over the world, for everyone came to know of this curious situation. After many tests it was discovered that her body had started producing electricity. The body has many batteries. If they are working in order, we do not feel anything. If the order is disturbed, a great deal of energy is produced—released.

You take energy from the food you eat, and this energy charges the batteries in your body. Therefore, many times you feel the necessity to recharge the batteries. A man is tired and spent by the evening. A good night's rest recharges him. However, he does not know what it is that recharges him in sleep. During sleep, some influences are at work upon him. All this information has been obtained, and we know that forces work on him in sleep. If a man wishes he can take the advantage of these influences in the waking state. Then he is capable of giving you shocks that are not even magnetic, but which are of the body's electricity. You can mistake this for Shaktipat.

There are many other ways of Shaktipat that are equally false. They are in no way connected with the actual transmission of power If a person has no knowledge of body magnetism, of body electricity, but he knows the secret of breaking the electric circuit of your body, he can give you shocks then too. There are many ways of breaking your body's electrical circuit, and when this is disturbed you receive a shock. Nothing comes from the other person toward you, but you feel the shock. It is the shock of your own body electricity which has been disturbed.

I cannot tell you everything in detail, for it is not proper to do so. All that I say is incomplete. Even the false methods I talk of are not completely described, for it is very dangerous to speak extensively and completely about them as there is the temptation to try them out. Our curiosities are very shallow. One fakir has referred to curiosity as sin. There is only one sin in man—the sin of curiosity. He has no other sin. Man commits so many sins entirely out of curiosity. We are not aware of this, but it is curiosity which makes him commit, God knows how many crimes.

There is a story in the Bible that God told Adam to eat the fruits of all trees but one. This one curiosity, put him into difficulties. The original sin was the sin of curiosity, and he found himself in trouble. What was the secret ? In such a large forest filled with trees of delicious fruits, what could be so special about the fruit of this ordinary looking tree ? But this one tree began to have a meaning to him, and all the rest became meaningless. His mind was hovering round this one tree until he could no longer remain without tasting the forbidden fruit. Curiosity got the better of him, and Christianity says that this was the original sin that man committed. Now what sin could there be in tasting the fruit? The original sin was his curiosity.

Our minds are filled with curiosity, but it rarely inquires. Search only takes place when there is no curiosity. Remember, there is a fundamental difference between curosity and inquiry. A curious man never inquires. He is only filled with curiosity about everything and does not see one thing in its entirety. He hardly glances at one thing when ten others draw his attention. Then he is never able to investigate.

The false methods I have talked about are not complete. Some important parts of these methods have been purposely dropped. It is necessary to do so, for our minds coax us with the curiosity to try them out. There is no difficulty in performing these experiments. When false seekers go in search of power, in search of God, they come across false givers of power also. Then it is like the blind leading the blind. The blind are bound to fall and also the long line of blind people that are after them. Then the harm done is not only of a lifetime, but of many lives. It is easy to break a thing, but very difficult to set it right again.

Therefore, do not try in this respect to investigate out of curiosity. Prepare yourself in the right context. Then what is necessary for you will come your way.

[Text of a discourse given on July 9, 1970, evening, in Bombay, India]

16

FROM THE PHYSICAL PLANE TO NIRVANA—THE ULTIMATE DEATH

Questioner :

Yesterday you talked to us about the effect of Shaktipat (transmission of the life force) and kundalini awakening on persons whose first three bodies are not prepared for it. Please explain further what kind of effect will take place. Also, how should a sadhak (seeker) prepare his physical, etheric and astral bodies for the event?

Bhagwan Shree Rajneesh :

The very first thing to be understood in this connection is that complete harmony in the first, second and third bodies is absolutely essential. If there is no friendly relationship between these three bodies, kundalini awakening can prove harmful. There are a few things which are very necessary in order to bring about this harmony, this relationship.

Firstly, as long as we are insensitive toward the physical body, this body cannot establish harmony with other bodies. By "insensitiveness" I mean we are not fully aware of the body. When we walk, we are hardly conscious of the fact that we are walking. When we stand, we are hardly conscious of the fact that we are standing. When we eat, we are hardly conscious of the fact that we are eating. Whatever work we do with the body, we do in unconsciousness and slumber. If we are unconscious about this body we must be doubly unconscious toward the others, for they are more subtle. If we are unaware of this gross body which is visible to the eye, the question of your being aware of the invisible subtle bodies does not arise. It is impossible to be aware of them.

Harmony cannot be without awareness. Harmony is possible only in a state of awareness. In a state of sleep all harmony is broken. So the very first thing is to be aware of the body. With whatever small action the body performs remembering is absolutely necessary. There should be mindfulness with all that we do. As Buddha used to say, "When you walk along the road, be aware that you are walking. When you lift the right leg, your mind should be conscious of the fact that the right leg has been lifted. When you sleep in the night you should know when you change sides."

There is an incident in the life of Buddha when he was still only a sadhak. He was passing through a village with a companion. They were both talking when a fly sat on Buddha's neck. He was in the midst of discussion when he lifted his hand to drive the fly away. It flew away, but Buddha stopped suddenly. "I have committed a grave error", Buddha told his companion. Then he lifted his hand again in the act of driving away the fly. The fellow sadhak exclaimed in surprise, "What is this you are doing ? The fly is no more there." Buddha replied, "Now I am driving the fly away as I should have. Now I am fully aware of what I am doing. Now as the hand lifts, I am fully aware that it is being lifted and that it is going in the direction of my neck to drive the fly away. That time I was talking to you, and hence my action was mechanical. I committed a sin against my body."

If we begin to do all our physical acts with full consciousness, then the identification with the physical becomes broken. If you lift one hand upward with full attention, you will feel yourself apart from the hand—because the one who lifts is very different from that which is lifted. The feeling of being apart is the beginning of the knowledge of the etheric body. Then, as I said before, you should be fully conscious toward this second body aslo.

Now suppose there is an orchestra playing. Many types of instruments are played in an orchestra. If there is a man in audience who has never heard music he will only hear the drums, for this is the instrument that makes the loudest sound. He will not be able to catch the softer notes of other instruments. But if he begins to become aware of the music he will slowly catch the softer notes. As his awareness increases he will begin to catch the most delicate subtle notes. Then as his awareness increases further he will not only catch the notes, but he will become aware of the gap between two notes—the silence between two notes. Then will he have grasped the music completely. The interval, the gap, is the last thing to grasp. Then it can be said that his grasp of music is complete.

The interval, the silence, the stillness between the two notes, has its own meaning. In truth the notes of music are meant only to accentuate this stillness, this silence. How much this silence is projected and emphasized is the real thing in music.

If you have seen Japanese or Chinese paintings, you must have been surprised to note that the painting is always in one corner; the rest of the canvas is left bare. Nowhere in the world do we find this method of painting, for nowhere in the world has the artist painted with such concentration. In fact, nowhere except in China and Japan have meditative people taken up painting. If you ask this artist why he has wasted such a big canvas for such a small painting when he could have easily used 1/8th of its size, he will reply that in order to bring out the empty space of 7/8th of the canvas he specifically worked on the remaining 1/8th. In reality, this is the ratio.

Now, ordinarily, when a tree standing in the vast space is painted, the whole canvas is taken up. Actually, the tree should be in one little corner, for in comparsion to the vast skies the tree is very insignificant. This is the actual ratio. When the tree stands in its right spatial proportion on the canvas, then only can it be alive. Thus, all your paintings are out of proportion. If a meditative man produces music, there will be less of notes and more silence in it—for the notes are very small compared to the silence that joins them. The notes have only one use—to give a hint of the emptiness, the silence, and then they depart. The more you develop a knowledge of music, the more you will get a glimpse of voidness.

The purpose of our physical body is only that it gives us a perception of our more subtle bodies, but we never use it to this end. We remain fixed only at the physical body because of our sleepy identification with it. We are asleep, and thus we live in the body in a very unconscious manner. If you awaken to each and every action of this body, you will begin to feel the presence of the second body. The second body too has its own activity, but you will not know the etheric until you have fully awakened toward the activities of the physical body, for the etheric is more subtle. If you are fully conscious of the activities of the physical body, you will begin to feel the movements of the second body. Then you will be surprised that there are etheric vibrations within you that are active all the time.

A man becomes angry. Anger is born in the etheric body, but it manifests in the first body. Basically, anger is the activity of the second body; the first body is used as a means. Therefore, you can stop anger from reaching the first body if you wish. This is what is done in repression. Suppose I am filled with anger, I feel like beating you with a stick, but I can stop myself. Beating is an activity of the first plane. Basically, there is anger but now there is no manifestation of anger. I can withhold myself from the act of beating; I can even smile at you if I wish. But within, anger has spread throughout my second body. So in repression what happens is that we hold back on the plane of manifestation, but it is already present on its basic plane.

When you begin to understand the processes of the physical body, you will begin to understand the movements of love, anger and hatred within you; you will become aware of their presence. Until you grasp the movements of these emotions that rise from the second body, all you can do is repress them. You cannot be free from them, for you only become aware of them when they have reached the first body—and not even then many times: often you only become aware of them when they have reached another person's body. We are so insensitive that not until your slap reaches someone's cheek do you realize what you have done. After the slap you come to know that something has happened.

All emotions rise from the etheric body. Therefore, I also call the second, etheric body "the emotional body". It has its own momentum; it has its own movements for anger, love, hatred, restlessness. You will come to know these vibrations.

In fear the etheric body becomes contracted. The diffidence we feel in fear does not belong to the first body. The first body remains just the same; there is no change in it whatsoever. But the effect of this contraction of the etheric body becomes evident in the person's walk, in the way he sits. He looks subdued all the time. He will not stand straight: he will slouch. When he speaks, he will stammer. His legs will shake when he walks; his hands will tremble when he writes.

Now anyone can make out the handwriting of a man from that of a woman's; it is not at all difficult. A woman's handwriting will never be straight. No matter how symmetrical and well formed, there will always be signs of trembling in it. This is a very feminine characteristic and it comes from a woman's emotional body. A woman is fearful all the time; her personality has become stricken with fear. So without any difficulty one can recognize the handwriting of a woman from a man's. Also, we can find out how fearful a man is from his handwriting. There is no difference between the fingers of a man or a women, nor in the way they hold the pen. As far as the first body goes there is no difference between the two, but on the plane of the second body the woman is fearful.

Even the woman of today has not been able to be fearless within. As of yet, our society, our culture and the state of our thinking is such that we have not been able to grant fearlessness to a woman. She is fearful all the time, and the vibrations of her fear descend upon her complete personality. The degree of fearlessness or fearfulness in men can also be gauged from their handwriting. The state of fear is on the plane of the etheric.

I have asked you to be aware of each happening in the gross body, but you should likewise be aware of the processes of the etheric body. When you are in love you feel as if you have expanded. The freedom experienced in love is because of this expansion. Now there is someone before whom you need not be fearful. There is no cause for fear near a person you love. Really speaking, to love means to be free of fear in the presence of a person before whom one can blossom to one's full capacity, no matter what one is. Therefore, a feeling of expansion is experienced in moments of love. The physical body remains the same, but the body within flowers and expands.

In meditation there are always experiences of this body. One sadhak may feel that his body has enlarged—so much so that it has filled the room. However, his physical body remains the same. When he opens his eyes he is shocked: the body is just the same. But the feeling of the experience follows him and makes him realize that what he had felt was not false. The experience was clear—that he had filled the whole room. This is a happening of the etheric body, the proportions of which are limitless. It also expands and contracts in response to the emotions. It can expand so that it can fill the earth; it can contract so that there is enough place for it in an atom.

So you will start noticing the movements of the etheric body—its expansions and contractions, in which conditions it contracts and in which conditions it expands. If the sadhak begins to live in those processes in which it expands, a harmony will be created. If he begins to live in the conditions that contract it, harmony will not be established between the two bodies. Expansion is its innate nature! When it has extended to its full capacity, when it blossoms fully, it is connected to the first body by a bridge. When it becomes fearful and shrinks, all its contacts with the first body break and it lies separate in a corner.

There are other. processes of the second body which can be known by other methods. For instance, you see a man perfectly healthy, perfectly normal. Now if someone goes and tells him he is to be executed, he will turn pale at once. No change has taken place in his first body, but there is an immediate change in his etheric body. His etheric body is ready to leave the physical body. If the owner of a house comes to know that he has to vacate the house immediately, all joyfulness and brightness will disappear; everything will be disturbed. The second body has broken its connections with the first, in a sense. The execution is to take place after some time or maybe not at all, but its connection with the first body is broken.

A man attacks you with a gun or a lion attacks you in the jungle: even though nothing has yet happened to the physical body, the etheric body promptly makes arrangements to leave it and a great distance is created between the two. So you can observe the workings of the second body in a subtle way, and this can be done without difficulty. The difficulty lies in this, that we fail to observe the processes of the physical also. If we do so, we shall start feeling the movements of the second body.

When you have a clear knowledge of the working of both, this very fact will create harmony between the two.

Then there is the third body—the subtle, astral body. Its movements are definitely more subtle—more subtle than fear, anger, love and hatred. It is difficult to grasp its movements unless the knowledge of the second body is complete. It is difficult even to understand, for the gap is now greater. We are unconscious on the first plane, but the second body is nearer the first so we can understand a few things about it. With the third, however, the distance increases. It is just as if the second body is our neighbour. Sometimes we hear the clatter of utensils or the crying of a child next door. But the third body is the neighbour's neighbour from whose quarters we do not hear any sound.

The journey of the third is yet more subtle. It can only be grasped if we begin to capture the emotions fully. So I will not know that you are angry with me unless you show your anger, for I can only see it when it becomes an action. But you can see it well in advance. You can feel it rising in your etheric body. Now this anger that has risen has its own atoms that come from the etheric body. If these atoms do not come, you cannot be angry.

You can call the astral body a collection of vibrations. You will be able to understand the different conditions of this body better by an example. We can see water, and we can see hydrogen and oxygen separately. There is no trace of water in oxygen; there is no trace of oxygen in water. Neither oxygen nor hydrogen has any property of water. But these two combine to form water: each has a hidden quality that manifests when they combine. Anger, love, are not seen in the astral body; nor are hatred or fear. But they have vibrations which become manifested when combined with second body. So when you are completely aware of the second body, when you are completely awakened toward your anger, then you will know that some reactions have taken place before the advent of anger. In other words, anger is not the beginning. It is the next part of a happening that has already taken place elsewhere.

A bubble rises from the bottom of a lake and begins to travel upwards. When it rises from the sand at the bottom of the lake, we cannot see it. When it reaches half the depth of the lake, it is still invisible. When it is about a short distance from the surface where we can see down into the lake, it begins to be visible although it is very small. Then it begins to get bigger and bigger as it reaches the surface, for the weight and pressure of water decreases as it comes up. Also it becomes more clear to our view. At the lower depths the pressure of water kept it small, but as it travels upwards the pressure becomes less and less until it reaches its full size at the surface. But where it reaches its full dimension it also bursts.

So it has travelled a long way. There were places where we could not see it, but it was there all the same hidden under the sand. Then it arose from there, but it was still invisible because the water pressed it down. Then it came nearer the surface from where we could see it, though it was still very small. Then it swam to the surface where we could have a complete view of it, but then it burst.

So the bubble of anger develops fully and bursts by the time it reaches the first body. When it comes to the surface it reveals itself. You can stop it at the second (emotional) body if you so desire, but that would be suppression. If you look into your etheric body, you will be surprised to find that it has already travelled some distance. But in its place of origin, it is in the form of currents.

As I told you before, there are no different types of matter. Rather, there are different combinations of the same energy particles in this world. Coal and diamond are the same: the difference is only in the combination of energy particles. If you break any matter into its components, ultimately what remains is electrical energy. The different combinations of these energy currents bring about formations of different substances. All these substances are different on the surface, deep below they are all one.

If you awaken toward the etheric body and follow the emotions to their origin, you will suddenly find yourself in the astral body. There you will find that anger is not anger, forgiveness is not forgiveness: the same energy vibrates in them. The energy in the vibrations of love and hatred is the same, the difference is only in the nature of the vibrations.

When love changes into hatred and hatred changes into love, we wonder how two directly opposite feelings change into one another. For example, he whom I called my friend until yesterday has become my enemy today. Then I console myself that perhaps I was deluded—that he was never my friend, for how can a friend turn into an enemy ? The energy vibrating in friendship and enmity is the same; the difference is only in the rate of vibrations. The difference is in the structure of the waves. What we call love is love in the morning and hatred in the evening. At noon there is love, and this changes into loathing by evening. It is a difficult situation. The one we love in the morning we loathe by evening.

Freud was under the impression that we love those we hate and we hate those we love. The reason he put forward was correct to some extent, but since he had no knowledge of the other bodies of man he could not go further with his investigations. The reason he puts forward is very superficial. He says that the relationship with the mother is the first relationship the child experiences: the mother is the first object he loves. When the mother lavishes him with care and attention, he loves her. And he hates the same mother when she rebukes or punishes him. So two feelings fill his mind toward the same object—the mother: he hates her as well as loves her. Sometimes he feels like murdering her and at other times he feels that he cannot live without her—that she is his every breath. This dual thinking makes the mother his first object of love and hate. Thus, later in life, because of this association in his mind, whomsoever he loves he will also hate.

This is a very superficial finding. The bubble has been caught right on the surface where it is about to burst. If a child can love and hate his mother also, it means that the difference in love and hate is quantitative and not qualitative. Love and hatred cannot manifest together at the same time. If both are present, this can be possible only on one condition—that they are convertible: their currents can oscillate from one to the other.

So the sadhak only comes to know why the mind is filled with conflicting emotions in the third body. A man comes and touches my feet in the morning and hails me as "Bhagwan" (Divine). The same man comes in the evening, abuses me and says, "This man is Satan." The next morning he again comes and addresses me as "Bhagwan" and touches my feet. Then others come and advise me not to pay any attention to his words, for sometimes he calls me God and sometimes Satan.

I say that he is the only one fit to be relied upon. The man who speaks is not to be blamed; he is not making conflicting statements. Rather, his statements belong to the same spectrum. They are rungs of the same ladder, the difference being only quantitative. In fact, as soon as he says "Bhagwan" he catches hold of one part.

The mind is made up of pairs of opposites, so where will the second part go? It will lie under the first waiting for it to exhaust itself. The first gets tired after all, for how long can this man keep on saying "Bhagwan"? When he is tired, the second part comes up which prompts him to say, "This man is Satan." Now these are not two things: they are one. Until the time comes when we are able to understand that all of our conflicting emotions are forms of the same energy, we shall not be able to solve man's problems. The greatest problem that confronts us is that when we love we hate also. We are ready to kill the person without whom we cannot live. He who is our friend is our enemy also deep within. This is our biggest problem, and wherever there are relationships in life this poses a big question. One thing should be well understood, that the underlying energy in the different emotions is the same; there is no difference whatsoever.

Ordinarily, we look upon light and darkness as two opposite things, which is wrong. In scientific terms, darkness is the most minimum state of light. If we try, we shall find light in darkness too. There is no darkness where light is not. It is a different matter if our instruments of investigation fail to recognize it. Our eyes may be incapable of discerning the light in the darkness, but light and darkness are on the same plane, they are different forms and vibrations of the one energy.

It will be easier to understand it in another way: we believe light and darkness to be absolutely opposed to one another, but we do not believe cold and heat to be opposed to each other to that extent. It would be interesting to carry out an experiment. Let one of your hands be heated over a stove and keep the other on ice. Now put both hands in a bucket of water at room temperature. You will find it difficult to decide whether the water is hot or cold. One hand will say it is hot and the other will say it is cold. You will be at a loss to decide, for both hands are yours. In fact, cold and heat are not two different things. They are relative experience.

If we call something cold, it only means that we are warmer. That we call it warm only means we are colder: we are only expressing the quantitative difference of temperature between that object and ourselves—nothing else. There is nothing hot and nothing cold. Or, that which is hot is cold also. In fact, hot and cold are misleading terms. We should speak in terms of "the temperature" : that is the right expression. The scientist also does not use the words hot and cold. He says that "the temperature of a thing is so many degrees". Hot and cold are poetic words. They are dangerous for science, for they convey nothing.

If a man enters a room and says it is cold, we cannot know what he means. It is possible that this man has fever, and the room feels cold to him though it is not at all cold. Therefore, until this man knows the condition of his body temperature, his assessment of the temperature of the room is meaningless. So we say, "Do not comment upon whether the room is hot or cold. Just say what is the degree of temperature of the room." The degree gives no indication of hot or cold. It only informs you what the temperature is. If the degree of temperature is less than your body temperature, you will feel cold; if it is more, you will feel hot. The same holds true for light and darkness: it depends upon our ability to see.

The night seems dark to us, but not so to the owl. The owl finds the day very dark. It must be wondering, "How strange a creature man is ! He keeps awake in the night." Generally, man, considers the owl foolish, but he does not know what the owl's opinion of him is. For the owl, the day is at night and it is night when it is day. He must be wondering at the foolishness of man ! He thinks, "There are many wise men among human beings, yet they remain awake at night, and when it is day they go to sleep. When it is the real time to be up and doing, these poor creatures go to sleep." The owl's eyes are capable of seeing at night. Because it can see at night, the night is not dark for it.

The vibrations of love and hate are like those of darkness and light: they have their own ratio. So when you begin to be aware of the third plane, you will be in a strange condition: it will no longer be a matter of your own choice to choose whether to love or to hate. Now you will know that these are two names of the same thing. If you choose one, you automatically choose the other; you cannot escape the second choice. So if you ask for love from a man of the third plane, he will ask if you are prepared for hatred also. You will, of course, say, "No, I want love only. Please give me love!" He will reply that it is not possible, for love is one form of the vibration of hate. In fact, love is the form that is pleasing to you whereas hate is that form of the same vibrations which is displeasing to you.

So the man who stands on the third plane begins to be liberated from the pairs of opposites. He will come to know for the first time that what he had looked upon as two opposite things are one and the same. Two opposite branches became part of the same trunk of the tree. Then he will laugh at his stupidity for trying to destroy one in order to keep the other. But then he did not know that this was impossible and that deep within the tree was the same. Only after awakening in the second plane can the third plane be known, for the third body has very subtle vibrations. There, there are no emotions—only vibrations.

If you come to grasp the vibrations of the third body, you will begin to have a unique experience. Then, upon seeing a person, you will directly be able to tell what vibrations possess him. Because you are not aware of your own vibrations, it is not possible for you to recognize those of another person. Otherwise, the vibrations emanating from the third body are gathered around every person's head. The halo depicted in pictures of Buddha, Mahavir, Ram and Krishna is the aura seen around their heads. These have special colours which have been detected. If you have the right experience of the third body, you will begin to see these colours. When you begin to see these colours, you will see not only your own, but those of others as well.

In fact, the deeper we begin to see ourselves, the deeper we begin to see inside others also—to the same extent. Because we know only our own physical body, we know only the physical bodies of others. The day we come to know the etheric body, we shall begin to be aware of the etheric bodies in others. Before you become angry, you can know well in advance that you are going to be angry. Before you express love, it can be easily predicted that you are making preparations for love. So what we call getting to know the feelings of others is not such a great thing after all. By becoming aware of one's own emotional body, it becomes easy to grasp the feelings of others, for we begin to see all its conditions. By awakening into the third plane things become very clear, for then we can see the colours of the personality also.

The colour of the clothes of sadhus and sannyasins were chosen by the colour seen from the third body. The choice was different in each case, according to which body was favoured. For Instance, Buddha chose yellow because he stressed the seventh body. The aura around the person who has attained the seventh plane is yellow. Therefore, Buddha chose the colour of yellow for his *bhikkhus* (monks). It was because of this colour that Buddhist *bhikkhus* found it difficult to remain in India. The yellow colour is identified with death. And in fact, it is the colour of death, for the seventh plane is the plane of ultimate death. So the yellow colour is connected with death deep within us.

The colour of ochre gives the feeling of life. Therefore, ochre-robed sannyasins looked more attractive than the yellow-robed ones; they appeared alive. This colour is the colour of blood and the colour of the aura of the sixth body (the Cosmic body): it is the colour of the rising sun.

The Jains chose white, which is the colour of the fifth body—the spiritual body. The Jains insist on leaving God alone—on leaving God out of discussion and on leaving Nirvana out of discussion—because scientific discussions are possible only up to the fifth body. Mahavir was a man of a scientific bent. Therefore, he talked about matters as far as they could be solved mathematically; beyond that he refused to talk. He did not wish to talk where his words were liable to err, so he refused to elaborate on mysticism. Thus, he did not talk of the planes after the fifth. Mahavir chose white, therefore; it is the colour of the fifth plane.

From the third plane, you will start seeing colours which are due to the effect of the subtle vibrations within. In the very near future it will be possible to photograph them. If they can be seen by the naked eye, it follows that they cannot escape the eye of the camera for long. Then we shall develop a wonderful ability to judge people and their character.

There is a German thinker by the name of Bluschev who has studied the effect of colour on millions of people. Many hospitals in Europe and America are using his experiments, the colour you choose tells of your intimate personality. A man with a particular disease prefers a particular colour: a healthy person choose quite another colour; a tranquil man prefers yet another colour; an ambitious man quite another than a non-ambitious person. With your choice you give a hint of what is happening within your third body. Now it is an interesting fact that if the colour that emanates from your third body is grasped, and if your preference of colour is then tested, it will turn out to be the same colour: you will choose the colour that is spread around you.

Colours have wonderful meanings and uses. It was not known previously that colours could be so meaningful that they can speak of your character. Also, it was not known that the effect of colours can touch your inner personality. You cannot escape from them. For instance, the colour red : it is always connected with revolution. It is the colour of anger and it is difficult to escape from it. Therefore, the revolutionaries carried red flags. There is an aura of red colour around a wrathful mind : it is the colour of blood, the colour of murder, the colour of anger and of destruction.

It would interest you to know that if everything in the room were coloured red, the blood pressure of all of you sitting here would rise. If a man lives continuously with the colour red, his blood pressure can never be normal. The colour blue causes the blood pressure to fall: it is the colour of the skies and of supreme tranquillity. If there is blue all around you, your blood pressure will fall.

Leave aside man: if we fill water in a blue bottle and keep it in the sun, the chemical composition of the water will change. The water absorbs the blue colour which changes the composition of the water. This water has an affect on man's blood pressure. Similarly, if we fill a yellow bottle with water and put it in the sun, its characteristics will be different. The water in the blue bottle will remain fresh for days whereas the water in the yellow bottle will turn foul at once. The yellow colour is the colour of death, and it disintegrates things.

You will begin to see the circles of all these colours around you This will be on the third plane. When you are awakened and are aware of these three bodies, that very awareness will bring about a harmony between them. Then Shaktipat of any kind will not be able to bring harmful results. The energy of Shaktipat will enter your fourth body through the harmonious layers of the first three bodies; this will be the highway along which it will travel. If this path is not ready, there can be many dangers. Therefore, I said that the first three bodies should be strong and fit; then only is progress achieved.

Questioner : *If a man who is established in the fourth, fifth, sixth or seventh chakra (centre) dies, what will be the condition of his chakras in the next birth? If persons who have attained the bodiless state are reborn, then on what plane must the person to whom they are born be on? Do bodiless beings have to be reborn as human beings for the final attainment?*

Bhagwan : Now we shall have to understand some things from afar. I talked to you about the seven bodies. Keeping these in mind, we can divide the whole of Existence into seven parts. In the entire Existence, all of the seven bodies are forever present. Awake or asleep, active or dormant, ugly or beautiful, they are always there. Take a piece of metal—say, a piece of iron: all of the seven bodies are present in it, but all of the seven are asleep; all of the seven are dormant—non-active. Therefore, a piece of iron looks dead. Take a plant: its first body has become active—its physical body. Therefore, we get the first glimpse of life in plants.

There is the animal: his second body has become activated. Therefore, movement, which is not in plants starts in animals. The plant strikes its roots and stays in one place always. It is not mobile because for that the second body must be activated—the etheric body from which all movements come. If only the physical body is awakened, it will be immobile, fixed. The plant is a fixed animal. There are some plants that move a little. That is a state between plant and animal.

In the lagoons of Africa, there are certain plants that slide over a distance of twenty to twenty-five feet in a year. By means of their roots they can clutch the ground and let it go and thus perform movement. This is the revolutionary link between the plant and the animal. The second body has also begun to work in the animal. This does not mean that the second body has reached awareness : it only means it has become activated. The animal has no knowledge of it. Because of the second body being activated, it experiences anger, it can express love, it can run, defend itself, it experiences fear, it can attack, and it can move.

In man, the third, astral body is activated. Therefore, not only does he move bodily, but also with the mind: he can travel with his mind. He travels in the past as well as in the future. There is no future for the animal, and therefore, it is never worried, never tense, for all anxiety is of the future. What will happen tomorrow is our greatest worry. But for animals there is no tomorrow; today is everything for them. Even today does not exist for them in a way, for what does today mean to one for whom tomorrow has no meaning ? What is, IS. In man a more subtle movement has taken birth—the movement of the mind. It comes from the third, astral body. Now he can think of the future with the help of the mind. He can also worry about what will be after death—where he will go, where he will not go. He also reflects upon whether he was or whether he was not before birth.

The fourth body is active in a few persons, not in all. If a person dies after his fourth body is activated, he is born on the plane of the "devas"—the gods (or you can give it whatever name you want to give it) where there are many possibilities for the activation of the fourth body. If the third body remains active, only then does a man remain as a man. From the fourth body, birth on higher planes begins.

But with the fourth there will be a difference that must be understood. If the fourth body is activated, there is less possibility of acquiring a physical body again and more possibility of a bodiless existence. But as I said, remember the difference between activation and Consciousness. If the fourth body is merely activated and one is not conscious, we shall call it the plane of "pretas" (evil spirits). If it is activated as well as fully conscious, we shall call it the plane of the "devas" (godly spirits). This is the only difference between pretas and devas. An evil spirit is not aware that its fourth body is activated whereas a godly one is. Therefore, the preta can cause a great deal of harm with the activity of its fourth body, both to itself and to others, for unconsciousness can only bring harm. The deva will cause many acts of beneficence, both to itself and to others, for awareness can only be beneficial.

He whose fifth body becomes active goes beyond the existence of devas. The fifth is the spiritual body. On the fifth plane, activation and awareness are one and the same. No one can reach the fifth plane without awareness; therefore, activation and awareness take place simultaneously here. You can reach up to the fourth without awareness also. If you awaken, the journey will take a different turn : it will go toward the deva plane (the plane of the gods). If you go on sleeping, your journey will be in the realm of the evil spirits.

On the fifth plane activation and awareness are there simultaneously, for this is the "Atman sharir" (the spiritual body) and unawareness is meaningless so far as the Atman (Self) is concerned. "Atman" means consciousness. Therefore, the other name of Atman is "consciousness". Here unconsciousness has no meaning.

So from the fifth body, activation and consciousness are one and the same thing, but before that the two ways are separate. The difference between male and female is there until the fourth; the difference between sleeping and waking is there until the fourth. As a matter of fact, duality and conflict are there only up to the fourth body. From the fifth the non-dual begins—the undivided. Unity starts from the fifth. Before this there is diversity, difference. The potential of the fifth comes neither from the plane of pretas nor from the plane of the devas. This should be understood.

The fifth body is not possible for pretas for theirs is an unconscious existence. They do not have that body which is necessary for consciousness, and they do not have the first body which is the first step toward awareness. For this reason the preta has to return to a human form. Therefore, the human existence is in a sense at crossroads. The plane of the devas is above it but not beyond it, for to go beyond it is necessary to come back to the human existence. The preta has to return in order to break its unconsciousness, as for this a human form is absolutely necessary. The devas have to return, because in their existence there is no suffering whatsoever. Actually, it is an awakened existence. However, in such an existence there cannot be the pain and suffering that spur the longing for sadhana. Where there is no suffering, there is no thought of destroying or of achieving.

So the heavenly existence is a static existence where there is no progress. This is a peculiarity of happiness : it blocks all further progress. In pain and suffering there is motivation, progress. Suffering goads us to find ways and means of deliverance from pain and sorrow. In happiness all seeking stops. So this is indeed a very strange state of affairs, and people usually cannot understand this.

In the lives of Mahavir and Buddha, there are descriptions of devas coming to them in order to be taught, but these are very exceptional happenings. It is strange that "devatas" (devas or gods) should come to human beings, for it is an existence above the human existence. It seems strange, but it is not, for the existence in heaven is a static existence from where there is no progress. If you wish to go ahead, then just as you take a step back before you jump you have to step back to the human existence.

Happiness is peculiar in the sense that there is no further movement. Another thing : happiness becomes boring. There is no other factor that can cause as much tediousness as happiness. Unhappiness is not boring : an unhappy mind is never bored. Therefore, an unhappy man is never discontented, nor is a society where pain and misery prevails. It is only the happy person or the happy community that is dissatisfied India is not as discontented as America. The reason is only this, that they are affluent and happy whereas we are poor and miserable. There is nothing to look forward to in America and there is no suffering to goad them to further progress. Besides, happiness is repetitive. The same forms of pleasure and enjoyment over and over again become meaningless.

So the existence in heaven is the peak of boredom. There is no place more boring in the universe, and there is much, too much boredom there. But it takes time for the boredom to develop. Besides, it depends upon the sensitivity of the individual. The more sensitive a person, the sooner he will get bored; the less sensitive a person, the later he will get bored. It is also possible that he may not get bored at all. The buffalo eats the same grass every day and is not tired of it.

Sensitivity is very rare. The boredom will be proportionate to the sensitivity of the being. Sensitivity always looks for the new: it seeks more and more that is new day by day. Sensitiveness is a kind of restlessness, and this in turn is a kind of aliveness. So existence in heaven is a kind of dead existence, and so also is the existence of the pretas. But existence in heaven is more dead, for in the world of the pretas there is a lot of suffering (and ways to inflict suffering as well as "the pleasure" of making others and oneself to suffer). There are enough provisions for restlessness there, so there is no boredom at all.

Existence in heaven is very peaceful: there is no disturbance of any sort. So, ultimately, the return from heavenly existence can only be out of boredom. Remember, it is above human life, for sensitivity increases there. The pleasure that does not become boring to us over the years (in the bodily life) becomes stale and boring once it is enjoyed in the heavenly existence.

This is why it is said in the "Puranas" (Hindu mythological scriptures) that the gods yearn to be born as human beings. Now this seems very surprising, because here on earth we long to go to the realm of the devas. There are even stories where some deva (god) descends on earth to fall in love with a woman. These stories are indications. Some celestial maiden descends on earth and falls in love with a man. These stories are indications of the state of mind. They show that in that realm there is happiness, but it is insipid because there is just pleasure and enjoyment without a trace of pain or sorrow. Then it becomes tedious, dull and uninteresting. If one is given a choice between infinite happiness without a moment of sorrow and infinite sorrow and suffering, the wise man will choose the latter. We have to return from heavenly existence; we also have to return from the existence of the pretas.

Human existence is at the crossroads: all journeys are possible from it. The man who attains the fifth body, however, has not to go anywhere. He enters a state in which there is no longer any birth through any other source: he is not reborn through the womb of any mother. "Being born through a source" means entrance into a womb. So his birth does not take place through any source.

He who attains the Self has ended his journey in a sense. The state in the fifth body is a state of liberation. But if he feels satisfied within himself, he can stop at this plane for an infinite number of ages, for here there is neither pain nor pleasure, neither bondage nor suffering. There is only one's own being—not the universal Being, the All. So a person can languish in this state for an infinite number of ages until a time comes when he grows curious to know the All.

The seed of curiosity is within us; therefore, it arises. Therefore, if the sadhak nurtures the curiosity of knowing the All from the very beginning, he can escape the inconvenience of languishing in the fifth body. Thus, if you know the full science of the seven bodies, you will know that the inquiry should be full and final from the very beginning. If you start with a goal of halting in between, then when you reach (the fifth) you will feel you have come to the end of your destination, and that will be the end for you.

So the individual of the fifth body has not to take birth, but he is bound within himself. He breaks away from everyone, but remains bound to himself. He is rid of the ego, but not of a certain pride. Ego is a claim against others. Understand this well : When I say "I", it is to subjugate some "you". Therefore, when the "I" succeeds in subjugating a "you", conceit becomes manifested. When it is subjugated by the "I" of another, it whimpers pitifully. The "I" is always an effort to overwhelm the "you", so the ego is always comparing to the other.

Here (at the fifth) the other is no more and there is no longer any competition with it. Now this state of I-ness (*Asmita*) is self-contained. This is the only difference between ego and I-ness (*Asmita*). Now I have nothing to do with "you". There is no claim of "I", but still there is my being. I no longer need to stand against "the other", but "I am" although there is no "you" to be compared with. Therefore, I said ego will say "I" and the being will say "am". This will be the difference. In "I am" there are two concepts : the "I" is the ego and the "am", the being.

The feeling of "I-ness" is not against anyone: it is in favour of itself. The feeling is one of "I am, so let there be no one else in the world. Let there be a third world war and let all perish. but 'I' should remain." So though there will be no ego in me, the feeling of I-ness still will be: I know that 'I am', even though I will not say 'I' to others, for there is no longer any 'you' left for me whom I can say it too. So when you are absolutely alone, there is no other. Then too your feeling is one of "I am" in a sense.

The ego bows out in the fifth body and thus the strongest link in the chain of bondage falls. But the feeling of I-ness remains—free, independent, boundless and without any attachments. But the I-ness has its own limits. All other boundaries fade away except the boundary of I-ness. At the sixth this too disintegrates or is crossed. The sixth is the Cosmic body.

The question of being born in a womb ends with the fifth body, but birth still must be taken. This difference should be properly understood : One birth is from within the mother's womb and one birth is from within oneself. This is why, in this country (India), we call the Brahmin "*dwij*"—twice-born. This term was actually used for the "Brahma Jnani" (one who knows the Brahman—the Cosmic Reality). To call such a person, "Brahmin" is unnecessary. When a second birth of an entirely different kind was gone through by a person, he was called *dwij*—"twice-born".

So one birth is from another and one is from one's own self. Once the fifth body is attained, you cannot be born to another. Now you shall have to be born through the fifth body into the sixth body. This is your own journey, your own inner pregnancy, your own inner birth. Now there is no connection with an external womb or with any external means of creation. Now you have no father or mother. You are the father, you are the mother and you are the child. Now this is entirely an individual journey. So when a person enters the sixth body through the fifth, he can be called twice-born, and not before that. He is born without the external means of creation, without the help of an external womb.

One *Rishi* (sage) of the Upanishads says, prays, "Oh Lord, open the golden cover of this I-ness within which the Reality is hidden." The covers are definitely of gold. They are such that we do not want to throw them aside. They are such that we are eager to keep them. The I-ness is the most priceless cover that is over us. We ourselves will not like to part from it and there is no external obstruction to stop us. The cover itself is so lovable that we cannot leave it. Therefore, the *Rishi* says, "Remove the golden cover and open the womb that makes a person twice-born".

So "Brahma Jnanis" were called twice-born, and by "Brahma Jnani" is meant one who has attained the sixth body. From the fifth to the sixth the journey is one of being twice-born. The womb is different, the mode of being born is different. Now everything is wombless: the womb is one's own, and we are self-born now.

From the fifth to the sixth there is a birth and from the sixth to the seventh there is a death. Therefore, one who has undergone the latter is not referred to as twice-born; there is no meaning in it. Do you understand ? It is easy to follow now. From the fifth to the sixth there is birth through oneself; from the sixth to the seventh there is death through oneself. We were born through others—through the bodies of others, and the death that follows is also of others. This I shall explain.

If your birth is from another, how can your death be your own ? How can this be ? The two ends will be unrelated. If another gives me my birth, then death cannot be mine. When birth comes from another, death too is from another. The difference is this that first I appear through one womb and the second time I enter into another womb—but I am not aware. When I came into this birth it was apparent, but now my going is not apparent. Death precedes birth : you had died somewhere before you were born somewhere. Birth is apparent, but of death, you are not aware.

Now you were born through a mother and father: you obtained a body, an apparatus that will run for 70 to 100 years. After a hundred years, this instrument will not work. The day it will stop working is predestined from the movement of birth. It is not so important when it will fall: what is important is that it will fall. With birth it is decreed that you will die. The womb which brought you your birth brought along your death also. You have brought them along both together. In fact, death lies hidden in the birth-giving womb.

There is only an interval of a hundred years. In these hundred years, you will complete your journey from one end to the other and go back exactly to the place from where you came. The death of your body is received from another AT THE TIME OF YOUR BIRTH. Therefore, death is also from another. So YOU are neither born, nor is it you who dies. In birth there was a medium and in death too the same will be the case. When you enter the sixth, Cosmic body from the fifth (the spiritual body), you will be born for the first time. Then you will be "self-born" : your birth will be without a womb. But then "self-death" will at the same time await you —a wombless death also awaits you. Wherever this birth takes you, from there death will lead you even further ahead. The birth takes you to the Brahman and death to the Nirvana.

This birth can be very prolonged; it can be endless. Such a person, if he remains, will become "Ishwara" (God). Such a consciousness, if it travels for long, will be worshipped by millions; prayers will be offered unto him. Those whom we call Avatar, Ishwara (God), Son of God, Teerthanker (a World Teacher of the Jains), are those who have entered the sixth plane from the fifth. They can remain in that plane for as long as they wish, and they can be of great help. There is no question of any harm coming from them and they can be deeply informative. Such persons are for ever striving and labouring for others to travel through the preceding journey. The consciousness of people from the sixth plane can also relay messages in various ways, and those who have the slightest feel of such persons cannot place them anywhere lower than "Bhagwan" (God). "Bhagwan" they are : there is nothing lacking in their being Bhagwan, for they have attained the Cosmic body (the Cosmic Reality).

In this very life it is possible to enter the sixth plane through the fifth. Whenever anyone enters the sixth in this life, we call him a Buddha or a Mahavir or a Ram or a Krishna or a Christ. And those who perceive them as such look upon them as God. For those who cannot see, the question does not arise.

One man in a village recognizes Buddha as Ishwara (God); to another he is nothing—absolutely ordinary. He catches a cold like us; he falls ill just like us; he eats, sleeps, walks and talks like us; he even dies the same like us. "Then what is the difference between he and us ?" is how they argue. The number of those who do not see is infinitely larger, so those who see appear to be mad, "poor creatures," for they have to evidence whatsoever to offer as proof.

Actually, there is no evidence. For instance, this mike is before me. If you who are present cannot see it, how will I prove to you that it is there ? If I say it is and if you cannot see, I will be judged mad. To see when others cannot see is "a proof" that you are "not sound of mind".

We measure knowledge also by number. Here too we have the voting system. So Buddha is God for some. Those who cannot see him as God will say, "What madness is this ? He is the son of Shuddhodan, and so and so is his mother, and so and so his wife. He is the same Gautam. Even his own father could not see that he was Buddha. He looked upon him as his son, and said, "Into what kind of foolishness have you fallen ? Return to the house. What are you doing ? The kingdom is getting ruined and I am getting old. You return and take care of everything." The poor father failed to recognize that Buddha had become the ruler of an infinite kingdom. Those who had the eyes to see looked upon such people as a Teerthanker, Bhagwan or the Son of God. They will make use of some such word to address them.

The seventh body is never attained in this life. In this body we can at the most stand on the boundary line of the sixth body from where we can see the seventh. That jump, that Void, that eternity, is visible from there, and there we can stand. Therefore, in the life of Buddha two Nirvanas have been mentioned. One nirvana he attained under the Bodhi Tree on the banks of the river Niranjana : that was forty years before his death. This is called "Nirvana". That day he stood on the periphery of the sixth body—and he remained there for forty long years. The day he died is called the "Mahaparinirvana" (the day he cast off his physical body and entered the seventh plane). Therefore, when anyone asked him, "What will happen to Tathagat (a name of Buddha) after death ?" Buddha would reply, "There will be no Tathagat."

But this does not satisfy the mind. Again and again they would ask, "What will happen to Buddha in Mahaparinirvana ?" To this Buddha replied, "Where all activities cease, where all happening cease, that is call Mahaparinirvana." As long as something keeps happening it is the sixth body, it is the existence. Beyond this is the non-Existence. So when Buddha is not, nothing will remain. In a sense you may say he never was. He will fade away like a dream, like a line drawn on the sand, like a line drawn on water that disappears as it forms. He will be lost and nothing will remain. But this does not satisfy our minds. We say, somewhere, on some level, in some corner, no matter how far away, he should exist. But in the seventh he becomes only the Void.

There is no way of bringing news from beyond the seventh. There are people who stand on the borderline and see the seventh, who see that abyss. Therefore, all that is known of the seventh plane is what is reported by these people who stand at the boundary line of the sixth plane. It is not an account of people who have gone there, for there is no means to give any account. It is just as if a man standing at the borderline of Pakistan would look and report that there is a house, a shop, a road, some people, and he can see the trees and the sun coming out. But this man is standing on the Indian border.

To go into the seventh from the sixth is the supreme death. You will be surprised to know that the meaning of "Acharya" in the olden days was one who teaches the final death (the word is now used to mean Professor). There are aphorisms which say, "Acharya is death." So when Nachiketa reaches the God of death, he reaches the Acharya (an Upanishadic story). The God of death can only teach death and nothing else. "Acharya" is a designation from which only destruction, disintegration and extinction can be taught.

But before this death it is necessary for you to be born, for that which you consider as yourself is borrowed : it is not your existence. Even if you lose it, you were never the possessor. It is just as if I were to steal something then give it in charity. Since the thing did not belong to me, how can it be my donation? What is not mine, I cannot give. Therefore, one whom we call a renunciate in this world is not a renunciate at all, for he renounces that which is not his. And how can you be the renouncer of that which is not yours ? To claim to have left that which is not yours is madness. Renunciation takes place when you enter the seventh from the sixth. There you cast aside that which is YOU, for you have nothing else. You leave your very being.

The only renunciation that is meaningful is the entrance from the sixth plane to the seventh. Before that, all talk of renunciation is childish. The man who says "This is mine" is foolish. The man who says "I left all that was mine" is also foolish, for he still claims to be the possessor. Only we ourselves are ours, but we have no understanding of this.

Therefore, from the fifth to the sixth you will know who you are and from the sixth to the seventh you will be able to renounce that which you are. And the moment someone renounces that which he is, there is nothing more left to be attained, there is nothing more left to be renounced. The question is silenced for ever in that infinite stillness, in the eternal silence. After that one cannot even talk of bliss or peace; one cannot even talk of Truth or falseness, light or darkness. Nothing can be said : this is the state of the seventh.

Questioner : *If the fifth plane is attained in the physical body, in which form is the person reborn after his death* ?

Bhagwan : To attain the fifth body and to be Awakened is one and the same thing. Then you no longer need the initial bodies. Now you can work from the fifth plane; now you are an Awakened person. Hence, there is no difficulty. The initial bodies are required only up to the fourth body. If the fourth is activated and Awakened, the person becomes a deva—a heavenly soul. If the fourth lies idle and asleep, the person enters the realm of the pretas—the evil spirits. You will have to return to the human form from both of these states, for you have no idea of your identity as yet. And in order to know your identity you must still have a need for "the other". Only with the help of the other will you be able to know yourself.

To know yourself you need the other: without the other you will not be able to recognize yourself. The other will form the boundary from where you will know yourself. Therefore, up to the fourth plane you will have to take birth under any circumstances.

After the fifth the other is not necessary; it has no meaning. In the fifth it will be possible for you to be without the previous four bodies. But with the fifth the process of an entirely new kind of birth begins, and that is the entrance into the sixth plane. This is a different matter altogether and does not involve the first four bodies.

Questioner : *When a person enters the fifth from the fourth plane, does he not acquire a physical body again after death* ?

Bhagwan : No !

Questioner : *If a Teerthanker desires to be born, can he take a physical body* ?

Bhagwan : Now this is a different matter altogether. If a Teerthanker wishes to be reborn, a very interesting happening takes place: that is, before death he does not discard his fourth body. There is a way and a method of doing this, and that is by having the desire to be a Teerthanker. So when the fourth body is falling away, one desire has to be kept alive so that the fourth body does not drop. If the fourth drops, birth in the physical is impossible.

Then the bridge, the connection through which you came, is no more. So the desire to be a Teerthanker has to be kept alive before the fourth body. Not all who are worthy of becoming Teerthankers become Teerthankers: they go straight along their way without this. There are only a few who become such Teachers, and their number is fixed beforehand. There is a reason why their number is predetermined. It is predetermined that for a particular age so many Teerthankers would be enough for so many people.

So the desire of becoming a Teerthanker has to be very strong. It is the last desire, and if it slips the matter is over. So the seed of desire that "I want to teach others" must be very strong. One must feel, "I will show others the way; I will explain to others, I must come for others." Then the Teerthanker can descend into a physical body. But this means that the fourth body has not been left yet. He steps onto the fifth, but he fastens a peg in the fourth body. This peg can be quickly uprooted; hence, it is a very difficult task to maintain it there.

There is a process of making Teerthankers : they are made in schools; it is not an individual heppening. In the same manner that a school functions, a group of sadhaks perform sadhana. Then from among them, they find one who shows full promise of becoming a Teacher : he can express what he knows, he can impart what he knows, and he can communicate it to others. So the whole school begins to work on his fourth body : he is told to concentrate on his fourth body so that it should not disintegrate, because it will be useful in the future. Thus, he will be taught ways and means of saving his fourth body. And more labour and hard work goes into saving this body than in discarding it.

It is so easy to let-go, but when all the anchors are pulled up, when the sails are all drawn and filled with the wind, when the vast ocean calls and there is bliss and bliss everywhere, you can imagine how difficult it must be to guard one small peg. Therefore, when we address a Teerthanker, we say : "You are most compassionate."

This was the only reason why a Teerthanker was so called. The greatest part of his compassion was that when everything was ready for his departure, he stayed back for those who were still at the shore and whose boats were yet not ready to sail. His boat is absolutely ready; yet he bears the sufferings of the shores, he endures the stones and the abuses. He could have left anytime; his boat was ready to set sail. Yet, for no reason of his own, he preferred to be amidst those who are capable of harassing and even killing him.

So his compassion knows no bounds, but the desire for this compassion is taught in schools. Therefore, sadhaks working individually cannot become Teerthankers, for when the peg falls off they will not know about it. Only when the boat has sailed do they realize that the shore is left way behind.

Even persons who have attained the sixth plane, whom we call "Iswara" (God), sometimes help in the advent of a Teerthanker. When they find one worthy enough not to be let off from the shore, they try in a thousand ways to keep him back. Even devas (godly souls of the fourth plane) who, as I said, are helpful in doing good, take part in this venture. They go on influencing such a one to save one peg. They tell him : "We can see the peg; you cannot. But you have to save it."

So the world is not anarchic, disorderly. There are profound arrangements; there is order within order. Efforts of all kinds are often made, but at times the plans go amiss, as in the case of Krishnamurti. Great efforts were made with him to fix a peg, but they failed. The whole school of sadhaks made a a tremendous effort to drive in a peg in his fourth body, but all efforts failed. Other persons had a hand in this effort. Also, there was the hand of higher souls behind this and there was the hand of persons of the sixth and the fifth, and Awakened ones of the fourth plane. Thousands of persons took part in it.

Krishnamurti was chosen as well as a few other children who showed promise of becoming Teerthankers, but the opportunity passed away without bearing fruit. The peg could not be fixed, and so the world lost the benefit of a Teerthanker through Krishnamurti. But that is a different story.

[Text of a discourse given on July 10, 1970, evening, in Bombay, India]

17

KUNDALINI SADHANA AND THE ESOTERIC DIMENSIONS OF TANTRA

Questioner:

You have said that the difference of male and female ends with the fifth body. How do the positive and negative poles of electricity of the first four bodies become adjusted to bring about this happening? Please explain this in detail.

Bhagwan Shree Rajneesh:

In the context of the male and female bodies you have been told that the first body of the female is a female body while the second is male, and the exact opposite is the case with the male. Then the woman's third body is again female and the fourth male. I have told you before that the female body is half complete; so is the male body. These two together make a complete body. This union is possible in two ways. If the external man combines with the external woman, together they create a unit. With this unit, the work of procreation, of nature, goes on. If a man or woman turns inward and unites with the female or male within, a different journey begins which is the way toward the Divine. The external union, however, is a journey toward nature.

When the first body of the male meets his second etheric body which is female, these two make a unit. When the first body of a female meets her second, etheric body which is made of the male element, they also form a unit. This is a wonderful unity. The external union can only be momentary. Very briefly it gives a period of happiness, then the sorrow of separation is infinitely greater. And this sorrow brings about a fresh yearning for the same pleasure which again proves to be momentary; then again there is the parting which is long and painful. So the outer pleasure can only be momentary whereas the union within abides for ever. Once it takes place it never breaks.

Therefore, as long as the union within does not take place there is sorrow and pain. A current of happiness begins to flow within as soon as the inner union takes place. This pleasure is similar to that which is experienced momentarily in the outer union that takes place during coitus—a union which is so infinitesimal in its duration that it is over before it has hardly begun. Many a time it is not even experienced. It happens with such swiftness that it is not experienced at all.

From the point of view of yoga, when "inner intercourse" becomes possible, the instinct for outer intercourse immediately disappears. The reason is that this inner union is completely satisfying and fulfilling. The images of coitus depicted on temple walls are indications in this direction. Inner intercourse is a process of meditation. Therefore, opposition arose between the concept of internal and external intercourse. This was due to the fact that he who enters into inner union even once will lose all interest in outer intercourse.

This also should be remembered: when a woman unites with her male etheric body, the resulting unit will be female; when the male unites with his female etheric body, the unit will be male. This is because the first body absorbs the second body: the second merges in the first. But now these are male and female in a very different sense. It is not the outer man and the outer woman which we see. The outer man is incomplete, and, therefore, uneasy, unsatisfied. The external woman is also incomplete, and, therefore, restless, unfulfilled.

If we examine the development of life on earth, we will find that in primal organisms the male and female are both present. For example, the amoeba: the amoeba is half male, half female. Therefore, there is no other creature more satisfied in this world. No such thing as discontent ever arises in an amoeba. This is also the reason why it has failed to develop: it has always remained an amoeba. So very elementary organisms in biological development do not have separate bodies for each sex. Both male and female are contained within the same body.

When the first body of the woman unites with her male etheric body, a new woman comes into being who is a complete woman. We have no idea of the personality of a complete woman, for all the women we know are incomplete. We have no estimate of a complete man, for all the men we know are incomplete. They are all only half. As soon as this unit is completed, a supreme satisfaction pervades—a satisfaction in which all discontent diminishes and finally disappears.

Now it will be difficult for this complete man and complete woman to establish any external relationships, for outwardly there are only half men and half women with whom their personalities do not harmonize. However, it is possible for a perfect man, one whose first two bodies have united within, to form a relationship with a perfect woman, one whose first two bodies within have also united.

Tantra has tried many experiments for this relationship. Therefore, tantra had to go through a great deal of harassment and calumny. We could not understand what tantrics were doing. Naturally, it was beyond our understanding. When a woman and a man who are each united to the inner complementary body copulate under the circumstances of tantra, it is nothing more than ordinary intercourse for us. We could never evaluate what was happening.

But this is a very different kind of happening, and this was a very great help to the sadhak (seeker). It had a great significance for him. The external union of a complete man and a complete woman was the beginning of a new meeting; it was a journey toward a new union. One kind of journey was already over: the incomplete woman and incomplete man have been completed. A particular plateau of fulfilment was then reached, because now there was no thought of desire.

When a complete man and a complete woman meet in this way, they experience for the first time the bliss, the pleasure, of the union of two whole beings. Then they begin to understand that if such a perfect union can take place within themselves, there would be a torrent of unabounding bliss. The half man enjoyed the union with the half woman. Then he united with the half woman within himself, and he experienced unlimited bliss. Then the complete man united with the complete woman. Then it is but logical that he should set out to attain a perfect woman within himself, so he set out in search of the perfect woman within where the meeting of the third and fourth bodies takes place.

The third body of the man is again male and the fourth female; the woman's third body is female and the fourth male. Tantra has taken care to see that man does not stagnate after the perfection of one body is achieved. There are many sorts of perfection within us. Perfection never obstructs, but there are many kinds of perfections which are imperfect in view of the further perfections that lie ahead. However, they are perfections in view of the preceding imperfections. The previous imperfections may have vanished, but we still have no idea of the greater perfections that lie ahead. This may create a hindrance. Therefore, many methods have been developed in tantra which cannot be immediately understood. For instance, when there is intercourse between a complete man and a complete woman, there will be no loss of energy: there cannot be, for each forms a complete circuit within his or her own self. There will be no discharge of energy from the partners; for the first time they will experience pleasure without loss of energy.

The pleasure experienced in the physical union at the time of orgasm is invariably followed by the experience of pain. The gloom, the anguish, the fatigue, the remorse that follows with the loss of energy, is inevitable. The pleasure passes in a moment, but the loss of energy takes 24 to 48 hours or more to be regained. Until the energy is gained, the mind is filled with agony.

Tantra has evolved strange and marvellous methods for intercourse without orgasm, and it has worked very courageously in that direction. We shall have to talk separately on this subject some other time as tantric practice forms a complete network in itself. And since this network has been broken, the entire science gradually became esoteric. Also, it is difficult to talk about tantric practices openly and directly, for our moral beliefs have made this very difficult. Besides, our foolish wisemen who know nothing, but who are capable of saying anything, made it impossible to keep any precious knowledge alive. The knowledge of tantra thus had to be given up, or else it was hidden and work with it had to go underground. Thus, the current of tantric knowledge no longer flows clearly in our lives.

The intercourse between a complete man and a complete woman is a very different kind altogether. It is an intercourse in which there is no loss of energy. An entirely new happening takes place which can only be hinted at. When an incomplete man and an incomplete woman meet, both undergo a loss of energy. The quantity of energy after their intercourse is much less than it was prior to it.

Quite the opposite is the case in the union of a complete man and a complete woman. The quantity of energy after their intercourse will be more than the quantity that was there before it. The energy of both increases. This energy lies within them, and it becomes awakened and active by the nearness of the other partner. In the second happening, their own individual energy becomes awakened and active in the presence of the other; whatever lies hidden within each one's own self manifests fully. From this happening there is a hint whether a union of the complete man and complete woman can take place. The first union is a union of two incomplete beings. Now work has begun to bring together their third and fourth bodies.

The third body of the man is again male and the fourth female; the third body of the woman is again female and the fourth male. Now in their union, only the male will remain within the male; his third body will become prominent. Within the female, the female will remain prominent. Then the two complete females will merge into one, for now there will be no boundary between the two to separate them. The male body is required to keep them apart. Similarly, between the two male bodies, a female body is required to keep a distance between them. When the female of the first and second bodies meets the female of the third and fourth bodies, at the very instant of meeting they will merge into one. Then the woman achieves perfect femininity in double measure.

No greater womanhood than this is possible, for after this there is no further growth of femininity. This will be the perfect feminine state. This is the perfect woman who has no desire even to meet the Supreme Being.

In the first completeness there was the charm of meeting a second complete person, and the meeting of the two awakened energy. Now that too is over. Now even meeting God will be meaningless in a sense. Within the man also, both the males will merge into one. When the four bodies unite, what remains in the male is the male, and what remains in the female is the female. From then onwards there is no male and no female.

Therefore, the happening that takes place in a man and a woman on the fourth plane will be different; it is bound to be. The happening is the same, but their attitude toward it is different. The man will still be aggressive and the woman will still be surrendered. After the attainment of the fourth body a woman lets go completely; not even an iota will be withheld in her surrender. This surrender, this letting go, will take her to the journey of the fifth plane where a woman is no longer a woman, for in order to remain a woman it is necessary to keep something back.

In fact, we are what we are because we hold back a little of ourselves. If we were to let ourselves go completely, we would become something we never were before. But there is a holding back in one's being all the time. If a woman gives in completely even to an ordinary man, there will be a crystallization within her and she will go beyond the fourth body. This is why women have many a time crossed the fourth body with their love for very ordinary men.

The word "*Sati*" has no esoteric meaning. "*Sati*" does not mean a woman whose eyes do not fall on another man. "*Sati*" means that woman who no longer has the female factor left within her to look at another man. If a woman becomes so completely surrendered in love to even an ordinary man, she does not have to go through this long journey. All her four bodies will combine and stand at the doorstep of the fifth. Therefore, it was the women who went through this experience who said, "The husband is God." This does not mean that they actually thought that the husband was God. It means that the doors of the fifth opened for them through the medium of the husband. There was no mistake in what they said; what they said was absolutely correct. What the sadhak obtains through great effort she obtains with ease through her love. The love for one person alone takes her to that position.

Now take the case of Sita: She belongs to the category of women whom we call "*sati*". Now Sita's surrender is unique. From the point of view of surrender, she is perfect: her surrender is total. Ravan carried Sita away, but he could not touch her. Actually, Ravan is an incomplete man whereas Sita is a complete woman. The radiance of a complete woman is such that an incomplete man cannot dare to touch her. He cannot even set eyes on her, and only an incomplete woman can be seen in a sexual way by him.

When a man approaches a woman sexually, the man is not entirely responsible. This incompleteness of the woman is also inevitably responsible. When a man sexually touches a woman in a crowd, he is only half responsible. The woman who invites it is equally responsible. She incites it, invites it, and because she is passive her aggression goes unnoticed. Since the man is active, it is very evident that he touched her. But we cannot see the other side's invitation to it.

Ravan could not even lift his eyes toward Sita and Ravan held no meaning for Sita. Yet, after the war Ram insisted on the fire test (sitting in fire until it has burnt itself out) from Sita. Sita did not resist. Had she refused to go through the test she would have lost her position as "*sati*". She could have insisted that they both pass through the fire test, for if she was alone with another man, Ram too was roaming the woods alone. And who knows what women he may have met ?

But this question never arose in Sita's mind. She readily went through the fire test. Had she questioned Ram's authority even once, she would have fallen from her position—for then the surrender would not have been total: there would have been something slightly lacking in it. And had she raised the question even once and then passed through the fire, she would have been burnt; she would not have gone unscathed. But her surrender was total. For her there was no other man.

We, however, think it a miracle that she passed through the fire unharmed.

If an ordinary person also passes through fire while in a particular inner state, he will not burn. If in the state of hypnosis a man is told that fire will not burn him, he can walk on it and not be burnt.

An ordinary fakir walks on fire in a particular state of mind when the circuit is complete within himself. The circuit breaks with doubt. If a doubting thought crosses his mind even once, if he doubts that he will be burnt, the circuit breaks and he is bound to get burnt. If two fakirs jump into the fire and seeing them you feel, "If these two can jump and not be affected, how can I burn ?" then if you too jump into the fire, you also will not be affected by it. A whole line of people can thus pass through fire and not be burnt. The one who doubts will not dare enter the fire, but the one who sees so many passing through unaffected thinks, "If so many are unharmed, why should the fire harm me ?" Thus, for this reason he can go through, and the fire does not touch him.

If the circuit within us is complete, even fire has no means of touching us. So if fire did not affect Sita, it is quite plausible. After the fire test, when Ram turned her out of his kingdom, even then she did not question him. She had passed the fire test to prove her chastity. But Sita's surrender is so total, so complete, that for her there was no reason to question.

If a complete woman reaches a perfection of love for one person, she will jump over the first four steps of sadhana (spiritual practice). For a man it is very difficult, for he does not have a surrendering mind. But it is interesting to know that even aggression can be perfect. However, for aggression to be perfect many things are involved and not you alone. In surrender, however, you alone are responsible for its perfection and other things do not matter at all. If I wish to surrender to someone, I can do so entirely without telling him. But If I have to be aggressive toward someone, that someone will also be involved in the final result. Therefore, in our talk about Shaktipat, you may have felt that there is something slightly lacking in women, that there is a slight difficulty as far as they are concerned.

I had told you, there are rules of compensation in life. In the case of the woman, her shortcoming is made up for by her ability to surrender. A man is never able to love completely, no matter how much he loves someone. The reason is that he is aggressive and has less ability to surrender. So if a woman's first four bodies become complete and merge into one unit, she can surrender very easily at the fifth. And when a woman in this fourth state crosses these two steps of inner intercourse and becomes perfect, no power on earth can come in her way. Then no one except God exists for her. Actually, the one she loved in her first four bodies had also become God for her, but now, whatever is, is God.

There is a very lovely incident in Meera's life. Once she went to Vrindavan. There the priest of the great temple did not look at women, so ladies were not allowed inside that temple. Cymbals in hand, immersed in her Lord, Meera went right inside, however. The others in the temple hastened to tell her that the temple was closed to women as the priest did not look at women. To this Meera said, "That is very strange. I was under the impression there was only one man in the world—Krishna. Who is this other man ? Is there another man ?"

They went running to the priest and told him about Meera. When he heard all they had to say, he came running to Meera, fell at her feet, then said, "It is meaningless to call her a woman for whom there is only one man. The matter of man and woman is finished for her. I touch your feet and ask forgiveness. Seeing ordinary woman, I looked upon myself as man. But for a woman of your calibre my being a man has no meaning."

When a man reaches the fourth body he becomes a perfect man. He will have crossed the two steps toward attaining this perfection. From then onwards there is no woman for him; the term "woman" holds no meaning for him. Now he is only a force of aggressiveness, just as a woman who attains perfect womanhood in the fourth body becomes only the energy of surrender. Now they are only an energy of aggressiveness and an energy of surrender, respectively. Now they no longer hold the name of "man" or "woman": they are only energies.

Man's aggressiveness developed into various yoga sadhanas and woman's surrender blossomed into various paths of *bhakti* (devotion). Surrender becomes *bhakti*; aggressiveness becomes yoga. Both male and female are the same; there is no difference between them now. The difference of man and woman is now merely external and pertains only to the physical body. Now, whether the drop falls into the ocean or the ocean falls into the drop, the final result is the same. The drop of the man will jump into the ocean and merge with it. The drop of the woman will become an abyss and call upon the whole ocean to fill her. She will surrender and the whole ocean will drop into her.

Even before this, she is negative: she is completely a negativity. She is the womb that holds the entire ocean within itself. The entire energy of the universe will enter into her. Man, even at this stage, cannot be receptive. He still maintains the quality of strength, so instead he will take a jump and drown in the ocean.

In the intimate depths of their beings, their personalities will carry this male-female differentiation—right until the very end of the fourth body. The realm of the fifth plane is absolutely different, however. There only the soul remains. There is no longer any discrimination based on sex, and henceforth the journey is the same for all. Until the fourth there is a difference, and that too is only one of whether the drop falls in the ocean or the ocean into the drop. But the final outcome is the same: It makes no difference whether the drop falls into the ocean or the ocean into the drop. Until the last limit of the fourth body the difference is very apparent, however. There, if a woman wishes to jump into the ocean she will create difficulties for herself, and if a man wishes to surrender he will land himself in trouble. Thus, you should beware of the possibility of such an error.

Questioner : *In one of your discourses you had said that a long intercourse leads to the formation of an electrical circuit between the man and the woman. What is this circuit, how is it formed and what are its uses ? On the basis of the first four bodies, kindly answer this* *question. Also, insofar as meditation alone is concerned, what is the form of the above-mentioned happening ?*

Bhagwan: As I said before, woman is half complete and so is man. Both are energies, both are electricity. The woman is the negative pole, the man, the positive pole. Whenever the negative and positive poles of electricity meet and form a circuit, light is created. This light is of various kinds: it may not be visible at all, it may be visible only sometimes, or it may be visible to some and invisible to others. But a circuit is formed all the same. But the union of man and woman is so momentary that no sooner is the circuit formed when it breaks. Therefore, there are methods and systems of prolonging intercourse. If intercourse exceeds half an hour, the electrical circuit can be seen encircling the couple. Many pictures of this have been taken. There are many primitive tribes who go through long periods of copulation, and hence the circuit is formed.

Ordinarily, it is difficult to find this circuit in the civilized world. The more tension-ridden the mind, the more momentary the intercourse. Orgasm takes place quicker when the mind is tense. The greater the tension, the quicker the ejaculation, for a tension-ridden mind is not looking for intercourse but for release. In the West, sex serves no greater purpose than a sneeze. A tension is thrown out, a load is unburdened. When the energy is thrown out, you feel dissipated. To relax is one thing, to feel dissipated is quite another. Relaxation means the energy is within and you are resting, and to feel dissipated means energy is thrown out and you lie feeble and weary. You are weakened with the loss of energy and you think you are relaxing.

So, as tension increased in the West, sex became a release from tension, a freedom from the pressure of an internal energy. There are thinkers in the West who are not ready to consider sex as being any more valuable than a sneeze. The nose tickles and you sneeze, so the mind is relieved. In the West, they are not ready to give sex any more recognition than this. They are correct also, for what they are doing with sex is no more than this.

The East is also slowly veering toward the same state of

affairs, for the East is also becoming tense. Somewhere, in some distant mountain village, we might find a man who is not tense. He lives in a world of mountains and streams, trees and woods and is as yet untouched by civilization. There, even now, the circuit is formed. Also, there are tantric methods with which anyone can produce such a circuit.

The experience of this circuit is wonderful because it is only when the circuit is formed that you get the feeling of oneness. This man and woman becoming one is never experienced before the formation of this circuit. As soon as the circuit is formed the couple engaged in intercourse are no longer two entities. They become a flow of one energy, one power. Something is experienced as coming and going and revolving; the two separate entities disappear. Depending upon the intensity of this circuit, the desire for intercourse will lessen and its interval will increase. It can happen that once the circuit is formed, for one full year there may not be any desire for repetition, so fulfilling can the happening prove.

Or, take it this way: A man eats a meal and then regurgitates it. Then he will not get any satisfaction from the meal. Generally, we feel that the act of eating brings satisfaction. It is not so; satisfaction only comes when the food is digested. Intercourse is of two types: one that is of merely eating and another that is of digesting. What we generally know as intercourse is merely eating and regurgitating; nothing is digested. If something is digested, its satisfaction is long and deep. Absorption takes place only when the circuit is formed, however. The circuit indicates that the minds of the two partners have merged and become absorbed into one another. Now there are not two: they become one. There are two bodies, but the energy within each has become one; now it is flowing between them.

This condition of sexual satisfaction leaves a deep state of satisfaction: this is what I mean. It is very useful for yoga and also the sadhak. If such inner intercourse is possible for the sadhak, the need for intercourse becomes very much reduced. Then the intervening period leaves him free for his journey inward. Once the inner journey starts and the union takes place with the woman (or man) within, the external woman becomes useless, the external man becomes useless. For a householder, the term "brahmacharya" (celibacy) means that his act of intercourse should be so fulfilling that it leaves years of brahmacharya in between. Once this period of brahmacharya is attained and a sadhak sets out on the inward journey, the outer necessity (for intercourse) has faded away.

I am saying that this is the case for a householder. For those initiated into Sannyas (the traditional kind of Sannyas) for those who have not accepted a householder's life, the meaning of brahmacharya is "*antarmaithun*" (sexual union between the inner male and female). And for them there is a need for inner intercourse. Such a person will directly have to start finding a means for inner intercourse, or else he will shun the outer woman only in name while his mind will keep running. And he will lose more energy in his efforts to keep away from the outer woman than he would by intercourse. So the path is a little different for the traditional sannyasin. The difference is only this: the union with the outer woman is the initial step for the householder who he meets the woman within himself in the second step, whereas the traditional sannyasin unites directly with the woman within himself. The first step is not for him.

Therefore, it is foolish (in the traditional concept of Sannyas) to make anyone and everyone a sannyasin. Actually, initiation into traditional Sannyas is only possible when we can look within the person to see whether his first body is in a state of readiness to meet the woman of his second body. If it is so, only then should the initiation into brahmacharya be granted; otherwise this will only bring about madness and nothing else.

But there are persons who go about initiating indiscriminately. There is one guru of a thousand sannyasins, another of two thousand, and they do not know what they are doing. Are those whom they initiate, ready and fit for inner intercourse ? Far from it ! They do not even know that there is anything like inner intercourse. This is why, whenever a traditional sannyasin comes to me, his most profound and intimate trouble is sex. Householders I meet galore and they have other troubles too, but I have yet to come across a traditional sannyasin whose trouble is anything but sex.

Sex is one of the many worries of a householder, but it is the one and only affliction of the traditional sannyasin. Therefore, his whole consciousness is centered around this one point. His guru shows him many remedies to save himself from the outer woman, but he has no idea of how a sadhak can meet the woman within. Therefore, it becomes impossible to discard the outer woman. He can only make a show of shunning her, and it is very very difficult.

The electrical vital energy has to move somewhere. If it can go within, only then can it be prevented from flowing outward. If it does not go in, it is bound to flow out. It makes no difference whether the woman is present in substance or in imagination. It can flow out with the help of an imaginary woman also. The same goes for women, but here again there is a little difference between the two which should be kept in mind.

Sex is not such a problem for a "sadhika" (a female seeker) as for a sadhak. I am acquainted with many "sadhvis" (Jain nuns) and for them sex does not pose a big question. The reason is that a woman's sex is passive. Once it is awakened, it becomes a problem. If it is not awakened, she can go through a lifetime and never feel that there is any problem. A woman requires initiation—even in sex. Once a man takes a woman into sex, the energy rises sharply within her. But if this does not happen, she can remain a lifelong virgin. This is very easy for her because of her passive nature. Her own mind is non-aggressive; she can wait and wait indefinitely. Therefore, I believe that it is dangerous to initiate a married woman unless she is taught to unite with the man within her.

A virgin girl can be initiated. She is in a better position than a boy. She can wait indefinitely until she is taken into sex, for she is not aggressive. And if there is no aggression from without, gradually the inner man will begin to unite with the outer woman. Her second body is a male body which is aggressive.

So inner intercourse is much easier for a woman than a man : Do you understand what I mean? The second body of a woman is male and this body is aggressive. Therefore, even if a woman does not find an outer man, it does not matter to her. And if she does not experience sex from an outside source, the man within will begin to be aggressive. Her etheric body will begin to invade her; then she will turn inward and become immersed in inner intercourse. For man, inner intercourse is difficult, for his aggressive body is the first body whereas his second body is female. This body cannot assert itself over the first. Only when the first body goes to it will it receive him.

These are the differences, and once they are understood we shall have to change all our arrangements. If the householder succeeds in creating the electric circuit in intercourse, it will be very helpful to him. The same circuit will be formed in the case of inner intercourse also, so the energy which surrounds an ordinary man at the time of ordinary intercourse will, for all the twenty-four hours, surround the man who has united with his second body. Therefore, the circle of energy will become wider and wider at every plane.

No image was made of Buddha until 500 years after his death, and this kind of phenomenon has happened many a time in history. In Buddha's place an image of the Bodhi Tree was carved, and this was worshipped in the temples, but the place beneath the tree where Buddha was supposed to have sat was left vacant. Now those who study history and mythology are very much intrigued over why Buddha's image was not carved. Why was Buddha symbolized by a tree? And why was his image then installed after 500 years? Why was the place beneath the tree depicted as empty all that time? This is a mystery which neither the historian nor the mythologist can solve.

In Truth, those who had observed Buddha very keenly stated that on observing him with one-pointed attention Buddha could not be seen: only the tree remained and the aura of the energy. His physical body disappeared. Now, for instance, if you observe me keenly I too will disappear and only the chair will remain. So those who saw him deeply claimed that Buddha could not be seen, but those who did not, claimed that he could be seen. However, the statement of the former was more authentic. For 500 years the word of those who said that Buddha was never visible, and that there was only the tree and the empty place beneath it, was honoured. But this concept worked only so long as there were people who could see deeply. When this class of people began to diminish, it became difficult to worship the tree alone without Buddha.

Five hundred years after him his idol was installed. This is a very interesting fact. Those who saw Jesus deeply also could not see him: they could see only light. Those who saw Mahavir deeply could also see only light, and so was it with Krishna also. If people of this calibre are observed with full concentration, only the light of the energy will be visible: no person as such will be seen there.

After every two bodies the vital energy increases. After the fourth body it attains a fullness. At the fifth body there is only energy. At the sixth body this energy will appear not separate, but as one with the stars and the skies. At the seventh plane, even this will disappear. First matter will disappear, then energy. It is worthwhile to reflect upon this.

Questioner : *On which plane does the sadhak reach the "no-thought" state ? Are thoughts possible without identifying the consciousness with objects or is identity essential for thought ?*

Bhagwan : The perfect no-thought state is attained in the fifth body, but incomplete glimpses begin from the fourth body. Thoughts continue in the fourth body, but the intervening gaps begin to be observed. Before the fourth, there are thoughts and thoughts and only thoughts; we do not see the gap between the thoughts. In the fourth, the intervals begin to appear. Also, the emphasis changes. If you have observed gestalt images you will be able to understand this. Now suppose there is a picture of a flight of steps. It can be so drawn that if you look attentively you will observe the steps going up; then if you look again, you will see the steps coming down. But the most interesting part is that you cannot observe the steps going up and down simultaneously. You can see only one of the two. When you observe it a second time, the first picture will have vanished.

We can make a picture in which two faces can be seen facing each other, complete with nose, eyes and beard. One time it will appear as if two men are facing each other. Now paint the faces black leaving the intervening space white. Now say there is a flower pot in this intervening space, and the nose and eyes become the outlines of the pot. You will not be able to see the pot and the two faces at one time. When you see the two faces the pot will not be seen; when the pot is observed the faces will vanish. No matter how hard you try to see them all together, the gestalt will change its emphasis. When your emphasis shifts to the faces the pot will vanish; when the emphasis is on the pot the faces will vanish.

Up to the third body, the gestalt of our mind has its emphasis on thought. Ram comes, so Ram is visible and his coming is visible. The empty space between Ram and his coming, or the empty space before Ram's coming and after Ram's going, is not visible to us. The emphasis is on "Ram comes"; the intervening space is not observed. The change starts from the fourth body. All of a sudden it will strike you that Ram's coming is no longer very important. When Ram was not coming there was the empty space. The empty space begins to come within the focus of your mind: faces disappear; the pot becomes visible. And when your attention is on the empty space, you cannot think.

You can do only one of the following two things: as long as you see thoughts you will think, but when you see the empty space you will be empty within. However, this will keep alternating in the fourth body. Sometimes you will see the two faces and sometimes the pot: that is, sometimes you will see thoughts and sometimes the gap. Silence will come and so will thoughts.

The difference between silence and emptiness is only this: silence means thoughts have not yet ended, but the emphasis is changed. The consciousness has shifted from speech and takes pleasure in silence, but speech still remains. It is only that the consciousness has shifted: the attention has shifted from speech. Then the attention is on silence. But speech returns sometimes—and when it manages to draw your attention, again silence is lost and speech begins.

In the last moments of the fourth body, the mind will keep alternating between the two. On the fifth plane, all thoughts will be lost and only silence will remain. This is not silence, for silence exists in comparison to speech: silence means "not to speak". Emptiness means a state where there is neither silence nor speech. Neither the faces remain nor the flower pot: only the blank paper. Now if you are asked whether the faces are there or the flower pot, you will say neither. The state of no-thought occurs in its totality in the fifth body. At the fourth we get glimpses of this state; it will be observed off and on between two thoughts. At the fifth the no-thought state will become evident, and thoughts will disappear.

Now the second part of your question is, "Is identification necessary for the formation of thoughts, or can thoughts occur without any identification?" Up to the third body identification and thought come simultaneously. There is your identification and there is the coming of thought. There is no interval between the two. Your thoughts and you are one—not two. Now when you are angry, it is wrong to say that YOU are angry. It would be more correct to say that you have become anger, for in order to be angry it should also be possible for you not to be angry. Now, for instance, I say, "I am moving my hand." Then suppose you say, "Now stop your hand," and I say, "That is not possible; the hand keeps moving." Then you may well question what I mean when I say, "I am moving my hand." I should say, "The hand is moving," for if "I" am moving the hand, "I" should be able to stop it. If I cannot stop my hand, I cannot claim to be its owner: it has no meaning. Because you cannot stop your thoughts, your identification with them is complete up to the third body. Up to there, YOU are thought.

So up to the third body, by hitting someone's thoughts we are hitting the person himself. If you tell such a person, "What you say is wrong," he will never feel that what he says is wrong: he will feel HE is wrong. Quarrels and fights take place not because of a statement, but because of the "I", for there is complete identification. To attack your thoughts is to attack you. Even if you say, "It is all right if you do not agree with my way of thinking," within you will feel that YOU have been opposed. Many times it happens that the notion in question is left aside, and we begin to fight for it merely because WE put forth the view and not for any other reason. You uphold it merely because you have put it forth as your viewpoint, because you have declared it as your "*shastra*" (scripture), your principle, your argument.

Until the third body, there is no distance between you and your thoughts: YOU are the thought. In the fourth wavering begins. You will begin to get glimpses of the fact that you are something apart and your thoughts are something apart. But so far you are unable to stop your thoughts, for deep within the roots the association still exists. Above, on the branches, you feel the difference. You sit on one branch and the thoughts on the other, and you see they are not you. But deep within, you and thoughts are one. Therefore, it seems that thoughts are separate, and it also seems that if my association with them is broken thoughts will stop. But they will not stop. At some deeper level the association with thoughts will continue.

Changes begin to take place on the fourth plane. You begin to get a vague notion of thoughts being different and you being different. You still cannot proclaim this, however, and the thought process is still mechanical. You cannot stop your thoughts, nor can you bring them about. If I can say to you, "Stop anger and show that you are the master," it can also be said, "Bring about anger and prove that you are the master." You will ask, "How can this be done ? We cannot bring about anger." The moment you can you are its master. Then you can stop it at any moment. When you are the master, the processes of bringing on anger and stopping it are both in your hands. If you can bring on anger you can stop it also.

It is also interesting to note that stopping it is rather difficult, but bringing it on is easier. So if you want to be the master first begin by bringing on anger, for this is easier. In the situation of bringing it on you are tranquil, but in the situation of having to stop it you are already angry, and so you are not even aware of yourself. Then how will you stop it ? Therefore, it is always easier to start the experiment by bringing on anger rather than stopping it. For instance, YOU begin to laugh, but then you find that you cannot stop laughing: it is difficult. But if you are not laughing and you want to bring on laughter, you can do in a minute or two. Then you will know the secret of laughter—from where it comes and how—and then you will know the secret of stopping it also and it can be stopped.

At the fourth plane you will begin to see that you are separate and thoughts are separate: that you are not your thoughts. Therefore, whenever the no-thought state occurs (as I said before) the witness also comes, and wherever there are thoughts the witness will be lost. In the intervals between thoughts—that is, in the gaps between thoughts—you will realize your separate identity from the thoughts. Then there is no association between you and the thoughts. But even then you will be a helpless observer. You will not be able to do much, though all efforts are to be made in the fourth body only.

Therefore, I have defined two possibilities of the fourth body—one that is natural and the other that is obtained through sadhana (spiritual practice). You will be alternating between these two. The first possibility is "*vichar*" (thought) and the second is "*vivek*" (understanding). The moment you attain the second potential of the fourth body (*vivek* or understanding), the fourth body will drop, as well as the identification of consciousness with mind. When you attain the fifth body, two things will drop: the fourth body and this identification.

In the fifth body you can bring on thoughts or not bring them on, as you wish. For the first time, thoughts will be a means and will not depend on identification. If you wish to bring on anger, you can bring on anger. If you wish to bring on love, you can do so. If you do not wish to bring on anything, you are at liberty not to do so. If you wish to stop anger that is half-formed, you can order it to stop. Whatever thought you want to bring will come to you, and that which you do not wish to bring will not have any power to invade your mind.

There are many such instances in the life of Gurdjieff. People considered him a peculiar man. If two people were sitting before him, he would look toward one with the utmost anger and toward the other with the utmost love. So quickly would he change his expression that the two would carry away different reports about him. If both would meet him together, one would say, "He looks like a dangerous man," while the other would say, "How full of love he is." This is very easy on the fifth plane, Gurdjieff was beyond the understanding of people around him. He could instantly bring any of a thousand kinds of expressions to his face. There was no difficulty for him in this, but there was difficulty for others.

The reason behind this is that in the fifth body you are the master of yourself; you can bring about any feeling you please. Then anger, love, hatred, forgiveness, all your thoughts, become mere playthings. You can, therefore, relax when you please. To relax after play is very easy, but to relax from life is difficult.

If I am only playing at anger, I will not sit in anger after you leave the room. If I am playing the game of talking, I shall no longer be talking after you go. But if talking is my life-breath, then I shall keep on talking even after you leave. Even if nobody listens, I will listen. I will keep on talking, for that is my very life: it is not a play after which I can relax. It is my very life; it has taken hold of me. So such a man will talk even at night. In dreams also he will gather a crowd and speak. In dreams also he will quarrel, he will fight, and do all that he has been doing in the daytime. He will keep doing this all the twenty-four hours, for that is his life, that is his very existence.

Your identification breaks in the fifth body. Then, for the first time, you are at peace, you are empty, by your own free will. But when the need arises, you think also. So in the fifth body, for the first time you will be putting your power of thinking to use. It would be better to say that before the fifth body thoughts make use of you; after the fifth you make use of thoughts. Before that it is not correct to say, "I think". In the fifth body you also come to know that your thoughts are not your own: thoughts of people around you also enter your mind. However, you are not even aware that the thoughts you think to be your own could be someone else's.

A Hitler is born, and the whole of Germany is permeated with his thoughts. But each German feels it to be his own thought. A very dynamic person diffuses his thoughts into the minds of others, and they become echoes of the same. This dynamism is as serious as it is deep. For example, it is two thousand years since Jesus died. The thought waves that he left in the world still grasp the minds of Christians who think that these are their own thoughts. Similar is the case with Mahavir, Buddha, Krishna and others. Any kind of dynamic person's thoughts, whether they are of a good person or an evil one, can catch hold of the human mind. The hold of Taimurlang and Ghenghis Khan upon our minds has not yet been released, nor has the hold of Krishna and Ram. Their thought waves for ever move around us, and you are able to catch those thought waves that are conducive to your particular state of mind.

It always happens that a man who is very good in the morning becomes evil by noon. In the morning he moves in the waves of Ram; in the afternoon he may be caught by the waves of Ghenghis Khan. Receptivity and time cause the difference. The beggar always comes to beg in the morning, for the effect of evil vibrations are at their minimum at the time of the rising sun. As the day progresses and as the sun gets tired of its long journey in the skies, their influence gains strength. So the beggar has no hope of charity from others in the evening. If a beggar asks a man early in the morning to give two paisa, he will not be able to refuse right away. As the day progresses, it is more difficult to say yes to the beggar. By evening the man is tired with the day's work, so now he is fully prepared to refuse. The condition of his mind is quite different now; so also is the entire atmosphere of his surroundings. So the thoughts we feel to be our own also do not belong to us.

This you will experience only in the fifth body, and you will be surprised to see the way thoughts come and go. The thought comes, then it goes; it catches hold of you, then it leaves you alone. There are a thousand kinds of thoughts—and very contradictory ones too; therefore, there is confusion in our minds. Each and every person is confused. If thoughts were entirely yours, there would be no question of confusion. Your one hand catches hold of Ghenghis Khan and the other catches hold of Krishna, so there is bound to be confusion. Both of these sets of thought waves lie in wait for you, and as soon as you show your readiness they enter within. They are present all around you.

All this you will come to know when your identification with thoughts breaks completely. The biggest change will be that until this time you will have had thoughts, but now you will have "thinking". There is a difference between the two. Thoughts are atomic: they come and go, and they are always alien. To say that thoughts are always alien is quite correct. "Thinking" is ours, but thoughts are alien. This thinking will start within you after the fifth body. Then you will be able to "think": you will no longer be merely collecting the thoughts of others. Therefore, the thinking of the fifth body is never a burden upon you, for it is your own. This thinking that is born in the fifth body may be called wisdom or discrimination, as you like.

At the fifth plane you have your own intuition, your own understanding, your own intellect. At the fifth the influence of all outside thoughts will end, and in this sense you will be the master of yourself: you will attain your Being; you will become your Self. Now you will have your own thoughts, your own power of thinking, your own eyes and your own vision. After this, only what you wish will come to you; what you do not wish will never come near you. You can think just what you want to think: the other thoughts cannot invade you. Now you will be the master. Here the question of identification does not arise.

In the sixth body thinking also is not required. Thoughts are necessary up to the fourth body; thinking and wisdom are necessary in the fifth. On the sixth plane even these end, for there they are not required at all. You become Cosmic; you become one with the Brahman. Now there is no other. In fact, all thoughts are always related to the other. The thoughts before the fourth body are unconscious links with others. The thoughts of the fifth body are conscious links, but they are still related to others. After all, why are thoughts necessary? They are required only to establish a relationship with others. Until the fourth they are unconscious links; at the fifth they are conscious links. But at the sixth no "other" remains for establishing links. All relatedness is finished; only the Cosmic remains. "I" and "thou" are now one. Now there is no place, no reason for thought to exist.

The sixth is the Brahman—the Cosmic Reality where there are no thoughts. In the Brahman there are no thoughts; therefore, it can be said that in the Brahman there is Knowledge. Actually, the thoughts which exist up to the fourth body are unconscious thoughts : they contain a deep ignorance. It shows that we need thoughts to fight with this self-ignorance. At the fifth, there is Knowledge of the Self within, but we are still ignorant about that which is "other" to us; the "other" is still there for us. Therefore, there is the need to think in the fifth body. At the sixth there is no "inside" or "outside", there is no "I" or "thou", there is no "this" or "that". Now there is no distance to justify thoughts. Now, what is, IS. Therefore, at the sixth there is only Knowledge, not thoughts.

At the seventh Knowledge also does not exist, for he who knew is no more and that which could be known is no more. So even Knowledge is not on the seventh plane. The seventh plane is not "Knowledgeless", but "beyond knowledge". If someone likes he may call it a state of ignorance also. That is why it is always the case that a man of Supreme Knowledge and an absolutely ignorant person seem identical, for their behaviour is often similar. This is why there is always a great similarity between a small child and an old man who has attained Infinite Knowledge. They are not actually the same, but superficially they seem alike. Sometimes a Self-Realized saint acts childlike; sometimes in the behaviour of a child, we get a glimpse of saintliness. Sometimes an Enlightened One looks like an absolute ignorant person, an absolute fool, and it would seem that no one could be as foolish as he. But the saint has gone beyond Knowledge and the child is still below knowledge. The similarity lies in the fact that they both are "outside" of knowledge.

Questioner : *In which body is that obtained which you refer to as Samadhi ?*

Bhagwan : Actually, there are many types of Samadhi. One Samadhi will take place between the fourth and the fifth body. Remember, Samadhi is not a happening of one plane. It is always a happening between two planes; it is the "twilight" period. One may just as well ask whether twilight belongs to the day or the night. Twilight belongs neither to the day nor the night. It is a happening between day and night. So is Samadhi.

The first Samadhi occurs between the fourth and the fifth planes. This Samadhi that takes place between the fourth and the fifth leads to knowledge of the Self. One Samadhi occurs between the fifth and the sixth planes. The Samadhi that takes place between the fifth and the sixth planes leads to "*Brahma Jnan*" (Cosmic Knowledge). One Samadhi occurs between the sixth and the seventh planes. The Samadhi that occurs between the sixth and the seventh leads to Nirvana. So generally speaking, there are these three Samadhis that occur between three *shariras* (bodies).

There is one false Samadhi that has to be recognized also. It occurs in the fourth body, but is not Samadhi though it seems like Samadhi. In Japan, the Zen Buddhist term for it is "satori". It is false Samadhi. It is that state which a painter or a sculptor or a musician reaches when they are completely immersed in their art; they experience a great bliss. This is a happening on the fourth—the psychic plane. If, when looking at the morning sun or listening to a melody or looking at a dance of the opening of a flower, the mind is completely drowned in the happening, a false Samadhi takes place. Such a false Samadhi can be brought about by hypnosis or false Shaktipat. Such a false Samadhi can be brought about by alcohol and drugs like marijuana, LSD, mescaline, *charas* and hemp.

So there are four types of Samadhi. Actually, there are three authentic Samadhis, and they are of great value. The fourth is an absolutely false experience that appears like Samadhi. In this there is no actual experience—only a feeling of Samadhi that is misleading. Many people are misled by satori. This false Samadhi occurs in the fourth—the psychic plane. It is not the transitional process between the fourth and the fifth plane. It happens well within the fourth body. The three authentic Samadhis occur outside the bodies in a transitional period, when we pass on from one plane to another.

One Samadhi is a door, a passage, between the fourth and the fifth plane. In this Samadhi we attain knowledge of the Self. We can stagnate here. This first is a far cry from the final goal. Generally, people stop at the false Samadhi in the fourth body, for it is so easy. We have to spend very little energy, making no effort at all, and it is obtained "just like that". The majority of sadhaks, therefore, stagnate here. The first (real) Samadhi, which takes place from the fourth to the fifth body, is very difficult. The second, from the fifth to the sixth, is yet more difficult, and the third, from the sixth to the seventh, is the most difficult of all. The name chosen for the third Samadhi is "*vajrabhed*" (piercing of the thunderbolt). It is the most difficult one for it is a transition from Being into Non-Being; it is a jump from life into death; it is a plunge from Existence into Non-Existence.

So there are actually three Samadhis. The first you may call "*Atma Samadhi*", the second, "*Brahma Samadhi*" and the last, "*Nirvana Samadhi.*" The very first and false Samadhi you may call satori. This is the one you should guard against, for it is very easily attainable. Another method to test the validity of the Samadhi is that if it takes place within the plane, it is false. It must take place BETWEEN the planes. It is the door: it has no business to be inside the room. It must be outside of the room, adjoining the next room.

Questioner : *Why has the serpent been chosen as a symbol of kundalini ? Please explain all the reasons. In the symbol used by "Theosophy", a coiled serpent with his tail in the mouth is shown. In the symbol of the Ramakrishna Mission, the tail of the serpent touches the hood. Please explain the meaning of these.*

Bhagwan : The serpent symbol for the kundalini is very apt and meaningful. Perhaps there is no better symbol than this. Therefore, not only the kundalini, but also the serpent has undergone a great many travels in the symbol form. Nowhere in the world is there a religion in which the serpent has not been depicted somewhere. This is because the serpent has many qualities that tally with the kundalini.

The very first thing that occurs to the mind at the mention of the serpent is the motion of sliding—crawling. The very first experience of the kundalini is that of something sliding within. You feel as if something has moved within—just as a serpent slides. Another thing that comes to mind with the very notion of a serpent is that it has no legs, yet it moves. It has no means of movement, yet it moves. Kundalini too has no limbs, no means of movement ; it is sheer energy; yet it travels. The third thing that comes to the mind is that when a serpent sits, it forms coils. When the kundalini lies asleep within us, it too rests in the same manner.

When a long thing has to accommodate itself in a small place, it has to coil up; there is no otherway for it. A very big power is seated on a very small center, so it can only coil itself up. Now when the snake gets up, it unwinds the coils one by one. As it rises, the coil unwinds. In the same way, we feel the kundalini unwinding within when the kundalini serpent rises within us.

The serpent sometimes, out of sport, catches its tail in its mouth. The holding of the tail in the mouth is also a significant symbol. This is a valuable symbol and many recognized it as such. It is valuable because it suggests that when the kundalini is fully awakened, it will become circular and begin to form its own circuit within. Its hood will catch hold of its own tail; the serpent will become a circle. Now when a symbol is made to depict male sadhana, it will catch the tail by its mouth: it will be aggressive. If the symbol is derived at by female sadhana the tail will just be touching the hood. This is a surrendering tail: one that is not held in the mouth. This is the only difference and no more.

The hood of the serpent also became purposeful. The tail is very narrow whereas the hood is very broad. When kundalini awakens fully, it reaches up to the "sahasrar", (the seventh or highest chakra). It opens and spreads like the hood of the serpent; it expands to a great extent. It is as if many flowers bloom in it. Then its tail becomes very small. When the serpent stands up, it is a wonderful sight; it stands erect on the tip of its tail. It is almost a miracle. The serpent is an invertebrate, and yet it can perform this act. It can only be with the help of the vital energy within it, for there is no other substantial means for it to stand so erect. It stands by the strength of its own willpower, and it has no material strength to rely on. So also, when the kundalini awakens; it has no physical support; it is an immaterial energy.

These were the reasons why the serpent was chosen as a symbol. There are very many other reasons too. For instance, it is an innocent creature; hence, Shankara, who is also called "the guileless Shankara", carries it on his head. On its own the serpent never troubles anybody, but if it is disturbed, it can be very dangerous. The same applies to the kundalini. It is a very innocent power; it does not trouble you on its own. But if you disturb it the wrong way, you will find yourself in trouble. It can prove very dangerous.

So the thought remains within us that it is dangerous to disturb the kundalini in the wrong way. Keeping all this in mind, there was no other symbol more apt than that of the serpent. All over the world, the snake stands for the symbol of wisdom. Jesus has said, "Be clever and intelligent like a snake, and as innocent and guileless like a dove." The snake is a very clever creature—very alert, very watchful and very sharp and quick. These are all its qualities. The kundalini is also like this. You reach the ultimate peak of wisdom through it; it is as nimble and swift, and also as powerful.

In the olden days, when this symbol was chosen for the kundalini, perhaps there was nothing better than the serpent. Even now there is nothing better. Perhaps in the future there may be a new symbol—like the rocket. Some future concept may grasp the kundalini as being like the rocket. Its journey is the same; it travels from one firmament to another, from one planet to another, and there is void in between. It can become a symbol ! The age decides the symbol.

This symbol was chosen when man was very close to the animal kingdom. All our symbols of those times have been taken from the animals, for that was all that our knowledge consisted of. So we tried to find symbols in them. The serpent was thus the most apt symbol to define the kundalini.

In those days we could not say that kundalini is like electricity. Today, when we talk, we may say so. Five thousand years ago, kundalini could not be talked about in terms of electricity, for there was no notion of electricity. But the snake has the quality of electricity. This is hard for us to believe, for many of us have no experience of the snake. We may have no experience of the kundalini whatsoever, but we hardly have any knowledge of snakes either. The serpent is a myth for us.

Recently a survey was taken in London and it was found that seven million children had never seen a cow. Now these children who have not seen a cow cannot possibly have any idea of a snake. So their whole way of thinking and reflecting, and their symbols, will be quite different. Now the serpent is out: it is no longer an important part of our life. Once upon a time it was very near to us. It was our neighbour and was with us all the twenty-four hours of the day. It was then that man noticed its nimbleness, its intelligence, its movements, and the ease with which it carried itself about. It was then that man realized also how dangerous a creature it could be.

There are stories of a serpent guarding an infant, and it is so guileless. There are instances when it has bitten the most feared person and killed him, so dangerous can it be. So both of these possibilities are in it.

When man was very close to the serpent, he must have watched it closely. The subject of kundalini also began at about the same time, and both the serpent and the kundalini were found similar in their qualities. But all symbols are meaningful, and if they have come to us through the ages there is a suitability, a rhythm in them. But now it is bound to break. The symbol of the serpent, will not last long. We shall not be able to call the kundalini "serpent power", for now where is the poor serpent ? It is no longer our neighbour; we have no connection with it. We do not even see him on the roads. So as we have no connection with it whatsoever, this question arises. It could never arise before when it was the only symbol.

Questioner : *It is said that when the kundalini awakens it eats the flesh and drinks the blood. What does that mean ?*

Bhagwan : There is a meaning to this. The simile should not be taken literally. Actually, when the kundalini arises, many transformations take place within the body. Whenever a new energy arises in the body, its old composition undergoes a complete change. It is bound to change ! Now, for instance, the body functions in so many unknown ways of which we are not conscious. For example, take the case of a miser. Now miserliness is a quality of the mind, but his body will also become a miser. His body will begin to collect those substances that may be required by it in the future. It will keep on accumulating without any reason, until it reaches a point where it causes harassment and discomfort.

Now let us say that another man is a coward. His body will gather all the elements that are conducive to fear. Suppose the body wants to tremble in fear and it does not have the necessary requirements: What will it do ? You demand fear from the body and it does not have the necessary glands and enzymes: What will it do ? So the body keeps a ready store, for it knows your requirements. The body of a fearful man gathers glands of fear to facilitate his indulgence in fear. Now the man who perspires with fear will have very strong perspiration glands. He has a capacity to perspire profusely. This arrangement is absolutely necessary, for his demands can be many in the course of a single day. So the body stores things according to the requirements of our mind—and more.

When the mind changes, the body changes also. When the kundalini rises, there will be an all-out change. In that transformation many changes will take place. In that transformation your flesh may decrease and so also your blood, but it will decrease strictly to your requirements. So the body will be completely transformed. Only as much flesh and blood as is necessary for the body will remain; the rest will be burnt away. Then only will you feel light; then only will you be able to rise in the air. This will be the difference.

What has been said is correct. The sadhak has to have a special diet and a special arrangement for living, or else he will find himself in difficulties. When the kundalini rises a lot of heat is produced within, for it is an electric force. It is an energy that is of a very high voltage.

Just as I told you that the serpent is a symbol of kundalini, fire too is a symbol of kundalini in some places. This too is a very good symbol. So the kundalini will burn like fire within you and the flames will rise high. A lot of things will burn in this. A certain dryness can result from the awakening of the kundalini. Therefore, the personality should be very harmonious and some channels of softer qualities should be developed. Now, for instance, take a wrathful person: if his kundalini awakens, he will find himself in difficulty. He is a dry and coarse person, so if a fire should rage within him he will be in trouble. A loving person has a deep chemical harmony. There is a "lubricatedness" of chemical harmony within him. He will not be adversely affected by the awakening of the kundalini.

Whatever has been said has been with regard to all these details. Things have been put rather crudely, for the art of expression in the olden days was not very much developed and the approach was crude. So what has been said is very true: the flesh will burn and so will the blood and marrow, for you will change completely; you are going to be an entirely new person. All of your patterns, your composition, have to undergo a change. The sadhak has to keep this in mind and prepare himself accordingly.

[Text of a discourse given on July 11, 1970, evening, in Bombay, India]

18

511

OCCULT DEPTHS OF KUNDALINI AND SPIRITUALITY

Questioner :

In the Nargol meditation camp you said that the practices of yoga "asanas, pranayam, mudras and bandhas" (various yogic exercises of the body and breath)—were discovered in the state of meditation. In different states of meditation, different asanas (postures) are formed by the body from which the depth of meditation of the "sadhak" (seeker) could be told. Conversely, can the same inner state be brought about by forming the necessary postures ? In that case, can meditation be attained by the use of various asanas, pranayam, mudras and bandhas ?

Bhagwan Shree Rajneesh :

First came the experience of meditation. But with the experience of meditation it was found that the body assumed many postures. Actually, whenever the mind is in a particular state the body takes an appropriate corresponding posture. For instance, when you are filled with love your face, your expression, is one way, and when you are angry your expression becomes altogether different. In anger you grind your teeth and clench your fists, and the body is ready to fight. When you are in a forgiving mood the eyes are soft and the palms of the hand open. When a man is filled with forgiveness his fists will never clench. Just as clenching the fist is a preparation to fight, opening the fist and spreading out the palm is an indication of freedom from the urge to fight: it is an assurance of protection. To clench the fist is to frighten the other person.

The nature of the body is that it works in accordance with the state of mind. The body follows the mind: it always follows behind. So, ordinarily, we know what a man will do in anger and what he will do in love—also what he will do in faith and trust. But we do not know how he will react to the deeper states of mind.

When deep states are created within the mind, a great deal takes place in the body also. Various mudras (gestures through which inner psychic states are expressed) and also many asanas take place that tell of the changes within. In fact, the asanas are formed at the time of preparation for particular inner states. Mudras are formed later, and they give information about a person's inner state.

When changes occur within, the body has to find an equivalent adjustment to the inner changes. When the kundalini awakens within, the body will have to assume all kinds of unusual positions to make way for the energy. The spine will bend itself in many ways in order to allow the energy to ascend. The head also takes different positions when the kundalini awakens. The body assumes such postures as we have never taken before. It is just like when we are awake the body takes an erect position and when we sleep the body has to lie down: it cannot stand or sit.

Now suppose there is a man who has not known what it is to sleep since he was born: he will never lie down. If after thirty years he wants to fall asleep, he will lie down for the first time. For the first time his condition of mind will have changed in this respect, and he will go to sleep. However, he will be very much intrigued by the new posture, as his body has never before assumed it. Up to now he used to sit, stand, walk, but never did he lie down. Now he has to lie down so that the necessary conditions of sleep can take place within him. When the body is laid down, the mind finds it easier to slip into a particular condition. But different people have different ways of lying down because the state of mind of each person is different.

For instance, a man from a tribal area will not put a pillow under his head, but for a civilized person it is impossible to sleep without one. A tribal person does so little thinking that the flow of blood to his head is much less. For sleep, it is essential that the flow of blood toward the head be as little as possible.

If it is too much, you will not be able to sleep. If the nerves of the brain do not relax, it will be difficult for you not to be tense. The blood will keep on flowing to the brain. Then you add one more pillow and one more. The more educated and civilized a person is, the more he is cultured, the greater the number of pillows that he requires under his head. The neck should be almost vertical to prevent the flow of blood toward the brain.

The position of the body corresponds to one's state of mind. So with the awakening of the energy within and its movements in several ways, asanas begin to form. The different "chakras" (centers) also take the body into different asanas. Thus, various postures are formed. As a particular state begins to form within, the expressions of your hands, face and eyes change. This happens in meditation. As a result, the reverse has also come into man's deliberation: that is, performing these asanas, is it possible to go into meditation? It is necessary to understand this.

In meditation, these processes take place; yet they are not inevitable. In other words, all sadhaks do not pass through the same body processes. One condition has to be borne in mind: every sadhak's state of body and mind is different from the states of body and mind of others. Therefore, all will not pass through the same asanas. Now, for instancc, if the flow of blood is less toward the head of one sadhak, and if a greater flow is required for the awakening of the kundalini, he will at once, without knowing, go into "shirshasana" (the headstand). All sadhaks will not undergo this asana, for the rate of the flow of blood is different in each; each one has different requirements. So asanas will form according to the need of each sadhak.

When we ourselves select asanas and practise them, then we do not know which particular asana is favourable and necessary for ourselves. Asanas can be helpful as well as harmful. If they are not required in the case of a particular sadhak, they can prove harmful. If they are needed, they will be of help. One difficulty is that this is an uncertain thing. Another difficulty is that when something is happening within and simultaneously something begins to happen outwardly as well, then the energy will move outwardly. When we perform an act from the outside, it may remain nothing more than a physical performance.

Now as I said, in anger the fists clench automatically. But it is not necessarily the case that you can bring on anger by clenching your fists. We can put on an act of anger while there is no anger whatsoever within. Yet, if we want to provoke anger within, clenching of fists could be helpful, but we cannot say for sure that anger will result. If we have to choose between clenching and not clenching the fists, the possibility of bringing on anger is definitely more with a clenched fist. This little aid is possible.

When a person is in a state of tranquillity, his hands will take on the necessary mudra (psychic expression). But if a person practises the formation of this mudra of the hands, it cannot be said for certain that his mind will attain peace. Yet, particular states of the body help the mind to be peaceful. The body will show its readiness to cooperate; then it is left to the mind to do the needful. But changing the body does not mean that the mind will change, and the reason is that the state of mind precedes the state of the body. That is why, when the mind changes, the body follows suit, but an initial change in the body can at best create a possibility of a change in the mind. It is not a certainty.

So there is always the danger of delusion. A man may keep on performing asanas and mudras and think he has done all. Such cases have happened. For thousands of years people have been doing asanas and mudras thinking that they were practising yoga, then gradually the concept of meditation was lost in yoga. By "yoga sadhana" (yoga practice) what comes to mind is asanas, pranayam (breathing exercises), etc. If you ask someone what is yoga sadhana (practice), he will think of asanas pranayam, etc. Therefore, I always stress that if the requirements of a sadhak are properly understood certain body positions can prove helpful to him. But the result is not certain. This is why I am always in favour of working from within and not from without.

If something begins from within we can understand its meaning. Suppose a sadhak sits in meditation and I feel that inwardly he wants to burst out crying but he is holding it back. I can see that if he cries for ten minutes he will also begin to move and catharsis will take place.

However, he is afraid that he may burst out crying so he stops himself. Now if he is told not to stop himself but cry, he will first pretend to cry. But later it will become authentic for he was actually wanting to cry from within. The process of crying will break the barrier, and what was to flow out will flow from him.

Suppose another sadhak feels to dance but he holds himself stiff. If we tell him to dance, at first he will only be acting: as yet the dance will not have come out from within. Once he begins to dance it will give the dance an opportunity to burst forth. In a short while this will start and the dance within will merge into the dance without. But if there is no cause for dance within him and we tell the sadhak to dance, he will keep on dancing but nothing will happen.

So many things have to be considered. There are very many conditions to all that I have told you. If you keep these in mind you will understand. If you do not want to be burdened with all, this, the best way is to start from within and let things happen spontaneously. Do not stop the outer happening, do not fight with it. Then things will happen of themselves.

Questioner : *In the experiment you are presently conducting, what are the physical and psychic differences brought about by sitting or standing for the experiment* ?

Bhagwan : It makes a great difference. As I told you before, deep within every condition of the body is connected with a particular state of mind that corresponds to it. If we tell a man to remain awake when he is lying down, it will be difficult for him to do so. If we tell him to be alert when he is standing, this will be easy. If we tell him to sleep when he is standing, it will be difficult. If we tell him to sleep when he is lying down it will be easy. So there is a double process in this experiment. One side of the experiment is hypnosis in which there is the fear that the sadhak may fall asleep or become drowsy. If he stands, this will help to dispel this fear. If he stands, the possibility of drowsiness is less.

The second part of the experiment is the witness attitude—awareness. Initially, it is difficult to maintain awareness lying down. Later on it is easy. It is always easy to maintain awareness while standing. So you will be aware and also a witness when you stand. The initial process of hypnosis, which will take you into a trance instead, is very much reduced by standing up.

There are two or three things more. When you stand, the movements of the body are free; when you lie down your movements will not be so free. When you sit half the body will not be able to participate at all. Suppose you want to dance and you are sitting: the legs cannot dance. You shall not even know what they require, for the feet have no way of expressing themselves. There are subtle hints which we fail to catch. If you are standing, the feet will begin "lifting themselves" and you will know they want to dance. But if you are sitting, this is not possible.

Actually, the tradition of sitting for meditation was specifically meant to suppress all the resulting movements of the body. "Siddhasana, padmasana and the sukhasana" (various yogic sitting postures) had to be practised extensively before meditation was taught in order that the body movements could be stopped. So the possibility of the energy rising within is there from the beginning. A great deal happens as a result. You feel to dance, sing, jump, run. These conditions are always associated with the insane, however: some mad persons cry, laugh, dance, or jump. As the sadhak does the same, he will, therefore, appear mad.

Siddhasana and other sitting postures were intensely practised in order that the body would be in full control. Then the sadhak would not look mad to the world. Now the sitting postures of padmasana, sukhasana and siddhasana are such that they cause your legs to become stiff. Your weight is greater near the ground while away from the ground it becomes lesser. You become bottom heavy like a temple or a pyramid: broad at the bottom, narrow at the top. Then the possibility of movement is very minimal—almost nil.

Maximum movement is possible when you stand—when there is nothing that keeps you fixed. When you cross your legs and sit you form an immovable base. A large part of your body is fixed by gravity, which then catches hold of it. Then you place your hand in such a way that possibility of movement is minimized. The spine too is kept straight and fixed. Before you would be allowed to go into meditation, this type of asana first had to be perfected over a long period of practice.

I think just the opposite. For one thing I think there is not much fundamental difference between us and those who are mad. We are all suppressed madmen: ours is a suppressed insanity. You can say that we are insane in a "normal" way or that we are "average insane people". There is so much in common between us and the insane. Those who go a little further in their insanity find themselves in trouble, but insanity lies within all of us and it tries to find its own outlets.

When you are angry you are temporarily in madness. At such a time you do things you would never dream of doing when you are conscious. You shout foul abuses, throw stones, break furniture. You can even jump from the roof; you can do anything. If an insane person does these things we could understand, but when an average person does this we merely say that he was angry. Now this was the same "average" man, and if these things were not within him they would not have come out. This is all inside of us and we are all guarding it. My opinion is that before going into meditation it is necessary that all this should be thrown out from within. The more you are relieved of this insanity, the lighter your mind will be.

Therefore whereas the old method of siddhasana took years to yield results, this new method performs the same task in a matter of days. The old method took many births for its fulfilment; this one may take only months. The inner condition has to be released, but in the old method the catharsis was carried out in the etheric body instead of the physical. Now this is something altogether different, for laughing, crying, dancing, etc. are all within you, and it is imperative that this should come out.

If you have trained your physical body extensively to be absolutely still for hours on end, then you will carry out the catharsis through your etheric body. Then it will not be visible to others, but only to you. You have now protected yourself from society; now no one will know when you dance or sing, as you will only do so within. This dancing and singing will be as if in a dream. You will dance within, cry within, laugh within, but your physical body will give no evidence of what is happening inside of you. It will sit still with not a trace of the inner happening.

I believe it is not worth undergoing so much trouble for so small a thing. There is no point in making a sadhak spend years in body control before taking him into meditation. There are other possibilities also. If a man becomes very proficient in controlling his body and succeeds in suppressing his physical body completely, there is a possibility that no vibrations will arise in the etheric body and it may become absolutely inert. Under such conditions it is possible that no deeper process will take place within you, but you will merely become adept in the art of physical control.

Now under such conditions, when all processes are suppressed within, there is a fear of the individual becoming insane. The method I advocate, however, if practised even by a madman for a month or two, will bring him out of his madness. There is no likelihood of a normal person becoming mad when practising this method, for in it we are not suppressing the insanity within us. We are trying to remove it, to bring it out. The old methods of sadhana have turned many into mad men, and this fact was covered with many terms. We would say of such a person, "He is ecstatically mad; he is 'God intoxicated'; he has become a saint." But the fact remained that he had gone absolutely mad. He had suppressed some things within himself so badly that they became completely out of his control.

This method does two things. The first task it carries out is to throw out all the rubbish that is within you by means of catharsis. You have first to become light—so light that not the slightest trace of madness remains within; then you travel within. So what apparently seems like madness in this method is intrinsically a process of relieving you of all madness. I prefer that what is within you should come out, and with it the burden, the tension, the anxiety. Now the most interesting fact is that when madness comes upon you, you have no control over it. But you are the absolute master of the madness that you bring on by yourself. Once you are aware of this fact madness can never take hold of you.

Take a man who is dancing and singing or laughing and shrieking of his own free will: he is doing all that a madman would do. There is only this difference: to the madman things are happening by themselves whereas the sadhak is bringing them about. Without the full cooperation of the sadhak, this madness cannot last a moment. He can stop the moment he wishes to. Now this man can never go mad, for he has lived madness, seen madness, become familiar with madness. Now this has become a voluntary happening for him. Madness is now within the scope of his control.

Our culture has trained us in such a way that madness is beyond our control: it has become non-voluntary. Thus, when it happens to us we cannot do anything about it.

I consider this method very valuable for the future civilization, for all of civilization is heading toward complete insanity. Everyone will need this technique to get rid of his madness; there is no other way. If one throws out his madness in this way during an hour of meditation, people will gradually get used to this mode of meditation. People will know that this man is doing meditation. However, if a person performs a similar act on the roadside, he will be locked up in a jail. If he releases his anger among people, all his relationships will become ugly and broken.

This madness must come out one way or the other, or else he will be in difficulty. If he does not allow it to be released voluntarily, this madness finds a hundred ways of erupting. Sometimes a man becomes completely drunk in order for the madness to come out of him; sometimes he indulges in a frenzy of dance and song. But why go through all these disturbances ?

Now the new modes of dancing, like the twist, etc., are artificially cultivated and not spontaneous. Inwardly, the body wishes to move and we have not left any room for movement. Thus, it makes arrangements for itself and then weaves further webs within these arrangements.

Meditation is throwing the madness without these arrangements. In meditation we are not making arrangements or controlling anything. We are merely throwing out that which we know is within us and which we know should be thrown out. If we teach this method of catharsis to children along with the rest of our education, there will be a sharp drop in the number of madmen. Madness can be removed for all time to come, but instead we see it increasing day by day. As our society progresses further, it will get more and more rampant.

Our culture can only teach us to suppress. Etiquette does not allow us to weep loudly nor to laugh loudly; it does not allow us to dance or to shriek as we please. It puts pressures on us from all sides with the result that all that needs to happen within us is stifled. Then one day the accumulated pressure of these emotions explodes, and the situation goes beyond our control. Thus, catharsis is the first step in our method of meditation, and through it we release all our pent up emotions within.

Therefore, I advocate standing during the experiment, for then you will be aware of the slightest movement within and you will be able to move freely. Therefore, again I say that the sadhak should lock himself up in his room. He should not only stand, but he should be absolutely naked so that not a strip of cloth can become a cause of obstruction to him. He should be absolutely free to perform all movements. There should not be the slightest obstacle in any part of his personality to hinder his movements. Then he will make quick progress, and that which takes years to bring about through hatha yoga and other yogas will happen within the course of a few days by this method.

Now the long drawn out yoga practices will not do for the world. Now people do not have days or even hours to spare. We need methods that yield quick results. If a man makes a sevenday resolve, by the end of that period he should begin to feel that something has happened to him: he should become a different man in seven days' time. If an experiment doesn't bear results for seven births, no one will ever go near such an experiment. The old methods claimed results after so many births. They used to say, "Carry out the practices in this life and the result is bound to come in another life." Those were very patient and persevering people. They carried out sadhana even though the result was promised in later lives. Now you will not find a single man like this. Now, if the result is not attained this very day, no one is willing to wait even until tomorrow.

And who can rely on tomorrow ? Ever since the atom bomb fell on Hiroshima and Nagasaki, our tomorrow has vanished. Thousands of American girls and boys refuse to go to college. They say, "Will the world remain intact by the time we finish our education ? One never knows what might happen tomorrow." Thus, they feel it is a waste of time. They run away from schools and colleges. They argue with parents: "In the six years we spend at the university will the world remain the same ? Do you guarantee it ? Why should we not make full use of these six precious years of our lives ?

Where tomorrow has become so uncertain, it is meaningless to talk in terms of many births. No one is ready to listen, no one does listen. Therefore, I say practise today and feel the result immediately. If a man is willing to give me an hour for this experiment, he should get the feeling of the results after this very hour. Then only will he be able to give me an hour of his time tomorrow; otherwise it is uncertain that he will do it tomorrow. So requirements have changed for this age. In the world of the bullock-cart everything moved slowly, so sadhana also moved at a very slow pace. Now it is the jet-age now sadhana cannot afford to be slow. It has to pick up speed

Questioner : *Please explain the significance and meaning of the following with respect to the energy of kundalini: prostrating on the ground in obeisance to a holy person, touching his feet with the head or hands, offering worship at holy places, the blessings of a Divine person given by touching the head or back of a sadhak, the covering of the head by Sikhs and Moslems on entering the "gurudwara" (a temple of the Sikhs) or mosque.*

Bhagwan : There are many reasons for these things. As I said before, when we are filled with anger we feel like beating up someone; we feel like crushing his head under our feet. Since this is rather impractical, we do the next best thing: we throw a shoe at him. It is very difficult to get a man of 5′6″ to get under our feet, so we allow our shoe to be thrown at his head as the symbol of the urge of anger within ourselves. But no one ever questions what is the reason behind this shoe throwing. And this is not an act indulged in by any one sect or one country: it is universal. It is a fact that whenever one man is angry with another, his overpowering desire is to bring the head of the latter under his foot.

When man was still primitive perhaps he rested only after placing his foot on his opponent's head, since he had no shoes. So when you are in a state of anger, you feel like putting your foot on someone's head. However, the opposite is true also: when you are filled with faith and reverence, you feel to place your head at someone's feet. There are many reasons for this as there are for the former situation.

There are moments when you feel to prostrate yourself, and these are the very moments when you feel the vital energy flowing from someone toward you. In fact, whenever you want to receive any kind of flow you have to bend down. If you want to fill your pitcher from the river, you must bend down. One must bend in order to receive the flow of any current for all currents flow downwards. So if you feel that something is flowing from someone, the more your head is bowed at that moment the more effective it will be.

Also, the energy flows from the pointed extremities of the person : for example, from the fingers and toes. The energy does not flow out from all places. Electrical energy of the body, "Shaktipat" (transmission of energy through the medium of an Enlightened one) or for that matter any energy that flows out from the body, flows from the tips of the fingers and toes. It does not flow from the entire body, but only from the pointed extremities. So he who has to receive the energy will put his head at the feet of the Divine person, and he who means to give the energy will put his hands upon the one who is to receive.

These were very occult, deeply scientific matters. It is but natural that many will imitate the action. Thousands of people place their heads at the feet of others without any purpose, and there are thousands who place their hands on their heads, also without any meaning. Thus, a very deep principle gradually became a mere formality. When a formality continues for a long time, people are bound to rebel against it. They will say, "What is this nonsense ? What comes out of placing your head at someone's feet ? And what happens by merely touching the head ?" Ninety-nine per cent of the time it is just nonsense; one per cent is still meaningful, however.

There was a time when it was a hundred per cent meaningful for then it was spontaneous. Then you did not have to touch someone's feet because you thought you should. Sometime, when you feel you must fall at someone's feet, do not hold yourself back: fall ! And it was not that the other person HAD to place his hand on the recipient's head. It happens that in some moments the hand becomes heavy and something is ready to flow out of it. If the other was then ready to receive, then only was the hand placed on the head. But over a long period everything turns into a mere symbol, and then it becomes meaningless. And when it becomes meaningless it is criticized. These criticisms then hold a great deal of appeal because the science behind the tradition is lost. So this is very meaningful custom, but it belonged to people who were conscious, people who were really alive.

A man falls at the feet of a Buddha, a Mahavir, and experiences unique delight. He feels a downpour of grace upon him. No one will be able to see it from outside, for this is entirely an inner happening. What he has experienced is his very own. If others ask proof of it he has none to give. In fact, this is the difficulty with all occult phenomena: the individual has the experience, but he has no proof of it to put before others. And then this person appears to be a blind believer, for he says, "I cannot explain it, but something has happened." Those who have not experienced refuse to believe this, for they have not felt anything. Then they feel that this poor man is under an illusion.

If one of these sort of persons should fall at feet of even Jesus, nothing will happen to him and he will begin to proclaim loudly that this is all nonsense: he put his head at the feet of Jesus and nothing happened. It is just like a pitcher with an open brim which bows down to the water. Upon returning it then says, "I bowed down and was filled." Now another pitcher whose brim is closed may set out to try it for himself. It may go deep into the river, but it will return empty. Then it will maintain that it is all false and that no one gets filled by being dipped into the river. It will proclaim, "I bent myself over, I dipped myself in, but I came back empty."

It is a twofold happening. It is not enough that the energy flows from a person. It is equally important that you are empty and open. Many a time the flowing of the energy is not as important as your preparedness, your openness to receive it. If you are open enough, then even if the energy is absent in the person before you, the power of energies above the person will begin to flow toward you and reach you. So the most surprising thing is that if you let yourself go wholeheartedly even before a person who has nothing to give, you will receive energy from him. The energy does not come from him. He is only a medium and he is completely unaware of the happening that has taken place.

Now the second part of your question is about entering the gurudwara or mosque with the head covered: Many fakirs preferred to cover their heads and then practise meditation. It has its uses. When the energy awakens, there is a possibility of the head becoming very heavy. If you have tied your head with a cloth, this energy is not likely to flow out. Then this energy will create a circuit within you and thus intensify your meditation. So this tying of the head proved very useful. If you meditate with your head covered, you will feel the difference at once. Then what could be accomplished in fifteen days can be accomplished in five.

When the energy reaches the head, there are chances of its becoming diffused and scattered. If it can be tied, and if a circuit is then formed, your experience will be much more deep. But at present this covering of the head in mosques and gurudwaras is a mere formality; it has no meaning now. The fact remains, however, that there is a lot of meaning behind this custom.

Now it is understandable that some energy can be obtained by touching someone's feet or through his hand being raised in benediction. But a man bowing before a grave or before an image in a temple, what can he gain ? There are many things in this also, two or three of which should be well understood. Behind the creation of images and idols lies a very scientific arrangement.

Suppose I am about to die and there are a few people around me who love me, who have seen something in me, who have searched and found something in me. Now these people may ask me in what way they should remember me. So a symbol can be selected between they and I. It could be anything—an idol, a stone, a tree, even a platform, or my grave, or a cloth of mine, or my slippers—anything. But this should be decided beforehand between us; it is an understanding between us. It cannot be decided upon by any one party alone: I should be a witness. My acceptance, my endorsement, is necessary regarding the symbol. Then I can say that if they go before the symbol and think of me, I shall be present in the bodiless state. This promise I have to give, and all the work proceeds in accordance with this promise. And this is absolutely true.

Therefore, there are temples that are living temples and temples that are dead. The dead temples are those that are created by only one side. There is no assurance from the other side. It is our desire to make a temple of Buddha—but this will be a dead temple, for the hand of Buddha is not in it. There are living temples that have an assurance from the other side also, and at their foundation lies the declaration of some holy person.

There is a place in Tibet where Buddha's assurance holds good since the last 2,500 years. This place is now in difficulty, however. There is a group, a committee of 500 lamas, and when one of these 500 dies it is very difficult to replace him. This number of 500 is constant: it can neither be more nor less. When one of them dies one more is chosen, but only with the approval of the 499. And if even one of the 499 refuses to accept him he cannot be taken. This committee of 500 lamas gather together on a particular mountain on the night of Buddha Poornima (the full-moon night in May when Buddha's birthday is celebrated), and at the exact given time Buddha's voice is heard.

It is just as you would make a resolve before sleeping at night that you will get up in the morning at five o' clock. Then you do not need any alarm to awaken you. At five o'clock sharp you will suddenly get up. This is something amazing—and you can check it by your watch. The watch may be wrong, but not you. If your resolve is firm, you will surely get up at five. If you make a firm resolve to die on a cértain day of a certain year, no power on earth can stop you: you will die the moment decided upon. If your resolution is very profound and intense, you can fulfil your promises even after death. For instance, the appearance of Jesus after death: it was a promise fulfilled. This has caused a lot of difficulty for Christians, for they do not know what happened afterwards and thus they are not sure whether Christ was resurrected or not. However, this was a promise by him which was fulfilled after death.

Actually, places where certain living promises are still being fulfilled over thousands of years have slowly turned into "teerths" (holy places of pilgrimage). Then by and by occult promises were forgotten. Only one thing remained in people's memories—that they have to go and visit these places; that was all.

There are promises that Mohammed made; there are promises that Shankara made. So also, there are promises made by Buddha, Mahavir and Krishna and these are tied to special places, to special moments and to a special time. But we can yet establish a relationship with them. So you will have to bow in obeisance again at these places and surrender yourself completely. Then only can you establish this connection.

Holy places, temples *samadhis* (tombs of saints) all have their uses, but as with other things these useful places ultimately become a tradition, and then they become dead and useless. Then they have to be torn down so that new promises can be made that would give rise to new places of pilgrimage, new idols, and new temples. The old has to be broken down, for it has become dead. We have no idea of the processes that have been working through them.

There was a yogi in the South. An English traveller came to him. At the time of his departure he told the yogi, "I am leaving now and perhaps I shall never return to India. But if I want to see you what shall I do?" The yogi picked up a picture of himself and handing it over to him said, "Whenever you close yourself in a darkened room and concentrate for five minutes on this picture without blinking the eyelids, I shall present myself." Now the poor man could contain himself throughout the journey. He was possessed with one thought: to try out the experiment as early as possible. He did not believe such a thing could happen, but it happened. The given promise was fulfilled astrally. There is no difficulty in this. A living man can fulfil his promise and so can a dead person in this way. Therefore, pictures become significant, and also images. The reason for their significance is that through them some promises could be fulfilled. So there was a full science behind the creation of images and idols.

An idol cannot be made in any old way. There is a complete method behind it. Now if you were to observe the images of the 24 "Teerthankers" (World Teachers) of the Jains you would fall into difficulty, for they are all alike; only their emblems are different. Mahavir has one emblem, Parshwanath another, Neminath yet another, and so on. If these emblems are removed, it is impossible to tell one Teerthanker from another. However, it cannot be that they all looked alike. It is, therefore, possible that the Teerthankers that followed used the image of the first Teerthankers as their symbol. So there was no need to make different images. There was one seal of the Teerthankers that was utilized by all.

But this did not satisfy the devotees who were devoted to different Teerthankers, so they appealed to their special Teerthankers for at least a sign, a token to differentiate him from the others. Thus, different emblems were created for the different Teerthankers, but the image remained the same. One has a lion as an emblem, the other something else, and so on. So there is this difference in their emblems, and this too is a part of an understanding. From an image with a particular emblem only the particular person connected with the emblem could be contacted.

So the emblem is an understanding, and it works. For instance the sign of Jesus is the Cross. This will work. Now Mohammed refused to have his idol made. In fact, so many images were created during the time of Mohammed that he wanted to give his followers an entirely different kind of symbol. He told them, "Do not make a statue of me. I will establish a relationship with you without a statue. Do not make a statue of me; do not make a picture of me. I will be related to you without picture or a statue." This was a very deep and courageous method, but ordinary people found it very difficult to establish contact with Mohammed.

Therefore, after Mohammed the Moslems built mausoleums and tombs for thousands of their saints. They did not know how to establish connections with Mohammed directly, so they did it by making a tomb of some Moslem saint. Nowhere in the world are tombs and graves so extensively worshipped as by the Moslems. The only reason was that they had nothing of Mohammed to hold on to in order to establish contact with him directly. They could not make an image of him so they had to create other images, and they began to establish relationships through these.

All this is a complete scientific process. If this is understood scientifically, it yields wonderful results, but if followed blindly it is suicidal.

Questioner : *What is the occult significance of the process performed during "Prana Pratishtha" (the installation of an idol)* ?

Bhagwan : It holds a great significance. The very term "*Prana Pratishtha*" (occult installation of an idol) means that we have created a new image based on an old promise. Now we must discover through indications whether the old promise has been duly fulfilled. We, on our part, should follow the old arrangement faithfully; we should not look upon an idol as a mere idol, but as a living entity. We should make all arrangements for it as we would for a living person, and then we will begin to get hints and signs by which we can know that the occult installation of the idol has been accepted. But this second aspect has completely vanished from our knowledge. If these signs are not present, then although we have done the idol installation it has not been successful. There must be proof that the idol installation has been successful. So for this reason, some special occult indications were fixed. If these signs were found, it was understood that the idol installation has been accepted by the occult forces and that it is now alive and active.

Now suppose that you have installed a new radio in your house. The first thing is that the radio itself should be in good condition: all its components should be in the proper place. Then you connect it with electricity; yet you find it does not catch any station. That means it is not working. It is a dead instrument, and it will either have to be repaired or replaced. The idol too is a receiving point of a sort, through which a dead person fulfils the vows he has made to others. But if you keep an image, you have no way of finding out whether it fulfils the necessary conditions or not, so you never know whether the image is living or dead.

The process of installation of a living idol has two parts. The first part is fulfilled by the priest. He knows how many mantras are to be repeated, how many threads are to be tied, what prerequisites are required for its worship, what type of worship is to be performed, etc. This is half the work. The second part of this installation can only be carried out by a person of the fifth plane. When this person pronounces that the image is alive, then only does it become living. Now this has become well-nigh impossible in modern times. Therefore, our temples are not the living temples of yesteryear, but dead places. The new temples of today are certainly dead places.

It is impossible to destroy a living temple, for it is not an ordinary event. If it is destroyed, it only means that that which you considered to be alive was not alive, as for instance, the Somanath temple. The story of its destruction is a very strange one, and it is indicative of the science of all temples. There were 500 *pujaris* (priests) in its service and they were certain that the image within was a living one. Thus, they were certain it could not be destroyed. The *pujaris* carried out their part of the task, but this was onesided, for there was no one who could actually find out whether the image was dead or living.

One day the surrounding kings and chieftains sent word to the temple warning them about the coming of Gajanawi and offered them protection, but the *pujaris* declined their help saying that the idol that protected all was beyond their protection. The chieftains asked their forgiveness and kept away, but it was a mistake: the idol was a dead idol. The *pujaris* were under the illusion that a great power stood behind the image, and as they considered it to be living it was wrong even to think of its protection. Gajanawi came and with a stroke of his sword broke the idol into four pieces. Even then it did not occur to the *pujaris* that the idol was a dead one. This cannot happen to a living idol. Not a brick could have fallen if the image within were living. If the temple were a living one, it could not have been touched. But usually temples are not living ones because there are great difficulties in keeping them as such.

A temple becoming alive is a great miracle. It is a part of a very profound science. Today, however, there is no one alive who knows this science and who can carry out its various requirements. Nowadays the class of people who run temples as shops has become so large that even if there is someone who knows this science he will be shoved off the premises of the temple. Temples are now run along business lines, and it is in the interest of the priests that they remain dead. Living temples are not beneficial for a *purohit* (priest). He wants a dead god within whom he can lock up, and then he wants to keep the key himself. If the temple is connected with higher powers, it will be impossible for the priest to remain there. So priests are instrumental in the creation of these dead temples, as this provides them with a lucrative business. In reality, living temples are very few.

A great effort was made to keep the temples alive, but the large hordes of priests and *purohits* in all religions, in all temples, made it difficult to do so. This is what always happens, ultimately. This is the reason why there are so many temples; otherwise there would be no need for so many. If the temples and places of pilgrimage created in the times of the Upanishads had still been alive in Mahavir's time, there would have been no need for Mahavir to build new temples. But the temples and sacred places were completely dead by then, and there was a network of priests round them which could not be broken. These temples could not be entered, so there was no other way except to make new temples. Today, even Mahavir's temples are dead and the same kind of network surrounds them.

If the living principles of religion had been saved, so many religions would not have come into being in this world. But these cannot be saved, for all kinds of disturbances gather around and ultimately cause them to lose all their potential. Then, when the conditions on one side are broken, the promise on the other side also breaks. It is an understanding arrived at by two parties. We have to uphold our side of the agreement; then only does the other side reciprocate. Otherwise the promise will not be fulfilled and the matter ends there.

For instance, I say to you, "Remember me and I shall be there." But if you never think of me or if you throw my picture into the dustbin and forget all about it, how long will our understanding last? And if this pact is broken on your part, there is neither any need for me to uphold it. Thus, such pacts are always broken.

But the occult process of installation of an idol hold a meaning, and its significance is based on various tests and indications that determine whether the idol installation has been a success or not.

Questioner: *In some temples, water trickles down naturally over the images. Is this a sign of that such a temple a living temple?*

Bhagwan : The test of a living temple has nothing to do with this. The water will trickle whether there is an image underneath or not. These are false proofs, and because of them we assume that a temple is a living one. Where not a drop of water falls, there are temples that could be and are living temples.

Questioner : *In sadhana, "deeksha" (initiation) holds a very important place. Its special ceremonies are carried out under special conditions. Buddha and Mahavir used to give initiation. How many types of initiations are there? What is their significance and use and why are they needed?*

Bhagwan : A little talk on *deeksha* will be useful. For one thing, *deeksha*, initiation, is never given: initiation takes place; it is a happening. For example, a person stays with Mahavir, and it takes years for his initiation to take place. Mahavir tells him to stop, to be with him, to walk with him, to stand thus, to sit thus, to meditate thus. Then a moment comes when the person is fully prepared. Then Mahavir is only the medium. Perhaps it is not proper even to say that he is the medium. Rather, in a very deep sense he remains a only witness, and initiation takes place before him.

Initiation is always from the Divine, but it can happen in the presence of Mahavir. Now the person to whom it is happening sees Mahavir before him, but God he cannot see. It happens to him before Mahavir, so naturally he becomes grateful to Mahavir—and this is fitting also. But Mahavir does not accept his gratitude. He can only accept his gratitude if he acknowledges that he initiated him. So there are two types of initiations. One is that which happens and which I call "right initiation", for in this you establish your relationship with the Divine. Then your journey through life takes a new turn: you become someone else now; you are no longer the same that you were; everything within you is transformed. You have seen something new. Something new has happened to you, a new ray has entered you, and everything within you now is different.

In the real initiation, the guru stands aside like a witness and he can only confirm that initiation has taken place. He can see the full process, but you see only half. You can only see what is happening to you; he sees THAT from where the initiation takes place. Therfore, you are not a complete witness of the happening. All you can say is that a great transformation has taken place. But whether initiation has taken place or not, whether you have been accepted or not, that you cannot say for certain. Even after you are initiated you will still wonder, "Have I been accepted ? Have I been chosen ? Have I been accepted by the Divine ? Can I now take it that I am HIS? On my part I have surrendered, but have I been taken unto Him ?" This you cannot know at once. You will come to know after sometime, but this interval can be long also. So the second person whom we call "guru", can know this, for he has watched the happening from both sides.

Right initiation cannot be given, nor can it be taken. It comes from the Divine : you are merely the recipient. Now the other type of initiation, which we may call false initiation, can be given as well as taken. God is completely absent there;

there is only the guru and the disciple. The guru gives, the disciple takes, but the third, real factor is absent. Where there are only two present—the guru and the disciple—the initiation is false. Where three are present—the guru, the disciple and He from whom it takes place—everything changes. The prelude of giving initiation is not only improper, but also dangerous, fatal, because in this "illusion of initiation", right initiation cannot take place. You will merely live under the illusion that initiation has taken place.

A sadhu came to me who had been initiated by someone. He said, "I have been initiated by such and such a guru and I have come to you to learn meditation." I asked him, "Why then did you take initiation? And if you did not even attain meditation, what have you obtained from your initiation? All you received is clothes and a name. If you are still seeking meditation, then what is the meaning of your initiation?"

The truth is that initiation can only happen after meditation. Meditation after initiation has no meaning. It is like a man who asserts that he is healthy, and yet he knocks at the physician's door and asks for medicine. Initiation is the acceptance obtained after meditation. It is a sanction given of your acceptance —a consent. The Divine has been apprised of you and your entrance into his realm has happened. Initiation is only an affirmation of this fact. Such initiation is now lost, and I feel it should be revived again: initiation where the guru is not the giver and the disciple is not the receiver—where the guru is only a witness, the disciple the recipient, and the giver, God. This can be; this should be. If I am a witness to someone's initiation I do not become his guru: then his guru is God. If he is grateful, it is his business. But to demand gratefulness is senseless and to accept it is meaningless.

Gurudom (the web of the so-called gurus) was created by giving a new form to initiation. Words are whispered in the ears, mantras are given, and anybody initiates anyone. Whether he himself is initiated is also not certain; whether the Divine has accepted him is not known. Perhaps he too has been initiated in the same manner. Someone had whispered into his ears, he whispers into someone else's, and this one in his turn will whisper into yet someone else's ears. Man creates lies and deceptions in everything—and the more mysterious a happening, the more deceptions there are, for there is nothing substantial to produce as proof.

I intend carrying out this method also. About ten or twenty people are preparing for it: they will take initiation from the Divine. The others who are present will be the witnesses, and their work will be to confirm whether the initiation has been accepted by the Divine; that is all. You will experience, but you will not be able to recognize at once what has taken place. It is so unfamiliar to you, how will you recognize that the happening has happened? Confirmation can be made by the presence of the Enlightened One. This alone is the basis of its evaluation.

So the Supreme Guru is the "paramatman" (God) only. If the gurus in between would step back initiation would be easier, but the intermediary guru stands rooted to the ground. His ego exults at his making a god of himself and displaying himself as one. Many kinds of initiations are given around this ego. They have no value, however, and in terms of spirituality they are all criminal acts. If someday we should start punishing spiritual criminals, these should not go unpunished.

The unsuspecting sadhak takes it for granted that he has been initiated. Then he struts about with pride that he has received his initiation, that he has received his mantra, and that all which was to happen has happened to him. So all his search for the right happening stops.

When anyone approached Buddha, he was never initiated immediately. Sometimes it took years. Buddha would keep on postponing by telling him to perform this practice and that. Then, when the moment came, he would tell him to stand up for initiation.

There were three parts to Buddha's initiation. He who came for it went through three types of surrender. First he said, "I surrender unto Buddha!" By that he did not mean Gautam Buddha. This meant surrendering himself to the "Awakened One". Once a sadhak came up to Buddha and said, "I surrender unto Buddha." Buddha listened and remained silent. Then someone asked him, "This man says, 'I surrender unto Buddha', and you were only listening to him?" Buddha replied, "He is not surrendering to me. He is surrendering to the Awakened One. I am a mere excuse. There have been many Buddhas before me; there will be many after me. I am just an excuse, I am just a peg. He is surrendering himself to the Awakened One, so who am I to stop him? If he surrenders to me I shall certainly stop him, but he has said three times that he is surrendering himself unto the Awakened One."

Then there is the second surrender which is still more wonderful. In this the person says, "I surrender myself to the assembly of the Awakened Ones." Now what does this assembly mean? Generally, the followers of Buddha take it to mean Buddha's assembly, but this is not the meaning. This assembly is the collective gathering of ALL Awakened Ones. There is not only one Buddha who has become Awakened. There have been many Buddhas before and there will be many Buddhas after who will Awaken. They all belong to one community, to one collectivity. Now the Buddhists think this term means an association of Buddhists, but this is wrong.

The very first invocation, in which Buddha explains that the sadhak surrenders himself to "the Awakened One" and not to him as a person, makes everything clear. The second invocation makes it all the more clear. In this the person dedicates himself to the community of Awakened Ones. First he dedicates himself to the Awakened One who is right before his eyes. As he is there in front of him, it is easy to approach him, to talk to him. Then he surrenders himself to the Brotherhood of the Awakened Ones that have Awakened since long and whom he does not know, to those who have recently Awakened and whom he does not know, and to those who will awaken in the future and whom he does not know. He surrenders to all of them and, he proceeds a step further toward the subtle.

The third surrender is to dharma—religion. The third time the seeker says, "I surrender unto the dharma." The first surrender is to the Awakened One, the second is to the Brotherhood of the Awakened Ones and now the third surrender is to that which is the highest state of Awakening—to the dharma: that is, to our nature, where there is no individual, no community; where there is only the dharma (only the Law). He says, "I surrender unto that dharma."

When these three surrenders were completed then only was the initiation complete. This was not matter of mere repetition. When these three were completed (and Buddha could see whether they had been completed), only then was the individual initiated. Buddha remained a witness to the happening. Therefore, later on also Buddha would tell the seeker, "Do not believe what I say just because I am an Awakened One; do not believe what I say just because I am famous or because I have many followers or because the scriptures confirm it. Now only believe what your inner understanding tells you." Buddha never became a guru. At the time of his death, when he was asked for his final message, he said, "Be a light unto yourself. Do not go after others; do not follow others. Be your own lamp; this is my message."

Such a person as Buddha cannot be a guru. Such a person is a witness. Jesus has said many a time, "On the final Day of Judgement I shall be your witness." In other words, on the last day Jesus will testify, "Yes, he is a man who had striven to become Awakened. This man wanted to surrender to the Divine." This is talking in symbols. What Christ meant to say is also this: "I am your witness, not your guru."

There is no guru; therefore, beware of the initiation where someone becomes your guru. The initiation where you become immediately and directly connected with the Divine is a unique initiation. Remember, in this initiation, you have not to leave your house and go away, you have not to become either a Hindu or a Moslem or a Christian, nor are you required to be tied to someone. You remain where you are in your full freedom; the change will take place only from within. In the false type of initiation you will be tied to a religion: you will be a Hindu or a Moslem or a Christian. You will be a part of an organization. Some belief, some religious order, some dogma, some person, some guru will catch hold of you, and they will kill your freedom.

That initiation which does not bring freedom is no initiation. That initiation which gives you full freedom is alone the right initiation.

Questioner : *You have said that Buddha attained Maha-Parinirvan" (the death of one who lived in Nirvana), but also that Buddha is to come once again in human form and will be known as "Maitreya". How is it possible to take on a human form after reaching Nirvana ? Please explain this.*

Bhagwan : This is somewhat difficult; therefore, I did not speak about it yesterday. It requires a detailed explanation; yet I shall now give you a brief explanation.

It is not possible to return after reaching the seventh plane. There is no rebirth after the seventh body: it is a point of no-return; you cannot come back from there. But it is also true that Buddha has said he will come again in the form of Maitreya. Now both these things seem contradictory: I say you cannot return after the seventh body and Buddha has promised to come again. Buddha attained the seventh body and merged into the Nirvana. Then how is this possible ? There is another way. Now you will have to know and understand a few things.

When we die, only the physical body drops; the rest of the six bodies remain with us. When a person reaches the fifth plane, the first four bodies drop away and only three remain—the fifth, the sixth and the seventh. In the fifth body a person can make a resolve to keep his second, third and fourth bodies, and this can happen if the resolve is very intense and deep. And for a person like Buddha this was an easy matter: he can leave behind for ever his second, third and fourth bodies. Like a mass of energy, these bodies of Buddha keep on moving in space.

All the feelings that Buddha had acquired in his infinite lives are the property of the second—the etheric body. And the impressions of all the karmas that Buddha had in his previous lives are accumulated in the third—the astral body. The fourth body carries all the achievements of Buddha's mind. All of his achievements beyond the mind have been expressed by him through the mind, for all expressions are given through the mind. Whenever a man wishes to make known his attainments of the fifth or even the seventh body, he has to make use of his fourth body—for the vehicle of expression is the fourth body. So that which has heard Buddha more than anyone or anything else is his own fourth body. Whatsoever he has thought, lived and known is collected in his fourth body.

The first three bodies disintegrate very easily. When a person enters the fifth body, his first three bodies are destroyed. When a man enters the seventh body, everything of his is destroyed. But if a person of the fifth plane so desires, he can leave all the vibrations of these three bodies in space. It is just as we are now making stations in space. This collection of Buddha's second, third and fourth bodies will go on moving in space until they manifest themselves in an individual by the name of Maitreya.

So when a person of the required state for Maitreya is born, these three bodies of Buddha will enter into him. Until then they will await his coming. When these three bodies enter into that person, he will attain the calibre of Buddha, for they are an accumulation of all the experiences, all the emotions, desires and activities, of Buddha.

Now, for instance, suppose I leave my body behind here and it is well preserved. In America, a man died about three or four years ago. He left a trust of millions of dollars, and he willed that this be used to preserve his body until such time that science discovers the secret of resuscitation. Millions of dollars are spent to preserve his body so that it should not deteriorate the slightest bit. His body is preserved by a scientific process. If, by the end of century, we succeed in reviving the dead, this body will be brought back to life. But the soul will be different; it cannot be the same.

The body will be the same: his eyes, his colour, his features, his way of walking, all of his physical habits, will be the same. In a sense, the man who is dead will be represented in the body. If the man was centered around his physical body (which he must have been, or else this keen desire to preserve the body would not have been there) without any idea of the other bodies, another soul can act for him. It will act exactly as the dead man, and scientists will then say that it is the same man come to life. All his remembrances and recollections that are stored in the physical brain will awaken once again: he will be able to recognize the pictures of his mother and his son who will have long since been dead; he will recognize the town where he was born; he will point out the place where he died; he will also name the people that were present when he died. The soul will be different although the brain content will be the same.

Now scientists claim that very soon they will be able to transplant memory. This will be possible. If I die, the whole store of my recollections and remembrances are lost with me. But now it is possible to save the whole mechanism of my remembrances at the time of my death, just as we preserve eyes for transplantation. Tomorrow someone will be able to see with my eyes. And it is not that I alone can love with my heart: someone else may also love with my heart tomorrow. Now it is not possible to avow that "My heart is always yours", for this very heart can make the same vow to another in the distant future.

In the same way memory will also be transplanted. It will take time to bring this about, for it is very delicate and very subtle. But in future, as we donate eyes to an eye bank, there will be memory banks also. Then my memory will be translpanted into a small child who will then know all that I had to learn. He will grow up knowing, for my memory will be a part of his cerebral make-up. Then my thoughts will be his, my rememb-rances will be his, and in certain matters he will think the way I do, for he will have my brain.

Now Buddha has experimented in a different direction—a direction which is not scientific, but occult. Through this efforts have been made to preserve his second, third and fourth bodies. Buddha is no more the same consciousness. The "Atman" (soul) that lived within was lost at the seventh plane. But before the Atman was merged into the seventh, arrangements were made to see that these three bodies—the second, third and fourth—did not die. The momentum of Buddha's determination and promise was instilled in them. It is just as if I were to throw a stone with enough force for it to travel fifty miles, then I die soon after throwing the stone. But my death cannot interfere with the movement of the stone. It has the force I gave it to travel fifty miles, and that it will do whether I am there or not. The strength I exerted will keep the stone going.

Buddha has given a momentum to these three bodies, and they will live. He has also told how long they can remain. Now the time is ripe for Maitreya to take birth. This very experiment was carried out upon Krishnamurti so that he should attain these three bodies of Buddha. First this experiment was carried out on Nityananda, the elder brother of Krishnamurti, but he died in the process. This is a very unique process—one which is difficult to go through.

An effort was made to separate Nityananda's three bodies (second, third and fourth) and replace them with Maitreya's. Then Nityananda died. Then this same experiment was tried on Krishnamurti, but this also could not be. Then it was tried on one or two more people: George Arundale was one upon whom this experiment was tried by some who knew of this mystery. Among those who knew of this secret, Mde. Blavatsky was the most profound woman of our century as far as the knowledge of occult science is concerned. Annie Besant was another; Leadbeater also had a lot of understanding in occult matters. There are very few people who had this understanding.

These few people knew that now the power behind three bodies of Buddha was about to diminish. If Maitreya would not take birth, these bodies would not be able to hold on any longer: they would dispense. Now their momentum is about to end. Someone should now be ready to absorb these three bodies. Whoever absorbs these will in a way cause the rebirth of Buddha. The soul of Buddha will not come back, but the soul of the individual will take on the bodies of Buddha and work accordingly. That person will at once involve himself in the mission of Buddha.

Not every person can be in this state. Whoever he is, he should at least be of a level of consciousness that is almost as high as was Buddha's. Only such a one will be able to absorb his three bodies; otherwise he will die. So the experiment was unsuccessful, for there were many difficulties in the process. Endeavours still go on. Even today there are small esoteric groups who are trying to bring down these three bodies of Buddha. But now there is no extensive propaganda about it, for that proved harmful.

There was a possibility of the three bodies descending into Krishnamurti. He was worthy of it, and this was widely advertised. This progaganda was done in good faith. It was done for the reason that when Buddha's advent took place he should be quickly recognized. It was also done in order to revive the past-life memories of those now living who existed at the time of Buddha so that they could certify that this was the same man. But this propaganda turned out to be detrimental to the process. It created a reaction in the mind of Krishnamurti who has a modest, reserved and sensitive personality. It was difficult for him to be amidst a crowd. If this experiment had been carried out silently in a secluded spot, if nobody would have known about it until the happening took place, it is very likely that the happening have taken place.

But it did not take place, and this was a great blow to the occult science of our times. Such a vast and intricate experiment had never been performed in this world anywhere except in Tibet. This process has been carried out in Tibet for a long time, and many souls work through the medium of other bodies.

I hope you have understood what I said. There is no contradiction in it even though sometimes you might feel that there is. It is possible that you may feel something to be contradictory because I have talked from a different angle, but there are none.

[Text of a discourse given on July 12, 1970, evening, in Bombay, India]

BOOKS BY BHAGAWAN SHREE RAJNEESH

- The Mysteries of Life and Death
  (*Talks based on Interviews taken by foreign seekers*)
- Who am I ?
  (*Fourteen discourses on Dharma, the process of Education, Morality, Fear and Love, Non-violence etc. etc.*)
- Path of Self-Realisation.
  (*Discourses on the attainment of Truth*)
- Philosophy of Non-violence.
  (*One of the Discourses on fearlessness, meditation and salvation from the self.*)
- The Ultimate Alchemy : Vols. I and II
  (*discourses on the Atma Pooja Upanishad*)
- The Book of the Secrets : Vols. I, II, III and IV
  (*discourses on Tantra*)
- The Supreme Doctrine
  (*discourses on the Kenopanishad*)
- YOGA : the Alpha and the Omega : Vols. I, II and III
  (*discourses on Patanjali's Yoga Sutras*)
- VEDANTA : Seven Steps to Samadhi
  (*discourses on the Akshya Upanishad*)
- The Way of the White Cloud
  (*talks based on questions*)
- Roots and Wings
  (*talks based on questions*)
- The Empty Boat
  (*discourses on Chuang Tzu*)
- No Water, No Moon
  (*discourses on Zen*)
- The Mustard Seed
  (*discourses on the sayings of Jesus*)
- When the Shoe Fits
  (*discourses on Chuang Tzu*)

Neither this nor That
(*discourses on Sosan-Zen*)

- ...and the flowers showered
  (*discourses on Zen Stories*)
- Returning to the Source
  (*discourses on Zen Stories*)
- The Hidden Harmony
  (*discourses on the fragments of Heraclitus*)
- TANTRA : The Supreme Understanding
  (*discourses on Tilopa's song of Mahamudra*)
- The Grass Grows by itself
  (*discourses on Zen Stories*)
- Until you die
  (*discourses on Sufi Stories*)
- Just like that
  (*discourses on Sufi Stories*)
- TAO : The Three Treasures : Vols. I and II
  (*discourses on Lao Tzu*)
- Hammer on the Rock
  (*darshan diary*)
- Come Follow Me : Vol. I
  (*discourses on the life of Jesus*)
- I am the Gate
  (*talks based on questions*)
- The Silent Explosion
  (*talks based on questions*)
- Dimensions beyond the known
  (*talks based on questions*)

BOOKS ON RAJNEESH'S TEACHING
by DR. R.C. PRASAD

- Lifting the Veil (Kundalini Yoga)
- The Mystic of Feeling
  (*A Study in the Rajneesh's Religion of Experience*)